Tennessee Frontiers

A History of the Trans-Appalachian Frontier

Walter Nugent and Malcolm Rohrbough, general editors

Andrew L. Cayton. *Frontier Indiana*

James E. Davis. *Frontier Illinois*

R. Douglas Hurt. *The Ohio Frontier: Crucible of the Old Northwest, 1720–1830*

Mark Wyman. *The Wisconsin Frontier*

Tennessee
Frontiers

Three Regions in
Transition

John R. Finger

INDIANA UNIVERSITY PRESS   BLOOMINGTON & INDIANAPOLIS

This book is a publication of
Indiana University Press
601 North Morton Street
Bloomington, Indiana 47404-3797 USA

http://iupress.indiana.edu
Telephone orders   800-842-6796
Fax orders   812-855-7931
Orders by email   iuporder@indiana.edu

The paper used in this publication meets the minimum
requirements of American National Standard for Information
Sciences—Permanence of Paper for Printed Library
Materials, ANSI Z39.48-1984.

Manufactured in the United States of America

Library of Congress Cataloging-in-Publication Data

Finger, John R., date
   Tennessee frontiers : three regions in transition / John R.
Finger.
      p. cm.—(A history of the trans-Appalachian frontier)
Includes bibliographical references (p.   ) and index.
   ISBN 0–253-33985–5 (cloth : alk. paper)
   1. Tennessee—History. 2. Frontier and pioneer life—
Tennessee. 3. Pioneers—Tennessee—History. 4. Land
settlement—Tennessee—History. 5. Indians of North
America—Tennessee—History. 6. Indian land transfers—
Tennessee—History. 7. Tennessee—Social conditions.
8. Tennessee—Ethnic relations.   I. Title. II. Series.
   F436 .F56 2001
   976.8—dc21
                                          2001001387
1   2   3   4   5   06   05   04   03   02   01

FOR

Judi

Contents

☙ List of Illustrations

☙ List of Maps

Foreword

For most Americans "the West" refers to the western half of the nation. From the Great Plains across the Rockies and the intermontane plateaus to the Pacific Ocean, "the American West" conjures up a flood of popular images: trappers, cowboys, miners, and homesteading families; the Marlboro man and country-western music. This has been the West since the California Gold Rush and the migration of '49ers propelled the region into the national consciousness.

But it was not always so. There was an earlier American West, no less vivid and no less dramatic. Here the fabled figures were not John Charles Frémont and Geronimo, but Daniel Boone and Tecumseh; not Calamity Jane and "Buffalo Bill" Cody, but Rachel Jackson and Davy Crockett. Geographically, this earlier West extended from the crest of the Appalachian Mountains to the Mississippi River, from the border with Canada to the Gulf of Mexico. It was the West of Euro-American expansion from before the American Revolution until the middle of the nineteenth century, when the line of frontier settlement moved through the first West toward that new, farther West.

Initially the story of the first American West involved two sets of characters: first, the white people of European origin, and south of the Ohio River, African-American slaves, who were spreading relentlessly westward; second, the original settlers, the Native Americans, who retreated grudgingly before the flood. The first Europeans, French and Spanish, appeared on this landscape in the 1600s and early 1700s, and their interactions with the original native peoples involved both cooperation and conflict. The English arrived a half-century later. The Europeans were almost always a minority in number, so they and the Indians sought neither conquest nor annihilation, but mutual accommodation, joint occupation of the land and joint use of its resources. The system of contact allowed both sides to survive and even to benefit from one another's presence. Trade developed and intermarriage followed, and so did misunderstandings and violence. Still, a delicate balance supported by mutual interests often characterized relations among Europeans and native peoples.

When Anglo-Americans began moving through the Cumberland Gap from Virginia into what hunters called the Kentucky country in the 1750s, they soon tilted the balance between the two cultures, occupying large portions of Kentucky and pressing against native groups from Ohio south to Georgia. By 1780, the Anglo-Americans had also occupied the former French settlements of Cahokia in Illinois and Vincennes in Indiana. Despite strong resistance by several native groups, the seemingly unending reinforcements of white families made the Euro-Americans' gradual occupation of the trans-Appalachian frontier inevitable.

In the 1780s the infant American government issued ordinances spelling out how the land between the Great Lakes and the Ohio River was to be acquired from the native peoples, subdivided, and sold to the citizens of the new republic. The new residents of that region could establish a form of government organization that would lead to statehood and equal membership in the union. A parallel process was soon set up for Kentucky, Tennessee, and the lands south to the Gulf.

In the 1830s and the 1840s, the remaining native groups east of the Mississippi were removed to the West. The expansion of settlement into the trans-Appalachian frontier could now continue unchecked into Illinois, Wisconsin, Michigan, and the great cotton lands and hill country of Alabama, Mississippi, and Florida. The frontier period had been completed—as early as the 1820s in Kentucky, and within the next twenty years throughout much of the Old Northwest and Old Southwest.

In brief terms, this is the story of the trans-Appalachian frontier. Over scarcely three generations, the trickle of settler families across the mountains had become a flood; four million people, both white and black, had settled in the frontier regions. Beginning with Kentucky in 1792 and running through Florida in 1845 and Wisconsin in 1848, a dozen new states had entered the American union. Each territory and state had its own story, and it is appropriate that each will have a separate volume in this series. The variations are broad. Florida's first European arrived in 1513, and this future state was a frontier for Spain and the United States for over 350 years. Missouri had a long French and Spanish history before the arrival of American settlers, but Kentucky and Ohio did not; Americans in large numbers came quickly to the latter states through the Cumberland Gap.

The opening and closing of the settlement frontier is the subject of these volumes. Each begins with the world that existed when Europeans first made contact with native peoples. Each describes and analyzes the themes associated with the special circumstances of the individual territory or state. And each concludes with the closing of the frontier.

The editors of the series have selected authors who have strong reputations as scholars and interpreters of their individual territories and states. We believe that you will find this history informative and lively, and we are confident that you will enjoy this and other volumes in the trans-Appalachian frontier series.

John Finger's history of frontier Tennessee is a description and analysis of three hundred years of the formative period of the area that became the Volunteer State. He begins his account with a superb description of early Tennessee's first Indian peoples and the landscape that they occupied. From the beginning, these Indian peoples were traders. Finger shows how they accommodated themselves to the arrival of the Europeans and used their woodcraft and trading skills to benefit families and tribal groups. In his discussion of early Tennessee before the American Revolution, Finger skillfully blends large themes, personalities, and unfolding events. The American Revolution found Tennessee home to several powerful personalities that helped to shape a series of scattered communities thinking in terms of permanence and growth. Already land had become a central theme, as it was on so many of the frontiers of the trans-Appalachian West. Opportunities for land ownership and land speculation flowered with the close of the Revolution, and several fascinating personalities connived to shape the future of Tennessee to their own ends. That Tennessee lay to the west of the mountains and looked to the West and South for trade and expansion only increased the international intrigues.

Here is a cast of characters—tribal leaders, Indian fighters, diplomats, speculators, political figures—who would guide Tennessee in the fight for territorial status and later statehood. Finger's analysis of the organization of the territory and the struggle for statehood is remarkably effective; he weaves together the varied personalities and the separate settlements and districts into a single story, and he expertly describes ordinary people and their activities in families and communities. He recognizes the significance of each county and its many institutions for the first generation of Euro-American settlers. After Tennessee became a state in 1796, a full generation of its pioneer period still lay ahead, and Finger follows the story into the Western District and illuminates the Americans' ongoing negotiations with Indian peoples over land cessions, closing his account with the removal of the Cherokees. The removal was a physical and symbolic ending of a frontier that stretched across a vast landscape and involved growing numbers of people—red, white, and black—over five generations. This compelling story will draw the interest of anyone interested in Tennessee's history.

WALTER NUGENT
University of Notre Dame

MALCOLM ROHRBOUGH
University of Iowa

Introduction

More than a hundred years ago Frederick Jackson Turner presented a famous paper in which he contended that the frontier had provided the single most important catalyst for American development. He argued that a series of frontier zones, beginning with English settlement on the Atlantic coast, had carried whites ever westward until after 300 years they had conquered a continent and now gazed upon the Pacific. The evolutionary result of the westward movement and of adapting to these frontiers was the creation of a new person, the American, who exemplified such traits as coarseness, practicality, materialism, individualism, nationalism, and democracy. The American was a product of the physical environment.

Perhaps the most important of these frontier zones was the one immediately west of the Appalachians, which challenged white Americans in the late eighteenth and early nineteenth centuries. Turner believed its conquest was decisive in the shaping of the American identity; it separated us from our European forebears and turned our psychic energies from the past to the future.

Tennessee, as a crucial component of the trans-Appalachian frontier, attracted early scholarly attention. During the 1930s Thomas P. Abernethy, Carl Driver, Samuel Cole Williams, and others published an array of important works. Abernethy's *From Frontier to Plantation in Tennessee: A Study of Frontier Democracy* (1932) remains a landmark of frontier historiography. Since that watershed decade, scholars like Harriet Simpson Arnow and Walter Durham have written excellent studies of specific aspects of the state's frontier experience, but there has been no comprehensive coverage of the topic. In this volume I hope to remedy that lack by providing a sound, up-to-date overview of Tennessee's frontier experiences over a 300-year period, emphasizing those aspects I believe are most important.

For many years as historians have argued vehemently for or against Turner's assumptions, they have often ignored a central question: What *is* a frontier? Turner himself employed various definitions before concluding lamely that the term is "elastic" and "does not need sharp definition." Regardless of its precise meaning, some scholars believe the term is so heavily laden with racist, sexist, and nationalist overtones that we should simply discard it. I believe the critics protest too much. They are correct in noting many of the inadequacies of Turner's paean to the frontier (however defined), but they often ignore his insights, especially his suggestion of certain recurring patterns in the sequence of settlement zones. Modern scholars have discussed six of these parallel processes: "species shifting," the introduction of new flora, fauna, and pathogens within each new zone and their interaction with the "virgin" environment; "market making," the economic exchange among Native Americans and Europeans and the creation and satisfaction of new market demands; "land taking" by Euro-Americans (in my view the most important of the processes); "boundary setting," reflecting the Euro-American penchant for commodifying and distinguishing each person's land from that of another; "state making," a political process establishing organized local authority to legitimize and protect frontier gains; and "self shaping," defining a regional identity for the post-frontier period.

My intention is to consider some of the above processes, especially market making and land taking, in discussing the development and passing of Tennessee's several frontiers. These processes are components of larger themes which will appear throughout the book. This is a selective history of the Tennessee frontier. I have included no separate chapters on religion, transportation, or daily life, though those topics appear within other contexts. Nor do I dwell on the frontier's real or alleged role in the emergence of a more democratic America by the 1830s. Instead, I begin by briefly discussing a series of prehistoric frontiers involving millennia-long processes of adaptation and creativity by Native Americans. The rest of the book deals with Tennessee's historic period and defines its frontier era as that time when two processes are at work, usually simultaneously and in conjunction with each other. First is the early interaction of Native Americans and Euro-Americans, ending when the latter gained effective hegemony. (The African-American experience is subsumed within that contest for hegemony.) The second is Euro-American development lasting until the emergence of a market economy. In Tennessee these processes began at different times but concluded at almost the same moment.

The frontier era obviously began with the incursion of Hernando de Soto's Spanish army in 1540. When to date the "effective hegemony" of Euro-Americans is somewhat more problematic. One might argue for 1795, by which time Cherokee and Creek military resistance within Tennessee had ended, but I have decided instead on the late 1830s, when the Cherokees made their last land cession and the tribal majority moved westward over the Trail of Tears. Land, after all, was crucial to both Euro-Americans and Indians, and its final, decisive acquisition by whites best demonstrated their effective hegemony.

It is also difficult to pinpoint when a market economy emerged. The first Anglo-Americans in Tennessee participated in a worldwide fur and deerskin trade that emanated from the capitals of Europe. Likewise, in the 1790s an extensive commerce linked Tennessee farmers and town dwellers with the markets of Philadelphia, Baltimore, and Richmond. No white Tennessean, not even the fabled long hunter, was ever totally self-sufficient or removed from the market economy. Those acknowledgments made, I am defining the emergence of a market economy as that time when most farmers in a given region moved beyond subsistence production and became dependent on regional, national, or international markets. When this occurred obviously varied in a state as geographically disparate as Tennessee; each of its three grand divisions contains many discrete and dissimilar areas that produced sequential frontiers or zones where the advent and duration of subsistence agriculture differed. Though a few isolated areas did not leave the frontier stage until long after 1840, most of the state had made the transition by then.

Two major themes emerge in this book. The first is what I call access to opportunity, the belief of frontier people—and Americans in general—that North America offered unique opportunities for social and economic advancement. The foremost means of advancement was the acquisition of land for productive or speculative purposes. From the outset land was a coveted commodity which impacted most aspects of frontier life. The second theme is the continuing tension between local autonomy and central authority. Woven into the fabric of frontier life was a reliance on government at all levels: on Parliament, on the legislative bodies of individual colonies or states, on Congress, and on local ad hoc creations like the state of Franklin. Frontier people expected government to acquire land from Indians and foreign nations, to devise a liberal land policy, to provide military protection, to make internal improvements, and to create a unifying sense of purpose or identity. But even while seeking favors, frontier residents resisted imposition of outside controls.

The frontier was not only an arena of interaction between whites and Indians, but it was also a zone of cultural interaction *within* those two groups. Pervasive distinctions of class separated frontier elites from "lesser" whites, and the struggle for control divided the elites themselves. Similarly, native society was riddled by factional disputes over the proper course of action regarding relations with other tribes or with whites. Despite this discord, Indians were resilient, culturally innovative and syncretic, and able to devise rational responses to new situations. Yes, they ultimately lost in certain fundamental ways, but they adopted a variety of strategies that delayed those losses and enabled them to retain their own identity, albeit in modified form. Scholars should no longer depict Native Americans simply as victims of white aggression.

Frontier history, more than most academic fields, is interwoven with symbolism and mythology. Indeed, the frontier is a cornerstone of American popular culture and probably shapes our national identity more than any other myth. Whether or not Turner was correct in his analysis of the frontier, he tapped into the vast reservoir of popular belief that the frontier made Ameri-

cans different from other peoples. The Myth of the West has become linked with such enduring stereotypes as the Long Hunter,
Mountain Man, Pioneer Farmer, and Cowboy. In differing ways
all are seen as tamers of frontier savagery and agents of change,
progress, and civilization. Our popular culture often portrays
real-life individuals as representatives of these mythic figures
and thus as legitimate American heroes. Recently Indian leaders
have joined this pantheon of heroes, not as the vanguard of Euro-
American civilization but as opponents of white aggression. Tennessee has more than its share of such red and white idols. But
Attakullakulla, Nancy Ward, Daniel Boone, John Sevier, Davy
Crockett, Andrew Jackson, and John Ross are far more than
mythical figures; they tell us something very important about
their times and their cultures. Even an endearing rogue like William Blount offers an illuminating case study of frontier avarice
and ambition.

A few cautionary notes are in order. For the sake of consis-
tency and clarity, I have opted for uniform modern spellings of
place names outside Tennessee—Charleston, for example, rather
than the earlier Charles Town. I also refer to South Carolina and
North Carolina according to the present boundaries of those
states, ignoring the fact that for many years they were both part
of a greater Carolina. Likewise, I speak of *Tennessee* throughout
the text, even when discussing its earliest habitation and the time
during which it was part of North Carolina. This will avoid unnecessary confusion attending the fact that all or a portion of the state
underwent many incarnations. Where necessary I am more precise by referring, for example, to Watauga, Franklin, or the Southwest Territory. Similarly, the names of certain geographic features are consistent with modern usage; for instance, the stream
from the junction of the French Broad and Holston rivers down
to the mouth of the Little Tennessee I refer to as the Tennessee
River, though for many years it was regarded as an extension of
the Holston and was called by that name. And what was once
known as the Tennessee River is known today (and in this study)
as the Little Tennessee. I employ the terms East, Middle, and
West Tennessee to denote those geographic divisions as they pres-

ently exist, even though for many years Middle Tennessee was called West Tennessee because the area to its west was unceded Indian land.

To avoid undue repetition, I use the terms *Indian* and *Native American* interchangeably, though the currently preferred designation is *American Indian*. Likewise, I write of *mixed-bloods* and *métis* when referring to the offspring of white-and-Indian liaisons. Some scholars object to the former term because of its supposedly racist implications. I use it because it has obvious descriptive utility, and I do so without any racist or other derogatory intentions. When using Indian personal names, I usually opt for the ones that most commonly appear in documentary sources.

Finally, I hope to remember that Tennessee's frontier experience is a story of real people dealing with real problems and possibilities in often difficult circumstances. It is my intention to portray them as accurately and sympathetically as possible, to reach back into time and convey their humanity and complexity with understanding and empathy.

One who undertakes a project of this sort is inevitably beholden to many institutions and individuals. At the risk of omitting those who have graced me with their goodwill and competence, I wish to thank the following: the staff of the Tennessee State Library and Archives in Nashville, especially Ann E. Alley; Anne E. Bridges, Humanities Reference Librarian at the John C. Hodges Library of the University of Tennessee; James Lloyd and his assistants in Special Collections at the same institution; staff members of Knoxville's Lawson-McGhee Library; the staff of the East Tennessee Historical Society, especially Mike Toomey; my former research assistants, Forrest Marion and Linda Gail Frost; the College of Arts and Sciences of the University of Tennessee, for assistance in preparing maps and illustrations; and the helpful people of the Appalachian Archives at East Tennessee State University and the Mississippi Valley Collection at the University of Memphis.

My colleagues in the Department of History at the University of Tennessee have provided both personal and professional support, even when good-naturedly asking, "Your contract deadline was *when?*" I am also indebted to Paul H. Bergeron, Walter Nugent, and Malcolm J. Rohrbough for their careful readings of my manuscript and for their perceptive, helpful suggestions. The latter two are series editors for A History of the Trans-Appalachian Frontier, and they waited much longer for this book than any of us expected. They did so with patience and good humor and offered appropriate words of encouragement. Any errors of fact or interpretation in *Tennessee Frontiers* are of course my own responsibility. Finally, I wish to thank my wife, Judith Gaston, for her constant love and support. She has sustained me.

Tennessee Frontiers

I.

LAND, PEOPLE, AND EARLY FRONTIERS

People and land interact in many ways, producing fundamental changes in each. When writing of a region, then, especially of its frontier stages, it is essential to explore those myriad interactions and their consequences. In the case of Tennessee, that task is difficult because the state's 42,244 square miles encompass disparate geographic features which have attracted different peoples at different times. Scholars and politicians often acknowledge these geographic and historical peculiarities by referring to the three states or grand divisions of East, Middle, and West Tennessee.

East Tennessee, the most physically diverse of the regions, has witnessed the most complex frontier experiences as peoples of different races and cultures coped in their own ways with one another and with the dictates of nature. Officially this region stretches westward from North Carolina to the middle of the Cumberland Plateau. Its boundary with North Carolina is within a physiographic province, the Unaka Mountains, which includes the Great Smoky range and has peaks towering more than 6,600 feet above sea level. Although the mist-enshrouded mountains, lush flora, and cascading streams shaped a rich body of mythic lore for early Indians, this province offered few attractions for permanent habitation. Not until the early nineteenth century would small settlements of white pioneers intrude into narrow valleys like Cades Cove and become eddies in the major flow of westward migration.

Both whites and Indians favored the gentler, more productive landscape of the Ridge and Valley Province immediately west of the mountains. A series of valleys on a northeast-to-southwest axis separated by low ridges, this region is commonly known as the Great Valley of East Tennessee and is an extension of the Great Valley of Virginia. This is where Tennessee's first European visitors interacted with complex and highly accomplished Indian societies. The well-watered valleys were generally fertile, and around Indian villages they featured extensive fields of corn. Timber was abundant: thick forests of deciduous species like oak, chestnut, and poplar, as well as scattered expanses of conifers such as pine, cedar, hemlock, fir, and spruce. River cane flourished along the streams, providing forage and protection for livestock and wild animals alike. Game was plentiful and included turkey, squirrel, black bear, white-tailed deer, elk, and wood bison (buffalo).

Linking the valleys of East Tennessee is a broad network of streams coursing toward the southwest, some bearing Indian names, some rechristened by presumptuous whites. Among them are the Powell, Nolichucky, and Watauga rivers; they comprise a litany of frontier experience and flow into the even more famous Holston and French Broad rivers, which join to form the Tennessee just above Knoxville. (*Tennessee* is itself a probable bastardization of "Tanasee," the name of a Cherokee town.) Flowing southwestward, the Tennessee swells as it absorbs the Little Tennessee, Clinch, and Hiwassee rivers. At Chattanooga it takes a sharp jog to the northwest and makes a deep cut, the Grand Canyon of the Tennessee, into the Cumberland Plateau; it then loops southward and westward through Alabama and northward across Middle Tennessee and Kentucky to meet the Ohio River.

The Cumberland Plateau, an ancient elevated tableland, includes parts of northern Alabama and Georgia, widens through Tennessee, and expands even more to cover much of eastern Kentucky and a smaller area in Virginia. In Tennessee its breadth ranges from about forty to fifty-five miles, and its midpoint is the demarcation between the eastern and middle parts of the state. The plateau is steepest along its eastern front, Walden Ridge, which rises northeastward toward the Cumberland Mountains. At about 3,500 feet above sea level, these mountains are the highest part of the plateau. Separating Walden Ridge from the southern portion of the plateau is the narrow valley of the Sequatchie River, which follows a leisurely southwesterly course and joins the Tennessee near Chattanooga. The western part of the plateau is drained by numerous streams that flow into Middle Tennessee and is more broken and eroded than the eastern half. Throughout the plateau are countless caves, caverns, waterfalls, and narrow canyons, as well as many varieties of trees and wildlife.

Despite its natural beauty, the Cumberland Plateau has the dubious historical distinction of being an obstacle for humans wishing to go elsewhere. To the first white settlers, it was the "Barrens" or the "Wilderness," a dangerous and inconvenient barrier to the fertile valleys and basins beyond. This explains why the plateau's most famous feature is Cumberland Gap, that point in the Cumberland Mountains where Virginia, Kentucky, and Tennessee meet. For many generations the gap has offered Indians and whites convenient access to the Kentucky Bluegrass and Central Basin, also known as the Nashville or Cumberland Basin.

Resembling "the bottom of an oval dish," the Central Basin is roughly one hundred miles by fifty to sixty miles in dimension and has an elevation of about six hundred feet. It is the central feature of Middle Tennessee, which extends from the Cumberland Plateau to the Western Valley of the Tennessee River. Completely encircling the basin is the Highland Rim. On the east the rim is a transitional link to the plateau; about twenty-five miles wide, it consists of gently rolling plains and hills about four hundred feet above the basin and one thousand feet below the plateau. On the northwest the rim broadens into a slightly lower belt some seventy-five miles wide that separates the basin from the Tennessee River. Early white hunters were amazed by the basin's abundance of game and by its springs, streams, timber, and natural grasslands. They viewed the area as a hunter's paradise and extolled the rolling, fertile land—more abundant and better than that of East Tennessee. The basin became a symbolic Garden of Eden, with dangers nearly as ominous as those confronting Adam and Eve.

Both East and Middle Tennessee were crisscrossed by a network of well-traveled Indian trails that linked Native American societies in every part of the Southeast and well beyond. Because of the surrounding terrain the Chattanooga and Nashville areas became hubs of aboriginal travel, with trails radiating in all directions. The most important and famous was the Great Indian Warpath—or simply the Warrior's Path—which extended from Chattanooga up the Great Valley of East Tennessee into Virginia and then down the New and Kanawha rivers to the upper Ohio. One major branch continued down the Shenandoah River and into Pennsylvania, and another led through Cumberland Gap and Kentucky to the Ohio opposite the Scioto River. The latter route became increasingly important in the eighteenth century for red and white Tennesseans alike.

Though the Warrior's Path was used for every purpose, including trade and diplomacy, its name suggests a more dramatic import: it provided access for wide-ranging war parties on campaigns of blood revenge and martial glory. Cherokee and Iroquois warriors walked hundreds of miles between the southern Appalachians and upstate New York to sustain bloodletting campaigns so ancient that both groups understood them only imperfectly. Other important trails led from Chattanooga and the mouth of the Clinch River across the Cumberland Plateau and into the Central Basin. Another well-traveled route crossed the Tennessee River at Muscle Shoals, Alabama, and linked Middle Tennessee with the Chickasaw and Choctaw villages to the southwest. This would become part of the famous Natchez Trace. Farther to the west a trail connected the site of Memphis, a major crossing point on the Mississippi, with the Alabama-Tombigbee river systems and Mobile Bay.

Indians often combined these overland trails with the ample waterways, relying on dugout canoes—sometimes carrying twenty or more men—or lightly-framed craft covered with elm

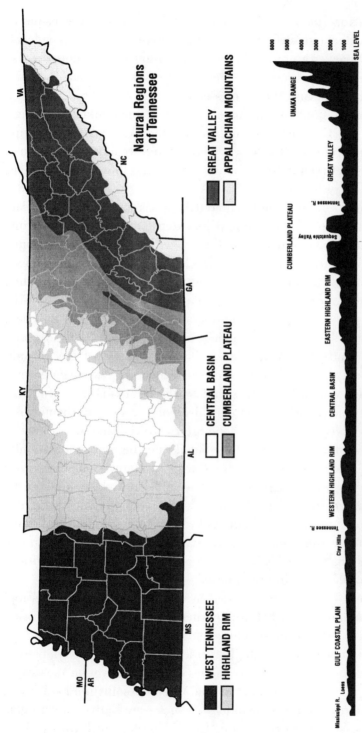

Natural Regions of Tennessee.

A cross section of Tennessee which compares the elevations of the different Natural Regions.

Natural Regions
of Tennessee

WEST TENNESSEE

HIGHLAND RIM

CENTRAL BASIN

CUMBERLAND PLATEAU

GREAT VALLEY

APPALACHIAN MOUNTAINS

or hickory bark. The Cumberland and Tennessee rivers were particularly important for extended travel. The former is laced with treacherous rapids in the plateau but becomes more domesticated and navigable as it enters the Central Basin. Both the Cumberland and the Tennessee cut large arcs through Middle Tennessee, and the distance between them gradually narrows until the Cumberland empties into the Ohio a few miles upstream from the Tennessee. Those three streams offered direct access between most of Tennessee and the Illinois Country and Mississippi Basin.

Early settlers usually entered East Tennessee by way of the Great Valley of Virginia and its extensions or by narrow trails from North Carolina through the Blue Ridge and Unaka Mountains. Most travelers going to the Central Basin followed the Warrior's Path through Cumberland Gap into Kentucky and then turned southward across the barrens to French Lick, a large spring where Nashville would arise. Others heading to the basin chose to float down the Tennessee. At optimal times the Tennessee's head of navigation was the Long Island of the Holston (present-day Kingsport), but low water often necessitated embarking well downstream. Then travelers had to brave two natural obstacles: first a gigantic whirlpool or "suck" in the narrows of the river's canyon and soon afterward the shallow and tricky stretch of water called Muscle Shoals. For those who successfully navigated these dangers, there usually followed an uneventful though arduous trip up the Ohio and the Cumberland to the basin. En route they would pass the mouth of the Red River, another navigable stream and the future site of Clarksville. Whatever route one took, the Central Basin—or simply "the Cumberland"—became a magnet even before East Tennessee was well into its frontier phase.

West Tennessee is bounded by the Tennessee and Mississippi rivers, and most of it is part of the much larger Gulf Coastal Plain. Its easternmost component is a narrow zone of hilly, broken upland bordering the Tennessee. From there the terrain gradually slopes downward to a series of bluffs above the Mississippi Bottoms, which are part of the Mississippi River Flood Plain. Those promontories include the Chickasaw Bluffs, which touch the Mississippi at four points from Memphis northward and are famous landmarks for river travelers. Major Tennessee tributaries of the Mississippi include the Big Hatchie, Forked Deer, Obion, and Wolf rivers. All offered access eastward a short distance into the interior, but they sometimes overflowed, and much of the surrounding terrain was swampy and marshy. The bottomland, though often unhealthy, was home to one of the most interesting and advanced prehistoric Native American communities in the state. White explorers, however, were more impressed with the geopolitical significance of the Chickasaw Bluffs, and they periodically built fortifications there. Later, speculators and settlers would extol West Tennessee's agricultural and commercial potential. The cession of the last Indian claims in 1818 opened the door to a new settlement frontier and the eventual emergence of Memphis as the state's largest city. By 1840 West Tennessee's cotton production was integrating the region into the national and world economies.

* * *

Clearly Tennessee's physiography, flora, and fauna helped to shape the frontier experiences of its people. Coping with the demands of nature, seeking reconciliation with the landscape or a tenuous hegemony over it, was a major feature of a series of frontiers stretching far back in time. Each culminated in or blended with a sometimes lengthy period of stable habitation and significant attainments before giving way to a new frontier produced by exploration, trade, migration, and the mingling of different peoples and cultures. These historical processes, which we normally associate with Eurocentric frontiers, occurred also during the thousands of years of pre-Columbian habitation in the Americas. Migration legends and other oral traditions suggest that ancestors of the Cherokees, Chickasaws, and Shawnees had participated in epic frontier adventures similar to those of Euro-Americans—whose ancestors had opened new frontiers in Europe. And these Indian frontiers continued to evolve simultaneously with, and partly in response to, those of Euro-Americans. Native American adaptability and creativity amid changing circumstances is one of the great underappreciated themes of frontier history.

Tennessee's first frontiersmen were the small bands of anonymous hunters who ventured into the region some twelve to thirteen thousand years ago. These nomads, called Paleo-Indians by archaeologists, were descendants of people who had appeared in North America during the last Ice Age, a time when gigantic glaciers formed, sea levels dropped, and a wide land bridge emerged linking Siberia and Alaska. Recent genetic and linguistic analyses point to three or more major movements from the Old World to New during that time. We know that the first and most important of these migrations occurred at least twelve to fifteen thousand years ago, and some scholars argue for much earlier arrivals some thirty to forty thousand years ago. Anthropologists categorize the Paleo-Indian period as the first of four lengthy eras of human habitation in the Southeast prior to white contact; the others are the Archaic, Woodland, and Mississippian periods.

Paleo-Indian artifacts, including the distinctive projectile points of the Clovis culture, are found in all parts of Tennessee. The otherwise scanty evidence suggests that small bands of nomadic hunters operated out of temporary base camps on river terraces and upland knolls or in caves and rock shelters. In many parts of the United States Paleo-Indians hunted large game animals like mammoths and mastodons, but no prehistoric habitation sites in Tennessee are indisputably associated with megafaunal kills, though further research at the Coats-Hines Mastodon Site in Williamson County may produce such a link. We should probably assume that early Tennessee hunters, like other Paleo-Indians, pursued large game animals when they encountered them but concentrated on hunting smaller mammals and foraging for wild plant foods. If this is so, their subsistence patterns differed from those of their Early Archaic successors only in degree rather than in kind.

By the advent of the Archaic period about ten thousand years ago Tennessee's climate, flora, and fauna were nearly identical to those encountered by the first Europeans in the mid-sixteenth century. Gone were the mega-fauna and extensive deciduous forests were common everywhere. During the next seven thousand years or so the hunter-gatherer economy shifted from small seasonal base camps to denser populations in semi-permanent camps or villages on favored riverine sites. Indians hunted game like deer, bear, and turkey, and the atlatl, or throwing stick, enabled them to propel their spears with great force. Dramatic dietary changes came with widescale gathering of nuts and wild fruits as well as consumption of fish, freshwater mussels, snails, and turtles. At the Eva site near the Tennessee River in Benton County, large midden heaps offer conclusive proof of the variety of foods available to the many generations of settlers between about eight and three thousand years ago. The site also reveals many of the increasingly complex cultural patterns of Archaic peoples: impressive stone technology, lithic workshop areas, and ceremonial burials of bodies arranged in flexed positions. During the late phase of its occupation, the site was part of a trade network that brought a few residents prestige items like marine shells from the Gulf of Mexico and pieces of copper from the Great Lakes area.

Cultural change accelerated with the advent of the Woodland period about three thousand years ago. By now Tennessee Indians typically resided in communities on the floodplains and on terraces of major streams. Subsistence still depended on hunting and gathering, but the bow and arrow, a major innovation, emerged sometime in the first millennium A.D. Whether this technological advance arrived by diffusion from the Old World or was reinvented in the Americas remains unknown. More important, Indian villagers embarked on the road to agriculture through increasingly systematic use of domesticated native plants like sunflowers, squash, and gourds. Though Indian corn, or maize, was introduced from the Southwest at an early date, it did not become important in Tennessee Indian diets until about nine hundred A.D. Beans appeared even later.

Woodland cultural complexity was striking. Ceramic pottery appeared and began an evolution that proceeded through distinct archaeological phases into the historic period. As the population increased, societies moved toward social stratification and loose unification, and burial mounds for important individuals became common. Palisades around towns indicate fear or wariness of neighbors, but trading links with distant peoples brought Tennesseans new products, ideas, and cultural patterns. Ritualism became more prevalent and complex, though its many meanings are probably lost forever. One example is the misnamed Old

Tennessee Hunters and Gatherers, ca. 5,000 B.C.
PAINTING BY GREG HARLIN. COURTESY FRANK H. McCLUNG
MUSEUM, THE UNIVERSITY OF TENNESSEE.

Stone Fort near Manchester, apparently constructed over a period of several centuries and completed some sixteen hundred
years ago. Most likely this large, open area bounded by steep
cliffs and embankments of earth and stone served as a ceremonial center. Even more impressive are the systematically arranged Pinson Mounds near Jackson, dating mostly from about
one hundred to three hundred A.D. and used for burials and ceremonies. One of these, Saul's Mound, is the second highest Indian
mound north of Mexico. Indians apparently traveled hundreds
of miles from other parts of the Southeast to participate in ceremonies there. Neither the Old Stone Fort nor the Pinson complex
served as sites of permanent habitation.

Around nine hundred A.D. the Woodland period began to give

way to the Mississippian period, so called because of startling new cultural developments throughout the Southeast that took an earlier, more dramatic form in the middle Mississippi Valley. The most famous example of these changes is the Cahokia site across the river from present-day St. Louis, where a large palisaded community dominated an extensive hinterland. Trade and an increasing reliance on corn enabled the population to increase during the late eleventh century to anywhere from fifteen to forty thousand people. Such growth brought more social stratification and cultural accomplishments. Eventually Cahokia and other incipient urban centers became chiefdoms ruled by hereditary leaders from distinguished clans or lineages. Some centers emerged as paramount chiefdoms and exercised tributary authority over smaller chiefdoms.

The most striking feature of these towns was the large pyramidal mounds with flattened tops that were used as platforms for temples and the residences of chiefs or priests. The largest of these is at Cahokia. Often the mounds overlooked a large plaza around which were lesser mounds, homes of villagers, and public buildings. Chucalissa Village, on the south side of Memphis, is an on-site reconstruction of an important Mississippian community, complete with mounds and Indian domiciles. So impressive were the Mississippian mounds that hundreds of years later, long after their parent culture had disappeared, white Americans assumed that no ancestors of contemporary Indians could possibly have produced them. Enlightenment-era men like Thomas Jefferson believed that an ancient race of mound builders must have immigrated from Europe, the Middle East, or even the lost continent of Atlantis. Only in the late nineteenth century did archaeologists prove that Indians had indeed built the mounds.

How and why this Mississippian culture appeared throughout the Southeast is a source of controversy involving theories of diffusion, migration, and on-site cultural adaptation. What is clear is that in the several centuries before the Spanish arrived a number of chiefdoms and paramount chiefdoms blanketed many of the larger river systems in the region. Moundville in Alabama and Etowah and Macon in Georgia are among the best known of such centers, and each is marked by impressive mounds. These

Toqua, a Late Prehistoric Town (ca. 1450 A.D.).
PAINTING BY GREG HARLIN. COURTESY FRANK H. McCLUNG
MUSEUM, THE UNIVERSITY OF TENNESSEE.

and certain other chiefdoms had already disintegrated well before Europeans arrived, reflecting the fluid nature of Indian society and of shifting pre-Columbian frontiers.

Among the many smaller mound sites in Tennessee is Toqua
on the Little Tennessee River. By 1400 this town had two mounds,
covered nearly five acres, and had a population of 250–300
people. The surrounding palisade separating it from outlying
fields reflected another feature of Mississippian chiefdoms: frequent warfare, conducted more for revenge and status than for
territorial expansion. By the mid-sixteenth century Toqua and
other East Tennessee communities appear to have been tributary
parts of a large confederation centered at Coosa, in northwestern Georgia.

At many different Mississippian sites archaeologists have found a variety of strikingly similar artistic and symbolic objects which, because they suggest common politico-religious beliefs, signify the Southeastern Ceremonial Complex or the Southern Cult. Many of these are ornaments like shell gorgets and other prestige items, and they are typically incised with intricate patterns and motifs like the Greek cross, feathered serpent, swastika, circles with scalloped edges, and the human eye depicted in the palms of hands or with chevrons and other designs. Scholars still disagree over the extent to which this Southern Cult derived from similar artistic and religious conventions in Mesoamerica, but many other features of Mississippian culture—most notably the mounds and such cultigens as corn, beans, and squash—had appeared earlier in central Mexico.

Despite fragmentary and sometimes ambiguous evidence, it appears that pre-Columbian Tennesseans had a significant impact on the natural environment. At some point in the Woodland period, they perhaps began to use fire to clear spots in the forest for rudimentary garden plots—or to encourage natural growth of desirable plants. Pollen samples from the Cumberland Plateau indicate that such open areas near ridgetops were repopulated by pitch pine, oak, walnut, chestnut and other fire-tolerant species of trees. Thus a "fine-grained patchwork of vegetation" appeared on the upper slopes, while on the less-disturbed lower slopes the older, moister ecology of hemlock, cedar, and basswood persisted. This raises the possibility that some oak-chestnut forests of the historic era resulted at least in part from aboriginal land management. There is also evidence of fire-induced clearings in the more heavily populated parts of southeastern Tennessee from the Woodland period to the sixteenth century, but it is unclear how many of these fires were from natural causes, were intentionally set, or were accidentally induced by other human activity such as tree felling. Several scholars suggest that intentional firing was probably infrequent and mostly confined to level areas in the more populous floodplains.

Circumstantial evidence suggesting such use of fire is the fact that Southeastern Indians understood how it cleared objectionable brush and litter, added nutrients to fields, and promoted good hunting and the growth of desirable plants (for example, river cane, which they used in massive quantities). Documentary evidence shows that Northeastern Indians employed fire in this way in the sixteenth century, and their knowledge could hardly have been a regional secret. Quite apart from their use of fire, Tennessee Indians reshaped the landscape in other ways. To support some of the larger communities, they must have cleared thousands of acres for planting corn and to provide timber for their palisades and houses. One estimate is that over a period of years an average-size Mississippian town would require the cutting of thirty thousand trees (some of which were probably second-growth trees sprouting in abandoned fields).

Clearly Tennessee's native inhabitants had a long and diverse history before they ever encountered whites. Their varied societies had succeeded in meeting their shifting needs, and during the Mississippian period they enjoyed their greatest prosperity, complexity, and cultural achievement. But there were internal problems—perhaps a combination of demographic, political, and economic changes—that are not entirely clear today. Well before the arrival of Europeans the Mississippian culture was declining in certain areas; the Spanish merely accelerated that process.

* * *

May 30, 1539, was a momentous day for the prehistoric Southeast. On that date Hernando de Soto, a Spaniard who had helped Francisco Pizzaro destroy the Inca empire in Peru, landed at Tampa Bay with some six hundred infantry and cavalry. Determined to acquire his own New World gold and other precious commodities, de Soto had won appointment as governor of Cuba and, more important, rights to explore and settle La Florida, which encompassed most of the Southeast. Neither hardship nor the prospect of death deterred him and his men. Mostly commoners, they represented a variety of occupations and included at least seven priests. At thirty-eight, de Soto was the oldest of this invading force, and the average age was probably less than twenty-five. Like many English, Scots-Irish, and German frontier people of later centuries, they were bound together by kinship and locality. The expedition enrolled brothers, nephews, and in-laws, and some of the men knew one another from previous campaigns in North Africa or Latin America. Data on 240 survivors of the expedition show that 41 percent were natives of Extremadura in southwestern Spain, a hardscrabble area which contributed many tough, ambitious men to New World adventures. Most of the rest came from other rural—even frontier—parts of Spain. There was also a sizable contingent of Portuguese, a few other Europeans, and a few blacks (both slaves and free men). At least six women are listed in the original company. The animal retinue consisted of approximately 220 horses, a number of hunting and attack dogs, and a herd of pigs for a mobile, emergency food supply.

De Soto's exact route is a source of great controversy because his quest for precious booty led him on an erratic course through Florida, Georgia, the Carolinas, and westward into Tennessee. One of the most common assumptions, that he followed the Hiwassee River into Tennessee and visited the chiefdom of Chiaha near today's Chattanooga, dates to an investigation of sixty years ago. But the most recent scenario, advanced by Charles Hudson and others, is that he and his men left the Indian town of Joara, near present-day Morganton, North Carolina, headed northwestward over the mountains, and entered Tennessee via the Toe and Nolichucky rivers late in May 1540, becoming the first European and African visitors to the state. The first village they encountered was Guasili, probably near present-day Erwin. The residents hospitably provided their guests with corn, small dogs to eat, and porters to carry their baggage. So pleasant was their stay that Spanish soldiers would later acknowledge a lucky roll of dice by calling out, "The House of Guasili."

After one night the Spanish departed from Guasili for the much larger town of Chiaha, where they arrived on June 5. Chiaha, if one accepts Hudson's calculations, was located on Zimmerman's Island in the French Broad River near present-day Dandridge; unfortunately, the site is now submerged by Douglas Lake, a Tennessee Valley Authority (TVA) reservoir. Whatever its location, most scholars agree that Chiaha was tributary to the paramount chiefdom of Coosa in Georgia. The Spaniards rested in Chiaha for more than three weeks and enjoyed a rare abundance of food: all the corn they could eat, a hominy-like gruel

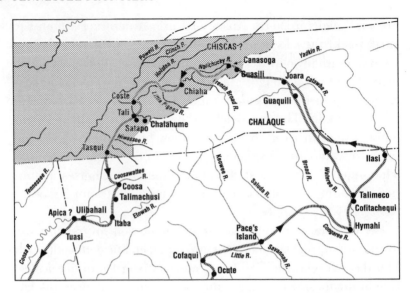

De Soto's Possible Route through Tennessee, 1540.
ADAPTED FROM CHARLES HUDSON AND CARMEN CHAVES TESSER,
EDS., *The Forgotten Centuries: Indians and Europeans in the
American South, 1521–1704*, © 1994 BY UNIVERSITY OF GEORGIA
PRESS.

called *sofkee*, honey, sweet-tasting bear's fat, and hickory oil
(which apparently caused flatulence). They swam, fished, and
collected mussels in the French Broad, while they and their
horses grew fat on the easy living. In the meantime two men were
sent northward to investigate stories about the Chiscas, who were
reputed to have copper and perhaps even gold.

There appears to have been no major trouble in these first en-
counters between Tennessee Indians and the Europeans, but de
Soto had the upper hand and made his customary demands for
food, information, and women. The last request created great
consternation, and many Chiahas fled their village, forcing de
Soto to threaten drastic reprisals unless they returned. They
complied with his demands, and he wisely settled for hundreds
of porters to accompany him on the next stage of his journey. No
doubt the Chiahas were glad to see the Spaniards depart on June
28. According to Hudson, de Soto's expedition headed down the

French Broad, forded the Holston River, and continued along the north bank of the Tennessee, passing through six or seven Indian villages on the way. On June 30 they bivouacked for a night in present-day Knoxville, and on July 2 they stopped at the Indian town of Coste on Bussell Island at the mouth of the Little Tennessee. Initially friendly, the inhabitants became threatening when the Spanish seized some corn and began rummaging for other things of value. Resorting to guile, de Soto tricked the chief and other principal men, then put them in chains and collars to ensure their good behavior. On July 9 the Spaniards finally resumed their march, heading up the north bank of the Little Tennessee to a point across from the chiefdom of Tali, probably the site of Toqua. The river was too swift to ford, but the men of Tali were nonetheless fearful; they piled their women, children, and valuables into dugouts and headed downstream. Somehow, perhaps by brandishing crossbows and primitive firearms, the Spanish were able to turn them back and convince the chief to provide canoes to ferry the soldiers across the river. After camping one night at Tali, the Spaniards continued southward and eventually crossed into Georgia near the present town of Old Fort, Tennessee. De Soto proceeded to the main village of Coosa where he remained for a month and took the paramount chief hostage.

The Spaniards then roamed westward for another two years, finding little wealth, making demands on their Indian hosts, and fighting bloody battles. It is possible, though not likely, that they reached the Memphis area and visited the site of Chucalissa. Hoping to reach Mexico, they ventured well beyond the Mississippi, then returned to its banks where the dispirited de Soto died in May 1542. The remaining Spanish again wandered far to the west before returning to the Mississippi and heading down to the Gulf in improvised boats. They finally reached Spanish Mexico in September 1543.

In April 1567 another Spanish detachment followed a slightly different route into Tennessee, attacked the Chiscas in upper East Tennessee (or possibly southwestern Virginia) and then proceeded to Chiaha, where the Indians treated them well (despite, or perhaps because of, their aggressiveness). The soldiers apparently constructed a small fort there, and if so, it was the first trans-Appalachian fortification built by Europeans. There they awaited their commander, Juan Pardo, who arrived from Santa Elena (Parris Island), South Carolina, on October 7. Pardo had an impossible mission, to find a feasible overland route from South Carolina to Mexico. His expedition got as far as the Little Tennessee before retreating under Indian threat back to the Carolinas. On his return through Chiaha he built a larger outpost, Fort San Pedro, where he left twenty-seven soldiers, who eventually returned to South Carolina. Pardo's men had seen enough of the fertile land, abundant and clean water, and wild fruit trees and grapevines to refer to East Tennessee as *"tierra de angeles,"* land of angels.

Whatever Tennessee's physical attractions, there is no clear-cut evidence that Europeans returned to Tennessee before the late seventeenth century. Scholars call the 150 years between the Spanish expeditions and the documented return of Europeans the Protohistoric period, a time when literate and preliterate societies first met, interacted, and thereafter existed in relative isolation from one another. But early contact had important consequences and required considerable adaptation on the part of Indians. Fortunately, this period has recently attracted serious study, and a spate of archaeological studies has opened tantalizing new vistas on these early contacts.

The dominant feature of the Protohistoric period was the widespread breakup of the Mississippian chiefdoms because of epidemic disease and internal stresses. The Spanish brought a host of diseases, such as smallpox, influenza, and measles, which killed thousands of Indians; it is even possible these contagions were introduced at the time of early coastal contacts and decimated some of the interior chiefdoms before de Soto arrived. Once again, necessity led to creativity. Amid the disruption and breakdown of Mississippian culture, surviving groups adapted rationally by moving out of afflicted areas and coalescing with other remnants. This partly explains the evolution of the Creek Nation, a sociopolitical bonding of diverse groups that originated during the latter part of the Protohistoric period and which wielded considerable power in the eighteenth century. Likewise, the Choctaws of Mississippi created a new polity, a confederacy of sorts, out of the chaos. The overall thrust of these changes was a remarkable adaptation (some call it a devolution) from the complexity and hierarchy of chiefdoms to the relative simplicity and autonomy of new tribal associations. The latter were also better suited to cope with the growing pressures from Europeans.

Among these emerging polities were the Overhill Cherokees of southeastern Tennessee, who figure prominently in colonial records of the eighteenth century. One controversial question is whether, as some anthropologists hypothesize, Cherokee ancestors had occupied the Tennessee River Valley for hundreds of years and evolved (or devolved) from the Mississippian breakup in situ. If so, they were the Tennessee Indians encountered by de Soto and Pardo. Other anthropologists believe most Cherokees resided in the Carolina mountains and foothills at the time of de Soto and that the most likely Spanish contact with them was at a conference near present-day Canton, North Carolina. A few Cherokee speakers might have resided within the borders of Tennessee, these investigators say, but linguistic analysis and other data suggest that mid-sixteenth-century East Tennesseans were primarily non-Cherokees of Muskogean linguistic stock who were related to today's Creeks.

If the latter argument is correct, most Protohistoric East Tennessee Indians migrated southward into Georgia and Alabama following the Spanish expeditions and eventually became Creeks. The move might have been the result of disease-related exigencies or because of pressures exerted by an expanding population of Cherokee speakers. The Cherokees themselves may have been moving partly to settle the attractive riverine sites in Tennessee and partly to escape increasing pressure from Eastern and Northern tribes that had been supplied with firearms and were procuring Indian slaves for English traders in Virginia and South Carolina. Whatever their reasons for migration, these Tennessee newcomers emerged as the Overhill Cherokees—so-called because they lived across the mountains from the Lower and Middle Cherokees, whose villages were in the uplands of South and North Carolina respectively. (The Middle Cherokees included another division known as the Valley Towns.) Not until the end of the seventeenth century can one establish with certainty a direct connection between these tribal components and the Cherokees of today. (The Cherokee tribal name itself is most likely a derivation of "Chalaque," the name of an Indian community in North Carolina visited by de Soto.) By 1715 the Overhill Cherokees had evicted the few remaining proto-Creeks from East Tennessee. At this time the various divisions of Cherokees totaled perhaps ten to twelve thousand people, a sharp decline (no doubt disease-induced) from possibly thirty thousand or more in 1685.

Tennessee's isolation from whites during the Protohistoric period was not complete. Local Indians managed to obtain some European goods from tribes closer to the Atlantic and Gulf coasts, and even by making occasional visits to Spanish Florida. A map of the period clearly shows a path from the Tennessee Valley to the Gulf Coast that was used by Shawnee Indians, and perhaps others, who provided deerskins and beaver pelts for a thriving trade between Florida and Havana. It also seems likely that some anonymous European—perhaps a Spanish soldier or miner, a wide-ranging French trader, or a wandering Englishman—ventured into Tennessee during this period. Cultural and ecological diffusion certainly intruded from coastal areas; early seventeenth-century archaeological sites in southeastern Tennessee contain peach pits, clear evidence that a Spanish foodstuff had already become a staple among Indians of the southern Appalachians. One of the more intriguing cases of possible diffusion involves the Melungeons, a dark-skinned people of obscure lineage, many of whom today live in Hancock County. A recent hypothesis is that they are descended from Spanish military personnel of Portuguese ancestry who had moved from the Atlantic Coast into the interior and intermarried with Indians.

But there is no evidence of whites returning to the state until July 1673, when two Englishmen, James Needham and Gabriel Arthur, after an arduous trek through the wilderness from tidewater Virginia, arrived in what many scholars believe was the Overhill Cherokee town of Chota. They were in the employ of Abraham Wood, a famous fur trader and the proprietor of Fort Henry, located on the present site of Petersburg; he was the most

active of Virginia frontiersmen in promoting westward exploration and the opening of direct trade with the interior tribes. The
Indians Needham and Arthur encountered, Cherokee or not, already possessed a few firearms they had probably obtained from
the Spanish in Florida. Needham was killed while returning to
Virginia, but Arthur had many adventures with his hosts—narrowly avoiding execution, accompanying them to Spanish territory, and being taken captive in warfare with a rival tribe
(perhaps the Shawnees). In the course of all this he might have
become the first white man ever to go through Cumberland Gap.
Within a year he was back in Virginia with a report that, as re-
told, is perplexing in its ambiguity regarding the places and
people he visited. If Arthur was the first Anglo-American frontiersman in Tennessee, he was also one of the most traveled, cov-
ering more than three thousand miles by horse, on foot, and in
dugout canoe. Despite his adventures and favorable reports, significant English trade with the Overhill Cherokees did not develop until the early eighteenth century. When it did begin, it
would initiate the most important phase of Tennessee's frontier
era, a time when Indians and whites experienced sustained interaction and the contest for hegemony was joined.

That contest also involved the French, who paid a quick visit
in 1673, the same year Needham and Arthur presumably con-
tacted the Cherokees. The intrepid Father Jacques Marquette
and his associate Louis Jolliet ventured partway down the Mississippi and skirted Chickasaw territory somewhere around Memphis. They encountered an Indian group called the Mouselas,
who possessed various European items, including weapons, and
who reported that the Gulf of Mexico was only about ten days
travel downstream. More substantive contact came in 1682, when
Robert Cavalier de La Salle's expedition paused at one of the
Chickasaw Bluffs a short distance above Memphis. Pierre Prudhomme, a member of the expedition, disappeared while hunting.
Because there were many paths in the area and other signs of
Indian visitation, La Salle constructed Fort Prudhomme on the
bluff as a temporary base while searching for his missing man.
Upon encountering two Chickasaws who appeared ready to flee,
one of the Frenchmen placed his gun on the ground as a sign of

peace and then, when the Indians approached, pulled out a hidden pistol and took them captive. Desiring peace and still seeking Prudhomme, La Salle sent one of the Indians with gifts and messages to the Chickasaw villages a few days away. Prudhomme finally appeared, and the expedition traveled downstream as far as Natchez with the other Chickasaw, who was well received by the Indians there. This kind treatment and his nonchalance about returning home by trail suggest frequent interaction and possibly even an alliance between the Chickasaws and the Natchez. La Salle continued to the Gulf of Mexico, where he proclaimed French possession of the vast Mississippi drainage and named it Louisiana in honor of King Louis XIV. His brief garrisoning of the Chickasaw Bluffs and his taking of Chickasaw hostages were a warning to Indians that the French—and indeed all Europeans—were prepared for war as well as for trade and diplomacy.

2.

TRADE, ACCULTURATION, AND EMPIRE: 1700–1775

For Tennessee Indians the 150 years following de Soto's expedition were fraught with unsettling portents. Demographic upheavals and the creation of new polities brought uncertainty and a hint of the greater transformations that were soon to occur. Sheltered by distance from the new European outposts on the South Atlantic and Gulf coasts, native Tennesseans nonetheless obtained a few manufactured items reflecting the material allures of white civilization. But soon the diffusion of European goods accelerated and assumed dangerous proportions. South Carolina businessmen were especially aggressive in pursuing the Indian trade, starting with tribes close to Charleston and then rapidly extending operations westward. By the end of the seventeenth century they were skirting the southern end of the Appalachians and taking their pack trains to the Creek towns of Georgia and Alabama and even to the Chickasaw villages of northern Mississippi. By the early eighteenth century they were visiting the Overhill Cherokees of Tennessee.

This far-flung trade, centered on the exchange of European goods for Indian slaves and the pelts of beaver and deer, became a crucial element in an imperial competition between English Carolina, French Louisiana, and Spanish Florida. On the Tennessee frontier Spain was relatively insignificant; English traders and their French counterparts, the *coureurs de bois*, were the spearheads—the agents provocateurs—of European rivalry. Sometimes, however, the traders' loyalties were suspect. The Frenchman Jean Couture, for example, schemed to use the Tennessee River as a commercial highway from the Middle Mississippi Valley to South Carolina, where English laws were less restrictive to individual traders than those of France. By 1699 Couture had become the first Euro-American of record to pioneer a water route linking the Southeast and the great interior basin . He went from the Mississippi up the Ohio, Tennessee, and Hiwassee (or perhaps Little Tennessee) rivers, made a portage to the headwaters of the Savannah, and then followed that stream down to South Carolina. By February 1700 he had led a party of Englishmen along the reverse route for the express purpose of encouraging trade between the Illinois Country and Charleston. The next year a party of three other *coureurs de bois* further demonstrated the feasibility of Couture's route by making a round trip from the Mississippi Valley. Nothing came from these efforts because French authorities were determined to prevent such a threat to their interests, but the traders' ventures into Tennessee gave Euro-Americans a better sense of its commercial and geopolitical possibilities.

As the imperial rivalry between Britain and France intensified, the Chickasaws assumed great strategic significance. Fierce warriors, they occupied villages in northern Mississippi but also claimed West Tennessee, which they used primarily for hunting. They could quickly interdict French communications along the Mississippi, and they were traditional enemies of the Choctaws, France's staunchest allies in the region. The Chickasaws' overland trade with Carolina was particularly troublesome for the French, who by the beginning of the eighteenth century had settled at Biloxi and Mobile on the Gulf Coast and by 1718 had established both New Orleans on the lower Mississippi and Fort Toulouse at present-day Montgomery, Alabama. The French intended to promote settlement in the region, to cement Indian loyalty by developing a mutually profitable trade, and to maintain strong links with countrymen in the Illinois Country and in Can-

ada via the Mississippi and its tributaries. Until the end of the
colonial wars they encouraged their Indian allies, especially the
Choctaws, to wage war against the Chickasaws and the Carolina
traders. War was preferable to peace because the constant inter-
tribal bloodshed increased the dependence of their client tribes
on French assistance and because the French lacked the goods
to accommodate both their allies and the Chickasaws.

On two occasions French forces landed on the site of present-
day Memphis to undertake major offensives against the Chickasaws. In 1736 a combined force of four hundred French soldiers
and Indian allies from the Illinois Country built a small fort on
the fourth Chickasaw Bluff and then marched toward the enemy
villages, expecting to link up with a larger force of troops and
Choctaws approaching from southern Alabama. The well-armed
Chickasaw defenders routed the Illinois invaders, then repulsed
those advancing from the south. Humiliated by these setbacks,
the French governor of Louisiana, Jean Baptiste Le Moyne de
Bienville, conducted an even larger campaign against the Chickasaws in 1739, using the fourth bluff as a staging area. There he
constructed Fort Assumption and assembled an army of some
3,600 French and African-American soldiers and their Indian
allies from the Illinois Country and lower Mississippi Valley—
probably the largest military force that had ever operated in the
interior to that time. In February 1740 the Chickasaws accepted
a French offer to negotiate, and both sides agreed to end hostilities and exchange prisoners. But it was a thinly disguised French
defeat: Bienville admitted that the impending winter rains would
have made military operations impossible, and he had no choice
but to withdraw his forces from the bluffs and allow the recently
constructed fort to return to wilderness. This single campaign cost
the French three times Louisiana's annual budget. For nearly
one hundred years afterward the fourth Chickasaw Bluff would
represent the western axis of the Tennessee frontier and serve
both military and diplomatic roles for Europeans, Indians, and,
after independence, Americans.

Farther to the east, active Cherokee involvement in European
trade and intrigue was delayed for a full generation after the 1673
visit of James Needham and Gabriel Arthur. In 1681 the first

Cherokees to arrive in Charleston came not as trading partners but as slaves, presumably the captives of Shawnee Indians recently relocated along the Savannah River. Two years later a Cherokee delegation of twenty chiefs appeared in Charleston to complain about slave raids by Carolina's Indian allies. Such problems limited early Cherokee trade with Carolina businessmen, and South Carolina's Council reported in 1708 that the "trade we have with these people is inconsiderable, they being but ordinary hunters and less warriors." Within four more years, however, relations had improved, and Carolina traders among the Cherokees were able to enlist a number of warriors to assist in the colony's war against the Tuscaroras, a troublesome North Carolina tribe. Later that same year Carolina's Commissioners of Indian Trade were concerned enough about Cherokee trading grievances to send two agents to settle the problems.

By 1713 the trading alliance had been cemented, and it now extended to Tennessee's Overhill Towns. The Partridge, head warrior of Tanase/Chota, repaid two traders, Alexander Long and Eleazar Wiggan, by giving them slaves seized in raids on a Yuchi town in Georgia. South Carolina objected to this unauthorized aggression, but the Overhill trade had become lucrative enough that both sides worked to resolve the problem. To reach the Tennessee villages, Charleston traders followed a well-trodden route to the Middle and Valley Towns in western North Carolina, passed through Unicoi Gap on the Tennessee border, and finally arrived in the Overhill Towns along the Tellico and Little Tennessee rivers. They enjoyed a near-monopoly of the trade, and despite their sometimes unscrupulous business tactics, they maintained a semblance of harmony with their clients by giving gifts and inviting disgruntled chiefs to Charleston for talks. In trade, as in all aspects of Cherokee life, harmony was central to the Cherokee cosmos and entailed an appropriate balancing of people, plants, animals, and the spirit world. Unfortunately, trade sometimes disrupted that balance by bringing misunderstandings or, worse, disease. A smallpox epidemic in 1738 significantly reduced tribal numbers.

Also involved in this early Tennessee trade were the Shawnees, a fragmented people whose bands were scattered over much of the eastern United States. Some of them moved from Ohio into Middle Tennessee during the mid-seventeenth century, and French maps of the period refer to the Cumberland as "Riviere des Chaouanons," or Shawnee River. The newcomers were undeterred by the fact that Middle Tennessee was already claimed by the Chickasaws on the west and by a confusing mix of proto-Creeks and newly intrusive Overhill Cherokees on the east. By the 1670s small groups of Shawnees lived and hunted in the game-rich Nashville Basin, from where they traded pelts as far south as Spanish Florida and as far north as the French outposts in Illinois. The Florida trade may have induced some Shawnees to migrate to South Carolina, where they began dealing with the English and became embroiled in a series of local Indian wars and intrigues. Those who remained in the Nashville area did business with Frenchmen such as Martin Chartier, who settled there around 1690, and Jean de Charleville, who operated a trading post at French Lick, on the site of Nashville, from about 1710 to 1714.

Trade had been a fact of life for Southern Indians for thousands of years, but its European phase had vastly more profound effects on native life. An array of abundant, relatively inexpensive items were now available not only to chiefs and other native leaders but also ultimately to every Indian man, woman, and child. Trade items still conveyed status, but the market was democratic: all who contributed to its expansion could share in its benefits. Though Indians at first employed some items in traditional ways that were quite unrelated to their intended uses in Europe, they quickly realized that "rational" usage of these goods made life easier. Firearms, the most dramatic and valued items, enabled their possessors to become more successful hunters and warriors; metal hoes, hatchets, and other utensils were superior to native counterparts made of wood, stone, and pottery; and woolen strouds and other fabrics were more colorful, easier to process, and more comfortable than deerskins and other peltries. Britain was in the early stages of the Industrial Revolution, so English goods were generally more abundant, less expensive, and better made than those of the French.

To pay for their goods many Indians at first captured and sold other Indians to coastal merchants as slaves, and prospective victims often fled and joined other groups. The slave trade rapidly declined when it proved destructive to both Indians and whites—and less economical to whites than enslavement of blacks. Indians increasingly paid for their goods with valuable furs and skins, which had a ready market abroad. Beaver pelts were important in the early years, but the skins of white-tailed deer quickly became the basis of trade. Right up to the time of the American Revolution many thousands of pounds of deerskins were shipped annually from Charleston. Overhunting threatened to deplete the deer population, but sometimes Indians were able to obtain goods by serving as diplomatic and military allies of their European suppliers. During such periods fewer deerskins were required, and herds had an opportunity to rebuild in the buffer zones separating hostile tribes because hunting there on a regular basis posed too many dangers.

On the other hand, these buffer zones and the hunting lands claimed by others were great temptations for aggressive tribes wishing to expand their trade. Several tribes—the Cherokees, Chickasaws, Creeks, and even the lordly Iroquois of New York—claimed or hunted in the Cumberland Basin, where game was abundant, but only the Shawnees occupied it in the early eighteenth century. As the market expanded, however, their presence became intolerable to both the Chickasaws and Cherokees, who ventured increasingly far from their villages to hunt deer. In 1715 those two nations combined to drive the Shawnees out of the region, and in 1745, after a few small bands had returned, they drove them out again.

Amid these developments Cherokee-European interaction took some curious turns. Perhaps the most peculiar involved the efforts of Alexander Cuming, an eccentric Scotsman who attempted to create an official alliance between the Cherokees and the English. Cuming was perplexed by Cherokee society. Each town was an autonomous unit whose inhabitants sought consensus on major issues. The Cherokees had no kings or princes to wield authority over loyal subjects. How could one negotiate effectively with such an atomized society? Cuming's response was to travel throughout the Cherokee country promoting a more unified polity. Perhaps because he was such an oddity, the Indians received him politely. In 1730 Cuming acted on his own initiative in council at the Middle Town of Nequassee and concluded preliminary articles of alliance between the Cherokees and Britain, proclaiming Moytoy, of the Overhill town of Great Tellico, "emperor" of all the Cherokees.

To legitimize his impromptu act of diplomacy, Cuming persuaded seven Cherokee warriors to accompany him to London, including Attakullakulla (The Little Carpenter), an Overhill leader who would later become one of the most famous Cherokee leaders. Cuming's Indian entourage remained in London for four months, where they were lionized by British society. Royal authorities were unwilling to recognize Cuming's pretensions, but they nonetheless accepted the formal Cherokee treaty of alliance, which became the basis for long-standing British recognition of the preeminent authority of specific Cherokee towns in Tennessee—at first Great Tellico, and later Chota. Yet despite British desires to create centralized authority among the Indians, the Cherokees themselves never recognized Great Tellico and Chota as supreme. They were the principal towns in terms of diplomacy and ceremony, but were only the first among equals. The ancient tradition of village autonomy continued.

A few years after Cuming's visit to the Cherokees, an even odder European arrived. Christian Gottlieb Priber was a German visionary who was fluent in French and English and wrote in Latin. He appeared in the Overhill town of Great Tellico around 1736 and almost immediately adopted native attire and customs, mastered the Cherokee language, and held his hosts spellbound with his personality, intellect, and imagination. He envisioned the Overhill country as a kingdom of paradise, a gathering place for all peoples. Overhill society would operate according to communist principles, with free love and with all things held in common. Acting as self-styled prime minister, Priber proclaimed that the Indians should zealously guard their lands, avoid dependency on the English, and move their government closer to the French in Alabama. Some Cherokees echoed his sentiments, and Carolina authorities concluded that he was a French agent. Priber's Cherokee friends would not allow the English to apprehend

Cherokee delegation to London, 1730. The Young
Attakullakulla at far right. COURTESY MUSEUM OF THE
CHEROKEE INDIAN, CHEROKEE, NORTH CAROLINA.

him, but in 1739 he made the mistake of leaving Great Tellico on
a mission to the French. Creek warriors who were allied with
Carolina traders captured him, and he ended his days in a Georgia jail. For years afterward, Great Tellico would be a center of
pro-French sentiment.

Trade served different purposes for Indians and whites. From
the Indian point of view, it was usually the dominant consideration in relations with Britain and France (and later with the
United States). Loyalty to any of these nations was conditional;
it was dependent on a ready supply of inexpensive goods. Even
the Chickasaws and Cherokees, both normally pro-English, sometimes threatened to switch their affections. Market demands created divisiveness when tribal factions loyal to one European nation intrigued against factions loyal to others. Britain and France,
on the other hand, viewed trade mostly as a necessary tool for
securing Indian political and military alliances in the escalating

imperial rivalries. This objective caused those governments to ameliorate the injustices of the trade somewhat, but it also involved Indians in wars that were far more sweeping and deadly than their traditional squabbles. These conflicts took many lives and disrupted normal subsistence patterns. Surviving combatants were unable to hunt on a regular basis, and women were exposed to the enemy while tending their fields. And when the wars were over and only one imperial power remained, Indians would be at the mercy of profit-minded traders who would charge whatever the market would bear and further ensnare their victims by providing alcohol and credit.

Although this trade inexorably led to growing Indian dependency, that dependency did not develop at the same time and in the same manner for all Southern tribes. No single dependency theory—no model, for example, of cores and peripheries within an expanding capitalist system—can adequately describe the variations. And yet Indians did become part of a market economy that emanated from Europe, was channeled through entrepreneurial or military middlemen along the Atlantic and Gulf coasts, and extended into the most distant reaches of the Southern backcountry. Dependency was a matter not so much of Europeans ensnaring unsuspecting economic naifs, but of fully rational Indians appraising the risks and taking their chances. They thought they understood the objectives of the competing Europeans and could devise strategies for dealing with them.

None of the Indians' strategies finally proved successful, but for most of the eighteenth century the Cherokees and other Southern tribes creatively delayed the consequences of dependency. They did this first through cultural syncretism, which entailed both being adaptable and maintaining a rough balance of power between the races. For most of the eighteenth century, Tennessee Indians greatly outnumbered whites and played a crucial role in imperial machinations. Whites still resided east of the Appalachians, or in the case of the French, in the lower Mississippi Valley. Whites who visited Tennessee were either small detachments of military personnel or traders and their employees and African-American slaves. Though few in number, these whites controlled the flow of trade goods. The power equation was roughly in balance, and because trade and alliances were considered mutually beneficial, both Indians and whites consciously created a middle ground that was not a particular geographic place, but a cultural construct. It was an unstated agreement that whites and Indians would each move toward understanding and dealing with the other for mutual benefit. As Richard White notes, the middle ground was the meeting place of European empire and Indian village republics. It represented a rational, adaptive strategy for both.

In Tennessee the middle ground meant accommodating the peltry trade to the respective obligations of Indian-European alliances; adopting certain rhetorical devices to connote understanding of their relationships; blending traditional Indian practices of gift giving and European bribery; and the sexual and cultural mingling of traders and Indians that produced a class of mixed-bloods, or *métis*. It also meant the presence of growing numbers of blacks who would become incorporated into Indian society. In the early years, at least, Overhill Cherokees largely defined the protocol of trade in their homeland, obliging white visitors to make the larger adjustments. But on both fronts traditional cultures were reshaped. The middle ground of mutual accommodation and benefit would help to stave off Indian dependency until the colonial wars ended and a rapidly growing white frontier population altered the balance of power forever.

Cherokee women played a crucial part in shaping the middle ground. They sold produce to traders, provided information, offered sexual favors on their own terms, and especially forged ties of kinship through marriage or long-term liaisons. In tribal society a woman's role was powerful, though it was separate from and complementary to that of a man. The woman was in charge of the family fields, owned the household, and could dissolve her marriage at any time (perhaps by unceremoniously dumping her husband's possessions on the ground). Certain prominent women had a voice in council and determined the fate of prisoners. One British officer marveled at the novelty, and a trader accused the Cherokees of being under a "petticoat government." Most important was a woman's role within the clan system. She belonged to one of seven clans (her husband belonged to another), and descent was matrilineal. Her children, being of her own clan, had no official relationship to their biological father; a maternal uncle was their closest male kin. For a white trader, marriage to a prominent Cherokee woman of the appropriate clan was crucial to acceptance and economic success. The mixed-blood offspring of such a liaison belonged to the mother's clan and were accorded full rights as Cherokees, and they became increasingly prominent as brokers between native and European cultures, a role that had both economic and political implications. Many of the most prominent Cherokees of the late eighteenth and early nineteenth centuries were products of such unions.

One significant aspect of the Cherokee kinship system was its relationship to tribal law. Because there were no courts and no police force, when a Cherokee was killed, whether accidentally or not, it was incumbent on members of the victim's clan to gain retribution by killing the perpetrator. Sometimes it was possible for the guilty party to atone for the deed by paying the aggrieved family. On the other hand, if the guilty party had fled, then members of the perpetrator's own clan were in danger. If enemy Indians killed a Cherokee, the clan of the victim was expected to take to the war path and kill someone from the offending tribe. If more than one Cherokee was killed, then the blood revenge was supposed to be proportionate. This "law of blood" was a universal tribal custom that reflected the Cherokee search for harmony and balance, and knowledgeable whites quickly became aware of its implications. If some unknown backwoodsman shot a Cherokee, then every white person was at risk until the offended clan had received its due.

Few people reflect the cultural syncretism of the Tennessee frontier as well as Nancy Ward, arguably the most famous Cherokee woman. During a 1755 battle between the Cherokees and Creeks, the seventeen-year-old picked up the weapon of her mortally wounded husband, Kingfisher, and continued to fight until her people prevailed. She thus gained recognition as a "War Woman" and eventually as "Supreme Beloved Woman," or *Ghigau*, a transition that perhaps came with the onset of menopause. As Supreme Beloved Woman, she increasingly assumed a prominent role as tribal counselor and arbiter. Ironically, considering how she won her renown, her chief duty was as a respected advocate of the "White Path," the road of peace. A fixture of the principal town of Chota, she was often the most effective diplomat in Cherokee-white interactions, especially after she married Bryan Ward, a white trader. In war, Nancy Ward could spare captives from certain torture and death by waving the wing of a swan. Her male counterpart was her uncle, Attakullakulla, who as the leading "white" chief also spoke for peace and harmony with Euro-Americans. By seeking the path of conciliation and understanding, both Ward and Attakullakulla fostered the middle ground. Many a white frontiersman in Tennessee should have given thanks to them.

Cherokees delayed dependency not only by pursuing cultural syncretism, but also by practicing realpolitik, mirroring European balance-of-power diplomacy by playing Britain, France, and Spain against one another. Sometimes they were successful enough to win the grudging admiration of their temporary pawns. By all accounts Attakullakulla was the most adroit practitioner of diplomacy. Whites described him as intelligent, eloquent, sly, artful, commonsensical, sagacious, and hypocritical. They called him a Solon, a noble savage, and a man whose diplomacy surpassed that of Cardinal Richelieu or Robert Walpole. During the mid-1750s Attakullakulla and several other Overhill Cherokees took advantage of the outbreak of the French and Indian War to extort a quid pro quo from both South Carolina and Virginia. From the former they demanded the garrisoning of a fort on the Little Tennessee River. Noncompliance would interrupt the thriving Carolina trade and perhaps force a tribal rapprochement with France, whose troops and Indian allies at Fort Toulouse were within easy range of the Overhill Towns. This was no empty threat because a major Cherokee faction at Great Tellico was already allied with the French.

As for Virginia, it was reeling from the recent victory of France and its northern Indian allies over British forces under General Edward Braddock in western Pennsylvania, an area that was claimed by Virginia. The colony's frontiers were now subject to continued Indian attack. Virginia was desperate for the assistance of Cherokee warriors. Attakullakulla and other leaders of-

fered to provide support if the colony would build a second fort
in Overhill country to protect Indian families during the absence
of Cherokee men who went to Virginia. The Cherokees also
wanted Virginia to trade more actively among them and thus end
South Carolina's virtual monopoly.

Both Virginia and South Carolina agreed to construct a fort
to defend their Tennessee allies against the French. The original
intention was to make it a joint venture, but when the Virginians
arrived in June 1756, no South Carolinians had appeared. Eager
to return home, they built a small log outpost across the Little
Tennessee from Chota and then departed; it was never garrisoned. Later that same year a much larger expedition arrived
from South Carolina to construct a proper fort on the south side
of the Little Tennessee near the mouth of the Tellico River and
about five miles below Chota. Designed by German engineer William Gerard de Brahm, the new post was operational by the summer of 1757; it was named Fort Loudoun in honor of the Earl
of Loudoun, the British commander-in-chief in North America.
Diamond-shaped, it occupied high ground overlooking the river
and was surrounded by a deep ditch and a palisade fifteen feet
high along the embankments; twelve small cannon, three at each
corner, provided formidable protection. It was the first British
fort of any significance west of the Appalachians.

Rather than wedding the Overhill people to the British cause,
Fort Loudoun quickly came to symbolize Cherokee distrust of
English intentions. Clearly, the fort was not so much for the benefit of Indians as it was a manifestation of the British struggle for
empire in North America. French intrigue contributed to Cherokee exasperation over deteriorating trading relations with Carolina, to their perception that they were being mistreated by colonial authorities, and to their growing fear that the British intended
to enslave them. Events on the Virginia frontier exacerbated
matters when Cherokee warriors serving as British allies became
entangled with settlers in mutual thievery and violence. A few
warriors were murdered by frontiersmen who tried to collect
bounties offered for scalps of pro-French Indians. Some Cherokees, following the custom of blood revenge, retaliated by taking
the scalps of settlers on the Carolina frontier. Late in 1759 South

Carolina authorities countered by imposing a trade embargo on the Cherokees, and British officers at Fort Prince George on the South Carolina frontier held a delegation of prominent Cherokees as hostages. One of these was Oconostota, the great warrior of Chota, who was soon released, but who understandably harbored great resentment against the English. These mutual provocations marked the beginning of the Cherokee War.

In January 1760 Cherokees from the Lower and Middle Towns began attacking scattered settlements and trading houses in the Southern backcountry, and in February warriors under Oconostota, hoping to free the other hostages, ambushed the commander of Fort Prince George. Soldiers within the fort promptly killed the remaining captives. Despite the persistent efforts of Attakullakulla and other peace advocates, the Cherokee War had escalated to critical proportions, and Fort Loudoun, deep in Indian country, became a lonely outpost amid a sea of enemies. A relief force of British regulars under Colonel Archibald Montgomery devastated a number of the Cherokee Lower Towns but ran into such strong resistance in the Middle Towns that Montgomery returned to Charleston. The Overhill Towns remained untouched by the British, who left Fort Loudoun to its fate.

For a time, the people of Chota played cat and mouse with the garrison. Unwilling to attack Fort Loudoun frontally and still awaiting possible assistance from French or Creek allies, Oconostota contented himself with periodic negotiations and a loose siege. Encouraged by Attakullakulla, Indian women, some of them wives of soldiers, continued to take food and information into the post as they pleased, often laughing at warriors who rebuked them. Captain Paul Demeré, the fort's commanding officer, maintained precarious contact with the outside world by dispatching a few daring messengers. One of these was Abram, the slave of a trader, who was promised his freedom if he managed to carry messages to the governor in Charleston. Somehow he made it safely, and amazingly he soon returned. By summer, however, the siege had tightened until it was difficult even to smuggle food into the post. Oconostota and others had tired of Attakullakulla's efforts in behalf of the garrison and expelled him from the Chota council. The soldiers of the garrison subsisted mostly on horseflesh and faced death by disease or slow starvation. On August 7 Demeré's emissaries negotiated terms of surrender at Chota town house, agreeing that the Cherokees would take the fort, its cannons, and the extra small arms, powder, and ammunition in return for allowing the garrison to keep their personal arms and proceed without harm to Fort Prince George or Virginia. Sick and disabled soldiers could remain behind until they had fully recuperated.

The British did not fully comply with the agreement. They buried or destroyed some of the fort's weaponry before evacuating Fort Loudoun on August 9 and marching fifteen miles to an encampment for the night. Early the next morning, they were attacked by an overwhelming force of Cherokees (and possibly some Creeks). Perhaps thirty or more soldiers died, including all the officers except Captain John Stuart, who was taken captive and then ransomed by his good friend, Attakullakulla. A short time later Attakullakulla employed a ruse to help Stuart escape, little knowing that his friend would soon assume a much more important role in Southern Indian affairs. The surviving enlisted men were all taken prisoner. According to reports brought back by the slave Abram and a few others, Captain Demeré met a grisly death. The Cherokees scalped him while he was still alive, forced him to dance, then chopped off his arms and legs. A Frenchman reported that the Indians had stuffed Demeré's mouth with dirt and said, "Dog, since you are so hungry for land, eat your fill." The ambush may have occurred because the Indians were enraged when the British failed to keep their promise, or perhaps the attack was a measured—though savage—response satisfying the Cherokee custom of blood revenge. The total number of fatalities was roughly equal to that of the Cherokee hostages killed by the British.

Despite their great triumph at Fort Loudoun, many Cherokees realized it was in their best interest to reestablish friendship and trade with the British as soon as possible. They lacked many essential items and found it aggravating that the Creeks had become beneficiaries of British largesse during the troubles. And although Oconostota continued to seek French support in Louisiana, by 1760 France had already lost the war in North America.

Fort Loudoun. Painting by Chester Martin. Courtesy
Historic Fort Loudoun State Park.

The Cherokees, who had a rare instinct for bad timing and for
choosing the losing side, found themselves without any real allies. Still, they were determined to hold out for acceptable terms
from South Carolina and Virginia even as Lieutenant Colonel
James Grant's army of British regulars, provincials, and Northern Indian allies marched from Charleston to express "His Majesty's Displeasure" with them. During the summer of 1761, despite stiff resistance, Grant's force destroyed fifteen Lower and
Middle Towns and some 1,500 acres of corn. The Overhill Cherokees remained unpunished, but they wisely followed Attakullakulla's shrewd diplomacy, and by the end of the year all tribal
divisions had made peace with South Carolina and Virginia. The
Cherokee War was over.

Upon concluding their peace treaty with Virginia at the Long
Island of the Holston River (present-day Kingsport), the Cherokees requested that a Virginia officer visit the Overhill Towns to

solidify the new amity between the peoples. Lieutenant Henry Timberlake volunteered to go, and he spent several months as a guest of the powerful Ostenaco at Chota before returning to Virginia in March 1762. A liaison with Ostenaco's daughter soon produced a son. A scrupulously honest observer of his hosts, Timberlake admitted "that it was the trade alone that induced them to make peace with us, and not any preference to the French, whom they loved a great deal better." This was understandable, he said, because the French were more diplomatic and willing "to conciliate the inclinations of almost all the Indians they are acquainted with." Nor did the French encroach on Indian land as relentlessly as the English, who "are now so nigh." As he noted, "The French lay farther off, and were not so powerful; from them, therefore, they had less to fear." Indeed, Timberlake himself was one of a number of British subjects to write early accounts of the attractive, fertile lands of East Tennessee. Another, William Gerard de Brahm, said that the rich soils of the valleys were "equal to Manure itself, almost impossible . . . ever to wear out."

The truth of Timberlake's remarks about Indian obsession with trade and Anglo-American obsession with land became apparent in the northern backcountry immediately following the French defeat. Even before the peace treaty of 1763 and British acquisition of French claims to Eastern North America, thousands of whites trespassed on transmontane Indian lands in western New York, Pennsylvania, and Virginia. These encroachments, along with heavy-handed trade restrictions imposed by the victorious British, were responsible for the eruption of a new Indian war in the spring of 1763. This conflict, named for the Ottawa war leader Pontiac, took perhaps two thousand Anglo-American lives in the backcountry before it was finally suppressed. It also reinforced London's long-standing desire to rationalize Indian-white relations on the American frontier so that such disasters would never occur again. The result was the Proclamation of October 1763, a triumph of naiveté, geographical ignorance, and wishful thinking. It drew a line—in effect a boundary—down the crest of the Appalachians and, except in the new colony of West Florida, restricted white settlement to the Atlantic

Cherokee Delegation to London, 1762 (Ostenaco, the
Great Warrior, in Center). COURTESY MUSEUM OF THE
CHEROKEE INDIAN, CHEROKEE, NORTH CAROLINA.

watershed, creating a supposedly inviolate Indian country west
of the line. The only whites permitted there were military personnel, licensed traders, and others authorized by the Crown. Officials in London realized the line would require some fine tuning,
but they ignored the larger fact that the Western lands belonged
to a number of seaboard colonies on the basis of their charters;
North Carolina, for example, claimed all of Tennessee. Even
more important, royal officials blithely defied reality by proposing to deny white Americans the one commodity they considered
most essential to their well-being—land and more land.

From the outset the Proclamation was a nullity as hunters,
speculators, and even imperial officials evaded or simply ignored
it. Encroachments on Indian lands continued unabated. In Ten-

nessee, they were the result of glowing reports from traders, hunters, explorers, and military personnel like Henry Timberlake. In addition to Carolina traders who had long been familiar with most of southeastern Tennessee, there were hunters and ambitious land speculators who had drifted into northeastern Tennessee from Virginia and North Carolina. In fact, speculators had been on the scene long before the Proclamation. As early as the spring of 1750 Dr. Thomas Walker, a prominent Virginia landjobber, had intruded on the fringes of Tennessee by leading the first party of whites through Cumberland Gap into Kentucky. More famous are the long hunters who prowled the wilderness of upper East Tennessee and the Cumberland Basin, hunting and exploring for months at a time, always at considerable risk. One of the earliest was Elisha Walden, who led a party of hunters into upper East Tennessee in 1761. Later that same decade Kaspar Mansker, Abraham Bledsoe, Michael Stoner, and others hunted both in East Tennessee and the Cumberland Basin, where the Frenchman Timothe de Monbreun had already established himself at French Lick. But these long hunters, accomplished in woodcraft though they were, paled in comparison to Daniel Boone.

Born in Pennsylvania in 1734 of Quaker parents, Boone had become a crack shot by his early teens and from his father had acquired an empathy, even an affinity, for Indians. When he was fifteen, he and his family joined the massive migration of whites down the Great Valley of Virginia and into the backcountry of North Carolina, settling near the Yadkin River. Daniel became a professional hunter and in 1755, along with other North Carolina frontiersmen, joined General Braddock's ill-fated army in western Pennsylvania. He narrowly escaped death in the debacle and returned to North Carolina, where he married Rebecca Bryan and earned a living partly as a wagoner but mostly by hunting and trapping. He and his growing family temporarily retreated to Virginia when their settlement was attacked during the Cherokee War in 1760. Returning home as the war was ending, he resumed hunting nearly full time and, accompanied by a friend, ventured into East Tennessee for the first time during the winter of 1760–1761. The most famous and controversial evidence of his

Tennessee exploits was the inscription carved around 1760 in a beech tree that stood for many years in Washington County: "D Boon cillED A. Bar." It was discovered before Boone gained renown, so it may have been genuine, but there are many spurious inscriptions attributed to him, and he consistently signed his name with a final *e* and, later at least, wrote "bear."

During the rest of the 1760s, Boone and a number of his North Carolina friends hunted and sometimes farmed as far west as the Holston and Clinch rivers. In 1771 he and his family squatted in East Tennessee, where he ran up a few debts for supplies (including two quarts of rum), and the following year he hunted as far west as French Lick. On several occasions in Tennessee and Kentucky, Cherokees and Shawnees complained about his hunting and forcibly took his accumulated pelts. Despite these losses and the gruesome death of his oldest son in a Cherokee ambush in 1773, Boone harbored little resentment toward Indians. Indeed, his ease with them, especially with the Cherokees, would later make him an important figure in Tennessee's and Kentucky's most famous land deal. It was in Kentucky that Boone achieved enduring fame. He became a cultural icon, a centerpiece of what might be called the Great American Myth about the frontier and its impact on an emerging national identity. Probably the most significant aspect of Boone and his fellow long hunters was their hard-won knowledge of the interior and willingness to share their expertise and enthusiasm. Without subscribing entirely to Frederick Jackson Turner's scenario of neat stages of frontier development, one might agree with the general observation that the long hunters played an important role in promoting early white settlement of Tennessee. A few of them put down permanent roots in the state.

By the late 1760s hordes of settlers following in the footsteps of long hunters forced British officials to adjust the Proclamation line. John Stuart, survivor of the Fort Loudoun massacre, was now the Indian Superintendent for the Southern Department and was responsible for implementing these changes. In 1768 Stuart presided over the Treaty of Hard Labor, in which the Cherokees gave up their claims to seldom-used lands in Virginia and West Virginia. The cession itself was not necessarily detrimental to Cherokee interests, but it immediately prompted white immigration well beyond the new boundary into southwestern Virginia as far as Wolf Hills (Abingdon) and even into upper East Tennessee. Among these migrants was William Bean, supposedly the first permanent white resident of Tennessee. He settled with friends and relatives along the Watauga River in 1769, but others arriving in Tennessee about the same time may have preceded him. All of the newcomers on both sides of the Tennessee-Virginia boundary were well beyond the treaty line. Some may have believed they were there legally because the Iroquois in New York had recently ceded their claims to lands as far south and west as the mouth of the Tennessee River. To the settlers it did not matter that the shadowy claims of the Iroquois were inferior to those of the Southern tribes.

These new encroachments, along with complex maneuverings by a number of speculators, forced Stuart to undertake a revision of the Hard Labor line. In the Treaty of Lochaber in October 1770, the Cherokees accepted modest compensation from Virginia in exchange for a cession bounded by a line extending along the northern boundary of Tennessee to a point near the Long Island of the Holston River and then northward to where the Kanawha River empties into the Ohio. The terms of this new cession, if adhered to, might have offered adequate protection to the Cherokees, but the boundary as surveyed violated those terms. White settlement in upper East Tennessee was already well established, so John Donelson's survey of 1771 accommodated some of these families by running slightly south of its intended route, diverting down the south fork of the Holston River. These "North of Holston" residents were led by Evan Shelby, who had settled at Sapling Grove (Bristol) in 1770 and who would become one of the most renowned public figures of Tennessee and Kentucky. Attakullakulla, ever a friend of the whites, supposedly agreed to the revised boundary because he "pitied" the settlers. North of Holston became the first officially sanctioned settlement of whites in Tennessee. It was an extension of the migration pushing through southwest Virginia, where political authority was already established, and for the time being North Carolina acceded to Virginia's governance of North of Holston.

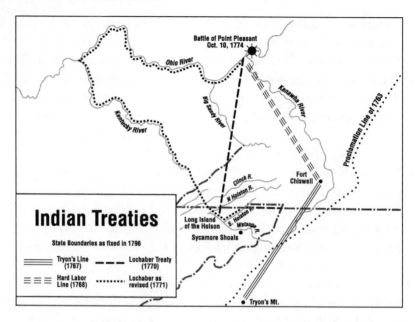

Indian Treaties, 1767–1771. FROM MAX DIXON, *The Wataugans* (1976). COURTESY THE TENNESSEE HISTORICAL COMMISSION.

An even greater deviation from the Treaty of Lochaber came when Donelson and his surveying party failed to lay out the prescribed northerly line to the Kanawha. Instead, he, Alexander Cameron, and the Cherokee observers agreed on a line that would open much of Kentucky to white settlement. This was apparently in accord with an offer the Indians had made at Lochaber in exchange for tribal retention of Long Island. Stuart had allowed them to keep the island but had refused their offer of compensation because it would have exceeded his instructions and set a bad precedent. Now, months later, Donelson and his associates believed the Crown would approve the extra cession and therefore headed northwestward from Long Island to the Kentucky River and followed it to the Ohio. Their actions, in terms of their original and still binding instructions, resulted in what is possibly the most inaccurate survey in the history of the American frontier. In his defense, Donelson claimed that Attakullakulla had suggested the deviation in order to encourage whites to settle in adjoining parts of Kentucky rather than in Tennessee. Regardless of the intention, Donelson's faulty survey of the Lochaber line left the North of Holston people as still the only legal white residents of Tennessee. His departure from prescribed guidelines of surveying perhaps explains why he and other members of his family soon became surveyors and land appraisers for some of Tennessee's most prominent speculators.

Hundreds of squatters remained in Indian country, and Alexander Cameron, John Stuart's assistant, ordered them to leave. These intruders included the upright William Bean and his neighbors who lived near Sycamore Shoals (present-day Elizabethton) on the Watauga River. Another group resided along the Nolichucky River and its tributaries, a short distance south of the Wataugans. The leading figure here was Jacob Brown, a merchant, blacksmith, and gunsmith who served whites and Cherokees alike. Farther west, Carter's Valley was still another center of white habitation; located on the west side of the Holston between present-day Kingsport and Rogersville, it was the namesake of John Carter, a Virginia merchant. Quite likely some of these early Tennessee settlers were former Regulators who had opposed the unfair taxation and undemocratic administration of the North Carolina backcountry, and who had attempted to regulate it themselves. In May 1771 they had suffered a decisive defeat by Governor William Tryon's army at the Alamance, near Greensboro, and their hatred for their former oppressors would have important repercussions during the American Revolution. It appears that some of these disgruntled souls were heading toward the Holston and the Nolichucky even well before the Alamance, and others came later.

Alarmed by Cameron's demand that they leave Indian country, Jacob Brown and others from Nolichucky quickly moved northward and settled among the Watauga residents, as did John Carter from Carter's Valley. Together they all pondered their options. They decided on a quintessentially American strategy: rather than leave their new homes, they would abide by the letter of the Proclamation, and to hell with its spirit. Prohibited from buying property beyond the Proclamation line, they would lease their lands from the Cherokees. They delegated James Robertson and John Bean to negotiate on their behalf at Chota. The two delegates took advantage of the fact that the Cherokees were, as usual, divided. They brought gifts for certain leaders, notably the aged Attakullakulla, who once again "pitied" the white settlers and agreed to accompany Robertson and Bean back to the Watauga for further discussions. To the surprise of many, John Stuart approved the idea, probably because it seemed the only peaceable solution to the problem. It was clear the Wataugans intended to stay anyway. In the final Articles of Friendship between settlers and Cherokees, the former offered various kinds of merchandise worth $5,000 to $6,000 in exchange for a ten-year lease of lands along the Watauga. The goods were probably underwritten by several prominent individuals within the community, and perhaps by interested parties in North Carolina. Both the settlers and Attakullakulla knew a good quid pro quo when they saw it. Emboldened, Jacob Brown soon met with Oconostota and other Cherokee leaders and worked out a similar lease of the Nolichucky lands.

While they were negotiating the Articles of Friendship, the Watauga and Nolichucky residents were also setting up a primitive system of government. They realized that their ultimate survival required political organization: a statement of principles, the creation of local offices, and above all a means of defending the land rights then under discussion with the Cherokees. In May 1772 they produced their Written Articles of Association, which established a five-member court and other local offices, including those of sheriff and clerk. It was an ad hoc government created by backwoods people who had a strong affinity for order and property and who found themselves beyond any established authority. They wanted to protect both their property and their reputation. Not for them an unorganized backwoods haven for debtors, deadbeats, and the lawless. The Watauga Association was not sanctioned by any existing law, but on the other hand, it did not violate any specific law. It was neither legal nor illegal; it was extralegal. Without making too much of it, the Watauga Association might also qualify as the first constitutional government west of the Appalachians. In the words of one royal official, the association acted as "a separate State; the consequences of which may prove . . . detrimental to the peace and security of the other colonies; it at least sets a dangerous example . . . of forming governments distinct from and Independent of His Majesty's authority." The association's precedents hearken back to the Mayflower Compact of 1620, and its frontier successors include two similar associations in Tennessee and a host of other ragtag, on-the-make squatters groups. The Watauga Association represents the intersection of backwoods culture, European culture, and frontier expediency.

Unfortunately, no copies of the Articles of Association or any of Watauga's other records have come to light, but it is clear from other evidence that the association's court was mostly concerned with land claims and individual rights. It operated according to the laws of Virginia (though Watauga was within the bounds of North Carolina) and presided over the normal business of people anywhere: legalizing marriages, probating wills, punishing miscreants, supervising militia service, recording land claims and transfers. It also handled relations with the Cherokees and outsiders. During the two years after the association's inception, the Watauga population continued to grow, and the wilderness became a pastoral landscape dotted with cabins and stump-riddled fields.

Though the emerging society approximated a yeoman's dream, the Cherokees were appalled. By 1774 they were complaining about being run off their lands and deprived of traditional hunting grounds. They said that the lease they had granted applied only to the original Wataugans, not to all of the newcomers. Besides, only a minority of their chiefs had ever approved of the transaction. Matters worsened when a white man murdered a Cherokee who was attending races and games at Sycamore Shoals. The killer was from Wolf Hills, not Watauga, but local residents were alarmed enough to send James Robertson to Chota to apologize and to promise punishment of the guilty party—a promise they couldn't fulfill. This diplomatic mission prevented immediate Cherokee retaliation, but the Indians still wanted the Wataugans to leave. They complained to Cameron, who complained to Stuart, who complained to North Carolina's

Governor Josiah Martin, who told all settlers in Tennessee below the south fork of the Holston River to leave immediately. The settlers ignored him.

Events along the Ohio River served as a sobering lesson for the increasingly restive Cherokees. In Kentucky and western Pennsylvania speculators, settlers, and colonial officials were pushing Shawnee toleration to its limits. The Shawnees were a widely-traveled people who by the mid-eighteenth century mostly lived in southern Ohio. Their primary hunting grounds were in Kentucky, where the Cherokees and other tribes hunted less frequently. Before long, however, explorers and long hunters like Daniel Boone had spread the word: Kentucky was another Eden. Every other part of the West was nothing in comparison. A host of prominent speculators, including Virginia's royal governor, Lord Dunmore, connived to enrich themselves by acquiring as much land there as possible. Virginia claimed both Kentucky and the region around Pittsburgh, and despite protests from Pennsylvania authorities, Dunmore's lackeys assumed control at the forks of the Ohio and quickly goaded the growing white population into violence against the Shawnees and other nearby Indians. In 1774 the smoldering collection of Shawnee grievances ignited into the aptly named Lord Dunmore's War.

The Shawnees had long been seeking alliances with other tribes and had sent delegations to the Cherokees asking them to forget old tribal animosities and to recognize the common dangers posed by whites. Many Cherokees seemed interested. At the same time the Watauga emissaries visited Chota, Cherokee warriors were in the Ohio country discussing a possible alliance with the Shawnee leader Cornstalk. The situation was volatile, and the wily John Stuart used an effective diplomacy of cajolery and threats to prevent Southern tribes from allying with one another or with the Shawnees. The Shawnees were without any significant Indian allies as Governor Dunmore and Colonel Andrew Lewis led two armies of Virginians to the Ohio River. Lewis's militia included a unit under Evan Shelby from North of Holston, reinforced by some twenty Watauga volunteers. In October 1774 Tennesseans participated in the decisive Battle of Point Pleasant at the mouth of the Kanawha, where for a full day

Cornstalk's warriors and the militiamen savaged one another. Though the battle was evenly fought, the Shawnees finally retreated across the Ohio, demoralized. The war ended a short time later when Governor Dunmore forced the Shawnees to cede their claims to Kentucky, cease hunting there, and refrain from attacking travelers on the Ohio. The Shawnees had no intention of abiding by these terms, and for many years they would continue their resistance to the growing white presence. What was different, however, was that they were able to enlist other tribes as allies. Among them were the Cherokees.

Shawnee concessions in Lord Dunmore's War offered a convenient excuse for whites to move into Kentucky, even though they were forbidden to purchase lands there. Speculators confidently believed that that small obstacle would soon be overcome. Among the landjobbers anticipating a bonanza was Richard Henderson, a lawyer and entrepreneur from the rapidly developing backcountry around Hillsborough, North Carolina. Appointed by Governor Tryon as a judge in 1768, Henderson had been a staunch defender of property rights and of creditors, and he had earned the hatred of the Regulators. At some point during the 1760s he and two other men organized Richard Henderson and Company for speculation in Kentucky, and they hired Daniel Boone as their expert land appraiser and wilderness adviser. By the early 1770s Henderson and his associates had added a few more partners, expanded their vision, and rechristened themselves the Louisa Company, reflecting the former name of the Kentucky River.

When Lord Dunmore's War ended, the Louisa Company was ready to make its move. After the Shawnee cession only the Cherokee claim to Kentucky was a serious obstacle to white occupation, and Henderson and his associates learned from Daniel Boone (who was informed by James Robertson) that some prominent Cherokees might be agreeable to a deal. Henderson immediately opened negotiations with them for a long-term lease of an enormous tract in Kentucky and Middle Tennessee, no doubt believing that the leaseholds could be converted to ownership whenever Britain formally opened the region to settlement. Ever confident of success, he published advertisements with liberal inducements for people to settle on the Louisa Company's lands. By January 1775 Henderson and his partners, now reorganized as the Transylvania Company, had adopted a more grandiose plan: they proposed to *buy* the lands. The purchase would violate the long-abused Proclamation and ignore the claims of Virginia and North Carolina, but so what? The mounting discord and confusion that led to the outbreak of the American Revolution offered a unique opportunity for speculators to grab what they could get and hope for the best. As a safeguard, Henderson worked out an elaborate and highly implausible legal defense of the proposed purchase.

The Transylvania Company invited Attakullakulla and some other Cherokees to come to North Carolina to inspect trade goods worth some ten thousand pounds sterling that would be offered in exchange for the real estate. Agreeable as ever, the old chief was satisfied. Immediately Henderson sent out invitations for Cherokees to attend a treaty conference beginning on March 1 at Sycamore Shoals on the Watauga, a traditional gathering place for Indians and whites. A startling array of characters showed up for what was to be one of frontier Tennessee's greatest spectacles. During the next two to three weeks an estimated 1,000 to 1,200 Cherokees visited the conference site. Chiefs such as Attakullakulla, Oconostota, and Willanaugh were dressed in eclectic ensembles featuring European coats, ruffled shirts, and traditional Cherokee leggings, and they usually sported a British medal or two. Heavily tattooed warriors eagerly eyed the goods that had been laboriously transported across the mountains and displayed by the Transylvania Company. Some six hundred white settlers had also gathered from near and far, hoping to savor every minute of the spectacle and the festivities. They had an economic stake in the proceedings as well: at Henderson's request they had provided enormous quantities of food for the guests.

Serious negotiations took place between March 14 and 17, as Cherokees and speculators shadowboxed over terms. Tribal leaders at first seemed less compliant than Henderson had expected. In exchange for the tantalizing array of trade items, he wanted them to sell the area between the Kentucky and Ohio Rivers southward to the divide between the Cumberland and Tennessee rivers—a tract of some twenty million acres encompassing most of Kentucky and Middle Tennessee. Kegs of rum and other gifts were lavished upon the Indians, but discussions came to an embarrassing impasse when Attakullakulla's son, Dragging Canoe, arose in council and accused his elders of endangering their people's survival by considering the cession. Other tribes, he said, had "melted away like balls of snow before the sun" after submitting to white requests for land. And would this latest sale satisfy the whites? No, their demands would never end. With that dramatic speech, Dragging Canoe made it very clear that he would never accommodate whites the way his father did; his words were a stinging rebuke of Attakullakulla's entire career. Nonetheless, after taking some time to reflect upon the matter, tribal elders signed the Treaty of Sycamore Shoals on March 17, 1775. They agreed to sell all the land Henderson requested, as well as a two hundred thousand acre "Path Deed" connecting the Holston River and Cumberland Gap.

Just two days later the Wataugans, taking a cue from Henderson and the Transylvania Company, converted their 1772 lease into an outright purchase by paying the still-compliant Cherokees two thousand pounds for about two thousand square miles encompassing the original leasehold and an area extending to the North Carolina Blue Ridge Mountains. Oconostota and Attakullakulla were the major Indian signatories and conveyed the land to Charles Robertson, who was acting as trustee for the Watauga Association. John Sevier was one of seven white witnesses; "linguister" (translator) James Vann was another. Almost immediately, the Wataugans opened a land office and began converting leaseholds into deeds and offering the remaining land to newcomers. Jacob Brown was not to be outdone. On March 25 he purchased two adjoining tracts along the Nolichucky that together were nearly as large as the newly-expanded Watauga.

Even before the Treaty of Sycamore Shoals was signed, the confident Richard Henderson had sent Daniel Boone with a party of woodsmen to build a crude road through Cumberland Gap to Henderson's new empire in Kentucky. This would become the famous Wilderness Road, heavily traveled by a full generation of immigrants pushing toward the promised land. Henderson, however, would find it difficult to profit from his supposed purchase. John Stuart and Alexander Cameron, speaking for the Crown, immediately denounced the purchase as illegal, as did authorities in Virginia and North Carolina who rightly viewed it as a violation of their colonial charters. And settlers would have little patience with Henderson's baronial pretensions. Even more troublesome was the ominous presence of Dragging Canoe. As his elders sold their tribal birthright, he had pointed toward Kentucky and warned that it would be a dark and bloody ground for settlers. Then he had stalked out, never again to meet with Americans in council. His words proved prophetic, for he and his supporters would take their revenge during the American Revolution.

3.

THE REVOLUTIONARY FRONTIER: 1775–1780

By 1775 the white threat to the Cherokee land base in upper East Tennessee was apparent. An estimated two thousand white settlers lived there, about three-fourths having arrived from the Great Valley of Virginia and the rest by way of the difficult mountain route from North Carolina. The earliest came on horseback and on foot, usually driving a few head of livestock. Though they were an ethnically diverse group, the majority were of English stock. A few of the wealthier immigrants brought along a slave or two. To the horror of the Cherokees, these newcomers transformed the landscape by girdling and cutting trees, building cabins, and planting crops and orchard trees. Settlers continued to hunt deer and bear for food and sport, but they increasingly depended on meat from domestic livestock. Cattle and hogs fed widely, especially among the tall cane that flourished along the streams. After the first few years a rough road system linked the new settlements with Virginia and distant cities like Philadelphia and Baltimore, but except for occasional drives of livestock to outside markets, traffic was mostly one-way. The few merchants in the area included John Carter on the Watauga, Evan Shelby at present-day Bristol, and Jacob Brown on the Nolichucky.

The most visible symbol of white control over the Tennessee landscape was the ubiquitous log cabin. When neighbors gathered to raise a new family residence, it was something more than mere work or an occasion to socialize. The construction, especially the notching and interlocking of logs, symbolized the way frontier residents were tightly linked in a mutual endeavor to tame the land and defy the supposed savagery of Indian hegemony.

In East Tennessee the typical early cabin was a rectangular "single-pen" of about sixteen by twenty feet, with a roof ridge parallel to the cabin front, side-facing gables, and an exterior chimney made of sticks and stones. Sometimes the logs were left in their natural rounded state, and sometimes they were hewn on two sides to provide a flat surface for the inside and outside walls. They were joined by distinctive corner notches, especially the V-notch. Both it and the saddle notch came by way of the Great Valley of Virginia. The half-dovetail notch came from Virginia and western North Carolina, and the square notch was a cultural marker of the latter state. Settlers usually filled the spaces between logs with various kinds of chinking, daubed over with mud or clay that was mixed with a binder of straw or grass. Roofs were made of oak clapboards held in place by a series of parallel poles, while floors were at first earthen and later replaced by puncheons. Outbuildings such as corncribs were built of unhewn logs and remained unchinked. Despite their makeshift character, the cabins and fields of white frontier people demonstrated both their adaptability and expansionist tendencies; they were prepared to remain in East Tennessee.

Confronted with this reality, the Cherokees and other Southern Indians had little choice but to support the British Crown as a split between Britain and the colonies became imminent. Few whites or Indians on the Tennessee frontier paid much attention to the philosophical and ideological foundations of the American Revolution. Instead, they saw the unfolding struggle in more concrete terms, centering on the issue of land and who would possess it. Most white settlers opposed Parliament's attempts to limit expansion in the backcountry, while Native Americans saw the impending conflict as an opportunity to support British imperial policy against the escalating encroachments on tribal domains. The fight in the backcountry, James H. O'Donnell rightly asserts, "was over the land, a struggle not new and not finished." Indeed, the Revolution both whetted and abetted white land hunger, and the Tennessee frontier expanded even amid a savage war.

The Indians would be a formidable strike force against the frontier, especially if the tribes could overcome their traditional animosities and unite. The four major Southeastern tribes—Choctaws, Chickasaws, Creeks, and Cherokees—had a combined population of perhaps forty thousand in 1775, with the Cherokees of the Lower, Middle, Valley, and Overhill Towns numbering between eight and twelve thousand people. The Overhill Towns posed the most immediate threat to Tennessee settlers. Assuming that one-fourth of all Indians were able-bodied adult males, the combined number of southern warriors was about ten thousand. Additional warriors from north of the Ohio River could lend support as part of a pan-Indian resistance to whites, but their actions, like those of Southern Indians, would be shaped by the aspirations and personalities of prominent individuals and differing notions of tribal self-interest. American agents would strive to prevent the creation of Indian alliances, and tribal unity would remain an elusive goal.

One of the major variables influencing Indian loyalty was trade. During the preceding century, Southern tribes had become dependent to varying degrees on the guns, fabrics, and other European objects obtained in exchange for deerskins. Indian support for British control of American settlers was tempered by the realization that patriot forces might prevent British goods from arriving in the interior. Besides, favorable trading relations had been established with certain colonial businessmen. Whichever side could guarantee a consistent supply of goods at reasonable prices would have an important advantage in dealing with the Indians.

After the clash at Lexington and Concord in April 1775, colonists and British officials alike prepared for full-scale military operations, and colonial leaders asserted that Indians should stay out of this dispute among white brothers. To promote tribal neutrality, the Continental Congress established three Indian districts in the backcountry, the southernmost having jurisdiction over relations with the Cherokees and other tribes on the Tennessee frontier. Five men from Virginia, North Carolina, and South Carolina served as commissioners for the district. Given the sorry colonial record of land grabbing, the commissioners quickly realized they would have to rely on "rum and good words" in their Indian diplomacy. Despite the Cherokees' natural inclination to support the British, they were worried about disrupting long-established trade with the colonists and the certainty of savage retaliation by settlers. Both the British and Americans pledged to continue the trade, the former to cement their Indian alliances and the latter to promote tribal neutrality.

The Revolution enormously complicated John Stuart's personal life and his duties as the Crown's Indian Superintendent for the Southern Department. Formerly a respected citizen of Charleston, he was forced to flee in the summer of 1775 because of the growing revolutionary fervor. He reestablished his headquarters first in St. Augustine in East Florida and eventually in Pensacola. Though realizing the British had an advantage in Indian diplomacy because the tribes saw the Crown as their only bulwark against eventual dispossession, he was afraid the Indians might not discriminate in waging war against the settlers, that in their fury they might attack those still loyal to Britain and push them into the enemy camp. Stuart's strategy was thus to counsel Indian allies to delay attacks on the backcountry until British troops were in the area and could act as a restraining influence. This policy conflicted with the wishes of military officers and loyalists in the backcountry who favored more aggressive actions against patriot frontiersmen.

Stuart had particular difficulty restraining the Cherokees, especially younger militants who were increasingly resentful about the incursions of "Virginians," as they called all land-hungry settlers. Richard Henderson's controversial acquisition of the vast area between the Kentucky and Cumberland rivers infuriated leaders like Dragging Canoe, as did the growing white population in upper East Tennessee. There were occasional murders on both sides, and in June 1775 the venerable war leader Oconostota attributed the killing of two whites by Indians to "evil minded" settlers who were not obeying the law—obviously a reference to violations of the Proclamation and Donelson lines. Nevertheless, he insisted that the Cherokees wished to live "in perpetual peace and friendship with our brothers the whites."

Some whites recognized the justice of Cherokee discontent. Henderson's agent warned that the recent settlement of white families in Powell's Valley violated the proprietors' orders and had resulted in bloodshed. He was directed to take action against such settlers, but this did little to assuage Indian anger. In August 1775 Oconostota delighted Alexander Cameron, John Stuart's agent to the Cherokees, by giving "a hell of a talk" in support of the British. But Stuart was still cautious and reiterated his request that the Cherokees postpone attacking the colonists until British troops and loyalists could offer support and guidance.

The most loyal Cherokee ally of the British was not the aging Oconostota, Attakullakulla, or Ostenaco, but Attakullakulla's son, Dragging Canoe, who was in his early forties. Since delivering his impassioned words at Sycamore Shoals, he had emerged as leader of those younger warriors opposing all compromise with the settlers. His very name bespoke his fierce determination. As a young boy, he had begged his father for permission to join a raid against the Shawnees. When Attakullakulla refused, the child slipped away and hid in a canoe at a portage he knew the Cherokees would use. Finding him there, his father said the youth could accompany them if he could carry the canoe across the portage. Too small to do that, he began dragging it instead. The warriors were impressed by his tenacity and shouted encouragement, one crying out, "Tsi.yu Gansi.ni," meaning "He is dragging the canoe." And so the boy became Dragging Canoe, and he was later head warrior of the Overhill village of Island Town. From the Treaty of Sycamore Shoals until his death in 1792, he would be the most implacable enemy of the Americans on the entire Southern frontier. His pockmarked visage, souvenir of a smallpox epidemic, inhabited the nightmares of an entire generation of white Tennesseans. Dragging Canoe would also prove to be an inspiring leader who paradoxically divided his own nation.

Most Tennessee settlers supported colonial resistance to British policies, and during 1775 North of Holston residents participated in patriotic meetings in Fincastle County, Virginia. Because the Holston people lived north of the Donelson line and the Virginia–North Carolina boundary in that area was still unsurveyed, Fincastle County exercised jurisdiction over them. That county had a revolutionary Committee of Safety, supported actions of the Second Continental Congress, and had appointed Evan Shelby to oversee a local boycott of British goods. Settlers on the Long Island of the Holston and in Carter's Valley were on the Indian side of Donelson's line, but in 1776 they invoked their revolutionary ardor in a successful petition for inclusion in Fincastle County.

Most exposed to possible Indian attack were the Watauga and Nolichucky settlers who, despite their recent purchases from the Cherokees, were illegally residing deep in Indian Country. Like other settlers, they sought security through political organization and formed a thirteen-member Committee of Safety, headed by John Carter. They patriotically called themselves the Washington District, the first political area named in honor of the new commander of the Continental army. The Committee of Safety blended its authority with that of the Watauga Association's court, which continued business as usual. The following spring, still anxious about their safety, inhabitants of the district appealed to Virginia for annexation.

Meanwhile, in British Florida John Stuart prepared to solidify Indian allegiance to the Crown by sending ammunition and goods into the interior with Henry Stuart, his brother and deputy superintendent. At Mobile in March 1776 the younger Stuart met Dragging Canoe, who complained about white encroachment, the lack of trade goods, and other matters. "The white men," the volatile chief said, "have almost surrounded us, leaving us only a little spot of ground to stand upon." He blamed the older chiefs for bargaining with Richard Henderson, and he was determined to attack the Watauga and Nolichucky settlers. When Henry Stuart arrived in Chota on April 24, he and Alexander Cameron found the other chiefs almost as incensed as Dragging Canoe over white trespassing. The two officials offered to communicate these concerns to the settlers and asked the Indians to keep the peace in the meantime. Ironically, they also distributed twenty-one pack loads of ammunition, but they warned that it was to be used only for hunting and defense.

In an effort to defuse the situation, Stuart and Cameron wrote to the Watauga and Nolichucky settlers about Cherokee distress over their illegal settlements. If they wanted good land and were truly "good and peaceable subjects," they could obtain free grants of land from the Crown in West Florida. Stuart and Cameron attempted to persuade them that immediate removal was necessary: "We are sensible that your removing at this season of the Year must be attended with a great deal of trouble and inconvenience, but this consideration is but trifling when compared to the danger to which Yourselves your families and effects must be exposed from a Mercyless & enraged Enemy, if you should think of remaining longer on their land, to which the Indians will never acknowledge your claim." The last sentence was succinct and ominous: "The Indians expect that you will remove in twenty days." Accompanying this message was a similar statement by the Cherokees.

Isaac Thomas, an American trader, delivered the letter and soon returned with an ambiguous reply from John Carter to the effect that the Wataugans were loyal subjects of the King, living on lands legally acquired from the Indians, and in the event they still had to move, would need more time. Stuart and Cameron sent a second message, saying the Cherokees had agreed to extend their deadline another twenty days but warning that trespassing was illegal even for loyalists. The Wataugans were neither loyal nor inclined to abandon their homes. They rejected the Fincastle Committee of Safety's recommendation that they move across the Donelson line and attempted to win support by fabricating a message from Stuart that threatened them not for trespassing but for being revolutionaries. It indicated that British troops would land at Pensacola, march through Creek and Cherokee territories, and attack the frontier with the aid of their Indian allies. Homes of British loyalists were to be marked in a special way so they might be spared. The apparently fraudulent message was sent to the Fincastle County Committee of Safety and eventually to the Virginia and North Carolina conventions and to Congress. It created widespread indignation and confirmed the belief that the British were inciting an Indian attack on the frontier.

In truth, Henry Stuart and Alexander Cameron continued to urge Cherokee restraint, but circumstances undermined their efforts. In June, while the Cherokees awaited a response to their second message to Watauga, a fourteen-man delegation of Northern Indians—Shawnee, Delaware, Mingo, Ottawa, and Mohawk—arrived at Chota for a council attended by Cherokees from all parts of the nation. The main speaker, a Shawnee, displayed a huge wampum belt from Cornstalk, recently defeated at Point Pleasant, who had issued a dramatic call for war by spilling vermilion paint over it. His emissary harangued the Cherokees as fellow Indians to take up the hatchet against the Americans, who intended to exterminate them all. Appealing to Indian nativism, he declared that because their cause was just, the Great Being would likely favor them. Dragging Canoe, painted black, eagerly accepted Cornstalk's belt and struck the war pole, while other Cherokees seized smaller belts offered by the visitors. Together the Cherokees and their guests sang a war song. These "ritually sanctioned actions" symbolized an alliance between Cherokee and Northern militants. From the time of that meeting at Chota until 1794, they would often fight side by side against whites on both sides of the Ohio.

The events at Chota revealed the deep divisions between tribal militants and the accommodationists, who were accustomed to making the best possible deals with British and Americans alike. The accommodationists, including older chiefs who had agreed to the Henderson sale, realized they had lost the initiative, and they now sat "dejected and silent." Despite insisting that they never understood the nature of Henderson's requests and had accepted his goods only as compensation for old injustices, they were often scorned by fellow Cherokees.

Stuart and Cameron realized an attack at this point would mean the deaths of innocent whites, including loyalists, and that the Indians would suffer fierce retaliation. The two agents still believed they could avert hostilities, but their hopes were undone when Cherokees launched attacks on the Carolina side of the mountains. The American commissioners for the Southern district had hosted a Cherokee conference that April in South Carolina, but only the Lower and Valley people attended in significant number. Most Overhill Cherokees had refused the invitation because they were preparing to meet Henry Stuart and Alexander Cameron. One of the commissioners, Willie Jones, correctly surmised that trouble was imminent. Lower Cherokees who had heard the Northern Indians speak at Chota returned home eager to take up the hatchet. Late in June war parties from the Lower Towns attacked settlers in the South Carolina backcountry, and by the end of July nearly forty whites had died on North Carolina's Catawba frontier.

Word of the initial attacks and receipt of a condescending and threatening letter from the Fincastle Committee of Safety spurred Overhill militants to prepare for war. The letter told the Cherokees to abandon their British advisers, control Dragging Canoe, and discuss the situation with the settlers face to face, or suffer an invasion of their country. Enraged, the Cherokee militants quickly planned an attack on the Tennessee settlements, agreeing to spare any Tories who joined the Indians or surrendered peaceably. Several traders, including Nathaniel Gist and Isaac Thomas, were dispatched to warn the loyalists, but instead they spread the alarm throughout an already alert backcountry. Nancy Ward, Beloved Woman of the Cherokees and resident of Chota, had apparently told Thomas the Cherokee plans. Her actions reveal the prominent role assumed by male and female Beloveds in Cherokee society and especially in Chota, which, despite its leading role in the Cherokee War of 1759–61, was traditionally dedicated to peace, diplomacy, and sanctuary. But Ward's functions were ambiguous, for she was also a War Woman with certain prerogatives in councils of war and decisions regarding clemency for captives.

Nancy Ward's relationship with white traders also raised questions. Her second husband was a trader, and she was known to whites by his surname. Other traders had also become part of the tribal kinship system through intermarriage. They supplied Indians with necessary goods and were crucial conduits of information between the two races. Indeed, both sides depended so much on such information that both were justified in suspecting traders of double-dealing. As the Revolution got under way, it was difficult to discern the actual sentiments of many traders. Usually they spoke the native language, lived comfortably in the villages, and had Indian spouses or consorts; their children were probably more familiar with Indian ways than those of white society. Alexander Cameron, John Stuart's assistant, was an anomaly as a trader. He resided on a South Carolina estate before the Revolution and remained forthrightly loyal to the Crown. His fellow Scotsman John McDonald was also unequivocally loyal, as was James Colbert, the most prominent Chickasaw trader. In contrast, Joseph Martin and Isaac Thomas reflected some of the ambiguities inherent in the cultural middle ground; both served the patriot cause but exhibited great sensitivity toward and concern for their Cherokee friends and relatives. Others like Nathaniel Gist played both sides when it suited their purposes. Not surprisingly, Dragging Canoe and other militants increasingly found the uncertain roles of female Beloveds and some traders intolerable.

The settlers in East Tennessee meanwhile sought outside assistance for the impending hostilities. On July 5, 1776, after unsuccessful pleas for annexation by Virginia, more than one hundred Wataugans signed a petition written by William Tatham asking North Carolina to annex and protect them. They had already dispatched a small company of militia to Charleston to help repel an anticipated British attack, but because of imminent danger at home they thought it wise to retain a larger company of riflemen under James Robertson "in defence of the common cause, at the expense and risque of our own private fortunes, till farther public orders." While appealing to Virginia and North Carolina, settlers worked at constructing several stockades, including Fort Watauga, overlooking Sycamore Shoals; Fort Lee, close to Jacob Brown's Nolichucky store; and Fort Eaton, near Long Island. Defenders realized any immediate assistance would likely come through the Great Valley and that Virginia was committed to protecting the lead mines at Chiswell, which were vulnerable to Cherokee and Shawnee attack. That state had already dispatched six companies of militiamen under Colonel William Russell to augment the troops patrolling the troubled region near Long Island. For its part, North Carolina instructed its frontier militia commander to be vigilant but not cross the line into Indian country unless attacked first.

Like patriots in other areas, Tennessee settlers took decisive steps to stifle dissent in their midst. It was well known that certain individuals at Watauga and Jacob Brown's Nolichucky settlement were loyalists. An alliance of discontented whites, Indians, and British would be extremely dangerous and threaten all settlers who aspired to become property owners. Community well-being and personal ambition thus intersected. Frontier elites throughout the backcountry legitimized their authority by denouncing loyalists as "white Indians" and banditti and by taking stern measures against them. At the request of John Carter, probably the most eminent resident of Watauga, Charles Robertson's riflemen and a unit of Fincastle militia under John Shelby (Evan's brother) forced more than seventy suspected loyalists on the Nolichucky "to take an oath to be true to the rights and liberties of America." Those who refused were drummed out of the settlements.

The Cherokee assault came in July. The leadership and size of the Indian force, numbering perhaps seven hundred warriors, indicated widespread agreement among the Indians. It appears that tribal accommodationists now perceived war against the settlers as a means of showing their solidarity with Britain and the militants, restoring Cherokee harmony, and perhaps of regaining their own prestige and influence. The attacking Indians followed a simple but sophisticated plan. The Raven, principal war leader of Chota, split off with fewer than one hundred warriors and attacked the settlers in Carter's Valley, who quickly fled into Virginia. The Indians burned cabins and killed livestock, then broke into smaller groups that raided almost to Abingdon. The main force of Cherokees, under Old Abram of Chilhowee and Dragging Canoe, proceeded up the Nolichucky to strike the other Tennessee settlements. Lieutenant John Sevier was attempting to finish Fort Lee, but half of his thirty-man garrison joined the flight of residents to Fort Watauga or Virginia. Sevier himself wisely decided to fall back on Fort Watauga. The Cherokees destroyed the abandoned Fort Lee and then divided their force, Dragging Canoe taking nearly two hundred warriors to attack the North of Holston settlers and Old Abram advancing on the defenders at Fort Watauga.

As Dragging Canoe and his warriors approached Eaton's Station near Long Island, a militia force under Captain James Thompson sallied forth to engage them at Island Flats. It was July 20, 1776, less than three weeks after the signing of the Declaration of Independence. In the ensuing battle militia leaders claimed to have killed at least thirteen Cherokees while only four soldiers were seriously wounded. Dragging Canoe was shot through the leg but managed to escape in the Indian retreat. Meanwhile Old Abram's group continued toward Fort Watauga, occupied by 150–200 men, women, and children, both whites and slaves, under Colonel John Carter and his subordinates James Robertson and John Sevier. The Indians attacked early on July 21, surprising some women who were milking cows just outside the gates. Catherine Sherrill was unable to make it back inside and instead was pulled over the palisade by Sevier amid a hail of bullets and arrows. Later, he would marry her. The attack lasted for about three hours before the warriors were driven back. The Cherokees then kept the post under siege for about two weeks while sending small raiding parties into neighboring areas and killing a few unwary or luckless whites. They finally withdrew as a relief force approached from Virginia. One of the most famous incidents in this campaign was the capture of Mrs. William Bean, who was taken into Cherokee country and was about to be burned to death when Nancy Ward exercised her prerogative as Beloved Woman and spared her. Oral tradition says that Mrs. Bean, before being returned to her family, stayed at Ward's house and taught her how to make butter.

Even after their general withdrawal, the Cherokees remained a potent threat, and some whites feared the Creeks would join them. Few settlers dared venture very far from the scattered forts or stations because small parties of warriors continued to menace the backcountry. John Stuart and Alexander Cameron no longer vacillated and now encouraged the Cherokees to continue their attacks. Reaction in the colonies was predictably forceful. Virginia's Governor Thomas Jefferson declared his hopes of driving the Cherokees beyond the Mississippi as an example to other Indians. Officials in Virginia and the Carolinas now viewed the Cherokees as British allies, and Congress concurred, resolving on July 30 that the Southern colonies should go to war "with all possible vigor against those savages."

The plan that emerged was for militias from the Carolinas to cooperate in campaigns against the Lower and Middle Towns, and for Virginia troops, with the possible assistance of North Carolina, to attack the Overhill communities. South Carolina acted first, quickly raising some 1,100 men under Colonel Andrew Williamson, who moved unsuccessfully to capture Alexander Cameron, reportedly leading one of the Cherokee war parties. Then in a ten-day campaign beginning August 2 Williamson burned and plundered the Lower Towns. Many of the inhabitants fled across the mountains to the Overhill villages and warned their brothers that they would suffer the same fate. A force of 2,500 men under North Carolina's General Griffith Rutherford destroyed most of the Middle Towns in mid-September and then, reinforced by Williamson, razed the remaining Middle and Valley communities.

Virginia was already preparing to send an army under Colonel William Christian against the Overhill villages. North Carolina militiamen would rendezvous with him on the Holston. William Russell and three hundred Virginia rangers awaited the soldiers at Long Island and built Fort Patrick Henry to accommodate them. The combined forces from Virginia and North Carolina arrived there in late September and found a few warriors lurking about the post. Christian's army began its trek to the Overhill Towns on October 1 and was soon joined by Watauga and Nolichucky militiamen under captains James Robertson and Valentine Sevier. These troops and those from Long Island constituted a battalion under Major Evan Shelby, making a total of about 1,800 men in Christian's command. They were all infantry except for a company of horsemen under Sevier. Isaac Thomas, the Cherokee trader, served as a scout.

The army reached the French Broad River on October 13,

crossed unopposed, and continued its march toward the Overhill Towns. At this point Cherokee factionalism again became apparent. Hard-liners like Dragging Canoe, backed by Alexander Cameron, wanted to continue the war. But most chiefs, including the newly chastened Raven, reverted to the earlier accommodationist strategy of accepting the best deal available. They favored making peace with Christian before they experienced the same devastation as the towns across the mountains. To Dragging Canoe's disgust, the peace faction prevailed and sent Nathaniel Gist to negotiate with the invaders. Christian and his men were suspicious of Gist but quick to take advantage of his information. While pondering the appropriate terms to impose on the Indians, Christian continued his march and finally camped on the Tennessee near Dragging Canoe's home village of Island Town. There was no opposition, only hurried retreat as inhabitants abandoned homes, food, and livestock. Christian sent a message to the Raven demanding that the Indians accept his terms or face destruction of all their towns. Nothing would save the villages that had most actively supported Dragging Canoe and Cameron. As militiamen burned Island Town, they found seven scalps in Dragging Canoe's abandoned home. The truculent chief had already gathered his loyal followers and retreated southward with Cameron.

In a preliminary settlement with Christian, the peace chiefs promised to release all prisoners, return the property taken in their attacks, deliver fellow Cherokees as hostages, cede part of their lands as compensation for the war, and attempt to deliver for punishment Dragging Canoe, Cameron, and other supporters of the British cause. Christian demanded that the Indians sign a formal treaty with Virginia authorities the following spring and pledged that in the meantime he would forbid unauthorized whites from venturing into the Overhill territory. Satisfied, he began his march back to Virginia in mid-November. Despite his promise to keep whites off Cherokee lands, his military success whetted their appetite for more of East Tennessee. As his militiamen marched to the Indian towns, they were quick to note likely sites for settlement.

While the Cherokee war raged through the summer and early

fall, North Carolina's revolutionary Council of Safety considered the Washington District's appeal for annexation. American independence had already been declared, and the former colony was about to write its first state constitution. The Tennessee settlers had demonstrated their loyalty to the Revolution and were within the chartered limits of North Carolina, so the council invited the Washington District to send five delegates to the constitutional convention in Halifax in November 1776. Wataugans promptly elected John Carter, Charles Robertson, John Sevier, John Haile, and Jacob Womack, and the convention voted 153–1 to seat them. Four of the five new delegates participated in drafting the state constitution, which proclaimed North Carolina's sovereignty over lands as far west as the Mississippi. With colossal oversight—or perhaps hubris—the convention simply ignored Indian ownership of Tennessee.

The new constitution placed almost all of present-day Tennessee and a small part of present-day North Carolina within the newly created "District of Washington." A special ordinance appended to the document appointed twenty-one justices of the peace for the district's new court. Tennessee voters quickly elected John Carter to the senate and John Sevier and Jacob Womack to the house of the first North Carolina state legislature. In 1777 the district became Washington County, which included Tennessee but none of present-day North Carolina.

North Carolina's fundamental dilemma for Tennessee was how to satisfy the settlers' insatiable desire for more land and also allay Indian fears and resentments. The latter was the most pressing problem. Though the Cherokees had pledged to appear at Long Island for a formal peace treaty, Dragging Canoe and others hoped to enlist allies to continue the struggle. But the Northern tribes were busy fighting elsewhere, and the Cherokees' recent humiliating defeats served as a powerful deterrent to other Southern tribes. About all that John Stuart was able to do was obtain a promise that a portion of the Upper Creeks would attack the backcountry the following year if they were supplied by the British. For the present, however, the Cherokees would have to stand alone, and the division between militants and accommodationists was wider than ever before. The latter, reluctant to fight in the first place, again moved to the forefront and opposed military resistance. Some of them no doubt privately sympathized with Dragging Canoe, but his implacable hostility to the settlers would prove to be a major diplomatic problem for his elders.

The devious nature of Cherokee diplomacy was apparent in April 1777 when the wily Attakullakulla and some twenty-five warriors appeared early at the Long Island council ground. Unperturbed by the charges of his son, Dragging Canoe, that he was a lackey of whites, the old chief was effusive in his goodwill toward the settlers. According to John Carter, colonel of the Washington County militia, Attakullakulla and his men said five hundred warriors stood ready to assist North Carolina and Virginia against the English or hostile Indians. Formal peace negotiations between the Cherokees and commissioners from Virginia and North Carolina began at Long Island on July 1. About four hundred Indians attended, including Attakullakulla, Oconostota, and Old Tassel, but Dragging Canoe was conspicuously absent. The brutal murder of a visiting Cherokee, apparently by the relative of a victim in the recent war, briefly delayed the council. Mortified officials could not positively identify the killer, but the Cherokees were finally mollified enough to sit down for talks. Tennessee's first Fourth of July celebration—marked by a parade, the discharge of musketry and cannons, and whiskey for whites and Indians alike—provided a festive interlude.

In the final Treaty of Long Island the Cherokees proclaimed themselves at peace with the revolutionaries and neutral in the settlers' war with Britain, and despite an eloquent protest by Old Tassel, they agreed to cede part of their land. A minor complication was Richard Henderson's defense of his company's claims, but both Virginia and North Carolina ignored his arguments. The Indians negotiated a separate treaty with each state, agreeing to boundaries that would put the white settlements within the limits of either. The two states would survey their common line later. Until then, Virginia would administer the North of Holston, Long Island, and Carter's Valley settlements, while the Nolichucky and Watauga communities were clearly within North Carolina. Virginia and North Carolina appointed Joseph Martin and James Robertson, respectively, to serve as state agents among the Overhill Towns. About that time Martin married Betsy Ward, the daughter of Nancy Ward. They settled on the lower end of the Long Island, where he would have quick access to the Overhill Towns.

Despite professions of goodwill, the treaties were mere scraps of paper because of continual trespassing by whites and Dragging Canoe's belligerence. Encroachment sometimes occurred under pretense of law and often in blatant disregard of it. Following the Treaty of Long Island, North Carolina opened a state land office in Washington County, with John Carter serving as entry taker. Individuals could buy land at the rate of fifty shillings per one hundred acres; a head of household could acquire up to six hundred forty acres, plus another hundred acres for a spouse and each child. Additional lands could be purchased at the rate of five pounds per one hundred acres. The state would recognize no land claims beyond the Indian boundary established in the recent treaty, but whites were already crossing that line by late 1777. Inhabitants of the Nolichucky and Watauga regions became more secure and self-confident now that North Carolina had extended its authority, and the land acquisitions made under the Watauga Association were quickly repurchased at Carter's land office.

More clearly than any other Cherokee, Dragging Canoe perceived the unrelenting nature of white expansion, and he was determined to resist it. Early in 1777 he and his followers established several communities farther down the Tennessee River near Chickamauga Creek at present-day Chattanooga. The new towns had convenient access to British trader John McDonald's post and to John Stuart's headquarters in Pensacola; they were also less accessible to white enemies in upper East Tennessee. Dragging Canoe's secession was both a repudiation of the traditional ethic of harmony and a reaffirmation of it. He consciously spurned older, more traditional leaders and polarized Cherokee society. Indeed, the Chickamaugas distinguished themselves from other Cherokees by calling themselves *Ani-Yunwiya*, "the Real People." On the other hand, Cherokees who could not conform to important consensual decisions traditionally removed themselves. It is possible that some of the older, pacified chiefs encour-

aged Dragging Canoe's secession in order to avoid making good
on their promise to turn him over to American officials, and to
deflect blame for his continuing resistance, which they could not
prevent. To their credit, colonial officials usually distinguished
between the "Chicamoggy" and the Tennessee Cherokees who
continued to reside in the old Overhill Towns.

It would be a mistake, however, to view the Chickamaugas
and the Overhill Cherokees simply as two distinct divisions of
the same tribe. So-called peaceful members of the latter group
actually occupied the spectrum of sentiment. At one end were
those who were openly sympathetic to Dragging Canoe and who
occasionally joined his war parties. At the other end were the
accommodationists, who were unhappy about white transgressions and expansion but opposed any overt action that would
result in savage retaliation. Such retribution would fall most
heavily on towns like Chota that were close to white settlements,
and the head men of these towns were often shrewd diplomats
who could both disavow violence and articulate Indian grievances to white authorities. Instinctively, they continued to seek
consensus, even where it was impossible. Whites were therefore
justified in their skepticism about a clear-cut division between
hostile and peaceful Cherokees; tribal society was much more
nuanced than that.

The Chickamaugas were not limited to Dragging Canoe's fellow Cherokees, nor were they confined to the towns along Chickamauga Creek. Their numbers included disparate groups of refugees who had gathered along the nearby upper Coosa River
after the Treaty of DeWitt's Corner. The latter included Cherokees from the Lower and Middle Towns as well as Upper Creeks.
Also affiliated with the Chickamaugas were Shawnees and Delawares who moved back and forth across the Ohio, a few blacks,
and a range of white traders, British agents, French boatmen,
and frontier loyalists. Thus the Chickamauga villages resemble
in many respects the contemporaneous "multi-ethnic village republics" in the Great Lakes country. The amorphous Chickamaugas also exemplify the pan-Indian and pan-ethnic character
of resistance to American expansion on the trans-Appalachian
frontier. Their total number was about five hundred warriors and
their families.

Dragging Canoe's dogged defiance was an inspiration to other Cherokees, especially the young warriors who periodically left the pacified towns and joined Chickamauga raids. Even while Attakullakulla, Old Tassel, and other tribal elders were negotiating the Treaty of Long Island, Dragging Canoe's warriors had kept the Holston settlers close to their fortifications, and it was questionable whether the whites would be able to harvest their crops. Among those killed by prowling Indians were the grandparents of Davy Crockett. That same year—"the year of the three sevens"—Dragging Canoe's prophecy of Kentucky becoming a dark and bloody ground came true, as Daniel Boone and other settlers withstood attacks by Shawnees and Chickamaugas alike. When the beleaguered Kentuckians pleaded for assistance, forty-five Watauga militiamen marched through Cumberland Gap and reinforced Boonesborough and Harrodsburg.

Continuing white encroachment on Overhill lands also heightened tensions, making it difficult for young warriors to abide by the peace so tenuously established in the Treaty of Long Island. In the fall of 1777 the North Carolina council tried to ameliorate the situation by instructing James Robertson to tour the Indian country and to bring a delegation of leaders to New Bern for talks. Robertson found the Cherokees outwardly hospitable, but he acknowledged the problems: Alexander Cameron's continuing influence, white encroachment, systematic cheating of Indians in trade, and white condescension and contempt toward the Cherokees. The general assembly of North Carolina again warned settlers not to trespass on Indian lands and attempted to diminish tensions in the backcountry by disbanding most of the militia forces there.

For the Tennessee frontier 1778 was a relatively quiet year as Dragging Canoe's warriors operated mostly in the Georgia and South Carolina backcountry. Though most Cherokees resisted the blandishments of John Stuart and Alexander Cameron to take up the tomahawk, Attakullakulla visited Stuart in Pensacola and promised Cherokee assistance in helping the British to guard the Ohio River, an offer that was perhaps a ploy to obtain renewed British trade. Stuart's refusal to supply the Cherokee towns that had been pacified by the Americans was obviously a sore point, and it resulted in an extraordinary event. Joseph Martin wrote Stuart to denounce Wataugan encroachments, claiming that the Cherokees remained neutral only out of fear of American retaliation, which was probably true, and asked Stuart to resume the trade. Perhaps Martin saw British trade as a lesser evil than the consequences of America's total inability to provide necessary goods. Or he may have written the letter simply to help his Cherokee friends and kinsmen.

But always it was the land that determined Cherokee attitudes toward the Americans. An exasperated Raven complained to Governor Richard Caswell of North Carolina that the Wataugans were "marking trees all over the country," even near his Chota home. Caswell merely replied that he had warned the settlers not to encroach on Indian lands. Virginia, on the other hand, was willing to make at least a few concessions. Fearful that the Shawnees might goad the Cherokees into a joint war against their state, officials obliged the Cherokees by refusing to recognize Nathaniel Gist's claim to sole ownership of Long Island. For the moment at least, the Overhill Towns resisted British and Creek pleas for them to attack the backcountry. They recovered from their defeats and waited to see what would happen. Britain's Indian allies in the Southwest were also mostly quiet. The Chickasaws and Choctaws supposedly guarded the Mississippi River against American incursions, but early that year Captain James Willing led a small force downstream, hit a British post south of Natchez, then continued on with dispatches from the Continental Congress for American officials in Spanish New Orleans. The Yankee raid was so swift and unexpected that Henry Stuart had fled in his nightshirt.

Despite the failures of British-backed Indian warfare on the Southern frontier, British officers continued to believe they could exploit the long-standing Indian antipathy toward white settlers. One of the more ambitious schemes envisioned coordinated Indian assaults in the Northern and Southern backcountry that would drive settlers back to the more populated areas and create massive confusion while British troops launched a major offensive in the South. Lieutenant Governor Henry Hamilton, operating out of Detroit, wanted the Southern and Northern tribes to meet at the Ohio River, reconcile any differences, and begin their attacks. John Stuart was confident that the Chickamaugas, at least, were ready for action and that loyalists in the backcountry would cooperate with them.

The continuing machinations of Stuart's subordinate, Alexander Cameron, coupled with a steady stream of information from Joseph Martin and friendly Cherokees, convinced American authorities that a preemptive strike was necessary. In January 1779 Virginia's Governor Patrick Henry ordered Evan Shelby to raise three hundred men to destroy the Chickamauga towns, and at his request North Carolina agreed to send an additional two hundred volunteers from the Washington County militia under Charles Robertson. After attacking the Chickamaugas part of the Virginia contingent would continue down the Tennessee River and join with Colonel George Rogers Clark's force in the Northwest. The Virginia and North Carolina forces rendezvoused on the Holston, built an armada of boats, and began their descent to the Chickamauga villages on April 10. Assisted by high waters, they made a quick trip and arrived just after a number of Chickamauga warriors had left to join a loyalist force marching to Savannah. The remaining Indians fled after losing perhaps half a dozen men, and militiamen systematically burned the towns, destroyed crops, and unearthed British goods that had been cached for future raids. Clark's reinforcements then continued on their way while the other militiamen returned to the settlements. The warriors who had left for Savannah were barely into South Carolina before receiving word of the attacks and returning to their smoldering villages. Most histories state that Shelby's campaign caused the Chickamaugas to relocate farther downstream, but their migration occurred unevenly during the next three years. Some hostile Indians remained in small communities near Chickamauga Creek.

Unchastened by Shelby's raid, Dragging Canoe again welcomed Shawnee delegates in 1779 and promised to continue fighting the Virginia "Long Knives." Some of the Northerners joined the Chickamauga towns, while parties of Cherokees fought with Shawnees in the North and helped block American use of the lower Ohio River. For the moment pan-Indian solidarity was real. Small Chickamauga war parties continued to menace whites in upper East Tennessee, and that summer a larger force joined Cameron's loyalists on another march into South Carolina. Encountering a force of some seven hundred patriot light horsemen under General Andrew Williamson, the Indians retreated despite Cameron's entreaties. Williamson promptly advanced into Chickamauga country and burned the easternmost towns, apparently those occupied by Lower and Middle Cherokees on the upper Coosa.

By this time British administration of the Southern Indian superintendency had undergone significant reorganization, triggered by John Stuart's death in March 1779. Alexander Cameron continued to work among the Chickamaugas for a few months before assuming jurisdiction over Choctaw and Chickasaw affairs, while Lieutenant Colonel Thomas Brown, superintendent of the new Atlantic District, administered Cherokee and Creek relations out of British-occupied Savannah. Both he and Cameron were subordinate to the ranking military officers in their districts, and both would operate under severe financial limitations, for Parliament was appalled by the spiraling costs of Indian diplomacy.

The Revolution in the South changed dramatically in 1780. The Spanish, who had long intrigued out of New Orleans with the Choctaws and Chickasaws, were now openly at war with Britain. In February they seized Mobile, and Pensacola was their next logical target. Farther to the east, British forces under Sir Henry Clinton laid plans in Savannah for a major campaign that Clinton hoped would bring the colonists to their senses. The offensive would open with an attack on Charleston. Clinton told superintendent Thomas Brown that their Indian allies should remain alert and await orders for coordinated attacks on the backcountry. Eager to support the British cause—and to receive gifts—about three hundred Chickamaugas arrived on the Georgia coast in March, only to confront a smallpox epidemic. They quickly accepted their presents and official British gratitude, then fled back to their homes. Both they and their east Tennessee enemies would find more pressing threats elsewhere—for the Indians, the new settlements in Middle Tennessee; for the whites, the advance of a British army into the Carolina backcountry.

4.

Expansion Amid Revolution: 1779–1783

The periodic lulls in backcountry warfare allowed settlers to consolidate their treaty gains and prepare for renewed expansion beyond the existing frontier. Especially alluring were the lands along the Cumberland River in Middle Tennessee, nearly two hundred miles west of the Holston and Watauga settlements. Unlike the larger Tennessee River, which roughly parallels it to the south and west, the Cumberland was never seen as a highway linking Atlantic coastal areas with the Mississippi Valley. Instead, it attracted attention because of the area's fertile soil and incredible abundance of game animals: buffalo, deer, bear, elk, squirrel, beaver, turkey, and waterfowl. Indeed, early visitors found buffalo and other game animals so thick at the salt licks that their bellowing "resounded from the hills and forests."

During the late seventeenth century wandering bands of Shawnees hunted and trapped along the Cumberland and sometimes settled long enough to plant a crop or two of corn. Accompanying them were a few Frenchmen down from the Illinois Country or the Wabash River. These individuals were mostly shadowy figures, but one of them was Martin Chartier, a well-traveled jack-of-all-trades who in 1690 began a two-year adventure with some Shawnees that took them throughout the Cumberland valley. A few years later another Frenchman operated a small trading post near present-day Nashville and served the needs of resident Shawnees. He was eventually assisted by an eager young countryman named Jean de Charleville. But the Cherokee and Chickasaw menace was becoming more dangerous, and a Chickasaw ambush in 1714 ended French trade and Shawnee habitation in the area. Around 1745 Peter Chartier, the mixed-blood son of Martin, apparently led some Shawnees in an attempt to resettle near Nashville, but the fierce Chickasaws again forced them out. After that the Cumberland area was a no-man's-land. The fat buffalo and other game animals continued to attract hunters from several tribes, but such visitors had to be prepared for fight, flight, or death. It was a dangerous region.

By the mid-1760s white hunters and traders were reappearing in the basin. A young Frenchman named Timothe de Monbruen began boating up the Cumberland, hunting extensively and collecting hides and tallow. On one occasion he and few employees followed a buffalo herd to several salt licks on the upper river. One became known as Big Salt Lick, or French Lick; the latter name was also used for early Nashville, which grew up there. Though he was not a permanent resident until much later, de Monbruen built a small log storehouse near the lick and traded with many of the American hunters who arrived after the French and Indian War. Perhaps the earliest was Henry Scaggs, who explored throughout the region in 1765. The following year the American invasion began in earnest. Michael Stoner and James Harrod, both Pennsylvanians, hunted there as well as some Virginians under Isaac Lindsey. A separate party consisting of Uriah Stone, James Smith, and two others from Virginia's Holston country explored the lower Tennessee and Cumberland rivers from Stones River above Nashville to the Ohio. Smith, accompanied only by a black slave, and carrying a Psalm Book and Isaac Watts's *Upon Prayer*, chose to return home on foot, and his narrative is the first English-language account of the Cumberland.

In 1768 British commerce came to the region when the Philadelphia firm of Baynton, Wharton, and Morgan began sending boatloads of buffalo hunters from the Illinois Country up the

Cumberland as far as Carthage. The following year Lieutenant Thomas Hutchins, an accomplished cartographer assigned to Western guard duty, methodically mapped the river to a point above Nashville. Unfortunately, his map was not available to others who visited the region during the next few years. These were hunters endowed with sharp eyes and a sixth sense for Indians and game, men like Kaspar Mansker, Abraham Bledsoe, and Daniel Boone, who in the summer of 1772 broke the Cumberland silence and attracted the attention of a dumbfounded Mansker by singing loudly to himself while lying on a deerskin.

Some of these early visitors were farmers as well as hunters, men who readily appreciated what Lieutenant Hutchins described as the Cumberland's "luxuriant" lands and abundance of springs, salt licks, canebrakes, and timber. The first American of record to farm in Middle Tennessee was a man known only as Jones, who in 1769 cleared a small plot in Sumner County and raised some corn before being frightened off by Indians. Reappearing in upper East Tennessee at about the time the first settlers were arriving, he extolled the beauty and fertility of Middle Tennessee. Thus, even before the frontier of upper East Tennessee was well established, residents were hearing the siren call of the Cumberland Basin, a paradise of game and land. The dislocations of the Revolution merely whetted this anticipation. Some of the Wataugans who had defended the Kentucky settlements in 1777 had pursued the Chickamaugas as far as French Lick, and upon returning home they regaled neighbors with tales of the basin's natural attractions. Later visitors said the black loam of the Cumberland was "fine as flour" and the region was to East Tennessee as "the fertile plains of Flanders to the barren deserts of Africa."

Richard Henderson, James Robertson, and John Donelson were willing to heed the siren call. Henderson's interest was understandable, deriving from the Transylvania Company's 1775 purchase of the area between the Kentucky and Cumberland rivers. While attending the treaty talks at Long Island in 1777, he discussed with Robertson and Donelson the prospect of settling the Tennessee portion of his acquisition. When Virginia invalidated his claims to Kentucky the following year, he decided to

Cumberland Gap. From William Cullen Bryant,
Picturesque America (New York, 1874).

follow up on those discussions by determining whether French
Lick was within the charter limits of Virginia or North Carolina.
Most people assumed it was in Virginia, and the famous George
Rogers Clark had used that state's land warrants to claim a large
area there. In the spring of 1779 Henderson sent Robertson and
eight others, including a slave, on an exploratory trip to Middle
Tennessee. Robertson took along certain "instruments" to determine whether French Lick was within North Carolina, and if it
was, he was to plant a crop of corn as an initial step toward
settlement.

Robertson's little party followed the Kentucky Path through
Cumberland Gap, and upon reaching the upper Cumberland
River they built small canoes and floated down to the lick, where
they found de Monbruen's unoccupied cabin. The Frenchman
and several of his countrymen were hunting at the time, but soon
they had a friendly meeting with Robertson. The only other residents of the area were a few Tory families—refugees from the
turmoil back East—and a handful of patriot backwoodsmen like
Kaspar Mansker, Michael Stoner, and Thomas (Bigfoot) Spencer,

an eccentric long hunter who lived in a hollowed-out sycamore. Robertson quickly decided that the area was well south of Virginia's extended boundary and therefore within the Transylvania Company's North Carolina claim. Leaving four men to plant a crop of corn on the site of present-day Nashville, he made a quick trip to the Illinois Country, perhaps to explore business opportunities, perhaps to see Clark about obtaining his claims. Then he returned to the Holston. His personal reconnaissance had convinced this esteemed citizen that the Cumberland offered much more for himself and his family than did East Tennessee.

The growing interest in the Cumberland Basin coincided with the long-standing confusion over boundaries in upper East Tennessee. In 1779 Virginia and North Carolina officials took steps to survey the long-delayed western extension of their common boundary (the northern line of present-day Tennessee). It was hardly a coincidence that Richard Henderson and two other members of the Transylvania Company were boundary commissioners. That Henderson was making additional plans for the Cumberland shows his confidence that the survey would go his way. He, Robertson, and Donelson conceived an ambitious scenario for a permanent settlement at French Lick. Robertson was to lead an overland contingent by way of Cumberland Gap which would include most of the able-bodied men (many of them young and single) and the settlers' livestock. This party would arrive at the lick first and begin the settlement. Donelson and about forty men would meanwhile take the women and children, including some of Robertson's family, by boat down the Tennessee River to Muscle Shoals in northern Alabama, where Robertson would provide an overland escort to the new settlement for his family and some of the others.

These expeditions happened simultaneously with Henderson's surveying, which proceeded well despite some disputes with the Virginia commissioners. Robertson's overland party left in October 1779 and soon linked up with other parties heading to the promised land, raising their number to some two hundred or more. The emigrants followed no specific order; some went ahead of Robertson by a few days while others tagged along behind. After leaving the settlements of central Kentucky and heading into the barrens, they crossed totally uninhabited terrain until coming to

Kaspar Mansker's place about twelve miles above the Cumberland River. By then the pleasant autumn had turned into a bitterly cold early winter, one of the most frigid on record. When Robertson's group arrived at the Cumberland at the end of the year, they crossed on the thick ice with all their livestock. Atop a bluff on the opposite side they began building Fort Nashborough, named for the late General Francis Nash. Other newcomers settled at nearby sites on both sides of the river. For these efforts and for his steadfastness in all the tribulations to come, James Robertson well deserves to be called the Father of Middle Tennessee.

While awaiting Donelson, the Cumberland settlers built rude cabins, scouted the surrounding area, and most important, attempted to find enough to eat. During that first winter, there were hardly any agricultural foodstuffs available in the Cumberland Basin, and corn imported from Kentucky reportedly sold for $165 a bushel in depreciated Continental currency. Only the incredible abundance of game stood between the settlers and starvation, but lead and powder were in short supply, and Indians intentionally dispersed buffalo and deer from the area. Venturing into the hinterlands to hunt was an obvious risk, but the returns were worth it: one hunting party spent five days near Caney Fork, twenty to thirty miles away, and took 105 bears, 75 buffaloes, and 87 deer.

Meanwhile, John Donelson was having his own problems trying to navigate the Tennessee. His log of the journey is one of the most famous documents of the American frontier, tersely detailing the daily monotony and terror of his expedition. His flotilla of makeshift craft, led by a large flatboat called the *Adventure*, left Fort Patrick Henry on the Holston on December 22, 1779, but a drop in water level limited significant progress until February. Once they were on their way they picked up an array of other hastily assembled rafts and boats filled with families who were also heading to new lands. Early in March 1780 the combined fleet reached the Chickamauga towns, where Dragging Canoe's people first feigned friendship, then attacked as the boats attempted to negotiate the treacherous waters near the suck. Several of the voyagers were killed by gunfire or drowning, and the occupants of a trailing boat, who were suffering from smallpox,

James Robertson. FROM W. W. CLAYTON, *History of
Davidson County, Tennessee* (PHILADELPHIA, 1880).

were all killed or captured; a number of Chickamaugas reportedly died from the disease, possibly from an earlier infection. To
make matters worse, James Robertson failed to appear at Muscle
Shoals. The voyagers had no choice but to continue down the
Tennessee, intending to reach French Lick by way of the Ohio

and Cumberland rivers. They finally arrived at the Ohio on March 15.

From the Ohio the voyagers faced a less dangerous but more arduous task: poling their craft about twelve miles upstream to the Cumberland and then ascending that stream to French Lick. Some decided instead to follow the Ohio and Mississippi downstream to the more populous Natchez country. As the rest of Donelson's group pushed up the Cumberland, they met Richard Henderson, who as boundary commissioner had recently confirmed that the long-awaited extension of the North Carolina–Virginia line put the Cumberland Basin safely within the former state. At the mouth of the Red River a small number of people under Moses Renfroe left Donelson's group and settled on the point of land where Clarksville now stands; unfortunately for them, the Chickasaws claimed that area. Not until April 24 did Donelson's log conclude: "This day we arrived at our journey's end at the Big Salt Lick, where we had the pleasure of meeting Capt. Robertson and his company. . . . Though our prospects at present are dreary, we have found a few log cabins built on a cedar bluff above the Lick . . ." Most of the newcomers continued onward a short distance and settled on Stones River.

After the arrival of Donelson's group, the settlers lost no time reenacting the already familiar routine of American frontier people organizing themselves for mutual assistance and governance and creating an aura of legality. Henderson, delighted with the recent survey and hoping that North Carolina would confirm his company's claims, was especially insistent on quick action. On May 1, 1780, Nashborough hosted a general meeting of Cumberland Basin residents. The assembly approved a compact of government, written in Henderson's hand, which was like the Watauga Association of 1772: it was an ad hoc, extralegal covenant composed by men far beyond the effective authority of North Carolina. The Cumberland Basin was at that time part of Washington County, but the county court was two hundred miles to the east, across the wilderness of the Cumberland Plateau. Any traveler who braved that forbidding terrain would be perilously near the Chickamauga settlements to the south and in constant danger of ambush. Communications between the Cumberland and upper East Tennessee would for years depend on the long, roundabout route through Cumberland Gap that Robertson's party had taken.

A second meeting on May 13 modified this "Cumberland Compact," which was eventually approved by 256 adult male settlers, including a few who signed in German script. The compact provided for a tribunal of twelve men representing the cluster of tiny settlements near French Lick. Nashborough had three representatives, Mansker's Lick two, and the others one each. All free men over age twenty-one could vote, and all males over sixteen were subject to military service. Not surprisingly, the compact also dealt with the claims of Henderson's Transylvania Company and the myriad matters relating to land purchases. No payments were necessary unless North Carolina confirmed the company's title to the area. The settlers hoped to develop the new lands undisturbed, but they would soon find to their dismay that the American Revolution and its attendant Indian warfare extended to the Cumberland.

Besides resolving title to the Cumberland Basin, the recent survey of the boundary placed the inhabitants of North of Holston, Long Island, and Carter's Valley within present-day Tennessee, and in 1779 they became citizens of the newly established Sullivan County. That same year the North Carolina legislature enacted the charter of Jonesborough, Tennessee's first official town. Since Washington County was created in 1777, its residents had been discussing where to locate the seat of their new government. It was temporarily lodged at the home of Charles Robertson, which became, briefly, the political center of all Tennessee. Choosing a permanent site was not an easy matter because settlers along the Watauga vied for the honor with those near the Nolichucky. The settlers finally compromised, choosing a site on Little Limestone Creek midway between the two settled areas. The new town had a log courthouse, a jail, and stocks, and surveyors laid out neat, orderly lots in a grid pattern. Jonesborough, named after North Carolina political leader Willie Jones, quickly became the hub of an emerging road network in upper East Tennessee.

One perplexing problem for the county government was dealing with Tories. Beginning in 1776, local associations of patriots—in effect vigilance committees—would periodically force suspected loyalists to take oaths of allegiance. Matters became increasingly confused as patriots and Tories alike sought refuge from the chaos east of the mountains. The records of Washington County, which begin in 1778, show surprisingly few official actions—perhaps a fine, confiscation of property, jail time, or corporal punishment—taken against alleged loyalists. Noted firebrand John Sevier even pardoned two of his militiamen who had spied for the British. On the other hand, oral tradition and accounts of early historians, sources which tend to emphasize the Tory menace, indicate that punishment often took summary and brutal form: beatings, tar and feathering, and even executions. Whatever the loyalist threat in Tennessee, it did not approach that in the backcountry of New York, Georgia, or the Carolinas east of the mountains. And in the far-off wilds of the Cumberland Basin, leaders like James Robertson could be surprisingly indifferent toward people with loyalist sentiments as long as they took no overt action.

Any dramatic action against Tories in East Tennessee would have increased after 1779, when the Revolution threatened not only more Indian attacks, but also incursions by British military forces. The Crown's recent change of strategy now emphasized offensive operations in the South involving coordinated military operations by regular British troops, disgruntled Indians, and thousands of Tories in the southern backcountry. Patriots in upper East Tennessee realized they were at greater risk than ever before, and they mobilized to meet an anticipated British thrust to the Blue Ridge and the very portals of the Watauga and Nolichucky settlements. In the summer of 1780 about two hundred men from Washington County under Charles Robertson and another two hundred from Sullivan County under Isaac Shelby crossed the mountains and reinforced Colonel Charles McDowell in North Carolina. The Tennesseans and other patriot units forced the surrender of a loyalist post, Fort Thickety on the Pacolet River, and on August 8 acquitted themselves well while retreating before a superior enemy force at Cedar Spring. On August 18 the patriots fought a sharp engagement with loyalists and the British at Musgrove's Mill, killing more than sixty of the enemy and taking seventy prisoners while suffering only four fatalities.

Immediately following their victory the Tennesseans and other patriot militia heard the shocking news that General Lord Cornwallis's army of regulars had just defeated Horatio Gates's combined force of Continental soldiers and militiamen at Camden, South Carolina. The path to North Carolina's interior was open, and the aggressive Cornwallis was eager to take it. His able subordinate, Major Patrick Ferguson, a veteran regular officer, immediately pursued the retreating McDowell and his Tennessee supporters and nearly caught them before he gave up the chase. McDowell stopped a respectful distance from Ferguson, and Shelby and Robertson returned home. The sixty-day enlistments of their men were expiring, and though they were willing to campaign away from their farms for short periods, their first thoughts were of work undone and especially the safety of their families. Who knew what the Cherokees might be up to? The appearance of even a few Indians could cause otherwise reliable militiamen to defy orders, abandon campaigns, and return to their homesteads. Camden seemed too far away to be of major concern. For the present, they were content to maintain a messenger service across the mountains to ensure their ready availability should the enemy advance on them.

They did not have long to wait. First, British forces defeated Colonel McDowell's patriot units and forced the remnants to seek refuge across the mountains among the Wataugans. But much more alarming was Major Ferguson's thrust up the east side of the Blue Ridge to secure the left flank of Cornwallis's advance into North Carolina. Ferguson's men consisted almost entirely of Tories from coastal and piedmont Carolina. The imperious officer intended to forestall any opposition from what he contemptuously called the "back water," "back mountain," or "overmountain" men of Tennessee, who in his eyes were "barbarians," "the dregs of mankind," and "a set of mongrels." At the same time, he was honest enough to concede that they could be elusive and cunning and were "superior marksmen."

Believing bluntness was appropriate, Ferguson paroled a captured kinsman of Isaac Shelby and sent him to Tennessee with a warning to the inhabitants: if they opposed him, he would lead his army across the mountains, "hang their leaders and lay their country waste with fire and sword." Upon hearing the news, Shelby immediately rode forty miles to confer with John Sevier, Washington County's new militia colonel. Shelby and Sevier decided to fight Ferguson on the other side of the mountains and convinced William Campbell and his militia from Washington County, Virginia, to join them on the expedition. A small powder mill on a branch of the Watauga and some lead deposits near Sevier's home provided part of the necessary ammunition, and most of the backcountry population found ways to help: baking bread, slaughtering cattle, mending soldiers' clothing, and doing similar tasks. To secure desperately needed money, Sevier and Shelby stood as security for state funds provided by John Adair, the Sullivan County entry taker. The arrangement was clearly illegal, but the logic was impeccable: what good was the money if the British should prevail?

The Tennessee and Virginia militia units, along with McDowell's remnant force, gathered at Sycamore Shoals on September 25. A growing network of roads and trails facilitated their arrival from all parts of upper East Tennessee and southwestern Virginia. Most of these mountain irregulars had neither uniforms nor extensive gear, but most came armed with an abiding hatred of arbitrary and oppressive outside authority and, in the case of some, with accurate, long-range Deckard rifles from Pennsylvania. Shelby and Sevier each led about 240 men, and William Campbell's Virginians numbered some 400. McDowell's small unit pushed the total to more than 1,000 men. A smaller force commanded by Major Charles Robertson was to remain at home and guard against Cherokee attack.

On the morning of September 26, after a blessing by the Reverend Samuel Doak ("help us as good soldiers to wield the Sword of the Lord and of Gideon!"), the over-mountain men set out. They followed the Doe River, ascended Bright's Trace, crossed the Unakas northeast of Roan Mountain, then headed down into North Carolina. Along the way two of Sevier's men deserted and fled to Ferguson with a warning. Within a few days the over-

The Gathering of the Overmountain People,
Sycamore Shoals, September 1780. PAINTING BY LLOYD
BRANSON. COURTESY TENNESSEE STATE ARCHIVES AND LIBRARY.

mountain army was near Morganton, where it united with some 350 men from Wilkes and Surry counties. On October 4 they sent McDowell to General Horatio Gates of the Continental army to ask for a regular army officer to command the force, now numbering about 1,500 men; for the present, they agreed that Campbell should have command. As the over-mountain men moved to intercept Ferguson, a patriot force accompanied by several hundred famished women and children was making a frantic retreat across the mountains to the Watauga country. A combined British and Cherokee force had broken Colonel Elijah Clarke's siege of Augusta and then pursued him relentlessly, committing atrocities against his captured stragglers.

Alerted that the over-mountain force was coming, Major Ferguson retreated southward and took up a position on King's Mountain, a flat-topped hill some sixty feet high in York County, South Carolina, very near the North Carolina line. Ferguson's confidence that he could successfully defend his position against any force was misplaced. Campbell, Shelby, Sevier, and the other militia forces attacked on the afternoon of October 7 after Campbell had ordered them to "shout like hell, and fight like devils." They did. After retreating several times before determined bayonet charges, they closed in on the British and loyalist defenders. Ferguson and several other officers were killed before the carnage ended an hour or so after the first shots were fired. Though the forces appear to have been roughly equal, loyalist losses were much higher—an estimated 157 were killed and more than 700 taken prisoner. At least 28 patriot soldiers died. After burying their dead, the backwoodsmen marched with their prisoners into North Carolina, where Tory leaders were tried for earlier atrocities and nine were executed. Localism then prevailed as the triumphant over-mountain men quickly returned home to defend their families against Indians. The Battle of King's Mountain was a significant patriot victory in the American Revolution, delaying Cornwallis's advance into the Carolina backcountry and forcing loyalists there to keep the peace, at least temporarily.

In reaction to the loss at King's Mountain, Lord Cornwallis instructed Indian superintendent Thomas Brown to urge his Cherokee allies to strike the Watauga, Nolichucky, Holston, and Kentucky frontiers in order to prevent any more incursions by back-woodsmen. Brown had already met with the Raven in Georgia and believed that the Overhill Cherokees would join their Chick-amauga brothers in taking up the hatchet again. The promise of a steady supply of goods from Augusta solidified the British-Cherokee alliance. By late 1780 Indians were again killing whites on the Holston and in Powell's Valley and stealing horses along the Kentucky Path. William Springstone, an American trader in the Overhill Towns, was told the British now recognized the Raven, not Oconostota, as head chief, and that the Raven was committed to attacking the frontier. The warnings and assistance of Nancy Ward and other Indian friends enabled Springstone and several associates to escape from the town of Citico.

In response to the renewed Indian threat, John Sevier, recently returned from King's Mountain, immediately organized a force of three hundred men and marched toward Cherokee country. On December 16, just beyond the French Broad River, he fought an engagement in which twenty-eight Indians, but not a single militiaman, died. Sevier was soon reinforced by troops from Sullivan County and Virginia, the latter under Colonel Arthur Campbell, bringing the combined force to over seven hundred men. They destroyed Chota and other nearby towns without opposition, equivocated about a peace overture brought by Nancy Ward, then proceeded toward the Chickamaugas. They got only as far as the Hiwassee River towns before Sevier's exhausted force returned home. Campbell torched the Hiwassee villages and more than fifty thousand bushels of corn, but the Chickamauga towns remained untouched. As he turned for home, Campbell directed the Overhill people who wanted peace to appear at Long Island for treaty talks. His warning that any further trouble might bring permanent white occupation of Cherokee lands no doubt made a forceful impression, but not everyone applauded his fire-and-sword approach. William Fleming wrote Governor Thomas Jefferson that Campbell's campaign might create "irreconcilable enemies, and force them for sustenance to live altogether by depredation on our frontiers, or make an open junction with our foes, as the loss they have sustained in men is little or nothing."

The campaign was sufficient, however, to convince some Overhill Cherokees to reaffirm their sometimes wavering attachment to peace. A few surrendered voluntarily to Joseph Martin, Virginia's hardworking agent, and performed "valuable services" for him. The agent considered using them as spies and told Governor Jefferson they believed the British were deceiving them with promises. The venerable leader Hanging Maw even argued in council against the war and threatened to withdraw himself and his town to the protection of the colonists. But Martin admitted that reconciling the races would be difficult because some "disorderly" individuals had killed the two Indians attempting to deliver Hanging Maw's flag of truce.

Notwithstanding Hanging Maw's professions of friendship, other Cherokees continued their small-scale raids during the early months of 1781. Shawnees likewise made forays through Cumberland Gap. But the Cherokees were the foremost concern, and Arthur Campbell revived an earlier suggestion to establish a garrison somewhere on the Tennessee River, either at Chickamauga Creek or between it and the Overhill Towns. He had originally suggested a site at the mouth of the Clinch River, where years later a fort would be built on Southwest Point at present-day Kingston. In 1781, however, he advocated establishing a garrison at the mouth of the Little Tennessee. Such a post would keep the Cherokees "always at our mercy," prevent enemy emissaries from reaching these Indians, open communications with the Chickasaws and American posts on the Mississippi, protect the Southwestern frontier, and save money that could be used for prosecuting the war elsewhere. Campbell knew that such a post would cost more than Tennessee's frontier population could afford, and he suggested the Continental government undertake the project. Jefferson concurred, but nothing was done.

General Nathaniel Greene, the new commander of the Continental army in the South, realized that the Indian threat made frontier assistance against another British invasion of the Carolina backcountry unlikely. At Arthur Campbell's suggestion and in behalf of Congress, he commissioned four Virginians and four North Carolinians, including Sevier, to initiate a treaty conference with both the Cherokees and Chickasaws. Because of renewed Indian aggression, however, Campbell believed it necessary first to terrify the "perfidious" Cherokees into submission. In March 1781 Sevier led about 150 volunteers against the Cherokee Middle Towns east of the mountains. Taking the town of Tuskasegee by surprise, his men killed about twenty Indians, captured fifteen more, and then destroyed other towns nearby. At the same time militia from Sullivan County mounted a campaign to drive hostile Indians from the mountains south of Cumberland Gap. A force under Joseph Martin attacked a large war party below the gap, but the mounted soldiers could not pursue the fleeing Indians through the thick river cane.

Meanwhile the conflict was becoming nasty farther west, where the Chickasaws posed a growing threat. Before Spain entered the war in 1779, the Chickasaws had played only a nominal role by guarding the trails into British West Florida. After Spain seized that area, British loyalists and a small number of Indians had joined the Scottish trader James Colbert on the fourth Chickasaw Bluff, where they sporadically attacked Spanish and American shipping on the Mississippi. Their greatest success came when they captured a Spanish convoy headed upstream to St. Louis. Among the passengers was the wife of the lieutenant governor of Spanish Illinois, who remained an unwilling guest of Colbert until gaining her release. This comic-opera warfare turned deadly serious in 1780 when George Rogers Clark, now a hero for his exploits in the Illinois Country, constructed Fort Jefferson on the Kentucky side of the Mississippi just below the mouth of the Ohio. A few white settlers, believing they were safe, began clearing land nearby. This was a direct provocation against the Chickasaws, who claimed that area, hunted in it extensively, and viewed it as a buffer against enemies. Enraged, they attacked the fort, and only the wounding of Colbert saved the garrison from capture. A protracted siege followed before the famished and disease-ridden soldiers and settlers wisely evacuated the post in 1781.

Even before the issue of Fort Jefferson was resolved, Chickasaw warriors began targeting the Cumberland settlements, many of which were on tribal lands. At first simply a forbidding but unseen presence, they soon started killing livestock and chasing game animals away from the whites. Hunters who followed the game were likely to be waylaid. Matters took a turn for the worse in the summer of 1780 when the Indians hit Moses Renfroe's small community on Red River, killing about twenty stragglers who had delayed flight to the better-defended stations near Nashborough. In January 1781 warriors managed to open the gate at one station, and in the ensuing battle they killed Major Robert Lucas and one of James Robertson's slaves. This was the last Chickasaw attack, for Britain was about to concede American independence, and many tribal leaders preferred an American connection to one with Spain. Robertson took advantage of this sentiment and negotiated a peace that was confirmed by a formal treaty at the end of the Revolution.

But the Chickasaws had been only a minor part of the problem, for beginning in 1780 small bands of Chickamaugas, Creeks, Delawares, and Shawnees also menaced the Cumberland. Settlers neglected their crops and depleted their ammunition as they were forced to hunt miles away from home. Dragging Canoe's warriors were the most persistent threat, finding the Cumberland stations an easier target than the larger settlements along the Watauga and Holston rivers. John Donelson's family was among the many that moved to more secure stations in Kentucky. Only the calm resolution of Robertson and a few others prevented a mass exodus. In the spring of 1781, while Overhill Cherokees were preparing for peace talks at Long Island, Chickamauga attacks became more intense. Early in April they lured a force under Robertson out of Fort Nashborough, then ambushed them and blocked off retreat. Robertson's men might all have perished in this Battle of the Bluff if the Indians had not been distracted by chasing the soldiers' panicky horses and by dogs released from the fort.

Dragging Canoe's hatred of settlers was independent of geopolitical considerations, but as the British position in the South began to deteriorate, so did the enthusiasm of most of their Indian allies. On March 15, 1781, General Cornwallis won a Pyrrhic victory at Guilford Courthouse in the North Carolina piedmont, where a small contingent of Wataugans and militia from Washington County, Virginia, distinguished themselves. Despite winning the field, Cornwallis retreated toward the Southeast and gave up his plans to enlist backcountry loyalists. Matters quickly deteriorated even more for the British. In May Pensacola finally fell to Spanish attack, and the next month Colonel Thomas Brown was forced to surrender Augusta to American forces. His appeals for Indian assistance had fallen on deaf ears, partly because many Cherokees were preparing to attend treaty talks at Long Island. Brown returned to British-held Savannah, where he continued his appeals for Indian assistance. Whites in East Tennessee and southwestern Virginia feared he might succeed in enlisting a combined force of Tories, Cherokees, and Creeks to forestall the treaty by attacking the backcountry.

A central question for the Overhill Cherokees preparing to attend the conference at Long Island was how there could be peace while whites continually trespassed on tribal lands. One of the treaty commissioners, William Christian, admitted that agreement would be difficult because of the continued encroachment. The only hope for peace was to treat the Indians justly regarding their lands and to provide them with necessary food and supplies during the summer. Supplies, especially powder, were a critical factor in determining Indian allegiance. Fortunately, the war-weary Overhill Cherokees were willing to renounce the British, and they finally arrived at Long Island on July 31, 1781. Christian had somehow been able to obtain money from Virginia to entertain the hundreds of Indian guests. He and Joseph Martin were the only commissioners present, and the absence of North Carolina officials meant that no promises could be made about ending white intrusions.

Old Tassel, the Cherokee spokesman, got right to the point. Yes, his people had sided with the British, but only in response to white aggression and encroachment. As he had asserted prior to the 1777 Treaty of Long Island, he claimed that the real issue was land—Cherokee land on which the whites were daily trespassing. Christian ignored this point and insisted the Indians give up their prisoners, evict British agents and conspirators from the Chickamauga towns, and send a delegation to Congress to confirm the peace. Perhaps the most dramatic moment in the conference was Nancy Ward's plea to the whites: "We are your mothers; you are our sons. Our cry is all for peace. . . . This peace must last forever. Let your women's sons be ours; our sons be yours." Touched by the words of this woman who was such a friend to whites, Christian responded, "Our women shall hear your words, and we know how they will feel and think of them. We are all descendants of the same woman." His people, like the Cherokees, wanted peace. Though their words reflected the conscious accommodation and mediation typical of the middle ground, both Ward and Christian must have realized that the balance of power necessary to sustain that ground had already shifted decisively to the whites. Ominously, the conference ended without any substantive agreement about land. Nor could there be such agreement, for North Carolina was even then planning to force another cession.

Peace with the Cherokees remained precarious. In the fall of 1781, at almost the moment Cornwallis was surrendering his army at Yorktown, the Raven made his way to Savannah and told Thomas Brown that his people were still loyal to the British and only necessity had compelled them to negotiate with people who had "dyed their hands in the Blood" of Cherokee women and children. He insisted that Oconostota, then visiting Williamsburg, was merely feigning friendship with Virginia in order to protect Cherokee towns; after the harvest his people would attack the frontier again. Brown no doubt realized the Raven was once more playing both sides of the fence in an attempt to obtain British supplies. Certainly, the Cherokees could not escape retribution if they took up the hatchet again. When some Cherokees did raid the South Carolina backcountry in December 1781, Andrew Pickens quickly mounted a counterattack. Likewise, Georgia militiamen intercepted and routed a detachment of Cherokees and loyalist traders trying to sneak into Savannah. Still, the British alliance with Dragging Canoe's Chickamaugas remained a threat. Oconostota, apparently sincere in his desire for peace, warned that the Chickamaugas had recently received British supplies of gunpowder and lead and would likely join with Creeks in attacking the backcountry; he feared that he was among their intended victims.

By the spring of 1782 patriot control of the backcountry was secure enough that communication between the tribes and the British was difficult; the latter finally evacuated Savannah in the summer, and Thomas Brown moved his operations to St. Augustine. Northern Indians, probably Shawnees, conducted raids in East Tennessee that spring, but by summer they had turned their attention to a large American force under Colonel William Crawford which was invading their Ohio homeland. Chickamaugas helped the Delawares and Shawnees inflict a disastrous defeat on Crawford, who was then tortured to death. Arthur Campbell feared this debacle would bring increased Indian attacks on the Tennessee and Virginia frontiers. Once again events in the backcountry were directly tied to those elsewhere in the new nation.

Dragging Canoe's Chickamaugas confirmed Campbell's fears by stepping up their raids, and indiscriminate retaliation by some settlers threatened to drive even peaceable towns to the warpath. Two Holston residents murdered two friendly Indians who were trading pelts, and other settlers sanctioned the deed by refusing to allow the perpetrators to be tried. Several chiefs reassured Joseph Martin that the incident would not shatter their resolve to remain at peace, but of course their pledges did not bind the victims' relatives, who might demand blood revenge. Arthur Campbell attributed white lawlessness in Tennessee to the feebleness of North Carolina's administration and to residents' jealousy over Virginia's domination of Cherokee trade and diplomacy. Because Indian matters were a national concern, he suggested that Congressional supervision might be the only answer to North Carolina's incompetence.

As if to highlight Virginia's concerns about North Carolina's intentions toward the Indians, the latter state began organizing a military expedition to march into Cherokee country to punish hostiles, force major land cessions from the entire tribe, and impose other harsh terms. Partly in reaction to these preparations and partly because of British setbacks in the South, the Chickamaugas now proclaimed their desire for peace. Arthur Campbell believed that a full-scale invasion of their country was no longer necessary, but he feared the North Carolinians would "not properly discriminate" between peaceful and hostile Indians. These were strange words indeed from a man who so recently had devastated hostile and friendly towns alike.

Fortunately, John Sevier intended to act with discretion and to coordinate his movements with South Carolina's attacks on the opposite side of the mountains. In September 1782 he organized a North Carolina expeditionary force of 250 men. They marched to the Hiwassee and upper Chickamauga Creek, where they destroyed several villages and encountered no real opposition. Sevier then moved into northern Georgia and burned the towns on the upper Coosa occupied by hostile Lower Cherokees. On his return to the settlements, he held a conference with Overhill leaders at Chota and announced a pending council at which North Carolina intended to impose its demands on the tribe. Sevier's campaign and South Carolina's invasion of Cherokee country immediately afterward removed any doubt that most Cherokees would accept the new realities. Before the cowed representatives of the Lower and Middle Towns, South Carolina's Andrew Pickens delivered a simple ultimatum: submit or face destruction. The Indians submitted.

The American Revolution formally ended in January 1783 when the terms of the Treaty of Paris went into effect. Britain virtually abandoned her Indian allies, making no provision for them in the treaty; the best she could do was to suggest they make peace with the new United States. Not only had the United States gained recognition of its independence, it now had sovereignty over a vast backcountry stretching between the Appalachians and the Mississippi and southward from the Great Lakes to Florida, which Spain had acquired as a result of its war with Britain. But the central reality was the insistence of white settlers—and many political leaders—that the Indians, as former British allies, were defeated enemies. As punishment they would be expected to cede many of their western lands to American speculators and settlers.

Despite their losses in the war, many of the Indians in the Southern backcountry sought to avoid total American domination. The Chickamaugas continued their resistance to white expansion, while elements of the Creeks, Choctaws, and Chickasaws returned to the old strategy of realpolitik. The Chickasaws attempted to find maneuvering room amid the new geopolitical conditions following Spain's acquisition of the Gulf Coast and the Floridas. For the present, they recognized that some sort of accommodation with the Americans was necessary, though pro-Spanish and pro-American factions would intrigue among them for the next dozen years. But they were confused about which Americans to contact, because there was no clearly understood line of authority on Indian matters between the new U.S. government and its constituent states. Should the Chickasaws treat with Congress or with representatives of Georgia, Virginia, and other Southern states? The Indians feared the Americans would demand land cessions in Tennessee. In a message to Congress their headmen noted that "Our Brothers, the Virginians Call upon us to a Treaty, and want part of our land, and we expect our Neighbors who live on Cumberland River, will in a Little time Demand, if not forcibly take it from us, also we are informed they have been making Lines through our hunting grounds." They could only hope that Congress would stop these encroachments and provide them with the required trade.

Governor Benjamin Harrison of Virginia was the first to respond to the Chickasaw peace overture. He appointed Joseph Martin and John Donelson as commissioners to meet with Chickasaw leaders and to obtain a formal peace treaty and, perhaps, a land cession in Kentucky. In November 1783 Martin and Donelson met with a number of Chickasaw headmen at Nashborough, where the Indians formally reaffirmed the peace agreement earlier negotiated with James Robertson and promised to evict from their lands a few Delaware Indians who remained hostile to the Americans. They refused to make a formal cession of land, but accommodated existing white settlement in Middle Tennessee by recognizing that tribal claims extended only to the divide between the Cumberland and Tennessee rivers.

Unlike the Chickasaws, the Chickamaugas refused to make any concessions. Their recently established villages of Lookout Mountain Town, Crow Town, Long Island Town, Nickajack, and Running Water were at readily defensible sites near the common boundaries of Tennessee, Alabama, and Georgia. Here, where the Tennessee cuts through the Cumberland Plateau, Dragging Canoe's people commanded the heights above a dangerous stretch of river that featured whirlpools and rapids. Their communities, especially Long Island Town, were at the heart of a network of trails radiating throughout the Southeast and offering quick access to white settlements, especially those on the Cumberland. Congregating here were pan-Indian militants of the Chickamaugas, Overhill Cherokees, Upper Creeks, and Shawnees, who would continue to terrorize the Tennessee frontier.

Dragging Canoe's prominence reflects the centrality of land in Tennessee during the American Revolution. For many Cherokees that conflict began not with Lexington and Concord but with Richard Henderson's supposed purchase of a few months earlier. White Tennesseans likewise fought mostly because of land and their aspirations to acquire it. The actions of Dragging Canoe and his followers undermined the Cherokees' ethic of harmony, exacerbating tribal intrigue, jealousy, and factionalism to the point that some headmen were fearful of being assassinated. A deep generational chasm opened between younger militants and those older chiefs who favored conciliation and compromise and who played both sides of the fence. The split was also familial, for two of the strongest proponents of conciliation were Dragging Canoe's biological father, Attakullakulla, and Attakullakulla's niece Nancy Ward. Ward remained a prominent figure, but after the deaths of Attakullakulla and Oconostota near the end of the Revolution there was no male leader of similar status who could effectively guide his people along a suitable middle course. The specter of Dragging Canoe remained.

And so as the 1783 Treaty of Paris formally concluded the Revolution and white Americans prepared to take possession of Western lands, an older struggle awaited, "not new and not finished." A struggle for land.

5.

SPECULATION, TURMOIL, AND INTRIGUE: 1780–1789

Tennessee's frontier was a society shaped by aspiring elites, covetous men of vast ambition who saw the acquisition of land as the means of economic and social advancement. Virtually every leader of pre-revolutionary society recognized that supporting the patriot cause was the only way of making good his land claims in the face of growing British opposition. The cause of independence also sanctioned new campaigns against the Cherokees to soften their resistance to ever-increasing encroachment on tribal lands. With the Revolution finally won, land speculators circled Tennessee's landscape like vultures, seeking to profit from the end of British control.

Illustrious Tennesseans like John Donelson, James Robertson, and John Sevier were on this roster of elites and exchanged their unexcelled knowledge of local conditions for the economic and political support of prominent speculators in North Carolina and elsewhere. Foremost among the latter was William Blount. Born in 1749, he was part of a prominent family which was friendly with Judge Richard Henderson and had invested in his Transylvania Company. Blount served as paymaster for North Carolina's Continental troops during the Revolution while helping his family expand its business activities. He first won election to the state assembly in 1781, and the following year he was elected a state delegate to the Continental Congress. From the outset his politics and business were inseparable; for him there was no such thing as conflict of interest.

Throughout the 1780s Blount's business activities increasingly focused on North Carolina's Western lands, over which the state and federal governments were contending. The Articles of Confederation had been ratified in 1781 only after bitter controversy regarding the future of the American backcountry. The former colonies which did not have claims west of the Appalachians demanded that landed colonies cede their Western properties to the central government, arguing that the blood of all had been shed in the common effort against Britain and that all should profit equally from the development of trans-Appalachia. Virginia's decision in 1780 to cede most of its Western claims was the catalyst for ratification of the Articles and for the cession of other claims to the region north and west of the Ohio River. The ordinances of 1785 and 1787 (the latter the famous Northwest Ordinance) provided for the survey, sale, and political organization of that area.

Southern states faced pressure to make similar cessions of their claims. Before doing so, however, speculator-politicians in North Carolina were determined to extract maximum benefits from the Tennessee country on two levels—through land warranties for military service and through outright purchase. As early as 1780, while the Revolution was still underway, North Carolina, like some other states, had attempted to raise additional troops by offering its Western lands as a bounty for service. The legislature authorized creation of a military reserve in northeastern Tennessee where each volunteer who served his full three-year enlistment would receive a bonus of two hundred acres and a prime slave. However, the act did not establish procedures for claiming those lands; nor did it provide for the many settlers already inhabiting the reserve. Two years later, to reward "the Signal bravery, and persevering zeal" of the soldiers, the legislature appointed three commissioners to survey a different reserve in Tennessee and raised the land bounties on a graduated scale from 640 acres for a private to 12,000 for a brigadier general. The legislature also granted preemption to any settlers who had already located on the reserve by 1780. By 1790 this act would open 2.8 million acres to holders of 3,723 military warrants, 60 percent of which speculators acquired for a pittance. Among the most prominent of these landjobbers was William Blount, whose position on a soldiers claims committee offered unrivaled opportunity for contact with warrant holders.

Even while preparing to take advantage of the new state legislation, Blount was calculating how a political separation of the West might serve his speculative interests. As a member of Congress in 1782, he became familiar with the issues of land and taxation. The federal government was chronically hard-pressed for income and relied in part on a tax based on the value of lands within each state. Because North Carolina was rural, it would pay less per acre than more urban states. On the other hand, its surveyed lands west of the Appalachians would increase its tax quota. Once again, Blount's personal and political interests merged; he favored cession of the Western lands both to save his state from excessive taxation and to help himself and other speculators by enhancing their property values through federal benefits like protection against Indians. Blount and the other state delegate attending Congress in Philadelphia favored a conditional cession, but Governor Alexander Martin blocked the action.

When Blount returned home, he found that North Carolina's chaotic finances broadened the horizon for shrewd opportunists like himself. His chance came with the convening of a new state assembly in the spring of 1783. He and his brother, John Gray Blount, were members of that body, which was noteworthy for a series of actions known collectively as the Great Land Grab. Pursuant to the 1782 act, surveyors had already marked off the military reserve in the southwestern part of Tennessee, but had found those lands almost inaccessible and perilously close to the Chickasaw domain. As a member of the military committee, William Blount authored an act to change the reservation to an area bounded by a line running southward fifty miles from the Virginia (now Kentucky) boundary at the Cumberland River, west-

William Blount. Based on a miniature by Charles Wilson Peale. COURTESY CALVIN M. MCCLUNG HISTORICAL COLLECTION.

🦢 **103**

SPECULATION,
TURMOIL,
AND
INTRIGUE:
1780–1789

ward to the Tennessee River, downstream to the Virginia line, and along that boundary back to the point of origin.

The new military reserve encompassed the upper half of Middle Tennessee and clearly subverted most of Richard Henderson's claim, but it protected the Cumberland settlers by giving them the right of preemption. The act also specified how veterans could obtain grants, called for the opening of a land office at Nashborough, extended eligibility to soldiers with just two years' service, and blatantly wooed the support of Governor Martin by granting him two thousand acres. In response to a petition submitted by James Robertson on behalf of the Cumberland Association, the legislature created a county named for General William Davidson to provide local government for the grantees. Davidson County was detached from the newly created Greene County, which originally included part of East Tennessee and all the rest of the state west of Washington and Sullivan counties.

The procedure for locating military land bounties was cumbersome and time-consuming. First, North Carolina's secretary of state had to verify that an applicant was a veteran of the state's Continental line before issuing him a land warrant. Next, if the recipient actually wished to settle in the military reserve, he would find a suitable location and then send his description and warrant to Colonel Martin Armstrong, the chief surveyor and head of the military land office in Nashborough. Armstrong registered the claim and dispatched surveyors to define its boundaries by metes and bounds. This method, commonly used in the South, was dependent on shifting natural features and was much less precise than the rectangular survey soon employed north of the Ohio River. After making his calculations, the surveyor drew a plat of the claim, attached a description, and returned his survey to Nashborough. Armstrong's office would make two copies of the surveyor's report and forward them with the applicant's warrant to Raleigh, where the secretary of state's office would issue a grant to the warrant holder. The warrantee would then complete the final step, registering his grant in the appropriate county within the military reserve. Though the 1783 legislation stipulated that the entire process be completed within three years, North Carolina subsequently allowed numerous extensions of the deadline and was still issuing military land warrants more than twenty years after Tennessee became a state in 1796.

This unwieldy system of land distribution was rendered even more problematic by the rampant speculation in Tennessee. Most veterans of the Revolution were enlisted men who had little money, little knowledge of the West, and little inclination to move there. The regulations relating to the land bounties, moreover, made it difficult for an individual with a single claim to locate a specific tract within the reserve. Under such circumstances, large-scale speculators had little trouble inducing veterans to sell away their bounty rights for a fraction of their value. In addition, some speculators would prematurely enter claims, challenge existing claims, or even resort to bribery, forgery, and enrolling nonveterans for bounties.

As if the opportunities represented by military land warrants were not attractive enough, North Carolina speculators were determined to open most of the rest of the Tennessee country for sale to private investors. To accomplish this John Gray Blount introduced a bill in the 1783 session to reopen the state land offices, which had been closed since 1781, and to create a new one at Hillsborough for the sale of all lands in present-day Tennessee except for the military reserve and a Cherokee reservation bounded by the state's southern line; the Tennessee, French Broad, and Big Pigeon rivers; and the Great Smoky Mountains. The act totally ignored both Chickasaw claims to the western third of Tennessee and the 1777 treaty with the Cherokees, which North Carolina invalidated because some Cherokees had subsequently supported the British. The state intended to secure Cherokee assent by calling a treaty council, but it failed to do so, partly because of confusion attending creation of the state of Franklin in 1784. That failure would provoke disagreement with the Confederation government over control of Indian affairs. As newly independent states, North Carolina and Virginia jealously defended their prerogatives by formulating their own Indian policy and conducting diplomacy accordingly. The results would prove disastrous. North Carolina's unilateral diminution of the Cherokee domain would imperil eager settlers who moved onto lands promised to the Indians in 1777.

105

SPECULATION,
TURMOIL,
AND
INTRIGUE:
1780–1789

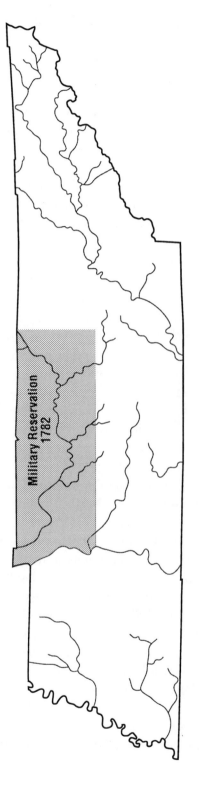

North Carolina Military Reservation, 1782.

The procedure for acquiring titles by purchase at the Hillsborough office was similar to that used for securing military land grants: the purchaser made a rough entry survey, obtained a warrant, and submitted a final survey to the secretary of state, who issued a grant that was endorsed by the governor. The final step was to record the grant in the register's office of the county where the land was located. The price was ten pounds per one hundred acres, but the money receivable for these lands—state and Continental bills and specie certificates—had depreciated so much that speculators could purchase property for less than $5 per one hundred acres.

The 1783 legislation dealt a final blow to Richard Henderson's claims in Middle Tennessee, prompting him to request compensation from his many friends in the North Carolina legislature. As an investor in Henderson's projects, John Gray Blount was sympathetic. He and three other prominent landholders served as house conferees on a committee that considered Henderson's memorial and recommended compensation of 400,000 acres (later reduced to 200,000 acres) in Powell's Valley. As speculators, the Blounts were loyal to their kind. Richard Henderson may have been devious and ambitious beyond presumption, but his activities had been crucial in opening Kentucky and Middle Tennessee to white settlement.

Whether they were interested in military lands or properties sold at the Hillsborough office, North Carolina speculators had to rely on the advice and services of Tennessee elites like John Sevier, James Robertson, and John Donelson, who had unexcelled knowledge of local conditions and opportunities. Such men were all too willing to cooperate with the Blounts and other landjobbers. Likewise, local men of prominence often held positions as surveyors and land registers or, like Joseph Martin, had considerable influence among the Indians. The successful speculator, then, was adroit in cultivating East-West alliances which linked men of influence in North Carolina with the specialized knowledge and skills of Tennesseans.

The complexity of such networks is nowhere more apparent than in the attempts of the Blounts and their associates to acquire lands at Muscle Shoals at the great bend of the Tennessee

River. At one time the "Bend" (or "Bent") was thought to be within North Carolina, but by 1783 it was acknowledged to be within the Western claims of South Carolina and Georgia. (Today it is in Alabama.) Strategically situated between the Ohio, Mississippi, and Alabama river systems, the Shoals and the surrounding area had long been recognized for their potential, and now William and John Gray Blount, Richard Caswell, and James Glasgow intended to acquire the region. This cabal enlisted John Donelson and Joseph Martin, both of whom, along with Isaac Shelby, had been commissioned by Virginia to hold peace treaties with the Chickasaws and Cherokees. Once again public service suited private need: development of the Bend required Indian acquiescence.

In their dubious dual roles as speculators and peace commissioners, Martin and Donelson met with twenty-two alleged Chickamaugas—twelve men, six women, and four chiefs—at Long Island in July 1783. They concluded a "peace," then privately arranged to pay the twenty-two Indians about $5,000 worth of goods for the Muscle Shoals land. William Blount and his associates planned to win Georgia's assent to a land grant and settlement in the Bend while Thomas Blount, another of William's brothers, went to Philadelphia to acquire the Indian goods. Again acting as Virginia commissioners, Donelson, Martin, and Shelby met with Chickasaw delegates at Nashborough in November and concluded a treaty confirming the earlier accord which recognized white occupation of the Cumberland and Chickasaw land claims as far east as the Tennessee-Cumberland divide. The Virginia commissioners thus endorsed tribal claims to an area outside of Virginia's jurisdiction, while North Carolina, which claimed the region, had ignored Chickasaw rights in its confiscation act of the previous May.

Whatever the understanding between the Chickasaws and the Cumberland settlers, the Chickamaugas and Creeks were in no mood for concessions and continued to raid Middle Tennessee. Indeed, their hostility provoked skepticism about Martin's and Donelson's recent conclusion of a treaty with a few Chickamaugas. Kentucky's Colonel Benjamin Logan wrote Virginia's Governor Benjamin Harrison of his suspicions and denounced the

Chickamaugas' continued depredations on the frontier. When Logan began raising a force of volunteers to punish them, both Donelson and Martin claimed that they had pacified the Chickamaugas and that the true culprits were the Creeks.

Questioned by Harrison about the Chickamauga negotiations, Martin disingenuously replied that the dealings at Muscle Shoals were a private venture separate from his official duties and that "the country is filling up with Inhabitants . . . so fast, that the Indians plainly perceived the Ground we purchased would be of no service to them." Considering the "licentious and ungovernable conduct" of the settlers, it was only sensible to clear Indian claims to the region by paying them a "reasonable" amount, ignoring for the moment that such logic could be used to acquire all Indian lands. Clearly, Martin's and Donelson's role as speculators overshadowed their role as public officials, hardly an unusual phenomenon on the trans-Appalachian frontier. But as they and their associates were to learn, those few Chickamaugas had no authority either to conclude a peace treaty or to cede any land to the whites. It was one thing to "buy" those lands and quite another to occupy them in defiance of Dragging Canoe's warriors and hundreds of hostile Creeks.

John Donelson's connection with the Carolina speculators was apparent in matters other than the Chickamauga treaty. He asked William Blount's assistance in having his sons appointed to surveyorships under the land grab legislation, and one son, Stockley, already the surveyor of Sullivan County, located choice sites near the French Broad River for Richard Caswell and James Glasgow. William H. Masterson calls it "a typical East-West agreement": Blount's group used the Donelsons in Tennessee while working to gain preferment for that family in North Carolina. Other East-West speculative alliances flourished in the Tennessee country. James Robertson, for example, located at least fifty thousand acres in Middle and West Tennessee with William Blount's military warrants in return for a one-fourth share of the business.

Land was the all-consuming passion in 1783 and 1784. Well beyond the boundaries of North Carolina, businessmen bought up depreciated paper currency to take advantage of the land grab legislation. Though an individual was entitled to a maximum of five thousand acres, it was easy to evade that limitation either by combining with other speculative groups or by committing outright fraud. Bribery of officials at all levels was rampant. Legal loopholes abounded, warrants were forged, and credit was illegally extended on sales. Almost four million acres of Tennessee land were sold under the terms of the 1783 legislation, in addition to the nearly three million acres claimed through military warrants.

In the spring 1784 session of the North Carolina legislature at Hillsborough, William Blount's group of independent speculators held the balance of power amid squabbling factions. Blount now furthered his long-term ambition by proposing that the state cede its Western lands to Congress on several conditions, including the recognition of prior entries. Recent congressional acceptance of Virginia's cession served as an important precedent. Blount's measure met stiff opposition but finally passed fifty-two to forty-three; it was "clearly the work of large speculators, with eastern support." The six Western representatives in the assembly no doubt objected to being labeled "offscourings of the earth" and "fugitives from justice" by Eastern conservatives favoring cession, and they were evenly divided on the bill.

At that same session Blount acted on James Robertson's request by introducing and helping to enact legislation renaming the Cumberland's principal settlement Nashville and making it the seat of government for Davidson County. The legislation also provided for the sale of town lots, created a court of oyer and terminer, and extended preemption rights to many settlers in the county. At the time the tiny community and its fort occupied a rectangular tract on the bluffs overlooking the Cumberland River and consisted of a few primitive cabins, including the store of the town's only merchant. The following year a visiting Spanish emissary reported there were only about forty residents, perhaps twenty who could bear arms. Surveyors, however, had grand dreams for Nashville. Like those in many other frontier towns, they followed Philadelphia's example by laying out streets in a checkerboard pattern surrounding the public square. Some of the street names copied those of Philadelphia—tangible evidence of local aspirations. Also indicative of community ambitions was James Robertson's 1785 success in obtaining a charter for Davidson Academy. The school was under the aegis of the Reverend Thomas B. Craighead, a Presbyterian, but it was more a dream than a reality until years later. Culture would have to wait. Despite Nashville's strategic location and the speculative bonanza promised by North Carolina's military reservation, the town remained an isolated outpost until the Indian wars ended.

Meanwhile William Blount was rewarding his business associates and political allies. He obtained a land grant for Robertson's son, Elijah, a representative from the Cumberland, and secured Stockley Donelson's appointment as surveyor of Tennessee's eastern district. He was also dealing with other Western leaders like Daniel Smith and William Cocke. By tending his political and economic garden, Blount ensured the continued success of his speculative ventures and cultivated Western goodwill that would redound to his advantage. But he could not foresee how a coalition of aspiring and well-established men in the West, including some of his friends, intended to use cession for their own ends. Since 1780 Arthur Campbell had advocated a separation of the transmontane region and had even attempted to create a new state in southwestern Virginia and adjoining portions of Tennessee. Frontier people were also well aware of congressional resolutions favoring the creation of new states in the West and sympathized with Kentuckians who were lobbying for independence from Virginia. They knew of a provision in the North Carolina constitution anticipating the creation of new governments in the West, and they were aware of the recent congressional ordinance authored by Thomas Jefferson providing for the division of the Northwest into territorial units that would someday become states. Some settlers had long resented the exploitative nature of North Carolina's sovereignty over them, and others, immigrants from Virginia, had never shown much loyalty to North Carolina. The Watauga Association of the 1770s, moreover, provided a precedent for local initiative in East Tennessee. Thus the 1784 cession act admirably suited the purposes of frontier residents who dreamed of greater political independence.

Immediately after word of the cession act reached Tennessee,

III

SPECULATION,
TURMOIL,
AND
INTRIGUE:
1780–1789

militia representatives met in Greene, Sullivan, and Washington counties to choose delegates to a general convention in Jonesborough. That August, forty delegates assembled there and elected John Sevier president of the convention and Landon Carter secretary. Contrary to Carl Driver's assertion that the delegates exhibited a "disdain for the conventions and institutions of the older sections of the mother state," they had a deep attachment to precedent and legality. After invoking the Declaration of Independence, the convention voted to declare the region's separation from North Carolina and to establish a new association which would possibly include part of southwest Virginia. They agreed to petition Congress for acceptance of the cession and for permission "to frame a permanent or a temporary constitution." In the meantime they could continue following all North Carolina laws that were not incompatible with their purposes. The delegates agreed to hold a constitutional convention that fall and then adjourned.

But even as Tennesseans planned their independence, there was a rising tide of opposition in North Carolina to cession. Some critics complained that cession would enrich a few speculators, and others noted that the cession act did not credit the state's expenses for conducting Indian campaigns against its financial obligations to the Confederation government. These resentments swirled in an angry brew of factional disputes and ancient personal animosities. William Blount, who was elected to the house speakership in October 1784, tried to quell the clamor for rescinding cession, and Alexander Outlaw, the representative from Greene County and recent delegate at Jonesborough, introduced a bill promising that the proposed new state would use its land receipts to pay North Carolina's war debts. But all such arguments and inducements were in vain. On November 18, 1784, the house voted thirty-seven to twenty-two to repeal cession. In order to assuage growing resentment in the West and to co-opt potential dissident leaders, it placed Davidson, Washington, Greene, and Sullivan counties within the newly-organized Washington District and named John Sevier brigadier general of the district militia and Arthur Campbell's brother, David, superior court judge. Creation of the new district meant that it was no longer necessary to make the long trip to eastern North Carolina for important legal cases. But repeal of cession also meant renewed need for the long-delayed Cherokee treaty, which had been under consideration in 1783 and 1784.

Unaware that cession was even then being repealed, Tennessee delegates reconvened in November to consider a new state, adjourned in confusion, then reassembled at Jonesborough on December 14. There, on the motion of William Cocke, they voted twenty-eight to fifteen in favor of organizing a new state, soon to be known as Franklin in honor of the famous citizen-patriot, Benjamin Franklin. Presiding over the proceedings was a rather uncertain John Sevier, who worried about the impact of separatism on the speculation at Muscle Shoals, in which he had become involved. Cocke, Joseph Hardin, and David Campbell were dominant figures in the Jonesborough proceedings. Neither Sevier nor Campbell knew that North Carolina had already appointed them to positions of authority in the new Washington District.

The Jonesborough delegates demonstrated a basic political continuity by approving a provisional constitution much like that of North Carolina. There was an obligatory declaration of independence justifying the delegates' actions on a variety of grounds: North Carolina's cession act and the congressional precedents encouraging creation of new states; North Carolina's dereliction in Indian matters, subjecting the frontier to danger; and the difficulty of communicating with eastern North Carolina because of the mountains. Sevier became temporary governor of Franklin until elections could be held. By now perhaps he saw a positive connection between Franklin and his Muscle Shoals venture; though the provisional constitution did not define the new state's boundaries, they might well extend south and, in blithe disregard of Indian occupation and Georgia's claims, include the Bend of the Tennessee.

Sevier was still ambivalent about separatism, however. Pleased upon learning of his appointment as brigadier general of the Washington District, he tried to dampen the Franklin tide, but it became too strong even for him. Realizing that his popularity—and prosperity—depended on his political leadership, Sevier set aside his misgivings and plunged into the affairs of state. "He opposed the movement until he saw that it would proceed without him and then grasped the reins of power." Perhaps he was also intrigued by some proposals William Cocke had made regarding economic possibilities in Franklin. As governor of the new state Sevier found himself in official opposition to North Carolina authorities, but this did not prevent him from continuing to work with the Blounts and Richard Caswell on the Muscle Shoals speculation.

The venture at Muscle Shoals, now called the Bend of the Tennessee Company, had expanded to involve Sevier, the Blounts, Caswell, James Glasgow, John Donelson, Joseph Martin, Wade Hampton of South Carolina, and Griffith Rutherford of North Carolina. William Blount remained the driving force, and in February 1784 he petitioned the Georgia legislature for a grant of three thousand acres for the company in return for settling three hundred families there within three years. The legislature established a new county, later to be named Houston and consisting of all Georgia lands north of the Tennessee River, and appointed a seven-member commission including Donelson, Martin, and Sevier to govern the area. The commission was empowered to issue generous land grants.

That May Blount attempted to stimulate the Muscle Shoals company by exhorting his associates to make it appear as though hordes of people were preparing to settle there, "whether true or not." He also wanted to circulate reports of outside interest in the lands. He advised his associates to use fictitious names to enter as many warrants for lands as possible, and he told them to offer the Georgia commissioners membership in the company. After all, their purposes were the same: "*I mean private Emolument,*" he wrote. In July 1784, Sevier was appointed colonel of the militia in the Bend; his brother Valentine Jr. was major, and John Donelson was lieutenant colonel. Other newly appointed officials were to oversee the disposal of lands. The following year, while serving as governor of Franklin, Sevier continued to tout the Muscle Shoals land, and his legislature passed an act encouraging an expedition to settle at the Bend under titles from Georgia. It was a marriage of convenience between Georgia and Franklin, arranged by speculators. Late in 1785 Valentine Sevier and ninety others arrived at Muscle Shoals, set up a land office, and issued warrants, only to leave early the next year because of Chickamauga hostility—disproving Joseph Martin's earlier assertion that those Indians had been pacified. Still, the area remained an enticement to speculators and settlers and would continue to loom large in early Tennessee history.

While looking after his Muscle Shoals interests, John Sevier solidified his leadership of Franklin. At the first general assembly in Jonesborough in March 1785, legislators elected him governor, Landon Carter secretary of state, David Campbell chief justice, and Stockley Donelson surveyor general. The assembly confirmed land titles, established a militia, created four new counties, and set up a rudimentary tax system that reflected the frontier's lack of hard money and the necessity of barter. Taxes and salaries could be paid in North Carolina money or in flax linen, woolen or cotton cloth, bacon, tallow, beeswax, rye whiskey, peach or apple brandy, sugar, tobacco, or the skins of beaver, otter, raccoon, fox, or deer.

Besides tending to these mundane matters, the Franklin legislators had to counter the growing hostility of North Carolina's Governor Alexander Martin. Answering his inquiry about their actions and intentions, they listed a series of grievances against the mother state, noted the ridicule they had suffered in debates over cession, reaffirmed their independence, and solicited North Carolina's assistance in gaining admission to the union. Martin's response in a manifesto of April 1785 was unequivocally negative. He asserted that the rescinding of cession removed even implied consent for separation from North Carolina, and he warned of retaliation if the Franklinites did not reaffirm their allegiance to the mother state. Fortunately for Franklin, Martin was soon succeeded by Richard Caswell, Sevier's friend and business associate. He was more moderate and diplomatic than his predecessor and even talked vaguely of an eventual negotiated separation, but he cautioned Sevier against assuming that he was "giving countenance" to the new state. Matters would have to await resolution in the North Carolina assembly. In the meantime, the two men privately reassured one another of their continuing cooperation in business.

Even as Franklin and North Carolina shadowboxed, the former was seeking support on the federal level. In New York on May 16, 1785, William Cocke presented a memorial to Congress requesting the admission of Franklin as a new state. Included was a petition from citizens in Washington County, Virginia, asking to be part of the new state—a proposal that quickly died when the Virginia legislature declared the action treasonous. A congressional committee which studied the Franklin memorial argued that Congress could accept the North Carolina cession anytime within the one-year limit specified by the original cession act and recommended that Congress do so. This action would have been a prelude to Franklin's admission as a state. Seven states voted for accepting the cession, two short of the nine votes necessary for enactment. Congress then asked North Carolina to rescind its repeal of the cession, a request the state ignored. Seven states voted for a resolution declaring the repeal law illegal, but only four of those states were willing to support accepting the cession despite its repeal. This was as close as Franklin would ever come to federal recognition. Frustrated, Sevier and other Franklin leaders again asked North Carolina to accept separation, but the dominant political faction there opposed conciliation and attempted to cause division by offering pardons to all people who reaffirmed their loyalty to North Carolina and by encouraging elections in Franklin for seats in the state legislature.

For those who believe the American frontier fostered political democracy, the state of Franklin presents an ambiguous case. In November 1785 a convention met in Greeneville, the new capital, to consider a permanent constitution to replace the provisional document. A committee headed by the Reverend Samuel Houston (a cousin of Sam Houston of Texas fame) drafted a document that was both politically liberal for the time and infused with "clerical influence and the rule of the righteous." Among its remarkable provisions were universal manhood suffrage, a unicameral government, popular election of the governor and certain other officials, registration of voters, voting by ballot, and a required referendum before enacting a general law. At Sevier's suggestion, however, the legislature voted to continue operating on the basis of the provisional constitution.

Historians disagree about whether the rejection of the Houston committee's proposed constitution was a victory for democracy or not. Some scholars argue that democracy prevailed because legislators feared religious interference in the political process, but others contend that elites opposed the proposed constitution because it was too democratic. But this dichotomy is too neat because some leading delegates, including Chief Justice David Campbell and Colonel John Tipton, favored the Houston constitution.

It is true, however, that Franklin's contending factions were dominated by landed elites, almost all of whom had business and political connections in North Carolina. Foremost was John "Nolichucky Jack" Sevier, whose personality and position as governor guaranteed that he would become a flash point of contention. One of his leading opponents was John Tipton, who had quickly disavowed his support for Franklin and proclaimed his loyalty to North Carolina. On the same day in August 1786 the Tiptonites and the Franklinites both held elections in Sullivan and Washington counties for the North Carolina assembly. The Franklinites participated because they still hoped to win North Carolina's recognition of their independence. Though Franklin's supporters received more votes, the North Carolina assembly seated the loyalists. As a state senator, Tipton was especially effective in arguing against William Cocke's appeal for recognition of Franklin.

North Carolina's general assembly continued to undermine the state of Franklin by promising pardons for loyalty oaths, remitting taxes, extending the period for surveys, establishing Hawkins County, and replacing those state officials who had taken positions in the Franklin government. The message was clear when John Sevier was replaced by Evan Shelby as brigadier general of the Washington District. Tipton's supporters gradually gained strength in Franklin's northern counties, while Sevier's group was strongest in the newly opened southern counties where settlers' claims rested on his extortion of land from the Cherokees. In Washington County, where both Tipton and Sevier lived, the two factions were roughly equal in power. Tipton, however, never enjoyed Sevier's enormous personal popularity.

Amid this political maneuvering, Sevier and other officials attempted to cope with the myriad problems involved in creating new opportunities for settlers and speculators. The foremost objective was to expand the available land base, so Franklin authorized the governor to negotiate with the Overhill Cherokees for a cession. Both North Carolina and the United States government were already planning their own treaty conferences, making it imperative for the Franklinites to act promptly. Some of the most prominent Cherokees refused to meet with Sevier because of the pending talks with federal commissioners, but in June 1785 the governor conferred with several chiefs at the mouth of Dumplin Creek on the French Broad River. According to the so-called Treaty of Dumplin Creek, the Indians agreed, in return for "reasonable and liberal compensation," to cede all lands south of the Tennessee and French Broad as far as the divide between the Little River and the Little Tennessee. One chief who was not present was Old Tassel, who later claimed that the young Indians attending the conference believed they had merely given temporary permission for some trespassers to remain in the area.

The net effect of this "treaty" was to legalize previous trespassing and open for additional encroachment an area recognized as part of the Cherokee reservation under North Carolina's 1783 law. Scores of new settlers crossed the French Broad and moved into the wide angle formed by its junction with the Tennessee. Ominously, Old Tassel protested that whites had built their cabins almost within sight and shouting distance of the beloved town of Chota. Both North Carolina and Virginia became alarmed over these trespasses and their implications for Indian affairs, but Sevier reassured Virginia's Governor Patrick Henry that he was doing all in his power to prevent the encroachments. He blamed North Carolina for having sold land so close to the Indian towns and ignored the fact that the Treaty of Dumplin Creek exacerbated an already difficult situation.

While North Carolina and Franklin argued over Indian affairs, Southern Indians sought another European ally to offset the British departure. By the mid-1780s they were meeting with Spanish officials in Mobile and Pensacola in an attempt to organize an alliance based on trade and opposition to American expansion. This was no mere case of Europeans manipulating

Native American puppets, for the Indians were acutely aware of their own needs and negotiated accordingly. Sometimes they also met with state and federal officials, seeking the best deal. The unsettled situation in the Southwest partly shaped Congress's decision in March 1785 to appoint five commissioners to hold treaty talks with the Southern tribes. This early assertion of federal primacy in Indian diplomacy created consternation in Franklin and North Carolina because both feared federal negation of their land claims. Along with Georgia, they denied the authority of Congress to treat with Indian residents of those states—a plausible argument under the Articles of Confederation.

Nonetheless, federal officials proceeded with their plans. In November 1785 at Hopewell, South Carolina, more than nine hundred Cherokees from every part of the nation except the Chickamauga towns attended their first treaty conference with representatives of the United States. Thirty-seven Cherokee headmen signed their marks to a treaty pledging to bury the hatchet forever, to forsake the law of blood revenge, to recognize the sovereignty of the United States, and to accept federal supervision of trade. In return, and much to the Indians' surprise, the commissioners upheld most of the Cherokee land claims. This did not discomfit most whites in Middle Tennessee, for the treaty recognized the validity of the Henderson Purchase and opened an additional area southward to the drainage between the Cumberland and Duck rivers. But East Tennessee was another matter. North Carolina's 1783 act reducing the Cherokee land base there was rejected in favor of the 1777 Treaty of Long Island's definition of a much more expansive tribal domain. Thus only the extreme northeastern corner of East Tennessee was legally open to white settlement. The Hopewell treaty also promised that Congress would look into the most troublesome matter—white trespassing south of the angle of the French Broad and Tennessee rivers—and allowed the Indians to punish other intruders as they wished. Within the next six weeks commissioners at Hopewell also completed treaties with the Choctaws and Chickasaws, but they failed to conclude an agreement with the Creeks. Indeed, Creek head chief Alexander McGillivray soon declared war on the state of Georgia, which exhibited land grabbing propensities rivaling those of North Carolina and Franklin.

In addition to raiding the Georgia backcountry, the Creeks joined Dragging Canoe's still-hostile Chickamaugas on forays into Middle Tennessee and Kentucky. Though the Cumberland settlements were within the area ceded by the pacified Cherokees at Hopewell, settlers there would find themselves in constant danger. During 1786 more than forty of them died at the hands of Indians. McGillivray's Creeks were supplied out of Pensacola, while the Chickamaugas received most of their supplies from French traders allied with Northern Indians and operating out of Detroit via the Wabash and Tennessee rivers. The Chickamaugas even built the town of Coldwater at Muscle Shoals as a residence for about thirty Frenchmen, who were protected there by Dragging Canoe's Shawnee and Delaware allies. Chickamaugas meanwhile ranged as far as the Great Lakes with the Northern tribes. Pan-Indian opposition to white expansion continued to be a reality.

In East Tennessee the Treaty of Hopewell proved useless for resolving Cherokee-white problems, both because Franklin and North Carolina repudiated the treaty and because settlers were already far beyond the 1777 line. William Blount had been present at Hopewell as a witness for North Carolina and had denied federal authority to conclude any of the treaties. Then, as a newly elected member of Congress in 1786, he attempted unsuccessfully to block their ratification. He and every other speculator in Tennessee claimed lands that were threatened by the Hopewell treaties, and John Sevier's state of Franklin faced the loss of two-thirds of its pretended domain. Even Franklin's new capital of Greeneville was well within Cherokee country as defined at Hopewell. One venturesome soul who found himself at odds with the federal government was James White, a Pennsylvanian who in 1786 settled on the north side of the Tennessee River just below the mouth of the French Broad; this was territory opened by North Carolina's 1783 legislation but deemed unceded Cherokee land under the Treaty of Hopewell. On a bluff overlooking a pleasant creek a short distance from the river,

White planted his crops and built a commodious cabin a story and a half in height. Eventually he erected a wooden palisade around his home, and it became known as White's Fort. A few years later it would become the site of Knoxville, the first capital of the state of Tennessee.

Whatever the confusion over the conflicting claims of the United States, North Carolina, and Franklin, white trespassers continued to swarm onto Indian lands. When Cherokees killed several settlers, Franklin's Governor Sevier sent an expedition into the Overhill Towns and in August 1786 dictated, on threat of annihilation, the Treaty of Coyatee, which cleared Indian claims to all lands north of the Little Tennessee River. Neither North Carolina nor the United States nor the Cherokees recognized the treaty, but the settlers remained. In 1787 Franklin opened a land office for the area and sold tracts for forty shillings per one hundred acres. The names given to the new counties south of the French Broad—Blount, Caswell, and Sevier—speak volumes about Franklin politics. Predictably, North Carolina refused to recognize the three counties.

The Creek hostilities against Georgia presented Sevier with a unique opportunity. He offered assistance to that state, presumably in exchange for Georgia's having allowed settlement at Muscle Shoals and for its support of Franklin's renewed efforts to obtain congressional recognition. Making good on the speculation at the shoals was no doubt foremost in the minds of Sevier and his North Carolina business associates. A Georgia commissioner visited Franklin in September 1786 and said that Sevier had solicited a joint alliance with the Overhill Cherokees and the Chickasaws against the Creeks. Sevier promised that Franklin could provide some one thousand riflemen and two hundred cavalry for the purpose. The threat from Northern Indians—notably the Shawnees—was not so great at the moment because an army from Kentucky was engaging them north of the Ohio. A Franklin alliance with Georgia remained a tantalizing possibility until late 1787, when Georgia ceded its claims to the Muscle Shoals area to South Carolina.

It also seemed possible that the Cumberland settlements would join Franklin, in part because of the constant threat from

Indians. Middle Tennessee's isolation was acute, and its only connection with East Tennessee and the rest of North Carolina was a
circuitous and difficult route along the Wilderness Road through
Cumberland Gap and a branch trail southward across the barrens to the Nashville Basin. This route was shaped like an oxbow
and was subject to attack by Indians from both north and south
of the Ohio. Recognizing Middle Tennessee's perilous position,
North Carolina in 1787 authorized construction of a much more
direct trail that would be ten feet wide to accommodate wagon
traffic. Peter Avery blazed most of this route, which went from
the south end of Clinch Mountain (near present-day Blaine)
across the Clinch River to the Wartburg area and then up the
Cumberland Mountains via Monterey to Bledsoe's Lick (present-
day Gallatin) and Nashville. Opened in September 1788, the Old
Road or Avery's Trace was little more than a rough pack horse
trail, and it was even more exposed to Chickamauga and Creek
attack than the Wilderness Road; safety required either a military escort or a large party of well-armed travelers. Andrew Jackson joined one of the first groups of immigrants to take the new
trail to Nashville.

In the meantime Sevier had to worry about renewed Indian
troubles closer to home. The Treaty of Coyatee had antagonized
the Overhill Cherokees, and in the summer of 1788 warriors
killed the family of John Kirk near the Little Tennessee. A son,
John Kirk Jr., had been absent and escaped death. Sevier retaliated by destroying a town on the Hiwassee and then encouraged
chiefs to come in for negotiations. Under a white flag of truce
Old Tassel, Old Abram, and a few others arrived for talks, but
in Sevier's absence they were savagely murdered by John Kirk
Jr. Old Tassel had been the one chief who consistently supported
peace and who was admired by all Cherokees, including the
Chickamaugas. His murder brought widespread condemnation
by whites and provoked many Overhill people to take up the
hatchet again, both independently and as allies of Dragging
Canoe.

Some Overhill Cherokees deserted their towns and reestablished themselves at Ustanali in Georgia, where they selected
Little Turkey as Old Tassel's successor. This move marked the

end of Chota as principal town; it began a rapid decline as white settlers pushed almost to its edges. Joseph Martin, Evan Shelby's successor as North Carolina's militia commander in East Tennessee, unsuccessfully attempted to placate the remaining Overhill Cherokees as well as those who had moved to Georgia. Deciding on a preemptive strike against the Chickamaugas before their new alliance with the Overhill people could become effective, he marched his troops to Lookout Mountain, where he was decisively defeated by well-entrenched defenders. Immediately thereafter Chickamauga and Overhill warriors moved in force against the Tennessee settlements and destroyed almost all of the habitations south of White's Fort. Detachments of raiders even penetrated as far as southwestern Virginia. A large force led by John Watts (a mixed-blood), Bloody Fellow, and Kitegisky was confident enough to go into winter camp near Jonesborough, but they were attacked in January 1789 by John Sevier's army. In savage fighting marked by hand-to-hand combat and the militia's fearsome swivel guns, the Indians suffered heavy casualties before retreating. Meanwhile, North Carolina officials' ongoing efforts to effect a truce finally succeeded. In March, Little Turkey, Hanging Maw, and even Dragging Canoe agreed to a cease-fire until formal peace talks could be held. It appeared that diplomacy might yet prevail.

By this time North Carolina's dual policy of opposition and conciliation finally promised to bring about Franklin's demise, not in a burst of glory but quietly, without a whimper. Since early 1785 many people in East Tennessee had opposed Sevier and held local positions under North Carolina's appointment. Two rival administrations vied for popular support, waging a noisy polemical war that sometimes strayed from pamphlets and broadsides and extended to physical threats, though North Carolina's local militia maintained a truce with the Franklin militia. John Tipton was a particular thorn in Sevier's side and as the senator from the Washington District consistently undermined Franklin in the North Carolina legislature. Nor had the Franklinites succeeded with their renewed pleas for statehood presented to the delegates who assembled in Philadelphia in 1787 to draft a new constitution.

There was also the problem of finding a leader to replace Sevier, whose term was expiring and whose abilities and forcefulness
had kept Franklin alive. In August 1787 the Franklin legislature
elected Evan Shelby as the next governor in hopes that he could
work out a reconciliation with North Carolina. Because Shelby
was a militia general for North Carolina, he properly refused the
honor, but he clearly favored a diplomatic solution to the stand-
off. His wishes were subverted, however, by John Tipton's enduring enmity toward Sevier. Early in 1788 their feud led to an
armed clash of their supporters that resulted in three deaths.
Months later Samuel Johnston, North Carolina's new governor
and no accommodationist where Franklin was concerned, ordered Sevier's arrest for high treason. Probably no one actually
intended to arrest the popular Nolichucky Jack, except Tipton,
who apprehended his old enemy and spirited him across the
mountains to Morganton, North Carolina. Embarrassed officials
there quietly released Sevier on bond and forgot about the
charges. They would await the imminent death of Franklin and
expect its erstwhile leader to resume his rightful role in North
Carolina.

Amid the shambles of a dying Franklin, Sevier participated in
a shadowy scheme involving other Western leaders and a possible alliance with Spain. This intrigue reflected the widespread
discontent in the Southwest. Harassed by Indians and lacking
protection from their mother state, Tennesseans realized the federal government could offer little support as long as North Carolina and other Southern states refused to cede their Western
lands. Besides, the national government was notoriously ineffec-
tual and seemingly little interested in the Southwest, although it
was busy establishing military posts and otherwise asserting itself in the new Northwest Territory. John Jay, Secretary for Foreign Affairs of the Continental Congress, had even suggested that
the United States temporarily waive the right to navigate the
Mississippi in return for certain concessions from Spain. Leaders
in Tennessee and Kentucky, in contrast, wanted Spain to stop
assisting the hostile Indians and to reopen the Mississippi to
American trade. Westerners realized their future prosperity depended on an uninterrupted flow of goods between the interior

and the Gulf of Mexico. If neither the United States nor individual state governments could guarantee peace and prosperity, perhaps it was time to seek an accord with Spain.

Another major consideration of Western elites was validation of their land claims, and here again they were dissatisfied with the status quo. Without the cession of Western lands to the central government, they would be at the mercy of political rivals in their home states, federal armies would offer little protection, and their lands would decline in value. Without cession they could not organize their lands as states. Statehood, with themselves as leaders, of course, would offer the ultimate political safeguard for their claims, as well as an opportunity to shape federal Indian treaties to their own needs. Short of cession, their only surety for life, influence, and property might be seceding from the United States and offering allegiance to Spain. Better yet, giving the appearance of secession might serve their purposes by helping to convince the states to release their Western lands to the United States. By the late 1780s, then, Westerners began a conspiratorial tiptoe with Spain that, despite professions of goodwill and respect on both sides, manifested self-interest most of all.

Among the conspirators were James Robertson and Daniel Smith from the Cumberland settlements, John Sevier of Franklin, and the ever devious William Blount. One of Sevier's letters to Diego de Gardoqui, the Spanish representative to the United States, suggests that one of their important objectives was Spanish pacification of the Southern Indians so that the Muscle Shoals venture could succeed. Whatever Sevier's intentions, he soon lost interest in the intrigue and acceded to North Carolina's wishes for a peaceful dissolution of Franklin and accepted the restoration of honors to himself. By mid-1788 the only remaining support for Franklin was among settlers living south of the French Broad River in defiance of North Carolina law and the Treaty of Hopewell. They drew up articles of association in January 1789 and affirmed their loyalty to Sevier, but in February Franklin's once and only governor took an oath of loyalty to North Carolina. Franklin was dead, but upon its ashes arose the certainty of a second and final cession of North Carolina's Western lands.

6.

THE SOUTHWEST TERRITORY: 1790–1796

William Blount was a member of the 1787 constitutional con-vention in Philadelphia, and he hoped North Carolina would share his enthusiasm for the finished document. Once again his ideol-ogy and business considerations blurred: a preference for stronger central authority coincided with a desire for North Carolina's cession of Tennessee to the new government and the expected increase in the value of his property. He remained discreetly quiet, however, as state delegates debated the Constitution in a special convention dominated by long-simmering factionalism and a general fear of overweening federal authority. In July 1788 delegates deferred acceptance of the document by offering a se-ries of amendments that Antifederalists realized would never be enacted. Alarmed, Blount and other Federalists quickly used skillful propaganda and the Constitution's ratification by other states to convince the assembly to reconsider the issue in the fall of 1789.

Cession and ratification were separate issues. Even while call-ing for a new convention, Blount promoted the idea of cession by continuing to intrigue with James Robertson and other Western-ers over a possible secession and alliance with Spain. They made little attempt at secrecy, and rumors abounded. Blount even sponsored and secured legislative approval for organizing Middle Tennessee as the Mero District, in honor of Don Esteban Miró, the Spanish governor in New Orleans (who perhaps was puzzled by the misspelling of his name). As far as Blount and some Westerners were concerned, the "Spanish Conspiracy" was mostly an attempt to inform easterners of transmontane concerns and create an impression that cession to a stronger federal authority was the only way to offset a growing Spanish menace to the West. Most Tennesseans favored ratification and cession so the new United States government could protect them from Indians, secure their right to navigate the Mississippi, and eventually, under the provisions of the Northwest Ordinance, grant them statehood. This scenario perfectly suited the wishes of nonresident speculators like the Blounts.

Westerners intended to play an important role in the unfolding drama, beginning with the reconsideration of ratification. In November 1789 a newly loyal John Sevier prepared to take his seat as North Carolina's senator from Greene County; despite a legislative prohibition against his holding public office because of his role in Franklin, he was seated and even reinstated to his old rank of brigadier general. He favored both ratification and cession. On November 23 the new convention accepted the U.S. Constitution, with only two Western legislators opposing it. Sevier's constituents quickly elected him congressman from western North Carolina even though they hoped his tenure would be short; once Congress accepted cession, his district would become part of a new federal territory.

Just three days after North Carolina ratified the Constitution, a bill was introduced for cession. Westerners overwhelmingly supported it, as did many Eastern conservatives who saw the West as a financial drain and its inhabitants as louts and brigands. The measure, passed in December 1789, was very similar to the cession act that had been repealed in 1784. It stipulated that all claims made under North Carolina law were to be protected, and—here was the joker—that if the military reserve lacked sufficient good land to meet the needs of warrant holders, they could locate elsewhere in Tennessee. The ceded area would be administered under the terms of the Northwest Ordinance, starting as a federal territory and eventually becoming one or more states. The ordinance's prohibition of slavery would not apply to Tennessee, for the peculiar institution was already well established there and specifically protected in the cession act.

While awaiting congressional action on cession, William Blount busied himself with political and business affairs. Failing to become one of North Carolina's senators in the new Congress, he contented himself in the state legislature with furthering his own interests and cementing goodwill among the transmontane population—supporting, for example, a resolution validating Franklin's Dumplin Creek treaty of May 1785 and its cession of Cherokee territory south of the French Broad. More important were Blount's hopes for a political position that might be even more advantageous than a seat in the United States Senate. Confident that cession would be accepted, he wanted to promote his burgeoning Western speculation by becoming federal governor of the new territory.

On April 2, 1790, Congress accepted North Carolina's cession and its stipulations, and on May 26 organized a government for "The Territory of the United States South of the River Ohio," usually referred to simply as the Southwest Territory. Except for later minor boundary adjustments, the territory included virtually all of present-day Tennessee. George Mason, Joseph Martin, and John Sevier were possible candidates for the new governorship, but William Blount's connections in George Washington's administration paid off. On June 8 the forty-one-year-old speculator-politician was appointed governor, and with typical candor he rejoiced because the office had "great Importance to our Western Speculations." It also gave him authority as superintendent of Indian affairs for the entire Southern department. Other appointees included Daniel Smith as secretary and David Campbell, John McNairy, and eventually Joseph Anderson as judges. Later, upon Blount's recommendation, James Robertson and John Sevier became brigadier generals of the Mero and Washington districts, respectively.

The Northwest Ordinance provided for a three-stage, evolutionary system of government whereby a territory would proceed from colonial status to statehood and full equality with other states. It was a process by which Americans could avoid the mistake that Britain made in trying to keep colonial peoples permanently subservient. The first stage began when the president, with congressional assent, appointed a territorial governor, a secretary, and three federal judges. During this phase the governor exercised supreme power over all inhabitants and was answerable only to the federal government. The second stage occurred when there were at least five thousand adult males living in the territory, at which time they could elect the lower house of a territorial legislature; members of an upper house were appointed from the territorial elite. The governor continued to hold the right of absolute veto over any legislative action. Preparation for the final stage could begin when the territory had a free population of sixty thousand. The free adult males would draw up a republican constitution, and upon its approval by Congress the former territory would join the union as a state.

How this political progression would actually take place was unclear, because the Northwest Territory, created in 1787, had not yet progressed to stage two. The bitter resistance of powerful tribes meant that extensive settlement and political development would take a while. Residents of the Southwest Territory, therefore, could not rely upon precedent; they would be establishing it themselves. They would also find that the federal government was far more involved with what was happening north of the Ohio River and seemingly little concerned with their welfare. This was partly because North Carolina's cession appeared more and more to be a white elephant. The federal government favored state cessions of the trans-Appalachian region because it hoped to generate revenue from the sales of public lands. Belatedly, it discovered that speculators had already claimed nearly 7.5 million acres of prime land in the Southwest Territory, leaving, except for unceded Indian country, a mere three hundred thousand acres of unappropriated "public" lands, and much of that was already occupied by squatters. In return for this questionable bequest, the federal government had to pay the costs of administering and protecting the new territory. It was a bad deal, and the Washington administration understandably focused its energies on the more attractive prospects of the Northwest Territory. Understandable or not, this attitude brought unrealized expectations in Tennessee, and the resulting frustration promoted alienation and an emerging sense of Southwestern regionalism. For nearly a generation any identification with the new American nation would be tentative and conditional. Some Westerners would continue to envision a possible connection with foreign nations should the federal government prove too inattentive.

In September 1790 William Blount left North Carolina to assume his new responsibilities; considering his longtime speculation in the area, it is surprising that this would be his first trip west of the mountains. Ever aware of political niceties, he first paid his respects to George Washington at Mount Vernon and then, in nearby Alexandria, he was formally sworn into office. In October he finally arrived in the Southwest Territory and established himself at Rocky Mount, William Cobb's home at the fork of the Holston and Watauga rivers. This comfortable nine-room house of white oak logs and glass windows was the first seat of government in the Southwest Territory. The many problems and past indifference of the federal government created a situation demanding all of the new governor's considerable skills. The resentful residents awaited Blount's arrival with a measure of skepticism. They would judge him by his deeds, not his words.

Blount was up to the task. From Rocky Mount he quickly familiarized himself with the conditions and needs of his constituents, traveling throughout the Washington and Mero districts and informing people about the Northwest Ordinance and, most important, generally confirming the authority of local residents who had long been exercising power. He was especially solicitous of the goodwill of James Robertson and John Sevier, which he received despite Sevier's initial ambivalence. In deference to the popular Nolichucky Jack, Blount paid less attention to John Tipton. In Middle Tennessee he obliged James Robertson's supporters, including the young Andrew Jackson, whom the governor duly licensed as an attorney. Blount's travels throughout the territory and his shrewd, self-serving appointments solidified his control. There, on the Tennessee frontier, he was creating a political machine.

Tennessee's first formal census was taken in the summer of

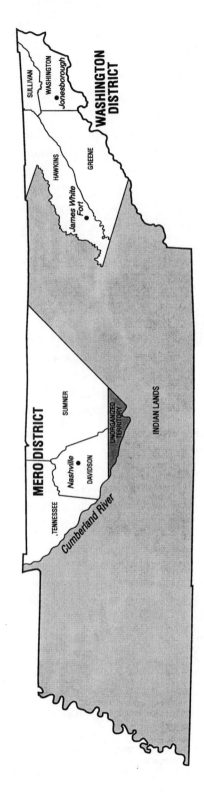

The Southwest Territory, 1791. Department of Geography and the Cartographic Services Laboratory at the University of Tennessee.

1791, but some people avoided the militia officers who served as enumerators, and several local returns were not filed in time for inclusion in the official figures; thus Blount believed the final total of 35,691 non-Indians in the Southwest Territory was perhaps 1,500 less than the true population. Slaves represented 3,417 of those enumerated, and there were 361 free persons of color. The Washington District had 28,649 inhabitants, including 3,619 south of the French Broad on Cherokee lands, while 7,042 people lived in the Mero District. The number of white adult males was 6,271, a significant figure because under the Northwest Ordinance it qualified the new territory for a legislative assembly. And yet Blount delayed taking steps toward that end for another two years, supposedly because citizens did not wish to pay taxes for governing themselves, but partly, no doubt, to give himself time to consolidate his authority.

The governor's most urgent objective, the measure for his success in office, would have tested the skills of the world's most sophisticated diplomats. He had to create friendly relations with the Indians, who were living amid an ever-expanding white population. The governor was in charge of federal Indian diplomacy not only in all of the territory's nearly forty-two thousand square miles, but also as far south as the boundary between Spanish territory and the United States, in an area claimed by Georgia. Blount's primary focus, however, was on the two widely separated zones of white habitation: the Washington District, comprising the narrow band of valleys in East Tennessee extending southwestward from Virginia to the Little Tennessee River; and, some 150 miles to the west, the Mero District of settlements clustered within a band twelve to twenty-five miles wide and stretching about eighty miles along the Cumberland River from Bledsoe's Lick westward to Clarksville. In both districts settlers occupied lands still claimed by Indians, and they were determined to take more.

The only Cherokee treaty recognized by the United States was the 1785 Treaty of Hopewell, but its land cessions had been hopelessly inadequate even when the agreement was signed. Whites had spilled far beyond those boundaries, beyond even the cessions Sevier had extorted for Franklin, all the way to within a few miles of the Cherokees' principal town of Chota. Those living south of the French Broad were a particular affront to the Upper Cherokees, and many young warriors were eager to join their Chickamauga cousins, who were biding their time before resuming raids in both districts of Tennessee. The most immediate Indian threat was along the Cumberland, where the Chickamaugas, Creeks, and Shawnees continued to oppose white encroachment on tribal hunting lands. The Upper Creeks were the worst menace; torn by internal rivalries and goaded by renewed Spanish intrigues, they repudiated the peace treaty Alexander McGillivray had signed in New York in the summer of 1790 and resumed their forays against the Cumberland settlers.

Large-scale speculators also contributed to the growing tension. Governor Blount was now in the ironic position of trying to head off attempts to settle Muscle Shoals and the Bend of the Tennessee by companies that were similar to his own venture of a few years before. In 1789 the Georgia legislature, a notably corrupt body, had granted several different speculative groups millions of acres from the shoals westward to the Yazoo and Mississippi rivers. The efforts of these companies antagonized the Indians and Spanish officials and worried the Washington administration, which feared full-scale hostilities in the South at a time when federal armies were attempting to subdue Northern tribes.

The war north of the Ohio was not going well and revealed the seeming impotence of the United States government. There, Northern and Southern warriors continued their pan-Indian resistance by fighting side by side. In the fall of 1790 a combined force of Indians, including some Chickamaugas, routed Josiah Harmar's federal army and exposed American military pretensions as laughable. Word of Harmar's defeat spread like wildfire among Southern Indians, inspiring further opposition to American expansion. The Washington administration prepared to field another army in Ohio and asked Blount to recruit men to serve under Brigadier General John Sevier in that remote theater, a levy that met widespread resistance from Tennesseans who resented federal emphasis on the Northwest and who feared for their own families. Southern Indians meanwhile well understood that a new Ohio expedition would limit federal military assistance to the Southwest Territory.

Secretary of War Henry Knox, Blount's superior in Indian affairs, hoped to defuse the volatile situation in Tennessee so that the United States could concentrate on the Northwest Territory. In August 1790 the Senate authorized President Washington either to enforce the Treaty of Hopewell or to negotiate a further Cherokee cession that would include lands occupied by white trespassers. The annual payment for such a cession was not to exceed $1,000. Knox promptly ordered the newly appointed Governor Blount to meet with the Cherokees under those broad guidelines (but within the framework of the Hopewell treaty) and also to attempt to thwart a proposed settlement by the Tennessee Yazoo Company at Muscle Shoals. Blount instead envisioned an entirely new treaty for obtaining additional lands that would possibly include the shoals. This would not be his last misunderstanding with Knox.

Blount asked the Cherokees to confer with him in the spring of 1791 below the junction of the French Broad and Holston, where James White had built his fort in 1786. Many Upper and Lower Cherokees were agreeable to a meeting, but certain resident traders—and even Andrew Pickens of South Carolina—warned that Blount meant to take their lands and perhaps massacre them. Of more immediate concern to Blount and the Indians was the attempt by speculators to settle at Muscle Shoals, within an area where Chickasaw, Cherokee, and Creek land claims overlapped. In March, Zachariah Cox, acting on behalf of the Tennessee Yazoo Company and ignoring Blount's warnings and threat of legal action, led thirty-one men down the Tennessee to the shoals. The Indians there were so threatening that Cox soon returned, only to begin planning another expedition to the area. Attempts to indict him for his actions were unsuccessful.

Despite all the concerns and various delays, treaty negotiations began at White's Fort in June 1791, with some 1,200 Cherokees, including many notable chiefs, in attendance. To the surprise of no one, Dragging Canoe failed to appear, but John Watts and Bloody Fellow were there to represent the Chickamaugas. Blount wisely catered to the Indian fondness for pomp and cere-

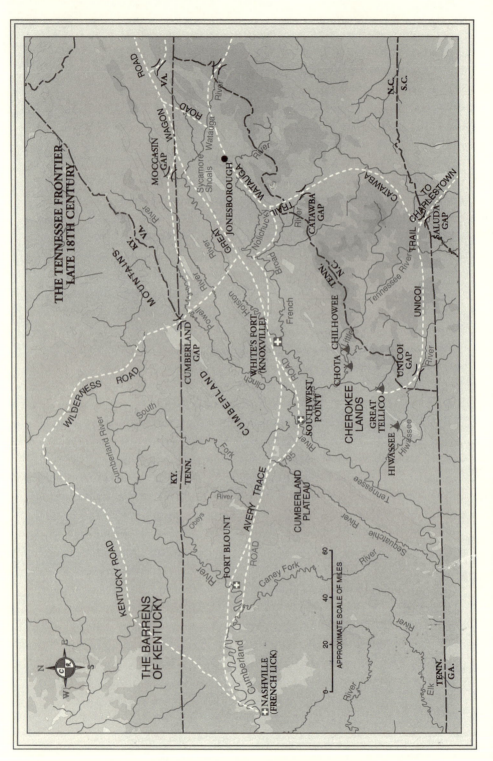

THE TENNESSEE FRONTIER
LATE 18TH CENTURY

mony by dressing in military uniform, holding court under a large marquee, and being formally introduced to each Cherokee leader. The Indians reciprocated by performing the Eagle Tail Dance, apparently for the first time since the American Revolution; with great drama and exaggerated movements, the gyrating men described their exploits in war. The formalities over, Blount bluntly informed the Indians that he wanted another cession. The Cherokees professed surprise, saying they had thought the meeting was simply to refine matters in the Hopewell treaty. After days of haggling and increasing rancor, the governor's forceful, and even threatening, manner finally resulted in the Treaty of the Holston. The Indians agreed to cede their lands east of the Clinch River and north of a line running eastward from near the mouth of the Clinch along the divide between the Little River and the Little Tennessee River to North Carolina, opening for whites new lands to a point just south of present-day Maryville. The Cherokees also confirmed their earlier cession of the Cumberland region, made in the Hopewell treaty, and agreed to a joint commission of Indians and whites to survey the new boundaries.

As compensation for these cessions, Blount persuaded the Indians to accept a temporary annuity of $1,000 while efforts were made to convince Congress to increase the amount. The treaty also dealt with crimes committed by Indians and whites against one another, stipulated that whites would have free and unimpeded use of the Tennessee River and the trail connecting the Mero and Washington districts, and specified federal gifts of agricultural and mechanical tools to help the Indians become more "civilized." From this point on federal Indian policy would have two interwoven objectives: acquisition of more tribal lands and the promotion of Indian "civilization," that is, weaning Indians away from their tribal societies and encouraging them to become more like whites.

For many whites and Indians, treaties were mere scraps of paper symbolizing brief meetings of mutual convenience for dissembling and misunderstanding. Even during the Holston treaty proceedings, Chickamaugas and Creeks raided in Middle Tennessee, and the treaty's subsequent ratification did not prevent continuing white trespasses and Indian depredations. Both Blount and militia officers within the Southwest Territory petitioned the federal government for regular troops, but Henry Knox was inclined to view the troubles as the work of "a few rascally Indians." Besides, the Washington administration's main concern was the escalating Indian warfare in the Northwest Territory, and Knox saw a general Indian war in the South as "an insupportable evil." His only response to pleas for assistance was to authorize the calling out of a minimal number of militia. Blount struggled to assuage the anger of his constituents over policies that might be fundamentally sound but still appeared detrimental to the interests of Tennessee.

Meanwhile troubles mounted, especially after a combined force of Indians routed a federal army under Arthur St. Clair north of the Ohio in November 1791. The loss of more than six hundred men, coupled with a panicky retreat, constituted what some historians believe was the most decisive defeat of American arms. The Southwest Territory shared both directly and indirectly in this debacle. Among St. Clair's army was a battalion of resentful militiamen who had answered the call of Henry Knox and William Blount and marched all the way from the Washington District. Among the victors were a number of Southern Indians who jubilantly carried news of their success back home. Once again, unified Indian militancy proved a potent factor on both sides of the Ohio.

Early in 1792, at a time when Indian bargaining strength was high, a delegation of Overhill Cherokees appeared in Philadelphia to complain about the Treaty of Holston and demand redress. Determined to avoid a two-front Indian war, Henry Knox cordially heard their complaints about white encroachment and their claims that some of the written provisions of the treaty differed from those agreed upon at White's Fort. The Cherokees disavowed any cession of the Cumberland, the traditional hunting land of several tribes, and insisted that whites abandon the area. Knox could not meet their demands but promised to delay surveying boundaries for the Treaty of the Holston, increased their tribal annuity to $1,500, and showered them with gifts to take back to their people. For their part, the Indians managed to keep a straight face and appear respectful when the secretary of war asked their support in new campaigns against the Northern tribes.

Knox's Indian strategy was sensible, but it was insensitive to the needs and wishes of white people in the Southwest Territory. His determination to concentrate on a final showdown north of the Ohio meant that he would agree to no more than limited federal assistance in Tennessee, promising to send a token force of regular troops and authorizing additional militia, arms, and ammunition for the Mero District, the area most exposed to danger. But he ordered that the militia remain strictly on the defensive and undertake no actions likely to provoke the Indians. For his part, Blount ordered draconian measures against white violators of the Holston treaty and urged the wisdom of a peace policy upon his dubious fellow citizens. Those who supported Blount's peace policy, even the popular James Robertson, faced public wrath. In one instance the governor issued a militia call only after a group of officers in the Mero District decided without authorization to send troops on a patrol south of the Cumberland River.

This limited and strictly defensive posture encouraged hostile Indians to expand their activities. They now had a powerful ally in Hector, Baron de Carondelet, the new Spanish governor at New Orleans, who aggressively sought to reestablish a coalition with McGillivray's Creeks and other Southern tribes to resist American expansion. As a Carondelet informant put it, "it has now become urgent to place an obstacle to the rapid westward progress of the Americans. . . . As soon as they are in a group, however small, they become dangerous; soon they want to run things." The Spanish Conspiracy was alive and well, but in an entirely different incarnation, and delegations of Southern Indians were enjoying Spanish hospitality at Pensacola, Mobile, and New Orleans. Between the Holston treaty of 1791 and the following spring, raids by assorted groups of Indians resulted in the deaths of more than fifty whites and the loss of much property, especially horses, which the Indians quickly transferred to unscrupulous traders for resale elsewhere. Indiscriminate retaliation by whites against inoffensive Cherokees of the Upper Towns simply exacerbated Indian resentment.

A major objective of Blount was to take advantage of Dragging

Canoe's sudden March 1792 death, the result of a wild celebration following a Chickamauga success on the Cumberland. The recalcitrant chief was about sixty years old and had not met white Americans in council since 1775, but Blount believed his successor, John Watts, was more amenable to reason—Blount's reason. Unlike the fiery Dragging Canoe, Watts, a mixed-blood, was at least willing to talk with whites, and he professed a desire for peace. In May 1792 Blount met with Watts and other prominent Cherokees at Coyatee, at the mouth of the Little Tennessee, where the recent Indian delegates to Philadelphia distributed the gifts by Henry Knox and George Washington. After elaborate ceremonies and copious drinking, Blount diplomatically referred to recent Indian attacks and called for peace and further talks. The governor left Coyatee convinced the Chickamaugas and other Cherokees favored peace, but Watts was soon meeting with Spanish officials in Pensacola and planning to join Upper Creek militants in further campaigns against the Americans. Equally ominous was a general Cherokee council the following month at Ustanali, Georgia, which revealed continuing resentment toward white encroachment and the Holston treaty.

The only Indians unequivocally favoring peace with white Tennesseans were the Chickasaws, who signed an agreement with Governor Blount in Nashville. Otherwise the violence on both sides continued, and an attack in summer 1792 by Chickamaugas, Upper Creeks, and Shawnees on Zeigler's Station in the Mero District resulted in the deaths of five whites and the capture of a number of others. The shocked Blount now raised the number of militia companies but found that many men were unwilling to leave their families and homes merely to conduct the defensive operations insisted upon by the Washington administration. They wanted a more aggressive policy. Blount's confidence—or hope—in John Watts had clearly been misplaced. At Willstown, the new Chickamauga headquarters near present-day Fort Payne, Alabama, Watts convened a mixed force of Indians, told them of promised Spanish support, and convinced them to issue a declaration of war against the United States. Reports circulated that as many as five hundred warriors would attack the frontier.

When Blount learned of the threat, he immediately ordered that defensive measures be undertaken in both the Washington and Mero districts. In an effort to fool the governor, Watts and other Cherokee leaders assured him the rumors were erroneous and that there was no planned attack. The governor momentarily let his guard down, only to learn that Chickamaugas, Creeks, and Shawnees under Watts were indeed marching to attack the Cumberland settlements. Fortunately, James Robertson had not been fooled and remained vigilant.

Indian unity quickly eroded as Watts and other leaders began arguing about whether it was best to attack Nashville directly or to concentrate on smaller outlying settlements. As Governor Blount later observed, such disagreements were "a rock on which large parties of Indians have generally split when consisting of more than one Nation." On a September night most of the warriors attacked Buchanan's Station, just four miles from Nashville. In furious fighting that left Watts seriously wounded, the relatively few defenders managed to repel the Indians, who split into smaller bands and harassed much of Middle Tennessee and Kentucky.

Blount now agreed with his constituents that only offensive operations by the militia or regular troops could end the Indian problem, but no one in Philadelphia, neither Knox nor Washington nor Congress, would authorize such aggressive and costly measures. Blount and his allies, including brigadiers Robertson and Sevier, incurred the wrath of many Tennesseans by loyally refraining from a direct challenge of the federal position. When Blount declined to authorize the use of scouts because such dangerous work entailed considerable expense, citizens in the Mero District compensated scouts by offering $100 per Indian scalp, to a maximum of twenty scalps.

The continuing official insistence on a strictly defensive posture led Sevier and his militia in November 1792 to build a fort at Southwest Point at the junction of the Tennessee and Clinch rivers, a position whose strategic importance had long been obvious. Located on the present site of Kingston, the fort was downstream from and readily accessible to all of the white settlements in East Tennessee. It was like a dagger poised at the Cherokee and Chickamauga villages, promising quick retaliation for any offense. It also offered refuge for travelers who braved the dangerous trail leading across the Cumberland Plateau between the Washington and Mero districts. The presence of militia there may have contributed to a temporary decline of Indian attacks late in 1792, but at the urging of Henry Knox, Blount deactivated most of Sevier's force, leaving only a small garrison at the fort. In February 1793 the first federal troops arrived in the territory, one understrength company of malcontents and potential deserters, and some of these soon garrisoned Fort Southwest Point. Until its abandonment in 1807, the post would be a center of federal diplomacy with the Cherokees.

Even while Blount grappled with the immediate Indian problems, he and other citizens of the Southwest Territory were continuing their speculation. One question of direct concern was where the permanent capital of the territory would be. Some argued for the Mero District, but Blount's speculative, strategic, and political interests dictated a site in East Tennessee, where most of the white and Indian population resided. Almost since his arrival in the territory, the governor had envisioned a new site well down the Tennessee River system, and regardless of its location, he intended to name the town after his immediate superior, Henry Knox. James White's Fort, where Blount had negotiated the Treaty of the Holston, seemed an ideal site. It was at the junction of the French Broad and Holston rivers, was near Indian country, and was accessible by wagon to Richmond, Baltimore, and Philadelphia—458, 543, and 638 miles away, respectively. Nashville was 205 miles to the west, though there was still no safe route between East Tennessee and the Cumberland country.

Once Blount's intentions were clear, James White hired Charles McClung to survey sixty-four lots overlooking the river in his new community and then disposed of these in a lottery on October 3, 1791, the date now accepted as Knoxville's birthday. The governor and his family established temporary residency there the following March, then moved into their new two-story wooden frame house. It overlooked a steep slope down to the river and, together with a separate office on the same lot, became the new territorial capitol. The home was a frontier wonder, per-

Blount Mansion and Executive Office, in today's
Knoxville. COURTESY BLOUNT MANSION ASSOCIATION.

haps the first of such size and construction west of the Southern
Appalachians; it had three brick fireplaces, had been built with
varying grades of yellow pine, and had poplar-clapboard siding
and a roof of cedar shakes. Its multi-pane glass windows were a
novelty in the backcountry and provided such a view and let in
so much light that dazzled Indian visitors called it the "house of
many eyes." Across the block from the capitol was a tavern built
by John Chisholm, Blount's confidant and sometime business
partner, who offered good cheer and room and board for Knoxville's early visitors. Blount Mansion still stands at the corner of
State Street and Hill Avenue.

Anticipating Knoxville's potential, George Roulstone and Robert Ferguson, who were enlisted by Blount himself, had established the *Knoxville Gazette* in November 1791. Because the de-

velopment of its namesake community was barely underway, the paper's first issues appeared in Rogersville. When Roulstone and Ferguson moved their presses to the new capital in 1792, they intended their biweekly to serve the governor and to legitimize Knoxville's urban pretensions. In June 1792 Blount further confirmed this latest advance of the frontier by authorizing the creation of two new counties comprising the lands acquired through the Holston treaty: Jefferson County and Knox County, which included the capital. Soon the new counties made up a new district named Hamilton, showing once again Blount's willingness to curry favor throughout the Washington administration.

Despite other disputes between residents of the Southwest Territory and the federal government, Indian problems remained the central point of contention. Tennesseans demanded protection. Following Alexander McGillivray's death early in 1793, Upper Creek raids, always a concern, became even more devastating in the Washington and Mero districts. To offset these attacks it was necessary for Blount to placate the Upper Cherokees and, if possible, keep the Chickamaugas neutral. In April 1793 the governor met with about sixty Cherokees, including a now inexplicably amiable John Watts, and entertained them with "eating, drinking and jocular conversation, of which Watts is very fond." The meeting was expensive because whiskey flowed like water, but Blount wrote Henry Knox he had "considered it the interest of the United States to be as liberal as Watts and his party were thirsty." Despite Blount's entreaties, the Cherokees expressed little interest in going to Philadelphia for a conference with federal officials. Nor could Watts's jovial professions of friendship prevent Chickamauga militants from continuing to raid the backcountry. He simply did not have the prestige of Dragging Canoe, his predecessor. Complicating matters were the frequent calls of Creeks and Shawnees for Cherokee assistance against the whites. By spring Creek leadership of mounting raids led the *Knoxville Gazette* to argue openly against Henry Knox's insistence on defensive measures only; either destroy the Creeks, it said, or face constant harassment from them.

Indeed, many Tennesseans now openly criticized federal policy and, at least implicitly, the local officials empowered to enforce that policy. Even the pro-Blount *Gazette* complained about an unhealthy "federal body politic" that was evidenced "by the pain and uneasiness which is felt in the extremities." The *Gazette* otherwise adhered to the federal line, admitting that problems within the territory often arose because of the penchant of certain Tennesseans to disregard the laws, "which is one cause why the general government is so backward in giving us that protection our exposed defenceless situation calls for, and has dictated the policy of half-war half-peace to the Indians."

The frontier people's disregard for federal Indian policy—and for the Indians themselves—was apparent in many ways. In May 1793 a delegation of friendly Chickasaws arrived in Knoxville to solicit American assistance in a new war between their tribe and the Creeks, and Blount was eager to promote an alliance. During the conference, however, whites attacked three Chickasaws within a few hundred yards of Blount's mansion, and one of the Indians died. Blount placated his guests by immediately offering a reward for the assailants and burying the deceased warrior with full military honors. But despite his best efforts, he could never identify the white assailants, and if he had, their white peers would never have convicted them. Equally outrageous was an unauthorized attack by Captain John Beard's Knox County militia on Hanging Maw's peaceable Upper Cherokee town, resulting in seven or eight deaths. Blount was away at the time on an official visit to Philadelphia, and acting governor Daniel Smith had to admit that public sentiment in the territory made prosecution of Beard impossible. A "Spirit for war against Indians," he said, "pervades people of all Ranks so far that no order of Government can stop them." He was correct, and within a year Beard would become one of Knox County's representatives in the first territorial legislature. Other groups of militia or irregular forces followed Beard's example by indiscriminately attacking any Indians they encountered, more often than not the Upper Cherokees who lived nearby. In vain Henry Knox warned that the United States would not support "a war brought on the frontiers by the wanton blood thirsty disposition of our own people." And he thought it was unfair for the United States to punish "banditti Indians" when "guilty whites escape with impunity."

One response of the Creeks and Chickamaugas was to renew their efforts to seek the support of other tribes. That summer a large delegation attended a major conference with Northern tribes at the rapids of the Miami River in Ohio, and a few months later representatives of the four major Southern tribes met on the site of present-day Vicksburg to sign a treaty recognizing Spanish sovereignty and creating an offensive and defensive alliance among the tribes. This Treaty of Nogales reflected both Governor Carondelet's desire to oppose further American expansion and Indian hopes to obtain vital Spanish trade goods. At best it was a shaky marriage of convenience, and the outbreak of war between the Chickasaws and Creeks meant those two tribes could never effectively unite. Furthermore, European geopolitics would soon dictate an end to Carondelet's scheme.

Of more immediate concern to the Southwest Territory than Spanish intrigues was the resumption of large-scale Chickamauga and Creek attacks. Late in August 1793 several hundred Indians attacked Henry's Station near Knoxville, and the following month John Watts returned to the area leading a much larger force of Creek, Chickamauga, and Cherokee warriors. Militia and federal troops were dispersed, and the few defenders in Knoxville could not adequately protect the town from possible attack. But just as had happened the previous year, the Indians quarreled among themselves over strategy. They gave up the idea of attacking Knoxville and, instead, on September 25 besieged Alexander Cavet's nearby station, killing thirteen defenders, including those who surrendered. Quickly responding to the demands for revenge was none other than Nolichucky Jack—John Sevier, brigadier of the Washington District, Tennessee's most renowned Indian fighter, and a loyal though reluctant adherent of Knox's peace policy. At the call of acting governor Daniel Smith, Sevier led a retaliatory expedition of about seven hundred men southward and destroyed several Creek and Lower Cherokee towns near present-day Rome, Georgia. The foray ultimately cost the federal government more than $29,000, and the fact that it had happened in an unauthorized campaign against the Indians angered the Washington administration; for years it refused to pay Sevier's militiamen.

Since returning from Philadelphia in the fall of 1793, Blount had been mulling over his options. His inability to elicit more federal assistance and the growing chasm between himself and the Washington administration convinced him that the only hope for Tennessee and his own political ambitions was in statehood. Even though this would end his tenure as territorial governor, the new state legislature would probably reward his constant efforts to win support for his constituents by electing him United States senator. (The even more popular John Sevier would presumably become governor.) To promote statehood, Blount first had to authorize the long-delayed convening of a territorial assembly, for which there was growing popular agitation. He called for election of thirteen members of a house of representatives. In accordance with the terms of the Northwest Ordinance, each voter had to own at least fifty acres of land and each prospective representative two hundred acres. The members of the new house convened in Knoxville in February 1794 and promptly nominated ten men—each of whom owned at least five hundred acres—as candidates for the council, or upper house. Of these ten President Washington appointed five to serve: Stockley Donelson, Griffith Rutherford, John Sevier, Parmenas Taylor, and James Winchester.

At the February meeting the new representatives also petitioned for more federal protection, noting that in the preceding three years Indians had killed some two hundred whites and destroyed more than $100,000 worth of property. The congressional committee for territorial defense responded by advocating construction of permanent posts along the Indian border, but Secretary of War Knox, while agreeing Tennesseans were entitled to protection, said the government was preoccupied with General Anthony Wayne's campaign against the Northern tribes. For the time being, he called for a more active militia defense in the Mero District and limited federal assistance in the form of a six small howitzers and two hundred muskets.

The first full session of the house and council—the general assembly—began late in August 1794 and dealt with education, taxes, political and judicial procedures, the need for roads, preemption rights for settlers on Indian lands, and, as always, requests for federal assistance. Heeding a plea in the *Knoxville Gazette* that it "take measures that this Territory may, as speedily as possible, become a member State of the Federal Union," the assembly called for a census to be taken in July 1795, ostensibly to determine territorial apportionment but also to see if the territory had the sixty thousand free inhabitants necessary for statehood. The assembly also elected Dr. James White (no relation to Knoxville's founder) as the nonvoting territorial delegate to Congress. White was the first person to hold this position under the Northwest Ordinance, and Congress was at a loss as to whether to seat him in the Senate or the House—or at all. The final decision, to give him a nonvoting seat in the House without requiring an oath of office, established a precedent for all later delegates.

Indian depredations in East Tennessee meanwhile declined significantly, thanks in part to the few federal troops garrisoned in Knox County and to Hanging Maw's sincere efforts to promote a lasting peace. By November 1794 Blount wrote that the settlers there "enjoy an entire peace—The friendly Cherokees serve as a guard against the hostile Creeks." Farther west, however, Chickamauga and Creek warriors continued to harass the Mero District. Despite the danger, Blount cautioned James Robertson to keep expenditures to a minimum. Reminding Robertson that economy was a republican virtue, the governor noted that it was costing about four times as much to defend the Cumberland settlements as those on the Holston.

A new federal treaty of 1794 reduced misunderstandings with peaceable Cherokees but did not assuage Chickamauga hostility toward the Cumberland settlers. In the face of federal indifference, Robertson and other Mero leaders—with at least tacit assent from Blount—secretly prepared for preemptive strikes against the hostile towns. On September 13 a force of some 550 mounted troops, led by Major James Ore and under orders from Robertson, surprised and burned first Nickajack and then the larger Chickamauga town of Running Water. Robertson defiantly justified the unauthorized action, assumed full responsibility for it, and resigned as brigadier general of the Mero District. In his report to Henry Knox Blount professed surprise about the attack, but there is evidence that he was fully aware of Robertson's plans and perhaps even masterminded them.

Whatever its origins, Ore's successful expedition had consequences beyond even Robertson's and Blount's wildest dreams. The destruction of Nickajack and Running Water serendipitously coincided with reduced Spanish support for Indian hostilities in the South and with General Wayne's dramatic victory over Northern tribes at Fallen Timbers in Ohio. Within a year the Spanish would sign a treaty recognizing a United States boundary far south of Tennessee, largely removing Spain as a prop for Creek and Chickamauga warriors. Wayne's victory demonstrated an unsuspected American military might and freed federal soldiers for possible duty in the South. The cumulative effect of these events was to end Chickamauga, and indeed all Cherokee, military resistance to white American expansion. The Creeks continued to raid Middle Tennessee for another year, and Blount's appeal for a federal offensive against them was brusquely rebuffed by Timothy Pickering, Henry Knox's successor as secretary of war. When the Creeks finally ended their attacks, it was not because of federal intervention but mostly because of their ongoing war with the Chickasaws and the dwindling Spanish support. By mid-1795 white Tennessee had peace at last.

Any pleasure Blount may have taken from the Indian peace was offset by his growing rift with Pickering, who lacked confidence in the governor, doubted his honesty, and seized every opportunity to attack him. Pickering even instructed David Henley, the war department's agent in Knoxville, to report any irregularities on Blount's part. Like Knox, Pickering complained about Blount's lack of attention to Indian grievances, especially regarding white land encroachments. Pickering's indifference to the needs of the Southwest Territory perhaps reflected his privately stated belief that frontier settlers were "the least worthy subjects of the United States," an assessment shared by many of his Federalist colleagues, one of whom publicly derided them as "semi-savages." But people in the Southwest Territory were neither stupid nor even poorly informed; their delegate, Dr. White, kept them up to date on matters in Philadelphia. Congress's do-nothing policy regarding the territory and the Federalists' tone clearly signaled the federal lack of concern.

Statehood was the answer, but what next? Did the initiative lie with Congress or the local assembly? From his vantage point in Philadelphia, Dr. White predicted congressional inaction but believed the widening rift between Thomas Jefferson's Republicans and the entrenched Federalists might work to statehood's advantage. Republicans suggested to him that the Southwest Territory should seize the initiative and attempt to gain statehood in time to support Jefferson's election as president in 1796. If the upcoming census showed a sufficient population, and if residents of the territory demonstrated their wish to join the union, Blount should go ahead and call a constitutional convention. Afterward, in accordance with their new constitution, people in the territory could elect officers who would simply appear before Congress to request their admission as an already functioning state.

Blount, discredited by the Washington administration and disgusted with Federalist antagonism toward the Southwest Territory, was willing to seize the opportunity and become a Jeffersonian Republican. His first step was to call a special session of the territorial assembly in June 1795, three months earlier than scheduled, and inform its members that their major task was to work for statehood. The obliging legislators quickly approved Blount's proposal that the forthcoming census include a specific question asking whether adults favored statehood. Because it was thought that Congress might consider admitting a state with fewer than the sixty thousand free inhabitants specified by the Northwest Ordinance, the census takers would merely ask respondents if they favored statehood even with a lesser number. In the likely event that the total exceeded sixty thousand, Blount was authorized to direct voters in each of the eleven counties to select five representatives to meet in a constitutional convention. The lone dissenting legislator was Thomas Hardeman from Davidson County, who feared statehood would mean higher taxes and bring no certain benefits. After addressing a few other matters, the second territorial legislature adjourned after only thirteen days.

The sharply increased flow of people into the territory attending the diminution of Indian troubles ensured a sufficient population for statehood. The 1795 census listed a population of 77,262 non-Indians, including 10,613 slaves. The 66,649 free inhabitants included 973 free blacks; slaves and free blacks together represented 14.9 percent of the total population. The eight counties of the Washington and Hamilton districts had 65,338 free people, and the three counties of the Mero District had a population of 11,924. The census referendum revealed that 6,504 voters supported immediate statehood even if there were fewer than 60,000 free inhabitants, while 2,562 voted against statehood under such circumstances. All three of the Mero counties decisively opposed the proposition, probably because people there feared political domination by the much larger population of East Tennessee.

Blount lost no time authorizing December elections for delegates to a state constitutional convention to be held in Knoxville in January 1796. The newly elected delegates included such luminaries as Governor Blount, who served as president of the convention, Daniel Smith, James Robertson, Andrew Jackson, and other future state and national politicians. With single-minded purpose the delegates wrote a constitution in less than a month and then proclaimed it fully operational. The document borrowed selectively from the U.S. Constitution and the constitutions of North Carolina and Pennsylvania. It had a Declaration of Rights similar to the U.S. Bill of Rights but added the inherent right to free navigation of the Mississippi. After considerable discussion, the framers dropped their idea of a unicameral legislature and opted for a senate and house of representatives, both reapportioned every seven years. Each candidate for legislative office had to own at least two hundred acres of land in the county he represented. Ministers of the gospel were prohibited from holding office, but so were people who denied God's existence or a future state of reward and punishment. Creating a similarly strange dichotomy, the constitution granted free manhood suffrage to all white and all free black adult males, but dictated that holders of most state and local offices be elected by the legislature or by quarterly courts. The machinations of William Blount and other large speculators were evident in one of the most troubling provisions: that all land except town lots would be taxed at the same rate, regardless of their value. Much less controversial was the matter of naming the new state. Tennessee had been in common use since 1793, when Daniel Smith published his *Short Description of the Tennassee [sic] Government.*

Without awaiting federal assent, voters elected legislators for the first Tennessee General Assembly, which met in Knoxville on March 28. It must have given Blount great satisfaction to inform Timothy Pickering that the territorial government had been terminated and to request immediate admission of the new state. Blount and his fellow citizens of the Southwest Territory had seized the initiative, and now they awaited congressional response to what they hoped was a fait accompli. President Washington presented Congress with Tennessee's constitution and request for admission, but he made no recommendation. The Federalist majority in the Senate saw Tennessee's request as an election-year maneuver by the Jeffersonians to gain political strength, and they were determined to postpone admission at least until the next session of Congress, after the elections. They argued that the hastily drafted Tennessee document conflicted in several respects with the federal constitution, and they especially denounced the territorial census for its lack of federal supervision. They also claimed that the census included many nonresidents because it was taken during the fall when movement through the territory was at its peak. The inflated figures, they pointed out, would entitle the new state to two representatives, giving it a total of four electoral votes. Not surprisingly, an investigative committee headed by New York's Senator Rufus King, a Federalist, concluded on May 5 that the Southwest Territory was not yet qualified for admission as a new state.

In contrast, the Jeffersonian-controlled House of Representatives readily voted to admit Tennessee. When the senate refused to concur, the House offered a compromise: Congress would admit Tennessee but reduce its number of representatives to one until the federal census of 1800 redetermined its population. The Senate rejected this, too, and several Federalist leaders, realizing the session would end on June 1 and believing the admission issue had been decided, made the mistake of leaving Philadelphia early. After their departure, the Senate agreed on May 31 to a House request for an immediate conference committee meeting, which led that same day to congressional enactment of the admission bill. President Washington signed the legislation on June 1, the last day of the legislative session.

Thanks primarily to the efforts of her own citizens and the self-interested support of the Jeffersonians, Tennessee became the sixteenth state to join the union, and the first to do so under the terms of the Northwest Ordinance. The Federalists, however, had attempted to subvert the ordinance, which called for federal solicitude and guidance through a territory's colonial bondage and its prompt admission into the national polity. Federalist indifference to the Southwest Territory had helped to foster a defiant localism and initiative, a determination to gain statehood as a means of attending to the residents' distinctive needs. Tennesseans had gained a measure of political autonomy largely through their own efforts, and their future relations with the United States government would reflect both their skepticism and a sometimes none-too-enlightened self-interest.

7.

THE SOCIAL FABRIC

Prior to the Revolution, Tennessee was a meeting place of whites and Indians who generally interacted peaceably as long as there was a rough balance of power. Whites were basically transients in an Indian landscape—traders, soldiers, a few long hunters, and occasional odd-ball visionaries such as Alexander Cuming and Christian Gottlieb Priber. The relationship between the Indians and the whites was no mere dichotomy of exploiters and victims but rather a process of mutual accommodation and adaptation, a cultural negotiation of expediency in which both sides attempted to gain advantages and maintain varying degrees of autonomy. The intercultural fluidity even allowed African-Americans a modicum of opportunity within both Native American and white society.

Following the Revolution, this landscape rapidly vanished as accommodation became less necessary for whites. Indians quickly learned that United States sovereignty meant the end of British support, and hordes of new settlers appropriated vast tracts of lands. Neither limited Spanish support nor the stubborn resistance of Creeks and Chickamaugas could restore the rough military parity of earlier days. By the turn of the nineteenth century the Indians had been neatly cordoned off by treaty-imposed boundaries, and they were no longer the dominant concern of white Tennesseans. African-Americans were now shackled by an expanding plantation economy. The demise of older modes of accommodation and adaptation reflected significant changes within all of Tennessee's social components.

Before, during, and after the American Revolution, patterns of deference to elites carried over from the older colonial societies along the Atlantic seaboard. In upper East Tennessee individuals like James and Charles Robertson, Evan Shelby, John Carter, and John Sevier assumed a mantle of leadership that extended to almost every facet of life. Carter, for example, served as colonel of the Watauga militia, chairman of the Washington District's court, senator in the North Carolina legislature, land office official, and chairman of the first Washington County court. Sevier, William Cocke, and (for a time) the Robertsons were only slightly less prominent as public figures in the same jurisdiction. Evan Shelby and his clan, along with Joseph Martin, Gilbert Christian, and William Russell, had similar prominence in southwestern Virginia and Sullivan County, while men such as James Robertson, Daniel Smith and, later, Andrew Jackson dominated political, business, and military affairs in the Cumberland region.

The understandable popular interest in illustrious leaders obscures the fact that the deference to them of their social inferiors was always voluntary and conditional. A major theme of colonial society was the determination of white men of all ranks to gain personal independence—freedom from the will of others—and to create "improved" societies which would guarantee that freedom and its fruits, including the right of independent individuals to exploit dependent ones. Late colonial societies, including those of frontier Tennessee, were not the supposedly egalitarian, idealized systems of the 1820s and 1830s. Instead, they hearkened back to the ordered systems of an earlier period, but tended to rank people according to merit and achievement rather than family background or legal priviledge. Thus Tennessee's leaders were men of varied background whose common links were personal enterprise and accomplishment and who had gained the respect of other aspiring whites. Deference was earned, conditional, and always subject to dispute. Most Tennesseans were concerned with private rather than public matters and were willing to leave political leadership to their supposed betters as long as the government was authoritative but not very intrusive, and as long as it promoted economic and social improvement.

A similar attitude prevailed in the Tennesseans' home state of North Carolina, where the hierarchical social structure had to accommodate the desires of its lower-class citizens. Because the latter had an unusual degree of autonomy, aristocratic privilege often existed side by side with a spirit of yeoman independence. In North Carolina's backcountry, including Tennessee, frontier elites had undisputed sway only over those matters that the lower classes ignored or disdained. Both groups mostly tended to their own interests. This meant that political legitimacy and the institutions that upheld it were always tenuous at best; would-be leaders were required to seek a popular base of support. As militia colonel, James Robertson validated his own authority among Middle Tennesseans by defying federal authority and authorizing attacks on the Chickamauga towns. Likewise, Governor William Blount was ultimately more responsive to his territorial constituents than to the Washington administration because he realized just how conditional his local support was. The deference and obligation of classes was mutual. As Jack P. Greene notes, greatness for backcountry elites required them to be "the servant of all."

Few of Tennessee's leaders were born to wealth or prestige, and they varied widely in temperament, education, and ethnic origins. They also came from many colonies, but especially Virginia, North Carolina, and Pennsylvania. What they had in common was determination, ability, and an understanding of—and rapport with—their constituencies. Almost all were obsessed with Tennessee's economic prospects, and the cornerstone of their business ventures and the raison d'être for seeking political leadership was land speculation, an orientation which shaped their actions during the Revolution. That conflict was the litmus test for their pretensions to leadership. People supported the patriot or Whig cause in Tennessee not so much because of their ideological principles, but because they realized that loyalty to the Crown meant forfeiting claims to Indian lands that had been acquired in blatant disregard of British law. The inevitable alliance of the Cherokees with Britain threatened not only the whole concept of frontier gain and improvement, but also life itself. Because a majority of whites from all social levels aspired to hold their lands—and indeed to acquire more—leaders could employ force to ensure loyalty to the cause of independence. They flexed their patriotic muscles by requiring loyalty oaths, forcing individuals into military service, drumming loyalists out of the country, confiscating loyalists' property, and otherwise upholding the patriot cause.

Following the Revolution Tennessee's leaders worked with elites in North Carolina to take advantage of North Carolina's land grab legislation and amass enormous tracts of land, especially in the Cumberland region. William Blount's arrival as territorial governor simply formalized and legitimized multiple and sometimes conflicting alliances based on land speculation. This evolving pattern in turn necessitated even more political and legal domination by local elites. Although Tennessee still offered opportunities for ordinary settlers—otherwise leaders would have lacked any basis of authority—the area was a happy hunting ground for individuals with wealth, political connections, and the personal charisma necessary to inspire others to follow.

The pattern of conditional deference was especially apparent in the dangerous first few years of the Cumberland Association. James Robertson's personal courage and business acumen made him preeminent in prestige, but most of the men making up the first Court of Notables were squires who ranked between the ordinary settlers and major speculators like Robertson. The eleven judges who were elected to the court between 1780 and 1783 had all demonstrated their overall competence and had at various times been long hunters, farmers, millers, physicians, or lawyers. (Many of Tennessee's elites practiced law—hardly surprising considering the litigiousness of late eighteenth-century America.) They were men of modest means, and some owned a few slaves.

When North Carolina formally organized Davidson County in 1783, the Cumberland settlements became integrated into Tennessee's already well-established system of county courts. These courts had several basic functions: to protect life and property; keep the appropriate records; encourage economic development;

and create an orderly, moral system of control. A varying number of justices of the peace made up the court, and they were typically assisted by a sheriff, prosecutor, clerk, register, and members of juries. The justices depended on the laws of North Carolina, William Blackstone's *Commentaries on the Laws of England*, and their own sense of right and wrong. Financial support for the system came from a poll tax levied on adult males, a tax on land, and a variety of fines for every conceivable offense. Frequently there was no cash available, and taxpayers and county officials were forced to rely on promissory certificates or payment in agricultural products. It was a makeshift system, and a county that had an adequate courthouse was fortunate indeed. In the early years justices commonly met at a tavern or the home of a prominent citizen. Their quarterly meetings were occasions for people from the surrounding area to gather for business and socializing.

The justices of the peace attended to almost every facet of local life: adjudicating legal cases; setting rates for ferries, taverns, mills, bed and board, and other economic activities; registering stock marks (usually distinctive slits in the animals' ears); offering bounties for wolves; appointing supervisors of new road districts; and improvising a rude system of public assistance for orphans, the mentally incompetent, and others who lacked family or means. The court records offer tantalizing insights into community values. In 1799, for example, Robertson County imposed poll taxes of six and one-quarter cents on whites, twelve and one half cents on blacks; taxed stud horses twenty-five cents each; and levied a whopping $6.25 on billiard tables, normally found only in taverns. In 1802 Sumner County taxed the tables at $10 each, twice the normal fine for assault and battery. Penalties in bastardy cases involved fines for both the woman and man (if known) and parental indemnification to the county for all charges and expenses incurred in raising the child. The court also routinely appointed guardians for orphans or bound them as apprentices to tradespeople. As Michael Toomey notes, the justices appeared to be firmly committed both to economical government and the well-being of county residents.

Failing to appear for jury duty, swearing, and other minor offenses brought small fines, but major crimes like horse theft and murder posed a problem because few counties had an adequate jail for lengthy incarcerations. A whipping post and public stocks were less expensive civic improvements, and public humiliation and physical punishment could be very effective. In Knox County one convicted horse thief received thirty-nine lashes on his bare back, had his ears nailed to the pillory and then cut off, and was branded with the letter *H* on one cheek and the letter *T* on the other. A murderer might be hanged or branded with the letter *M*.

Sometimes the loss of body parts did not signify criminal tendencies. Disfiguration could be a meritorious souvenir from "rough and tumble," the most spectacular and famous of all forms of frontier brawling. As its participants prepared for battle, they stirred the emotions of spectators with tales of their physical prowess and past victories and strove to destroy the self-esteem of their foes. The normal rules were no rules at all. Combatants could kick, bite, scratch, gouge, and chew one another until one of them gave up. It was common for a rough and tumbler to grow his fingernails long and toughen them up, the better to gouge out an opponent's eye. Some boasted of ripping out testicles ("abalarding" the opponent) or biting off noses or ears.

The more genteel observers of rough and tumble expressed horror and indignation but were nonetheless morbidly fascinated. Their sometimes exaggerated accounts echoed the boasts of the combatants and imparted a mythic quality to the mayhem. What few people could have appreciated at the time was that these contests validated the personal worth of individuals who stood apart from "respectable" society and lacked any other means of winning recognition. For a combatant a missing eye or ear might be a badge of honor. Others, however, might assume that they lacked certain body parts because they had been punished for criminal behavior. Thus deponents sometimes testified in court as to their losses in fights, and their claims were often corroborated by their rough and tumble conquerors.

Rough and tumble had a quasi legitimacy because it was an agreed upon contest, but assault and battery was a different matter. Official reaction to the offense often depended on the circumstances. In 1796 after Isaac Brown attacked James Stuart at a Robertson County race track, the two men stripped, went out in public, and fought "to the Terror of the good Citizens of this State & Against the peace & Dignity of our sd State." Brown was found guilty and fined six cents. The court could not condone the initial assault, but perhaps the small fine reflected the fact that both men had fought willingly afterward. In any case, the affront to Tennessee's dignity and to James Stuart's person was deemed a minor matter.

County courts were often dominated by lower-level elites— the petite bourgeoisie—but the influence of more prominent men was evident at the next highest level, that of representative to the state legislature. During the 1780s seven of the eight North Carolina representatives from the Nashville region were large-scale speculators; four of them were William Blount's collaborators. Elites were also prominent among the twenty-four Davidson County justices of the peace appointed by the legislature between 1783 and 1788. Among them was Daniel Smith, engineer, surveyor, and a graduate of William and Mary. Like Robertson, Smith would quickly emerge as a prominent leader in the Southwest Territory and the state of Tennessee.

Andrew Jackson was ideally suited to this milieu. Born in 1767 and educated in the law at Salisbury, North Carolina, he had the good fortune to have prominent friends like John McNairy, who in 1787 was chosen by the North Carolina legislature to be Superior Court judge for the Cumberland District. McNairy appointed Jackson prosecutor for the district, and in the spring of 1788 the two men and several others crossed the mountains and traveled as far as Jonesborough, where they stayed several months before continuing on to Nashville. In Jonesborough the young Jackson practiced law, attended several horse races, and, a bit insecure and defensive about his humble origins, played the gentleman. His volatile sense of honor prompted him to challenge Waightstill Avery to a duel. Avery was a prominent North Carolinian who frequently visited Jonesborough as state attorney, and he and Jackson served both honor and common sense by firing their pistols simultaneously into the air.

When Jackson finally arrived in Nashville in October 1788, he quickly became a major figure in local society and perhaps the

Frontier Rough and Tumble. Woodcut from The
Crockett Almanac, 1840 (Nashville, 1840). PHOTOGRAPH
REPRODUCED COURTESY OF LILLY LIBRARY, INDIANA UNIVERSITY.

hardest-working lawyer in what was now the Mero District. He
served as district attorney, often without pay, and handled a mul-
titude of cases in all three counties of the district; he was involved
in nearly one-half of all cases in Davidson County during his first
few years there and once he argued all thirteen cases on the
docket. Jackson's most lucrative work was collecting debts owed
to some of the prominent creditors of Mero. He quickly strove to
ingratiate himself with men like Robertson and Smith, and, as

expected for all would-be elites, he also assumed an active role in militia campaigns against the Indians.

When Governor Blount selected officials to serve in the South-west Territory, he cultivated the allegiance of Robertson, Smith, and Jackson, winning the latter's loyalty by appointing him attorney general of the Mero District. Among Jackson's responsibilities was prosecuting settlers who trespassed on Indian lands or otherwise violated federal treaties. Meanwhile he expanded his thriving legal business, developed a voracious appetite for land speculation, traded regularly in the Spanish Natchez District, and purchased a number of slaves. He also acquired a debt that would haunt him for years. In ironic counterpoint to his later national reputation, Jackson would become the quintessential frontier elite. In this respect he had much in common with his older counterpart, John Sevier, but the two would soon discover that Tennessee was too small a stage to share.

John Sevier was of French and English stock. His Huguenot grandfather had fled religious persecution in France and settled in England, where he anglicized the family name of Xavier to Sevier. He married an English woman, and two of their sons came to America around 1740 while they were still young. One son, Valentine, settled in the Shenandoah Valley, married, and founded New Market, Virginia. John, the oldest of Valentine's seven children, was born in September 1745. He married at age sixteen and acquired an easy ability to get along with people of all social classes and to handle every danger of frontier life. Exactly when he and his father moved to Tennessee is unclear, but they were on the Holston and then the Watauga by the early 1770s. On the Watauga and later the Nolichucky, John quickly distinguished himself as a natural leader. His courage and coolness at King's Mountain impressed many, as did his compassion, sense of justice, and ability to deflect men from excesses. After countenancing the execution of nine convicted Tories, he and Evan Shelby had intervened to save the rest of the condemned captives.

But Nolichucky Jack was best known for his prowess in fighting Cherokees. Encouraging his followers to whoop like Indians as they plunged into battle, he led thirty or more campaigns against the Cherokees, won them all, and was reimbursed for only one. While he was governor of Franklin Sevier could be devious and aggressive in acquiring Indian lands, but that was what frontier speculators did. Later, as six-time governor of Tennessee, he advocated still more cessions of land while remaining diplomatically correct toward the Indians, professing his friendship and dispensing frequent doses of advice to them. The patriarch of a large extended clan, including his own eighteen children, Sevier became the most famous politician-soldier of early Tennessee. He was also something of a dandy: handsome, urbane, fond of fine clothes, food, drink, and life itself. Most frontier whites loved Nolichucky Jack, and many Indians at least respected him. Andrew Jackson, however, came to despise him, perhaps because Sevier was too much like himself—a man of the people, and much more.

Below the upper class, of course, were whites of more modest standing who represented the majority of the backcountry population and who sometimes aspired to be elites. They were a mixed group in terms of background, status, and ideology. British and colonial officials had unfairly referred to many of the earliest settlers as fugitives from justice, offscourings of humanity, or rabble and complained about their frequent trespasses on Cherokee land. Frontier elites—in private, at least—occasionally used the same terms in describing them. During the Revolution some of these settlers were loyalists, threatening backwoods autonomy and making themselves convenient targets. Their alleged predations and possible alliance with Dragging Canoe led backcountry leaders to create vigilance organizations which tracked them down, punished them—even executing a few—and drove others away. After the creation of Washington County and the appointment of upper class officials, this persecution received political and legal reinforcement. Like most American vigilance movements, those in frontier Tennessee were bourgeois in origin, led by prominent men who knew that disorder threatened property as well as lives and ideological principles.

Like their social and economic betters, common folk came to Tennessee primarily for land. Imbued with a homestead ethic rooted in the notion that land ownership was essential to personal independence, and buttressed by a long-evolving Southern tradition of squatter rights, they believed that a man should be able to acquire family-size "vacant" tracts in the backcountry simply by occupying and working them. But how many acres were necessary for each family? Many Western Virginians believed four hundred acres was an appropriate number, though few could resist the impulse to acquire property beyond their immediate needs. Despite their frequent protests against large-scale speculators, even the lowest-ranking white settlers more often than not were themselves speculators; scale of enterprise was all that separated them from the economic elites. Their attachment to a particular place, like their loyalty to a particular leader, was not deeply rooted, and it was common for these settler-speculators to move about. An analysis of the census and tax lists for certain Washington County districts suggests that the steadily growing population there resulted more from immigration than from residential persistence and natural increase. Indeed, beginning in the early 1790s, over half of the individuals listed on each tax list were missing from the next. They might have moved elsewhere within the state—from East Tennessee to the Cumberland, for example—or to frontiers far beyond. The Hardeman family provides a classic example of this migratory pattern. Thomas Hardeman, a prominent businessman and political leader, was the patriarch of a clan that settled on the Watauga, then the Cumberland, and eventually in Missouri, New Mexico, Texas, Oregon, and other areas west of the Mississippi. In many ways the Hardemans were a microcosm of America's pioneer rootlessness.

Not all whites belonged to Tennessee's rural landholding majority. Some worked as tenants or hired hands in the countryside, while many others were confirmed town dwellers who found their opportunities on the urban frontier, in the new communities of Jonesborough, Greeneville, Knoxville, Nashville, or, later, Memphis. There was also an amorphous, transient group who contented themselves with hunting and made only haphazard attempts at farming. Some were former long hunters, like Daniel Boone in Kentucky, who lacked either the expertise or sustained will to acquire property and develop it over a period of years. Instead, they might drift off in search of other lands, other Xanadus, ultimately achieving stardom in the mythic drama of the American frontier. Others were simply hardscrabble, near-lawless men who, like the long hunters, were archaic remnants of an earlier time.

White and mixed-blood traders like John McDonald among the Cherokees and James Colbert among the Chickasaws were prestigious carry-overs from the intercultural accommodation of the earlier period. They put the war behind them, offered allegiance to the United States, and continued to shape affairs within their constituencies. McDonald's grandson, John Ross, who was only one-eighth Indian by blood, would become the most prominent of all Cherokee leaders during the nineteenth century. Nancy and Bryan Ward's daughter Elizabeth married Joseph Martin, Virginia's representative to the Cherokees, and thereby brought him into the web of relationships constituting the powerful Wolf clan. Another of the Wards' daughters also married a trader. These attachments were often casual and reflected the serial monogamy common among Cherokee women. Both Joseph Martin and Bryan Ward later returned to their white families, who were friendly toward—or at least resigned to—the Cherokee women. Nancy Ward was always welcome in her former husband's South Carolina household.

The Cherokee-related traders and their offspring served as cultural bridges, or brokers, between the races, but during troubled times their roles were often ambiguous. The man who perhaps best reflects this is Nathaniel Gist, who had helped establish the first white settlements in Fincastle County, Virginia, but also spent long periods as a trader among the Cherokees. He was accused of robbing fellow whites in Indian country, and yet sometimes he served honorably in colonial militia units. During the Revolution, when Gist appeared under a flag of truce as a Cherokee emissary to William Christian's advancing army, Christian's men had to be restrained from killing him. Afterward Gist's friend George Washington appointed him an officer of the Continental line. Gist was presumably the father of Sequoyah, another famous product of a Cherokee-white union. Sequoyah's loyalty to his mother's people was never in doubt, and he is renowned for his attempts to preserve Cherokee culture by adopting from whites what he considered their most important advantage: a system of writing.

Like the rest of white America, the Tennessee frontier was a man's realm; men dominated in the political, economic, and social spheres. In the hagiographic literature of the frontier, women usually appear in the Madonna Persona—as saintly mothers, wives, and daughters who sometimes, through force of dire circumstance, snatch up the weapons of their fallen men and repel the Indian hordes or confront other dangers. They are domestic heroines celebrated by courthouse statues throughout America and in special chapters of books by filiopietistic authors who feel an obligation to include women in what to them is basically a story of masculine conquest. Even the Cherokees, who accorded women an authoritative role in tribal society, attached special significance to the story of Nancy Ward, who fought against the Creeks in a dramatic battle that had already claimed the life of her warrior husband. She became a famous War Woman and later a Beloved Woman. Because she occasionally saved white captives from death, Tennessee's first historian refashioned the Madonna Persona motif by likening her to Pocahontas.

Another frontier woman whose role became mythologized is Catherine "Bonny Kate" Sherrill. According to legend, she was surprised by Indians outside Fort Watauga and barely escaped because John Sevier shot her closest pursuer and helped her over the fortress walls. When Sevier's wife died a few years later, he married Bonny Kate, threw a big wedding celebration, and then headed off to King's Mountain. The story of Sherrill's narrow escape from death and her marriage to Sevier was already well known when Theodore Roosevelt related it in *The Winning of the West*, and like the stories about Nancy Ward, the tale has become a staple of Tennessee folklore. Bonny Kate showed pluck and resourcefulness in escaping, but her real fame derives from Sevier's helping hand and proposal of marriage. Having displayed her mettle, Bonny Kate acceded to her proper role of helpmate and mother; she assumed the Madonna Persona. Another variation on this motif is the genuine heroism and endurance of the women participating in John Donelson's famous boat trip to Nashborough. They staved off Indians, helped muscle their craft over shoals, tended the ailing and wounded, and, along with their children, sometimes died.

The danger of the Madonna Persona is that it obscures the more fundamental reality of women's role on the American frontier. As always, women performed varied functions. They married, bore and raised children, farmed, tended livestock, cooked, provided all the other services expected of a frontier helpmate, and yes, on occasion took up weapons to repel Indian attacks. But usually theirs was a quiet role that was shaped by custom and seldom challenged by the women themselves. If there happened to be a store in the area, a married woman might have authority to do business there, but it was more likely that her husband handled the majority of even those responsibilities. An East Tennessee account book for 1800–1801 lists just 29 women and blacks out of a total of 374 customers. In the realm of law, women were clearly subordinate and in some ways suffered even more discrimination than free black males. Women could neither vote nor hold certain kinds of property. They were seldom mentioned in early court records except when they were licensed to run inns, when they were witnesses or administrators of their dead spouses' estates, or when they were mothers of "base born" or "bastard" children.

As far as the law was concerned, women were basically possessions of their husbands, a status leaving them little recourse should their home life deteriorate. Most had no choice but to tolerate the intolerable. A divorce could be obtained only through legislation, a costly, time-consuming, and problematic process. The first time the state of Tennessee granted a woman a divorce was in 1797. Desertion was a common method used by both husbands and wives to get out of unpleasant relationships, and it was often cited by husbands as justification for a legislative divorce. The most famous case of marital discord on the Tennessee frontier involved Andrew Jackson's wife Rachel and her first husband. When he left her, it was unclear whether he envisioned a permanent separation. It is also unclear whether Rachel and Andrew Jackson knew when they married that her first husband had not yet obtained a divorce from the state of Virginia. The bigamy haunted Jackson's later political career.

The customs, names, and languages of early Tennesseans reflect a mosaic of ethnic and national identities. Few of the settlers, however, had come directly from Europe; most of their families had been in America for two or three generations. During the 1770s, when families typically followed the Valley of Virginia to the Holston or the Watauga, the English heritage was predominant among newcomers. Also important were Scots-Irish families like the Robertsons that arrived from North Carolina and other colonies. Generations of fighting Irish Catholics, coupled with a stern Presbyterian Calvinism, had conditioned these people to a sometimes hostile New World environment, and some considered the Indians to be red-skinned Catholics. The Scots-Irish influence was strong, but some scholars have gone to absurd lengths in trying to prove a more pervasive Celtic culture. Others have stressed the impact of sober, industrious, and pious German-speaking settlers from the Rhineland, including some of the signers of the Cumberland Compact, or the influence of subgroups like the Moravians and Quakers. And what are we to make of Daniel Boone's Quaker origins?

But even while discussing major national, religious, or ethnic groups, we have to acknowledge that many individuals, such as John Sevier, of French Huguenot descent, and Welshman Evan Shelby, fall into the ethnic category of "other." There were many more such people than we sometimes assume, and they defy any neat language-defined or national categories. When describing German-speaking peoples, for example, we automatically think of Protestant peasants from the Rhineland, not such individuals as Christian Gottlieb Priber and William Gerard de Brahm. Priber, a free-thinking German communist and suspected Jesuit, had planned to establish the Kingdom of Paradise among the Cherokees in the 1730s. De Brahm was more sensible but no less imposing. Born a Roman Catholic in southern Germany in 1717, he had an excellent education and became a military engineer for Holy Roman Emperor Charles VII. Renouncing Catholicism, he came to America and was employed by the British to supervise construction of Fort Loudoun in 1756, just one facet of a remarkable life. Louis De Vorsey Jr. describes de Brahm as "a man whose versatility of genius went beyond even that of the typical

eighteenth-century dilettante: a surveyor, engineer, botanist, as-
tronomer, meteorologist, student of ocean currents, alchemist,
sociologist, historian and mystical philosopher."

The French were also well represented in early Tennessee,
with delegations of traders or soldiers periodically visiting the Overhill Towns or building temporary fortifications on the Chickasaw Bluffs. Their visits and permanent outposts and towns on the
fringes of Tennessee made them the European "other" of greatest
concern to the British until the end of the French and Indian
War. Well after the war French-speaking hunters, traders, and
boatmen from the Illinois Country and Vincennes were active
along the Cumberland and Tennessee rivers.

Whatever their origins, most of the whites who settled in Tennessee exhibited certain common cultural patterns. Though they
hardly constituted a frontier melting pot, neither were they so
disparate in their ways as to validate the metaphor of a frontier
salad bowl with separate and distinct ingredients. The cement
that bound almost all frontier groups together in an American
pioneer culture was threefold: the desire to obtain land in order
to secure and safeguard personal independence; incessant demands upon political and social systems to help secure that land;
and broadly similar patterns of adapting to the environment.

One recent argument is that pioneer culture emerged from
predominantly Finnish and Indian influences. The heartland of
this culture was the Delaware River Valley, where seventeenth-
century Swedish colonization included many native Finns who
had come from an area remarkably similar to that of the Delaware. The Finns were preadapted to the vast mesothermal forests. Their institutions had evolved until they were so well-
attuned to the environment that members of much larger ethnic
groups, including the Scots-Irish, incorporated Finnish patterns
into a common pioneering lifestyle. These patterns were supplemented by important adaptive strategies adopted from American
Indians, especially the Delawares.

Supporters of this argument downplay other influences and
claim too much for a Finnish-based pioneer culture, but they are
persuasive in their identification of certain features common to
American pioneer, Indian, and Finnish cultures. Tennessee's

slash-and-burn agriculture, for example, combines elements found in both Finnish and Native American societies, and the wormwood pattern of fencing so typical of trans-Appalachian pioneer settlements is nearly identical to a much earlier type common in Finland. Wormwood fencing required enormous amounts of wood and by today's standards was extravagantly wasteful. In the vast forests of Scandinavia and frontier Tennessee, however, it made economic sense, and there were few alternative forms of fencing. Perhaps the most convincing argument for this cultural influence involves the distinctive style of log cabin architecture that is found in Tennessee and many other parts of the woodland frontier, a mirror image of that in Finland. Even the famous dog-trot or open-passage style of cabin, consisting of two identical cabins connected by an open, roofed breezeway, had earlier equivalents in Finland. Most distinctive of all as a diagnostic trait is the V-pattern notching of logs that is common in both Tennessee and Finland.

Even if we acknowledge the connections between Finnish and pioneer American cultures, it seems most sensible to conclude that the latter was a composite of elements derived from several European and Native American sources. Whether discussing political institutions or backcountry housing, farming, herding, or ballads, it is hard to deny English, Scots-Irish, and a general Celtic influence. And the Cherokee and Chickasaw contribution to Tennessee's frontier culture is apparent in place names, foodstuffs, the roads of white commerce that originated as Indian trails, and an incredible variety of useful knowledge. For example, the Cherokees used and traded ginseng long before whites sought it out, and pioneer families acquired their knowledge of other medicinal plants from Indian neighbors. Native American contributions to the pioneer diet, especially corn, are so basic that they are almost forgotten. And sometimes Indians acted as cultural filters, taking an item from one European group, adapting it to the local environment, and passing it on to other Europeans. Peaches are a classic example. Southern Indians acquired them from the Spanish, made them an essential part of their domestic economy, and passed them on to white settlers, who also came to depend on them. American pioneer culture, then, was a mosaic of cultural patterns from varied sources that, taken together, enabled people to survive and perhaps even to prosper.

The powerful continuity of culture is reflected in almost every aspect of the daily lives of Tennessee settlers. They brought with them well-defined notions of proper governance and behavior and a desire to recreate many features of their previous lives, but in improved form. They wished to maintain cultural and economic links with their former homes east of the Appalachians and with the world beyond the Atlantic. They were hungry for news from those worlds, though the mail from Philadelphia usually took from three to eight weeks to arrive. Frontier life might force them to accept a lower standard of living, but that circumstance was expected to be temporary, for there was a common optimism that life in Tennessee would someday be better than life back east. In the meantime, families brought with them many tangible, meaningful mementos of their previous life, all affirmations of a cherished culture. Some unfortunates lacked almost any personal possessions, but most brought guns, tools, and a few head of livestock—the capital goods of pioneer farming. The "better sort" might also own a slave or two; a few pieces of silverware, pewter, or furniture; and books, most often the Bible, but also the classics. On special occasions a wealthier individual might even wear well-tailored clothes, with a watch, buckle, broach, or other accessories. (John Sevier was much enamored of fine style.)

Generally ignored in most discussions of pioneer culture are the slaves who made up the bottom stratum of frontier society. In the earliest years a slave was usually referred to as someone's Negro or servant. The slaves' backwoods masters treated them familiarly, and often counted them as trusted friends—socially inferior, yes, but friends nonetheless. Black men and women were unsung participants in every phase of early Tennessee history. Slaves accompanied Hernando de Soto, Christian Priber, and almost every trader heading to the Overhill Towns. One slave, Abram, performed heroic service as a messenger between the besieged Fort Loudoun and Charleston. Another, Jamie, accompanied James Smith on his 1766 return from the Cumberland, extracted a sharp piece of cane lodged in Smith's foot, gathered medicinal items, built a shelter, and helped hunt buffalo and cure the meat. For three months he was Smith's only human contact. During the Revolution, slaves helped to defend frontier posts and like their masters suffered scalping and death. James Robertson's faithful servant died on the Cumberland in an Indian attack, and his female slave protected his children during another. John Sevier's trusted servant, Toby, rode at his side in campaigns against the Cherokees. Black slaves were among John Donelson's passengers on the *Adventure* as they made their perilous voyage down the Tennessee, and they helped to construct some of the first homes on the Cumberland and Stones rivers.

The 1791 census of the Southwest Territory recorded 3,417 black slaves, less than 10 percent of the 35,691 non-Indian residents. In contrast, slaves already accounted for 16.5 percent of the population of the Mero District, the area best suited to commercial agriculture. Davidson County had the second highest number of slaves of any county; they represented 19 percent. But slavery was at a low ebb in the revolutionary era, and at the turn of the century race relations were more relaxed and fluid in Tennessee than in the Tidewater South, no doubt because blacks were a small minority and plantation agriculture had yet to take firm root. Men like James Robertson thought nothing of working side by side in the fields with blacks. Slavery seemed to be more of an incidental social arrangement than a pervasive aspect of the economy. True, leaders like William Blount and Andrew Jackson bought and sold slaves, and black chattels were often mentioned in probate inventories, but personal attachments between master and servant were still common. As in other parts of the South, slaves sometimes attended the same churches as whites or even became members of the congregations. They were also among the best jockeys on race courses throughout the South. One of them, a hunch-backed dwarf called Monkey Simon, was a fixture at the Nashville and nearby Clover Bottoms race tracks. He rode Jesse Haynie's formidable mare, Maria, to victories over a series of Andrew Jackson's horses (Jackson himself had several jockeys and a trainer who were slaves.) Simon felt secure enough in his prowess and self-worth to tease the general, who later remarked that one of his few regrets in life was not winning a race against Maria with Monkey Simon aboard.

Though Tennessee adopted North Carolina's restrictive manumission laws, it was not uncommon for early slave owners to free their property. During the first decade of statehood a number of antislavery advocates, often employing the rhetoric of morality and revolutionary patriotism, petitioned the legislature to pass more liberal manumission legislation. One such advocate was William Calvert, who in 1804 invoked humanitarian principle in seeking permission from the Washington County court to free several slaves once they had reached adulthood. Calvert insisted, however, that the slaves first compensate him for the costs of their rearing. And the 1796 state constitution tacitly acknowledged the citizenship of African-Americans by allowing free black males to vote and hold certain kinds of property.

These comparatively liberal sentiments persisted in Tennessee for many years, especially in the mountainous eastern sections where plantation slavery would never take hold. Some of the nation's earliest and most famous antislavery crusaders lived there, including Elihu Embree and Benjamin Lundy, both Quakers, and John Rankin, a Presbyterian. But theirs were voices increasingly dampened amid the rising tide of proslavery sentiment. With the end of the Indian wars and the influx of white settlers, slavery began to assume more ominous dimensions. By 1800, the number of slaves had risen to 13,584, nearly 13 percent of the state's population. In Davidson County alone, the slave population rose from 992 in 1795 to 6,305 in 1810, when they represented 40 percent of the total population of 15,608. (Free blacks numbered 130.) As commercial agriculture became increasingly important in Middle Tennessee and as West Tennessee opened, plantation slavery became firmly entrenched.

While it is easy to exaggerate the impact of religion on the daily lives of settlers, most backcountry residents at least unwittingly subscribed to emerging sectarian doctrines that reflected important frontier values. Most would also profess horror at Catholicism, the great bogeyman of Protestant America. For years Timothe de Monbruen was probably the only Catholic in Nashville. The Scots-Irish background of so many early settlers meant that Presbyterianism would be prominent, and that denomination's ministers were certainly the best educated. Samuel Doak, a Presbyterian minister and graduate of Princeton, established a school at his church near Jonesborough and shortly afterward invoked the sword of Gideon as he sent the over-mountain men off to King's Mountain. In 1785 Doak's Princeton classmate, the Reverend Thomas Craighead, established Nashville's Davidson Academy and in 1794 the territorial legislature chartered the Reverend Samuel Carrick's seminary, called Blount College, in Knoxville. Despite its name, Carrick's school was nothing more than a secondary academy. It would undergo various incarnations over many years before becoming The University of Tennessee. Remarkably, its early students included five young women, among them the daughter of Governor Blount.

Despite the Presbyterians' initial advantage with Scots-Irish settlers, their stern, uncompromising Calvinism and insistence on a well-educated ministry were not as well suited to frontier conditions as the theology and polity of some rival denominations. Notable among them were the Baptists, who arrived in Tennessee at the same time as the Presbyterians. The Baptists believed formal education was unnecessary if a man were called by God to preach, and often such untutored souls could speak a theology more direct and intelligible to backcountry residents than that of their Princeton-educated counterparts. Many frontier people liked the less structured organization of the Baptists, who preferred self-governing congregations to presbyteries, synods, or dioceses. Backcountry people increasingly wanted a religious autonomy that would match the personal independence they sought in their daily lives.

Speaking much the same message of personal autonomy were the Methodists, who arrived in Tennessee only a few years after the Baptists and Presbyterians. Their ministers generally had more education than the former and less than the latter. Like the Presbyterians, they had more organization and doctrinal structure than the Baptists, but their Arminian doctrine of free will and of people's capacity to achieve their own salvation suited the burgeoning new nation and especially its frontier citizens west of the

Appalachians. The Methodists also had an institution uniquely suited to spreading the gospel: the circuit rider, that fabled preacher who wore out countless steeds galloping from one isolated congregation to another in a predictable pattern of service to God and the faithful.

The first Methodist circuit rider to appear in Tennessee was Jeremiah Lambert in 1783, followed shortly thereafter by the most famous circuit rider of all. He was Francis Asbury, who had arrived in America in 1771 and stayed by his American flock through the Revolution. With the right combination of steel and compromise, he eventually emerged as the leader of American Methodism. He was ordained a bishop in 1784 but was not the sort of man to leave frontier proselytizing exclusively to his subordinates. Until the end of his life in 1816 he was the quintessential circuit rider, and Tennessee had many sinners who needed saving. Asbury made some sixty trips on horseback west of the Appalachians and usually included Tennessee on his itinerary. He was querulous and difficult, fixated on God and salvation, but he did pause from time to time to reflect on Tennessee and its frontier population. His complaints were legion: sleeping three to a bed in a backwoods cabin, being devoured by fleas, traveling the state's impossible roads, crossing the same stream twenty or more times a day, and facing harassment by frontier skeptics. Worst of all, as he admitted in 1797, "not one in a hundred" came to the trans-Appalachian backcountry to get religion; most came "rather to get plenty of good land," a fixation that would likely cost them their souls.

The crassness and materialism of such a people challenged Asbury's best efforts in his struggle with Satan, and he sometimes saw himself as literally a voice crying in the wilderness. Though there were always individuals of sterling character on the frontier whose hospitality he gratefully acknowledged, many others were "hardened" people who proved to be flinty soil indeed for the nourishment of Christian precepts. In Tennessee, for example, he spent a night with a distiller and could not resist the temptation (he probably did not try) to lecture him on the evils of demon liquor and slavery. The distiller took offense that a guest should presume to instruct him in the ways of righteousness. Besides, he said, the bishop preached so loudly that others in the house objected.

Asbury's pessimism regarding salvation on the frontier dissipated with the blossoming of the Second Great Awakening around the turn of the century. As part of this phenomenon, the Reverend James McGready, a Presbyterian, initiated the frontier camp meeting, or revival, where people would gather from miles around to spend anywhere from a night to a week or so listening to hell-fire and damnation sermons and joyfully experiencing the presence of God. The camp meeting was both a religious and a social experience, and it softened the sharp edges of frontier materialism and self-absorption. Asbury's Methodists were quick to use their talent for organization to develop the camp revival into its most effective form. Emotions ran high. One of the earliest revival meetings in Tennessee, in the fall of 1800 at Drake's Creek in Sumner County, attracted a thousand people over a five day period. Even as mainline Presbyterians backed away from the revivals because of their emotionalism, Methodists and Baptists extolled them as the "harvest time" for wretched souls. Who besides Presbyterians cared if these meetings lacked sophistication and reasoned theology? Some Tennessee Presbyterians agreed and split from the majority of their denomination to organize themselves as the Cumberland (or New-Light) Presbyterians.

A number of witnesses commented on the "falling exercises" of camp-meeting revivalism: shaking, jerking, rolling, screaming, barking, and speaking in tongues. The jerking exercise may have originated among the Methodists of East Tennessee, and they sometimes affected every worshiper present. Peter Cartwright, a famous preacher, noted with satisfaction that he had seen more than five hundred people at a time convulsing in ecstasy. Asbury did not consider such displays of enthusiasm to be sufficient evidence of conversion, but he believed the joy of the Holy Spirit was commendable as long as order was maintained. Yet it was difficult to encourage religious emotions while restraining other feelings. At some camps guards patrolled the premises at night to break up love trysts and to otherwise maintain Christian decorum. Though the fervor of camp meetings gradually subsided, the revivals continued to be a part of Tennessee backcountry religion for many years, a proof that good land and religion were not necessarily incompatible.

Tennessee Indians meanwhile were undergoing their own social changes, mostly in reaction to those among whites and African-Americans. If one likens the fabric of Tennessee society to a patchwork quilt, Native Americans represented less and less of the overall pattern while interlocking white and black patches limned new images and pushed the red to the margins. But the Cherokees were not helpless. Since 1700, when they had become part of a world economy, they had creatively rewoven their social and political fabric into patterns better designed to help them cope. For two or three generations, through realpolitik and cultural syncretism, they had ingeniously delayed the consequences of dependency. With the end of their military resistance in the mid-1790s, and amid unceasing threats to their lands, they continued to reshape their identity to enable them to blend traditional ways and values with those brought by whites and African-Americans. The institution of slavery is a case in point. Traditionally Cherokees had captured and enslaved other Indians. Sometimes they adopted these slaves as clan members, in which case they were no longer chattels. Those without clan protection remained slaves, people without identity. Because there was no capitalist incentive to accumulate surplus products for the market, there was no need to work them very hard. Slaves still had an important role in tribal society because, lacking clan affiliation, they were social deviants whose very presence reaffirmed to Cherokees the importance of their own kinship system.

With the advent of European trade, the economic significance of slaves became apparent to the Cherokees, and they and other Southeastern Indians captured one another for sale to Carolinians in exchange for goods. When African slaves became common in South Carolina, Indians quickly became familiar with them and learned their value. A major concern of Southerners was the possibility that black and red people would unite against whites, so slave owners attempted to make the two groups fearful and suspicious of one another. They offered lavish rewards to Indians for the recovery of escaped slaves and then systematically instilled in blacks a fear of the Indians. Despite this, Cherokees came to realize that they shared certain attitudes and values with blacks—a reverent linking of the spiritual and environmental worlds, for example, and the deep mythology and symbolism attached to animals. Indeed, those attitudes and beliefs may have been shaped and reinforced by the early interaction of Indian women and African male slaves. At least as early as 1540 black slaves on the de Soto expedition were having sexual relations with Native American women. The Spaniards had taken hostage the "Lady of Cofitachequi," the paramount leader of a Mississippian chiefdom in South Carolina, but she soon escaped and began cohabiting with a fugitive black slave. Other slaves who escaped at about the same time were supposedly "infatuated with native women." Later, during the Indian wars of the eighteenth century, whites were more likely to spare and enslave Indian women and children than warriors. Most of the imported African slaves, on the other hand, were males, and sexual unions between them and Indian women became common. Therefore, it has been suggested, certain features of African-American slave culture may be Indian in origin; the matrilineal kinship system of Southeastern Indians, for example, may help to explain the importance of women in black slave culture.

The Cherokees' growing involvement in the market economy fostered in them an appreciation for black slaves in terms of money and labor. Theft of slaves and horses for resale became commonplace, and by the 1790s many Cherokees exhibited the same racial prejudice toward blacks as whites did. The prominent leader Little Turkey linked African-Americans with Spaniards, telling William Blount that he found the latter to be "a lying, deceitful, treacherous people, and . . . not real white people, and what few I have seen of them looked like mulattoes, and I would never have anything to say to them." And an Indian captured on one of John Sevier's military expeditions was so mortified when his gun was given to Sevier's slave Toby that he objected strenuously. On the other hand, many Indians were more positive in their assessment of individual African-Americans. Jack Civil, a free black or mulatto, lived among the Chickamaugas as an equal. But the concept of blacks as property ultimately prevailed. Within a generation of Tennessee statehood, black slavery would become a fixture among the so-called Five Civilized Tribes of the Southeast.

The 1785 Treaty of Hopewell was the prelude to a new order imposed on the Cherokees by the federal government. Though the treaty was generally quite favorable to them, it limited their traditional freedom of action by proclaiming U.S. sovereignty and stipulating that Indians could no longer follow the law of blood revenge (a stipulation many Cherokees ignored). The 1791 Treaty of the Holston was an even bolder assertion of federal authority and, among other things, it initiated a "civilization" program that encouraged the Cherokees to adopt white lifestyles. One consequence of this policy was the continuing diminution of traditional roles for Cherokee women. Even without federal intervention, those roles had become more ambiguous during the American Revolution because of the growing schism between Dragging Canoe's militant followers and the traditional leadership, which included Nancy Ward as Beloved Woman. In most societies, her actions as an advocate of peace—even to the extent of warning whites of Cherokee plans—would represent treason, and many of the younger warriors interpreted her actions in that light.

Dragging Canoe believed that the Revolution was not a traditional war fought against another tribe with a similar culture, but a war of survival fought to preserve Cherokee identity. He was largely correct, and Ward's impassioned speeches for peace between the races carried little weight with him and his followers. For a brief time after the 1776 Cherokee attacks on Tennessee settlements, he apparently prevented Ward and other women from sitting in the Chota council. For Dragging Canoe, the institution and prerogatives of a war leader were more important than those of a Beloved Woman. Ironically, some of his bitterest white enemies agreed. Backcountry elites, Tom Hatley has suggested, may have found the relative freedom of Cherokee women offensive and even frightening, a threat to their own patriarchal leadership. The U.S. government was also suspicious of such a prominent role for females, although it made a small exception for Nancy Ward. At the Hopewell treaty deliberations she was introduced as a Beloved Woman who had fathered warriors, and though she was allowed to talk on behalf of all Cherokee women and urge the absent Thomas Jefferson to consider himself their son, she had no official role in the deliberations. Allowing her to speak was a gesture, a bow to an earlier time. Affairs of state were now considered a man's business.

By the 1790s more and more of the tribal population was shifting to the south and west, into northern Georgia and Alabama, where settlers were less of an immediate threat. So many of the tribal towns had been destroyed or put at risk by white encroachment that the remaining ones were smaller in size and lacked their former cohesiveness and vitality. By 1800 visitors to the former principal town of Chota found only a few buildings still occupied, mostly by older people who intended to spend their final days in familiar surroundings. Federal officials referred to the remaining Tennessee towns and those in Georgia and North Carolina as the Upper Towns. The villages farther down the Tennessee River, from the old Chickamauga bastions to Muscle Shoals, Alabama, were called the Lower Towns. Within Tennessee the Cherokees still had title to almost all of the Cumberland Plateau, a narrow band along its eastern margin, and the southeastern part of the state, but those lands were in jeopardy. Their only hope, many believed, was to embark on the white man's path and make themselves acceptable in the eyes of their neighbors. They would become civilized.

8.

THE FRONTIER ECONOMY

During its earliest frontier period Tennessee was part of an international economy centered on a thriving trade in furs and deerskins. With the arrival of the first white settlers, the peltry trade became less important, and land speculation on a massive scale came to characterize the economy. Restless men of wealth and influence vied and sometimes cooperated with one another to engross millions of acres and then to dispose of them at enormous profit. The speculators' machinations involved businessmen and would-be investors in every major city of the United States and many cities in Europe. For ordinary settlers the economy was radically different, initially featuring limited agricultural production geared to family subsistence or trade in small nearby markets. Eventually Tennessee farmers developed regional, national, and even international markets. But for both speculators and farmers, the economy throughout the state's frontier period depended on land and its productive potential, and production was measured in agricultural terms.

The first settlers in East and Middle Tennessee followed much the same routine: they cleared fields for corn, planted orchard trees and vegetable gardens, raised a few farm animals, and fenced their fields for protection against roaming livestock. By the 1790s farmers were exporting hogs, horses, and cattle to the Eastern states, and by 1800 nascent planters on the Cumberland were shipping tobacco and a small amount of cotton downriver to New Orleans—and ultimately to world markets. By the time war began with Great Britain in 1812, Middle Tennessee, with its abundant and fertile land, had already surpassed the eastern part of the state in population and agricultural productivity. It was an advantage it would never relinquish. By the 1830s plantation-based production of cotton for the export market was becoming increasingly significant both in the southern part of Middle Tennessee and in recently opened West Tennessee. Cotton soon became preeminent in the latter area, with Memphis emerging as a market center, while Middle and East Tennessee retained a more diversified agriculture. To supplement its commercial production of tobacco and cotton, Middle Tennessee grew other crops and raised livestock. In contrast, East Tennessee remained a bastion of smaller-scale, diversified farming and livestock raising because its soil and topography limited plantation agriculture. In addition to corn, farmers there raised wheat, oats, barley, flax, hemp, rye, timothy grass, a wide variety of vegetables, and even a small amount of cotton for local use.

Corn was a major product in all three regions, and when Tennessee's frontier era ended in 1840, the state ranked first nationally in its production. Corn provided the near universal sustenance for frontier families. The earliest settlers planted the kernels, and often flax, amid the stumps of recently cleared fields. Once planted, corn it required little or no cultivation, though women and children had to chase away squirrels and crows. Corn also offered an almost infinite variety of culinary possibilities. Most families especially loved the young roasting ears when the corn was in the milk, but they also used corn for Johnnycakes, hominy, ground mush, and as an all purpose boiled additive to beans and meat. Woven leaves and cornhusks had many household purposes, and the cobs were transformed into pipe bowls, fire starters, and a poor substitute for toilet paper. People enjoyed going to cornshuckings, or frolics, which featured drinking, dancing, and other merriment and were highlights of frontier social calendars. Corn was also used as fodder, becoming the most common replacement for the native river cane. In 1771 Evan Shelby had written his sons that except for his horses and a few milk cows, he sent all his livestock into the cane, so that feeding them "will be little cost to us more than salting." But the growing number of farm animals eventually depleted the enormous canebrakes, and farmers increasingly relied on corn for fodder.

Another major use of surplus corn was for the making of whiskey. Corn liquor was the ideal product—indispensable, easy to manufacture, easy to transport, and improving with age. At least two bushels of grain were required for every five gallons of whiskey, so by the early nineteenth century the distilling industry may have consumed one-fourth to one-half of all corn produced in some counties. People in the Tennessee backwoods also distilled rye, peaches, and apples. All echelons of frontier society, including women and children, used whiskey both as medicine and to lubricate social interaction. In those cash-starved times Tennesseans also paid their taxes with it. Indeed, the manufacture and consumption of liquor in all parts of the country was so prevalent that social historians refer to the early United States as "the alcoholic republic." This social and economic phenomenon attracted the attention of a needy U.S. government. In 1791 Secretary of the Treasury Alexander Hamilton persuaded Congress to pass an excise tax on distilled spirits produced in each of the states, and frontier people in the states saw the tax as a threat to their economy and local autonomy. But the law did not apply to the Northwest and Southwest territories, and John Sevier believed that inhabitants of the latter might be able to undersell whiskey distilled in nearby states and thereby induce more immigration into the territory.

After the tax was extended to the Southwest Territory in 1794, residents denounced it as taxation without representation and pilloried the U.S. government for being insensitive to their needs. In parts of the Northern and Southern frontier the occasional physical abuse of tax collectors and juries' flagrant disregard of federal authority threatened to make the whiskey law a dead letter. The Federalists considered sending U.S. troops into the South, then decided to punish lawbreakers closer at hand: the frontier distillers in western Pennsylvania, where the national government displayed its new strength by crushing the so-called Whiskey Rebellion. The tax remained in effect and applied to all distilleries within the Southwest Territory, some 450 of them by 1795–96. Seventy-four stills operated in Washington County alone, where 10 individuals owned two each and 54 others had one each. The largest had a capacity of 131 gallons. The proprietor of two distilleries totaling 187 gallons was taxed the most, $101, but there is no evidence he paid a cent. Though some Middle Tennessee distillers did pay the tax, other Tennesseans apparently continued to ignore the law and even smuggled untaxed whiskey to outside markets.

Distilleries remained important throughout Tennessee's frontier era. The 1840 census lists 1,426 of them, with a total capitalization of more than $218,000 and employing 1,341 individuals. Total yearly production was 1,109,000 gallons, an average of 78 gallons per establishment. Distilling was the state's most widespread manufacturing industry. Out of seventy-two counties, only five—four in West Tennessee and one in Middle Tennessee—reported no such businesses. Middle Tennessee also had six small breweries which produced 1,835 gallons of beer.

From the outset, merchandising was an essential economic activity. Though backcountry residents were isolated, they were never immune to consumerism, and itinerant peddlers and small-store keepers whetted their material appetites. Among the latter was Jacob Brown, founder of the Nolichucky settlement, whose log storehouse quickly attracted settlers and Cherokees alike. It is a near certainty that his customers included a slave or two, who were entrusted with errands for their masters, as well as a few female patrons who perhaps unwittingly enlarged women's traditional sphere. As transportation links between Tennessee and the outside world improved, stores became more common, offered more goods, and emerged as social centers, especially when they were designated as local post offices. There was a burgeoning consumption of material goods, and by the 1790s advertisements in the *Knoxville Gazette* touted a wide range of merchandise from Richmond, Baltimore, and Philadelphia. Some merchants operated on a regional basis, owning stores in more than one town.

Economic exchange on the Tennessee frontier relied on a bewildering array of monetary possibilities. During the American Revolution, paper dollars issued under authority of the Continental Congress depreciated to the point where they were virtually worthless (except for land speculation). Spanish milled dollars were the hard money standard and circulated widely. After 1791 the United States government coined its own silver dollars while retaining foreign money as part of its monetary system. North Carolina and Virginia currencies—calculated in pounds, shillings, and pence—both circulated in Tennessee prior to statehood, but their values fluctuated in relation to other monetary units. Estate inventories sometimes mention guineas, French crowns, sterling, sterling currency, and half Johannes. Usually a North Carolina pound was equal to $2.50 U.S. Written I.O.U.s and bills of credit were also common.

Early merchants, while favoring cash, had no choice but to extend credit, work out a barter arrangement, or go out of business. In 1794 a Knoxville merchant who had experienced credit woes closed shop and reopened the next day as "John Summerville's Cheap Ready Money Store, where no credit whatever will be given." He was willing to accept cash or agricultural products, but no deferred payment. It appears that the "Cheap Ready Money" concept was ahead of its time, for Summerville closed his store several months later. On the other hand, some merchants thrived on the barter system. Corn, beeswax, flax, wheat, rye, and bar-iron were common mediums of exchange and were sometimes legal tender. Valuable peltries were also taken in trade, and one merchant advertised that he would pay cash "for the best otter, black and grey fox, raccoon, wildcat, muskrat, and mink skins." Individuals also had the option of trading their labor for at least a part of their necessities. Farm workers, for example, might receive room and board as well as pay in the form of a small amount of cash each month.

Blacksmiths were probably the most common and indispensable craftsmen on the frontier, and some were also competent gunsmiths. Larger towns might even boast a goldsmith or silver-smith. Other skilled workers included carpenters, cabinet makers, joiners, turners, and wheelwrights. As early as the 1790s hatters, tailors, and tanners plied their trade in East Tennessee, as did itinerant stonemasons, some of whom did extensive work on John Sevier's home. Surveyors, wagoners, boatmen, and ferrymen were of course essential to the local and regional economies, and tavern keepers provided necessary lodging and libations. Lawyers were the most common professionals, but Tennessee would have been better off with more physicians. Records also list preachers and teachers, who, like many other professionals, often farmed as well.

Not until 1807 did the state authorize creation of its first private bank, in Nashville, and it was another four years before a second opened, in Knoxville. Between 1815 and 1817, with the return of good economic times following the War of 1812, the state chartered thirteen more private banks, and Nashville businessmen unsuccessfully attempted to establish a branch of the Bank of the United States. Like banks elsewhere, those in Tennessee issued paper money which was supposedly redeemable in specie, and like their counterparts, they often overextended themselves during those heady years. When the speculative fever collapsed amid the Panic of 1819, most were unable to redeem their notes in hard money. All except Hugh Lawson White's bank in Knoxville collapsed. Banking revived along with the economy in the mid-1820s, and a branch of the Bank of the United States opened in Nashville. Again during the flush economic times of the 1830s many banks overextended themselves, and again they collapsed, this time amid the Panic of 1837. The crisis threatened a host of proposed internal improvements in Tennessee and demonstrated clearly that the existing financial infrastructure was inadequate for easing Tennessee's transition from a frontier to an economically mature state.

The Age of Cotton arrived in Middle Tennessee in 1780 when John Donelson, newly arrived from the East, began planting it. By the middle of that decade farmers in the region were exporting cotton to Kentucky, and during the 1790s they were shipping it upstream to Pittsburgh for distribution in the Pennsylvania backcountry. A visitor in the Nashville area characterized the fiber as long and fine and said growers could expect about eight hundred pounds an acre, an exaggeration as it turned out. A few Tennesseans were using a prototype of the cotton gin even before Eli Whitney's invention of 1793, but there is no doubt that his machine (and pirated copies of it), along with expanding use of slave labor, boosted production of cotton considerably. By 1801 Tennessee was producing about one million pounds, and in that year the general assembly, aware of cotton's export potential, established an inspection system to certify both the quality of the product and where it was ginned. The assembly also purchased the right to use Whitney's gin by imposing a tax on each machine, but local growers were skeptical about Whitney's claims of invention and resisted the levies. Production continued to soar and totaled some three million pounds in 1811.

Middle Tennessee's tobacco production also grew, especially in the northern tier of counties where snuff and chewing tobacco proved well suited to European demands. As with cotton, the state initiated an increasingly rigorous inspection system. (A similar system for beef, pork, and lard proved unsuccessful and was abandoned.) Clarksville became a center of tobacco marketing, attracting buyers from all over the world to its annual sales, but Nashville remained the regional hub; its waterfront was crowded with boats headed to Natchez and New Orleans. This was part of a much larger trade which by 1801 included nearly six hundred vessels of all kinds carrying cargoes worth $3.6 million from the Ohio Valley to New Orleans. James Winchester was deeply involved in this both as a farmer and as a consignment agent at his estate upriver from Nashville. In 1801 he had orders for whiskey, pork, corn, and the construction of a new river boat that would be forty-five feet long and thirteen feet in the beam. By 1807, when trans-Appalachian cargoes to New Orleans exceeded $5 million in value, Winchester was dealing directly with a firm there which kept him informed about the latest commodity prices in Liverpool and other European markets. As Nashville grew, businessmen from outside the state eagerly inquired about their prospects if they settled there. By 1812, despite oppressive British maritime policies and a recent U.S. embargo, more than a score of merchants were involved in a far-flung trade that extended abroad. As was true in other cities of the Ohio and Mississippi valleys, Nashville's new elites were merchants rather than land speculators.

As late as 1802 one could still buy the best land near Nashville for no more than $5 an acre, and equally good tracts thirty or forty miles from town could be acquired for less than $3 an acre. Land owners often provided attractive credit for prospective buyers or offered rentals in exchange for payment in cash, kind, shares, or specified improvements. Similar liberal terms were available to hard-pressed settlers when West Tennessee opened a few years later. Renting made good economic sense for owner and tenant alike; the former saw his property improved at little cost to himself, and the latter, if lucky, might produce enough to buy his own property. Land costs went up during the flush times immediately following the War of 1812, especially in Middle Tennessee. In 1816 a Maury County resident said that land speculators had paid $4.50 an acre for unimproved land on which they fattened swine before driving them to South Carolina or Georgia. Apparently many landowners now insisted on receiving payment in cash, and in 1817 one prospective buyer advertised his complaint about the continuing demands for "ready money." He was giving notice (presumably tongue in cheek) that in lieu of such payment his wife, Jane, "will be exchanged for good arable land." An alternative to buying or renting land was to simply squat illegally on unoccupied tracts, as East Tennesseans did on Cherokee lands.

Stock raising was closely associated with early Tennessee agriculture and quickly became a major component of the state's economy. The most prestigious animals were horses, "the universal means of travel and pleasure" as well as most common source of heavy labor. Between 1777 and statehood in 1796, almost 91 percent of the estate inventories for Washington County show ownership of at least one horse, and the average was five horses. Likewise, in Middle Tennessee "Horses were more universally owned than household goods or farming tools." So essential were they that Indians and whites freely stole them from one another for resale to unquestioning customers elsewhere. Thus, in an unsanctioned way, the trade in horses became part of the frontier exchange economy.

Tennesseans had the same affinity for well-bred, fast horses as their Virginia counterparts. In the early 1770s Wataugans were attending local races, and breeding horses for speed and stamina became a minor industry in that area as well as in the Cumberland Basin. Tennesseans were at first devoted to straight racing along a quarter-mile course, but over time they turned to thoroughbred racing on oval tracks. Stud fees became an important source of income, as did buying and selling prime animals. As early as 1789 James Robertson sold a "high blooded horse" for "1,000 hard dollars," and in 1812 John Hardin paid $8,000 for a purebred Arabian. Good horseflesh and successful racing were a passion for Andrew Jackson as for many in Nashville. Only a few weeks after the Creek War began in 1813, Bishop Francis Asbury commented on the town's obsession: "Will it be believed that the *races* agitate the public mind notwithstanding the alarms of Indian wars?" Fine horses also reflected other facets of status, and in 1797 a traveler was surprised to encounter near Nashville a variety of carriages, including "two coaches, fitted up in all the style of Philadelphia or New York." In contrast, ordinary draft and pack horses were relatively inexpensive and often received harsh treatment.

Other livestock became even more important than horses in Tennessee's economy. Like horses, cattle were present on almost every farm, and in much greater numbers. Because their bloodlines were of little concern, the animals came in all colors, sizes, and dispositions. At first they fed on river cane and then, more and more, on the open range. Settlers often kept one or two milk cows and raised the rest of the cattle as beef for local and regional markets. Beef was plentiful, even cheaper than pork, and until about 1800 it was the preferred domestic meat. Cattle were rarely used as work animals, but their hides had a ready market in the many frontier tanneries.

In the early years fewer farmers owned hogs than horses and cattle, partly because pigs could not fatten satisfactorily without corn or other fodder. Pigs being pigs, they were always numerous and could fend for themselves in canebrakes and forests, or by rooting around. As corn production rose, the value of pigs rapidly increased until they exceeded all other farm animals in number. Sheep were also common in East Tennessee and were raised more for wool than for meat. During the early years they were less abundant in Middle Tennessee, but by the antebellum period the sheep in that region produced some of the finest wool in the world. In 1840 Tennessee's wool was worth nearly $3 million; only New York produced wool of greater value. Frontier households also owned geese, ducks, turkeys, chickens, an occasional mule, and almost always that faithful friend, sentry, and worker— a dog.

From a very early date Tennesseans began driving livestock to outside markets. In 1790, while riding southward through the Valley of Virginia to assume his duties as governor of the Southwest Territory, William Blount encountered some one thousand head of cattle being driven northward from the territory. Often, farmers in the Piedmont of Maryland or Virginia would purchase the animals for fattening and then drive them to the Baltimore and Philadelphia markets. An alternative to this pattern became apparent in 1796, when South Carolina's Governor Arnoldus Vanderhorst and Tennessee's John Sevier supported joint efforts to lay out a road from Greene County up the French Broad River to Buncombe Courthouse (Asheville, North Carolina), where it would connect with existing roads to South Carolina. Though the Tennessee legislature was unresponsive, livestock drives were apparently already following that route.

During the next quarter century the Knoxville area became the major gathering point in East Tennessee for livestock heading to market. Millions of animals filed through the French Broad Gap, ultimately reaching South Carolina, Georgia, and Alabama, where cotton producers preferred to use their acreage for farming rather than livestock. These drives included cattle, horses, mules, sheep, and even turkeys and ducks, but hogs were by far the most numerous. In droves numbering 300 to 1,000 animals, a total of 150,000 or more Tennessee hogs might go to market in a single season. Completed in 1828, the Buncombe Turnpike, said to be North Carolina's finest road, facilitated this traffic. Manufactured goods were imported into Tennessee by the same route, in large wagons pulled by teams of eight or more horses.

Some frontier stock raisers grazed cattle and other livestock on the higher elevations of the southern Appalachians, which they liberally salted to keep the animals from straying too far. Mountain grazing was a common feature of Scots-Irish herding practices and appears to be the best explanation for Appalachia's famous "balds," those open meadows whose origins have been a topic of much debate. Certainly one of the most famous of these is Spence Field, at an elevation well above 5,000 feet in the Great Smoky Mountains National Park. During the 1830s James Spence, who lived in nearby Cades Cove, created that mountain meadow by clearing and burning most of the trees and other vegetation. In the autumn herders would drive their animals down to the valleys and sell them to drovers. The disadvantage of high-elevation grazing was that the stock became half wild and were exposed to inclement weather and to the dangers of wolves and mountain lions. Whether stock roamed in the highlands or the lowlands, owners usually marked their animals' ears with dis-tinctive slits, which were registered with the county.

East Tennessee farmers not only profited from raising hogs and cattle, they also had a ready market for enormous quantities of corn to fatten the animals before they left the state. And while en route to market, the hogs required additional feed. They trav-eled an average of eight to ten miles each day and spent each night at one of the numerous commercial stands where drovers could rest, feed their livestock, and obtain lodging for them-selves. Drovers usually paid no more than five cents a pound for Tennessee hogs, and they needed an additional two cents a pound to make a profit. The price of cotton determined the final price of hogs. Livestock raising was also a major business in Middle Tennessee. The town of Columbia attracted buyers from throughout the South to its annual mule sales, and Tennessee mules could fetch as much as $300 a pair in Georgia. Livestock drives from the region radiated in all directions and included at least one turkey drive to Clarksville for shipment downstream to New Orleans. Another outlet for Middle Tennessee livestock was the Kentucky Stock Road, which connected Danville, Kentucky, and Huntsville, Alabama, and passed through the Cumberland Plateau. But feeding stock during the move through the relatively barren plateau was likely to be expensive. A drover taking horses from Nashville to Virginia in 1814 complained that farmers there charged a dollar a bushel for corn.

Not surprisingly, some of Tennessee's earliest industries were related to hunting and frontier defense. Foremost among these was the manufacture of gunpowder, a relatively simple though time-consuming process. Middle Tennesseans could buy gunpowder in New Orleans or from itinerant French or Spanish traders, but it was far cheaper to make their own. Fortunately, the limestone valleys of the Highland Rim had a number of caves that were rich in saltpeter, the basic ingredient of powder. Workers dug out the soil, crushed it between gin-like rollers, and leached it twice, the second time through hardwood ashes. The production of every one hundred pounds of finished saltpeter required about eighteen bushels of oak ashes, fewer if using elm. The watery mixture of potassium nitrate that resulted was boiled down, dried, and again crushed with rollers. The final step in making gunpowder was mixing the right proportions of ground nitrate with powdered charcoal and sulfur; the latter was readily available at country stores. East Tennessee also produced large quantities of gunpowder. Kingsport alone had four powder mills as early as 1806, and the War of 1812 brought a sharp increase in the mining of potassium nitrate throughout the southern Appalachians. By 1840, however, Tennessee had only ten small mills and produced barely ten thousand pounds of gunpowder a year. The industry quickly rebounded. In 1841 mining began at Alum Cave in today's Great Smoky Mountains National Park, and during the Civil War this famous site produced much of the Confederacy's gunpowder.

Powder and shot were both frontier necessities, but Tennesseans could not produce sufficient quantities of the latter. Though legend says the over-mountain men prepared for the Battle of King's Mountain by molding their ammunition from lead deposits on John Sevier's property, early residents usually imported their shot, mostly from the Chiswell mines in southwestern Virginia. So vital were those mines that during the Revolution back-country leaders took special precautions to protect them from British-allied Indians. For residents of the Cumberland, lead was especially difficult to obtain. Despite finding a few small deposits, they sometimes had to improvise to produce suitable material for their musket balls. One old-timer recalled that "my mother had to melt her pewter basins, cups and spoons to shoot the Indians." John Coffee, who like Andrew Jackson was a son-in-law of John Donelson, found it profitable to import lead from mines in the Illinois Country. He would take his small boats down to Shawneetown, across from the mouth of the Cumberland, and return to Middle Tennessee about three weeks later. A wide-ranging trader who took a variety of goods up and down the river systems, Coffee also brought lead back from New Orleans and the upper Mississippi.

One of Tennessee's earliest and most basic industries was the manufacture of salt, which was a necessity for cooking, livestock raising, and meat preservation. Middle Tennessee was blessed with a number of saline springs, or "licks," which attracted game animals and people alike. French Lick, Mansker's Lick, and Bledsoe's Lick are several of the better known, and James Robertson owned one of the best, producing one bushel of salt from about eighty gallons of water. But residents on the Cumberland resigned themselves to importing most of what they needed from the much larger saltworks in Kentucky. Those saltworks and others in southwestern Virginia also exported to East Tennessee, especially during the 1830s, when the Knoxville area required massive quantities of salt for its livestock industry. John Coffee also brought some salt to the Cumberland as incidental cargo because the salines of the Illinois Country were located near the lead mines which provided residents with ammunition. Still, despite their reliance on imported salt, most Tennessee frontier people at one time or another spent long hours at local licks. It was not without danger, and William Neely was ambushed and killed by Indians at his own lick. Salt making also consumed resources. The fires for boiling meant rapid deforestation of the surrounding area, and game animals, especially larger ones such as elk and buffalo, began to disappear.

Frontier Tennessee had a wide array of other industries directly related to its agricultural economy. Among the earliest was milling. Small water-powered mills ground corn and other grains and sometimes also operated as sawmills. They were especially numerous along the many streams of upper East Tennessee; in Washington County alone there were more than two dozen in the twenty years before statehood. The Cumberland region had less reliable water sources and therefore fewer mills. County courts recognized some mills as public and allowed their proprietors to charge tolls, often a specified percentage of the farmer's processed flour. The leisurely pace of milling offered customers an opportunity to socialize while conducting business. Barrel making and stave making were closely associated with milling, for flour and meal were often shipped in white-oak barrels, as were beef and pork. Farmers who had access to suitable groves of trees often made barrels when they had the time, and even the intrepid Davy Crockett, more noted for his hunting than his industry, cut staves for export down the Mississippi.

Rising cotton production and the state's acquisition of rights to Whitney's invention meant an increase in the number of cotton gins, especially in Middle and West Tennessee. As early as 1804 the state already had sixty-four gins, twenty-four of them in the Nashville area. By 1810 there were four cotton mills in that part of the state, producing goods worth a total of $9,500, as well as a fulling mill that yielded products valued at $2,700. But most of the state's fiber goods were manufactured within the home. The 1810 census credits families in Middle Tennessee with producing almost 1.8 million yards of cotton goods worth an estimated $900,000. During the next two decades mills proliferated. Even in East Tennessee, where cotton was not commonly grown, small spinning factories were operating in Knoxville and more rural locales by the late 1820s. By 1840 the state had thirty-eight cotton mills—twenty-five in Middle Tennessee alone—with a total of more than 16,800 spindles.

Besides agriculture, iron manufacturing was perhaps the state's leading industry. Early explorers had assumed that Tennessee was rich in mineral resources, and the Great Smoky Mountains were called the Great Iron Mountains well into the nineteenth century. In 1790 David Ross, an experienced ironworker from Virginia, moved to the South Fork of the Holston River and established Tennessee's first recorded iron manufactory. During the next two decades a number of iron mines, bloomery forges, and related enterprises arose, including an ironworks at Pactolus in Sullivan County owned by John Sevier and a partner, and another, the Cumberland Furnace, which James Robertson opened in 1797. Cumberland Furnace was Middle Tennessee's first ironworks and a source of profit for Robertson and his partners, who sold it to Montgomery Bell, the region's best-known iron maker. Meanwhile East Tennessee, even though importing iron goods from elsewhere, was shipping boatloads of iron-bar and castings to Nashville, Natchez, and New Orleans. One of the more profitable operations was that of Elijah and Elihu Embree, who acquired an ironworks at Bumpass Cove on the Nolichucky, expanded it, and did well selling nails, bar-iron, and castings at their general store.

The ironworks consisted of blast furnaces and smaller, much more common bloomery forges. The latter typically produced only a few tons of iron a year to make items like pots and pans, wagon rims, plow points, and wrought-iron bars for nails. Familiar Tennessee place names like Forge Creek and Pigeon Forge attest to the local significance of iron-making enterprises. Some of the proprietors used black slaves for the most onerous work, but at least a few slaves were among the most highly skilled iron workers. Apart from their obvious utilitarian nature, these iron smelters are most noteworthy for their tremendous impact on the environment. According to one estimate, a smelter required about twenty-two cords of hardwood to produce the charcoal fires for a single day. An acre of mature forest yields no more than thirty cords, and an average blast furnace required about three hundred acres of timber a year. The environmental impact of such an industry is apparent: "In 1820 alone," according to Donald Davis, "twelve small ironworks in Johnson and Carter Counties consumed 12,000 cords of wood, collectively eliminating more than 500 acres of hardwoods from nearby mountain forests." Such destruction probably explains why Tennessee passed a law in 1807 giving three thousand acres, "unappropriated and unfit for cultivation," to prospective builders of iron-works. The land was also tax exempt if the proprietor began operation of a forge within two years.

The burgeoning iron production led several Jonesborough-area merchants to begin a modest enterprise for the manufacture of farm tools. In 1825 they acquired the plans and rights to make a mould board plow which had been patented in the District of Columbia. The Embree brothers made the necessary castings at their Bumpass Cove ironworks, and several individuals scattered around Washington County constructed the implements, which were used throughout much of East Tennessee. At about the same time, a prominent businessman reported that a nail factory in Sullivan County was having a positive impact on the region, producing a necessity which previously had come by wagon from Baltimore and Richmond. During the next decade or so the iron industry surpassed agriculture in importance in some areas. By 1840 Tennessee had 34 blast furnaces which produced more than 16,000 tons of cast iron and 99 forges, bloomeries, and rolling mills which turned out almost 9,700 tons of bar-iron. Iron mining and iron making employed 2,266 individuals and had a total capitalization of $1,515,000.

Much of Tennessee's economic growth occurred in the major towns. By the late 1790s Knoxville was already a regional distribution point. Goods arrived by wagon from Eastern centers, and flatboats headed downstream to Natchez and New Orleans laden with whiskey, bacon, flour, and bar-iron. The waterfront around the mouth of First Creek bustled with the rhythm and hurly-burly of commerce. Visitors had mixed opinions of Knoxville. One out-of-towner happened to arrive on court day in 1798 and was aghast at the singing, dancing, and worst of all, the profanity, especially on Sunday. Whiskey and peach brandy flowed freely amid the flotsam and jetsam of frontier humanity—boatmen, wagoners, blanketed Indians, leather-jacketed woodsmen, gamblers, and women of dubious reputation shouting from doorways. The visitor repeated a story he had heard: the devil had gotten so old he couldn't travel very far, so he decided to spend his final years in Knoxville among his friends. On the other hand, during that same year a soldier found Knoxville to be "the most dull disagreeable place you can have any idea of."

Sometimes the boatmen taking cargoes downstream were novices, adventuresome souls entrusting themselves to the tricky currents and vagaries of weather. Martin Dickinson's 1797 journal offers a classic example of some of the difficulties inherent in the shipping business. A well educated young man, Dickinson agreed to take a load of iron and castings down the Holston and Tennessee rivers and then to Nashville. Beginning early in March, he and his fellow boatmen endured snow and pelting rain while they collected a cargo and awaited a rise in the river. They passed the time drinking, shooting squirrels, attending a barn-raising, wagering on marksmanship, wrestling, card playing, quarter pitching, and competing in foot races. Once, after a session of drinking at a local still, Dickinson, shooting offhand, was unable to hit a target from thirty yards and lost a pint of whiskey. His early trials with his boat were almost comical; once, lacking enough crewmen "and not understanding the business of rowing, we run on a bar of stones and stuck fast." They stayed there all night.

Not until May 6 was the water high enough for them to set out in earnest, and they managed to get to Knoxville by the 8th. On the 12th they passed Nickajack, where some "beggarly" Indians acquired whiskey from the crew. Between the 14th and the 19th they got stuck several times at Muscle Shoals and had to offload part of their cargo into a canoe. They received assistance from some Indian pilots and finally managed to continue their voyage, arriving at the Ohio on the 24th. Working their way upstream, they encountered numerous craft heading down to the Illinois and Natchez countries, and they endured "shocking bad water to drink" and mosquitoes "measured by bushels." Continuing up the Cumberland proved almost as difficult. Not until June 10 did they reach Clarksville, "a very trifling place," though its inhabitants danced "mightily." Finally arriving in Nashville on June 15, Dickinson spent his first night in two months sleeping in a bed. The next day he unloaded the boat and hired a black man to haul the cargo to a storage house. During the next month he delivered goods to clients in the Nashville area and settled his accounts, and then headed home on horseback. He reached Southwest Point in five days, and after a brief visit in Knoxville, he returned to Virginia.

Martin Dickinson was a relatively well-bred dilettante playing the role of a rollicking, hard-drinking riverman. But there was a class of drunken and violent men who conformed to the latter image, hard-bitten professionals who could terrorize a waterfront. In the early years of Memphis they often threatened town officials who attempted to collect wharfage fees and otherwise regulate them. All too often they conformed to the image of the half-horse, half-alligator western boatman exemplified by the real-life (and legendary) Mike Fink, who worked the Ohio and Mississippi in a keelboat. Mike could drink, fight, and shoot with the very best of any frontiersmen. He and his raucous, larger-than-life friends became a staple of antebellum folklore and represented nostalgia for a frontier that already appeared to be fading. Sometimes the riverman's exploits merge with those of another folkloric character, the backwoods rough and tumbler. Whatever their mythic significance, the rivermen played a major role in the frontier economy.

By the turn of the nineteenth century, the opening of new roads and the improvement of old ones contributed to the rapid growth of Nashville and the Cumberland Basin. After completion of Avery's Trace in 1788 travelers going from Nashville to East Tennessee no longer had to pass through Cumberland Gap; instead they could follow the more direct, though dangerous, route across the plateau. But Avery's Trace was merely a trail, and the 1791 Treaty of the Holston permitted construction of a road between the two regions. When Fort Southwest Point was activated in 1792, many Tennesseans believed the new road would begin there. Soon they were heading to the fort from David Campbell's Station, west of Knoxville, then following an unimproved trail through today's Rockwood and up to Avery's Trace near Cookeville. Both routes through the plateau remained dangerous because of Chickamauga hostility, and even normally peaceable Cherokees sometimes demanded tolls from travelers. In 1794 the territorial legislature authorized a lottery to finance construction of a true road between Southwest Point and Middle Tennessee. The scheme failed, so in 1795 the legislature authorized sale of public salt licks to support completion of the road. Later that same year George Walton finished the road's first link, from Carthage eastward to the Avery Trace in Putnam County.

The Cherokees protested the road building because it deviated in several ways from the Holston treaty, but as the Indian wars ended and Tennessee achieved statehood, traffic across the plateau increased considerably. In 1796 alone about twenty-eight thousand people paid ferry tolls to cross the Clinch River at Southwest Point. The general assembly was apparently impressed by these numbers; in 1799 it authorized completion of the new road's final link, between Southwest Point and Avery's Trace. Finished in 1801, the road became Tennessee's first toll road or "turnpike," so-called for the swinging pole which controlled traffic. Known as the Cumberland Turnpike, Cumberland Road, or Walton's Road, it was the most popular route between East and Middle Tennessee because the garrison at Southwest Point offered protection for travelers crossing what was still, until 1805, Indian country. Early improvements included removing stumps, widening the road to fifteen feet, leveling the grades as much as possible, and constructing bridges. The eminent Frenchman François André Michaux ventured across the road in 1802 and found it "as broad and commodious" as those around Philadelphia. The turnpike quickly fell into disrepair, however, and in 1815 the irascible Francis Asbury called it a swindle, just another of Tennessee's miserable excuses for a road. On another front, a "passable" road was open by 1809 connecting Middle Tennessee, the Chattanooga area, and the Federal Road in Georgia, saving travelers more than one hundred miles over the turnpike via Southwest Point and East Tennessee.

The most famous road linking Nashville with the world of commerce was the Natchez Trace, which angled southwestward to the busiest, most notorious town in Mississippi Territory. Under European jurisdiction Natchez had been the most significant center of trade on the Mississippi between New Orleans and St. Louis, and it remained so during the early years of American sovereignty. In the days before the steamboat, keelboatmen spent two months or more poling their boats back upstream, but the more numerous flatboatmen and rafters customarily dismantled their craft on the lower Mississippi, sold the lumber and fittings, and returned to the Ohio and Tennessee valleys by way of the Natchez Trace and Nashville. The trace itself was simply an improved pathway linking together various segments of longtime

Indian trails through Chickasaw and Choctaw lands. After the federal government created Mississippi Territory in 1798 it decided to make the Natchez Trace a major postal route between Washington and the territory, but even with a series of improvements, the route was often difficult, unmarked, and boggy. It took a hardy postal rider at least ten to fifteen days to cover the five hundred miles, and ordinary travelers took about a month. As traffic increased, a few whites and prominent Chickasaw mixed-bloods established taverns at widely spaced intervals to accommodate travelers.

The most famous incident along the Natchez Trace involved Meriwether Lewis and occurred in Tennessee. Renowned for the expedition he and William Clark had led between 1804 and 1806, Lewis endured repeated failures after returning to civilization. He proved inept in romance, inept in business, and inept as governor of the Louisiana Territory, and over time his deep-seated melancholy became more pronounced. Finally, in September 1809, he left St. Louis to return to Washington in hopes of repairing his finances and redeeming himself in the eyes of his friend and mentor Thomas Jefferson, who was now out of office. Lewis planned to return by way of New Orleans, but while traveling down the Mississippi had to be restrained from killing himself. At Fort Pickering, the location of present-day Memphis, Captain Gilbert Russell, the commanding officer, detained him for two weeks for his own safety. While convalescing there, Lewis became convinced that Britain's growing disregard of American rights on the high seas posed a distinct threat to himself and the valuable papers he was carrying. When he was well enough to resume his trip, he decided to head eastward to the Natchez Trace and return to Washington by way of Nashville. He was accompanied by a friend and two servants who would watch over him.

After reaching the trace, Lewis and his party headed northward until they came to Grinder's Inn near present-day Hohenwald, Tennessee, some seventy miles south of Nashville. Lewis's friend had remained behind that morning to retrieve some horses that had strayed. The two servants were lodged in Grinder's barn while Lewis was staying at the inn. That evening he behaved

very peculiarly, talking loudly to himself and pacing about the
grounds and in his room. Early in the morning of October 11, two
shots rang out. The first bullet only grazed Lewis's head, but the
second entered his chest and exited near the base of his spine.
While the terrified Mrs. Grinder remained in her room and the
servants slept in the barn, Lewis staggered out of his quarters,
called for assistance, lurched into the yard, fell, then somehow
made it back to his room. Not until sunrise did Mrs. Grinder
rouse the servants, who found Lewis still alive and slashing himself with a razor. They refused his request to blow his brains out,
and he died soon afterward. A lively controversy arose about
whether he committed suicide or was murdered, but those who
knew him best—Clark, other officers, and Jefferson himself—
never doubted that he had ended his own life. Near the place
where he died, an impressive monument marks Lewis's grave.

The Natchez Trace quickly faded in significance with the
dawning of the steamboat era in the West. Introduced to the Mississippi River in 1811, steamboats revolutionized transportation.
The shallow draft typical of western steamboats enabled the vessels to travel throughout the Mississippi drainage, wherever there
was even a few feet of water. Travelers heading upstream could
now accomplish in two or three weeks what would have taken
several months in a keelboat. Flatboats continued to be important until the Civil War, but their crews no longer had to use the
Natchez Trace to return from the lower Mississippi. Throughout
the trans-Appalachian region merchants were eager to benefit
from the new technology. In 1818 a group of investors headed by
William Carroll, a future governor of Tennessee, attempted to
reach Nashville in the *General Jackson*. Stopped a few miles
short by snags in the Cumberland River, the boat returned the
next year and on March 11, 1819, finally arrived at Nashville's
waterfront. In the words of a witness, "the whole population,
men, women and children, collected on the bank of the river, and
loud cheers rent the air. . . . The first ship that crossed the Atlantic, and touched the shores of America, was not an object of more
wonder to the astonished natives, than was this steamboat to the
people of Nashville." It was now possible to get to New Orleans
in just seven days and to return in seventeen. After Nashville's

trade experienced severe setbacks as a result of the Panic of 1819, it revived with a flourish. In 1825 the city shipped thirty thousand bales of cotton, worth $1 million, and by the 1840s as many as fifteen steamboats a week docked there. But Memphis was even more favorably situated for navigation, and it would become the chief beneficiary of the steamboat as cotton production in West Tennessee soared.

Knoxville was at a distinct disadvantage as a shipping point because water levels on the upper Tennessee fluctuated and because Muscle Shoals was a difficult obstacle. After a cash prize was offered for the first steamboat to make it upstream to the town, a small side-wheeler, the *Atlas*, somehow navigated both the shoals and the suck near Chattanooga and reached Knoxville in March 1828. It took more than two weeks after crossing the shoals, mostly because the crew had to stop frequently to cut firewood for the boilers. Knoxville hosted a great celebration, marked by a dinner, thirteen formal toasts, and a good many more impromptu ones. Despite the hopes of residents, however, the promise of profitable steam navigation on the upper Tennessee never materialized. Muscle Shoals were too hazardous, and most goods had to be offloaded and taken by wagon around them. A canal bypassing the shoals did not help much, but completion in 1834 of Alabama's Tuscumbia, Courtland, and Decatur Railroad provided a more effective link between the upper and lower sections of the river. Unfortunately, offloading cargo between boats and a train was also expensive, and Knoxville remained at a major disadvantage compared to Nashville and Memphis.

Middle Tennessee—and Nashville in particular—seemed content to rely on the growing network of roads and the burgeoning steamboat traffic, but the less developed regions, East Tennessee and West Tennessee, agitated for improved transportation connections. Frontier regions were always dependent on governmental assistance for their internal improvements, and they aggressively sought that support. While some Tennesseans, notably President Andrew Jackson, were philosophically opposed to federal appropriations for most internal improvements, they often made an exception for certain projects that had national import—military and postal roads, for example. Few complained at the turn of the century when the United States spent money to improve the Natchez Trace, and later to create new links to the Federal Road.

Ultimately it was the responsibility of the State of Tennessee and its citizens to take the initiative for internal improvements. Between statehood and the late 1830s the Tennessee General Assembly deliberated about incorporating private turnpike companies, improving the navigability of rivers, building canals, and conducting railroad surveys. In 1836 Knoxville leaders, realizing the inadequacy of their existing river and road system, hosted a convention which called for railroad connections with Atlantic and Ohio River ports. The state chartered a number of private railroad companies during that decade, but the Panic of 1837 effectively killed these and similar projects throughout the West. Not until completion of a North-South railway during the 1850s did Knoxville gain independence from a transportation network which was both time-consuming and expensive. Memphis, an increasingly important river port, had grander ambitions by 1840. It wanted to link its waterfront with transcontinental railroads, making the town a great interior entrepôt. By the time of the Civil War both Memphis and Nashville, now equally enthusiastic, had railroad connections with the South Atlantic, the Gulf of Mexico, and the upper Midwest. But no railroad directly connected Tennessee's three largest cities. If anything, modern technology simply reinforced the state's regional distinctiveness.

But Tennessee's geographic diversity hardly made it unique. Many states had multiple personalities. And what Tennesseans had in common was what they shared with people in most frontier areas. By 1840 Tennessee was still overwhelmingly agrarian—even Middle Tennessee, its most developed section. The state's economy was grounded in the basics: its topography, richness of soil, climate, and all the other vagaries of nature. And most residents retained an abiding assumption that land and its bounties offered the main route to economic and social advancement. That assumption was a powerful force indeed.

9.

Statehood to Nationalism: 1796–1815

John Sevier was the most noteworthy transitional figure in Tennessee's early history, occupying a position of authority from the Revolution to statehood and then holding various political offices until his death in 1815. He served six terms as governor, one as state legislator, and was elected three times to the U.S. House of Representatives. His career after 1796 echoes many themes of Tennessee's early frontier: the striving to retain political and moral authority in the face of strong opposition from elites and upstarts alike; the emphasis on land acquisition at the expense of Indians; the intrigue with foreign powers; and the frequent demands for assistance from a young federal government that coincided with a defiant defense of local autonomy. In his later years Sevier also witnessed much that was new: the rise of thriving commercial towns; the growing importance of cotton cultivation and its iniquitous bedfellow, slavery; the emergence of the Nashville Basin as the center of population and political domination; the gradual shift from old patterns of social and political deference; the forced recasting of Indian identity toward an idealized model of "civilization"; and even in the midst of a fierce localism, the emergence of a nascent nationalism that would make Tennesseans some of the strongest defenders of U.S. honor and dignity.

When he assumed office early in 1796, Sevier made it plain that one of his primary objectives was to continue the systematic acquisition of Indian lands. Though the Cherokees occupied only the southeastern part of the state and the Chickasaws resided in northern Mississippi, those two tribes still owned about three-fourths of Tennessee. The Cherokees retained large, connected chunks of East and Middle Tennessee, while the Chickasaws held the western one-third of the state. This was of great concern to Sevier and other leaders in light of the "truly flattering" rush of prospective settlers into Tennessee. Adding to the problem was the difficulty of defining the precise boundaries of Indian lands within the state. The 1791 Treaty of the Holston specified Chero-kee cession of the lands east of the Clinch River and north of a line from present-day Kingston to North Carolina along the di-vide of the Little River and the Little Tennessee River. The sur-vey of the ceded lands was delayed because of Indian hostilities and other matters, and in the meantime some whites pushed into the lands south of the specified divide. Farther to the north, squatters were also ensconced in the Powell Valley, another un-ceded area.

Even before commissioners finally made the survey in 1797, Governor Sevier realized that the boundary would probably leave many whites in Indian country, and he conscientiously pleaded the settlers' case with the secretary of war. Referring to the settlers as adventurers rather than as trespassers, he sought either compensation for their claims or another Cherokee cession to accommodate them. When the general assembly contemplated taxing Indian lands as a means of forcing cession, Sevier and others managed to block the measure, which would have put the state squarely at odds with federal law. But Sevier's meaning was clear when he wrote the secretary of war that Tennessee would observe all federal treaties with the Indians "so far as they are not pernicious, odious nor iniquitous."

While Sevier lobbied Congress to effect additional Cherokee cessions, he dutifully strove to avoid the costly consequences of

John Sevier. Portrait by Charles Wilson Peale. From the Tennessee Historical Society Collection. Courtesy Tennessee State Museum.

inciting the Indians to warfare. Though recently defeated, the Cherokees in particular remained a strong force and were capable of inflicting great harm on citizens if pushed too far. Remaining tribal landholdings enfolded the areas of white settlement and included the entire Cumberland Plateau, presenting a barrier between East and Middle Tennessee. Travelers along the Cumberland Road were sometimes robbed by wandering Cherokees, while the Indians claimed their hunters were often targets of frontier people. Governor Sevier received reports of random murders on both sides and, more frequently, of Indians and whites stealing horses and slaves for resale elsewhere. Horse theft was the most frequently cited provocation between the races. Various treaties specified that animals stolen by the Cherokees would be valued at $50 to $60 each, with the total to be deducted from tribal annuity payments. On one occasion Sevier told the Cherokees that the trail left by horses stolen on the Cumberland headed directly to their towns. He admitted that whites were not blameless and advised, "It will be best for your people not to hunt too near our settlements, for it often times gives an opportunity on both sides for stealing of horses and other mischief to be done by bad people."

Violence was the worst possible "mischief." The situation was so volatile that in April 1796 Sevier assured the Cherokees that if several of their warriors had been murdered by whites as suspected, the state would punish the guilty parties for "so wrong and black a deed." But he warned the Indians against taking their own revenge, reminding them that "you are only a handful of people, and that war will ruin you if ever you enter into it again." A keen student of Cherokee ways, Sevier was particularly concerned that the Indians would honor their obligation to avenge the killing of any kinsman. If the guilty party could not be found, then any member of the murderer's clan could be slain in retaliation. By extension, this meant that innocent whites might suffer for the indiscretion of one violent individual. Sevier held this system of retribution "in the utmost detestation" and affirmed instead traditional English jurisprudence. Punishment should be meted out only to the guilty.

In the meantime, the governor well understood that a few

whites could destroy the uneasy peace. He continually warned fellow citizens against abusing the Indians and advocated punishing those who did so. His sensitivity to interracial relations was such that he was willing to issue a proclamation to protect representatives of the Creek Nation who wished to buy ammunition and other necessities on the Cumberland. He must have known, however, that warnings and proclamations would not deter some Tennesseans from violence against Indians, and that other whites were not likely to prosecute, much less convict, them. The easy acquisition of whiskey by Indians and whites alike was also a concern, as was the frequent interracial mingling for political and commercial reasons at Knoxville, the capital.

As Sevier realized, the maintenance of peace on the frontier depended on federal assistance. Since the days of the Southwest Territory, Tennessee officials had not had much luck in their efforts to secure significant aid from U.S. officials. The Northwest Territory, in contrast, received extensive assistance from the government, mostly because that region offered millions of acres of prime agricultural land that were still under the jurisdiction of the United States. Federal lands in Tennessee were limited and access to them was often severely encumbered by the claims of North Carolina and various speculators. Tennesseans had a love-hate relationship with the Federalist administration in Philadelphia. They recognized the necessity of federal support for defense and the acquisition of Indian land, but that dependency offended them. After the establishment and recognition of the new state government, it seemed likely the United States would withdraw some of its troops from Tennessee, and any such move would lead Indians to believe the federal government was no longer protecting the Southern frontier. Sevier called on the United States for assistance in the form of additional troops, especially cavalry, to supplement the small militia units and help maintain the peace. But first the Tennessee militiamen who had served in the campaigns of 1793 needed to be paid by Congress. Sevier, a veteran Indian fighter, believed most federal treaty negotiators were young, callow, unable to understand the Indian psyche, and lacked adequate translators. And besides, he believed the "savage" Indian nations were unlikely to observe the treaties anyway.

Another problem was the federal government's recent decision to establish federal trading posts, or "factories," throughout Indian country. The factories would offer a variety of goods at standardized and regulated rates and would thereby, in theory at least, remove one of the foremost irritants in Indian-white relations. Not surprisingly, the factory system immediately came under bitter attack from private traders and other entrepreneurs who viewed it as an unwarranted and damaging imposition of national authority. The federal trading post among the Tennessee Cherokees was Tellico Blockhouse, on the north side of the Little Tennessee River. Sevier was careful to couch his protests against the blockhouse in terms of the *Cherokees'* opposition to it and that of their influential white trader friends. He said the Cherokees ridiculed the president and Congress by calling them peddlers and viewed the factory system as a state-run monopoly. Indian commentary about the avarice of both private and government traders sometimes took earthy and colorful form. In 1772 a noted Chickasaw had complained that traders cheated his people with short-measures of fabrics, leaving the warriors' breechcloths so skimpy that "they don't cover our secret parts, and we are in danger of being deprived of our manhood by every hungry dog that approaches." A generation later Sevier quoted Red Headed Will, a mixed-blood Cherokee leader who said that federal traders were "scratching after every bit of a rackoon skin in the nation that was big enough to cover a squaw's —." Red Headed Will believed the Cherokees' hunting days were fast disappearing and next the whites would take their lands.

Tennessee elites were acutely attuned to national and international events, especially if such developments might affect their attempts to enrich themselves by obtaining more lands. Contrary to the common assumption that frontier regions are by definition isolated, Tennessee was part of a global economic and diplomatic network from its earliest days. Beginning in the early eighteenth century traders, diplomats, and military personnel had worked to enlist Cherokee and Chickasaw support for either the British or the French during the colonial wars. Later, global trade had been a crucial consideration for those same Indians during the American Revolution. In 1786 Westerners were shocked by negotiations between John Jay and Spain's Don Diego de Gardoqui which proposed long-term abandonment of American rights to navigate the Mississippi. And during the late 1780s elites like Blount, Sevier, and Robertson had intrigued with the Spanish while pressuring North Carolina and the U.S. government to address the needs of the West. In 1793 Tennessee leaders were aware of plots involving "Citizen" Edmond Genet, revolutionary France's minister to the United States, and his overblown plans to enlist frontiersmen to conquer Spanish Louisiana and Florida. They had rejoiced over the 1795 treaty in which Spain ceded much of the Southwest, granted Americans unrestricted navigation of the Mississippi, and secured the right of deposit in New Orleans. They also bemoaned the Jay Treaty of 1794, seen by many as a triumph of British interests over those of America. Andrew Jackson, still only in his twenties but already a prominent citizen of Nashville, railed at the Jay Treaty as an unconstitutional usurpation of authority by President Washington. And in 1798, amid the infamous XYZ Affair and the threat of war with France, Governor Sevier commented learnedly on the diplomatic skills of French Foreign Minister Talleyrand.

In 1796 the war raging between Britain and revolutionary France gave rise to one of the more bizarre episodes of foreign and domestic intrigue in Tennessee. Many Westerners, including Tennessee's Senator William Blount, heard rumors that as a result of the conflict France might pressure Spain into returning the Louisiana country, ceded to it in 1763, as well as East and West Florida. Also, France might rescind American rights of navigation and deposit on the Mississippi. The Tennesseans were reassured by their belief that Britain also had an interest in those lands and would be far more accommodating toward Americans. So it was that John Chisholm—Knoxville tavern owner, husband of a Cherokee, Blount acquaintance, and former British subject—suggested to the British minister in Philadelphia that London provide financial backing for American settlers in the West to seize Florida and Louisiana in behalf of Britain. In return the

Westerners would receive land grants and navigation rights on the Mississippi and would have access to New Orleans and Pensacola, which would become free ports. Reports circulated that Chisholm was going to muster one thousand men at Knoxville in preparation for an attack on the Floridas. Amid the rumors, Blount emerged as leader of the conspiracy, partly because he was a natural plotter and partly because fears of a French presence in the West threatened the value of his massive landholdings. If the scheme succeeded, Blount would be a hero, and new political vistas would perhaps open for him. By spring 1797 he was deeply involved in the intrigues, unaware that authorities in London had rejected the plan.

Never a particularly cautious man, Blount was indiscreet enough to write a letter revealing details of the scheme, and despite telling his associate to read it three times and burn it, the incriminating document fell into the hands of enemies in Knoxville, who forwarded it to President John Adams, who sent it to the U.S. Senate. Blount's evasions as to his authorship did no good. The Senate expelled him from office, and the House of Representatives impeached him for violating American neutrality, undermining federal authority over the Indians, and other offenses. Before the Senate could try him, Blount returned to Tennessee, where he was welcomed warmly by Andrew Jackson and other opponents of the Federalist administration. Though Blount was no longer in the Senate, that body considered trying him anyway but concluded that it had no jurisdiction and dismissed the impeachment early in 1799. Thus William Blount's long and varied federal service ended ingloriously. He was elected to the state senate and briefly served as its speaker before he died early in 1800. The Blount Conspiracy was a perfect reflection of the man's boldness, energy, and lack of character. But before dismissing it as the crackpot scheme of a notorious scoundrel, one should consider the possibility that it prompted a faster Spanish evacuation of the region ceded to the United States in 1795, and the conspiracy certainly brought national attention to the West and its needs.

The settlers' foremost need was to keep the Indians pacified while acquiring more of their land—a delicate balancing act indeed. Much to the dismay of Tennesseans, after the federal government finally surveyed the Treaty of Holston line, it enforced the removal of whites who had settled in the Powell Valley and near the Little Tennessee River. After continued entreaties, however, the Adams administration agreed to open negotiations with the Cherokees for an additional cession which would include the recently evacuated lands. While the lengthy deliberations were still underway in 1798, Sevier resorted to flattery. He wrote to President Adams that he appreciated "your friendship and attachment to the interest and welfare of our state, and particularly towards our unhappy frontier settlers, who have been obliged to remove from their farms." The president's "readiness to relieve their sufferings" made Tennessee hope "for an opportunity to repay with gratitude the munificent and paternal services rendered . . . in your administration." A month later Sevier wrote a friend that the president's solicitude toward Tennesseans "has gained him much friendship, and should he continue to manifest his regard, he will become much admired by the people."

The new treaty was finally concluded at the Tellico Blockhouse in October 1798. George Walton of Georgia and Colonel Thomas Butler, commander of U.S. troops in Tennessee, were the federal negotiators, and the forty-one Cherokee signatories included the redoubtable Bloody Fellow, the former Chickamauga leader who was the equal of William Blount in cunning and duplicity. The new cession included all lands north of the Little Tennessee to a point east of Chilhowee Mountain, as well as almost all the area between the Clinch River and the base of the Cumberland Plateau; the latter section included the recently vacated Powell Valley settlements. The Cherokees also agreed that both the Cumberland and Kentucky roads through their lands would be "free and open" for the use of U.S. citizens. With this treaty, virtually all white Tennesseans east of the Nashville Basin now resided on land cleared of Indian title. Nor was it a moment too soon; emigration into Tennessee during the first half of 1798 was "beyond the most sanguine expectation." Growth continued, and in the four years between statehood and 1800 Tennessee's population grew from slightly more than 80,000 to 105,602, including 13,584 slaves. Much of that increase came in Middle Tennessee, where several new counties had been created; Davidson County's population alone grew more than 36 percent, to 9,965. Middle Tennessee's population in 1796 had been little more than 15 per- cent of the state's total, but by 1800 it represented nearly one- third.

Clearly the growing population necessitated additional cessions of Indian lands and other assistance that only the U.S. government could provide. The Federalists had spent relatively little time or money addressing the needs of Tennessee, and they had even attempted to block or delay the state's admission to the union. During the 1796–97 legislative session in Philadelphia, securing federal approval for the compensation of Tennessee militiamen for their Indian campaigns of the early 1790s required almost Herculean efforts by Congressman Andrew Jackson. An angry Jackson clearly revealed his anti-Federalist sentiments when he joined the minority who voted against a report effusively praising President Washington as he prepared to leave office. After 1798, when President Adams proved unwilling to force more Indian cessions, Tennessee's support for the brusque New Englander, never extending beyond Sevier's transparent flattery, dissipated quickly. Governor Sevier and other leaders had higher hopes for Thomas Jefferson, the new Republican president elected in 1800.

Though Tennesseans seemed to be united in opposition to the Federalists, the apparently harmonious state political system created by William Blount was beginning to fray. Factions began to coalesce around two towering symbols of the frontier. One was the well-established and beloved John Sevier, who was fifty-five years old in 1800. Nolichucky Jack squared off against the other symbol: thirty-three-year old Andrew Jackson. While Sevier's faction was gradually distancing itself from the Blount machine, Jackson remained a staunch Blount loyalist. The personal rivalry of the two men apparently began in 1796 when Jackson, recently elected to the House of Representatives, offered himself as a candidate for major general of the state militia. But Governor Sevier, once head of the militia himself, helped to engineer the election of George Conway to the position. Furious, Jackson said some things which Sevier found "scurelous." But the governor wrote

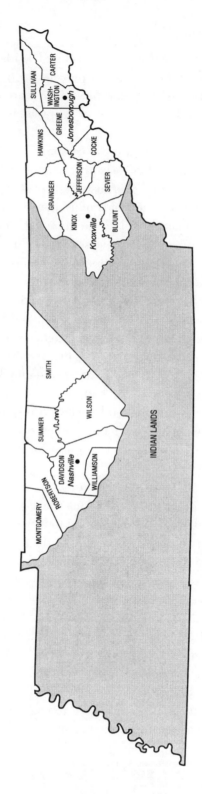

Tennessee, 1800. Department of Geography and the Cartographic Services Laboratory at the University of Tennessee.

to a friend that as a man of accomplishment and distinction he cared little about the charges of a "poor pitifull petty fogging Lawyer." Months later, when Jackson found out about the slur— imagine, Jackson a pettifogging lawyer!—he was calm enough to send Sevier a measured remonstrance, to which the governor responded with equal forbearance. The two appeared to patch up the squabble, and in 1797 the legislature, with Sevier's acquiescence, selected Jackson to replace Blount in the Senate. When Jackson resigned from that body the following year and wished an appointment to the Superior Court of Tennessee (the state's highest), Governor Sevier graciously assented, saying it would "give general satisfaction" to citizens. Still, the two men remained wary of one another.

As might be expected in disputes among frontier elites, round two of the Sevier-Jackson feud centered on land. This affair involved North Carolina's lavish grants of military land warrants in Tennessee since the early 1780s. By 1790, shortly after North Carolina made its second and final cession of Tennessee to the United States, the mother state had issued 3,723 warrants for a total of almost 2.7 million acres in Tennessee. North Carolina continued to issue warrants even after Tennessee achieved statehood, and by 1798 there were more than 5,300 of them. However, thousands of the warrants had been sold to speculators for a fraction of their value, lands remained unpatented, and many veterans or their heirs had yet to file claims. If there was insufficient tillable land within the military district of Middle Tennessee, individuals had the right to claim other unappropriated lands within the state. Speculators had already filed many claims within the Chickasaw domain in West Tennessee—so-called potentials for the time when those Indians would surrender their lands. Also vexing were the unsystematic methods of locating claims and the imprecise metes-and-bounds survey used by North Carolina, producing a patchwork of overlapping and poorly defined claims.

The possibilities for corruption in such a chaotic system were apparent, and in 1797 Andrew Jackson heard stories about massive fraud in the Nashville land office. He informed the governor of North Carolina, and officials there immediately began investigating records in both Raleigh and the Nashville office. As the evidence unfolded, Jackson gradually came to believe that the corruption extended to Governor Sevier and Jackson's own brother-in-law, Stockley Donelson. (The latter discovery allegedly inspired Jackson to remark, "When you set a bear trap, you never can tell what particular bear is going to blunder into it.") Sevier blocked transportation of the Nashville records because he feared they might be compromised, so North Carolina officials copied them. Reports in 1798 and 1799 detailed massive and flagrant fraud involving officials in both states. The Nashville office had recorded more warrants than North Carolina had issued. Sevier remained in the background because the records relating to him were ambiguous in their import. Jackson, still convinced of the governor's culpability, chose to remain silent about his beliefs until an opportune moment. Stockley Donelson avoided extradition to North Carolina, and two of William Blount's brothers were cleared of charges brought against them, but North Carolina Secretary of State James Glasgow was forced to resign because of his role in the frauds. The scandal heightened the tension between Tennessee and North Carolina over the latter's continuing use of military bounty lands, and the uncertainty of titles and confused system of survey understandably depressed land values wherever the warrants were used.

Jackson waited several years before attacking Sevier for his alleged role in the land corruption. The Tennessee constitution required the latter to step down as governor in 1801 after finishing three consecutive two-year terms, and Jackson's friend Archibald Roane became the new governor. But Sevier was not prepared to leave public service. He confidently became a candidate for major general of the militia, a position that had become vacant when General Conway died. Andrew Jackson also wanted the position, and his growing political acumen had gained him prominent allies. When the militia officers cast their ballots, Jackson and Sevier each received seventeen votes, while James Winchester got three. Governor Roane, following state law, broke the tie by choosing Jackson. Sevier was outraged that he had lost to a pettifogger with no military experience. What he did not know was that Jackson, at almost the same time as his appointment, conveyed to Roane certain documents which he said proved Sevier's malfeasance in the land scandal. It was a windfall for the governor, who knew that Sevier would likely oppose his bid for reelection. When Sevier did indeed become a candidate for governor in 1803, Roane made the documents public, and General Jackson supported him by using the *Knoxville Gazette* to accuse Sevier of bribing James Glasgow to gain his assistance in several major land transactions. Sevier vehemently denied wrongdoing, and if anything the actions of Roane and Jackson worked to his advantage. He easily defeated Roane and was inaugurated as governor on September 23.

A direct confrontation between Sevier and Jackson was inevitable. That dramatic moment occurred in Knoxville barely a week after Sevier's inauguration. Jackson, in his capacity as judge, was in town to hold court, and by chance he encountered his enemy in the public square. After mutual insults, some involving Rachel Jackson and therefore certain to enrage her husband, a near brawl ensued. The next day Jackson, still seething, penned a formal challenge to Sevier for a duel. The governor said he would oblige his rival, but not on the soil of Tennessee, which had outlawed such "affairs of honor." Jackson wanted to meet him in Knoxville, where the offenses had occurred, but finally, after using the *Gazette* to call Sevier "a base coward and poltroon," he assented to finish the matter in an adjoining state or the nearby Indian country. The two men finally agreed to meet in Indian country near Southwest Point, and there Jackson impatiently waited until Sevier and his entourage showed up. What followed was a true comic opera. Both men dismounted, then they cursed one another, stomped around, and so frightened Sevier's horse that it ran away with the governor's pistols. When Jackson drew his own pistol, Sevier scurried behind a tree, and others produced their weapons. In the words of Robert V. Remini, "It was quite ridiculous. Jackson's second was aiming at Sevier's son, who was aiming at Jackson, who was aiming at Sevier, who was hidden behind a tree." Everyone seemed to recognize the situation's absurdity, and cooler heads persuaded the two antagonists to avoid violence. Jackson and Sevier never reconciled, but the two giants of frontier Tennessee agreed to coexist as their state continued to grow.

Chastened by his experiences with Sevier, Jackson soon surrendered his judgeship and seemed satisfied to serve as major general of the militia. In peacetime, however, he had little opportunity to demonstrate his leadership and gain renown. The once-promising Middle Tennessean was in danger of sinking into obscurity—or worse, notoriety. Though his officers admired his fiery manner and continued to stand by him, two events led some citizens to question his morality, dignity, and even loyalty. The first was his duel with John Dickinson, a charming and socially prominent young man. The two had had a long-simmering feud involving bets on horse races and Dickinson's drunken allusions to Rachel Jackson and her bigamy with Jackson. The "affair of honor" took place in May 1806, just over the Kentucky line. One of the best marksmen in Tennessee, Dickinson snapped off a quick shot that lodged in Jackson's chest. Severely wounded, Jackson managed to remain standing. He took careful aim at his antagonist and squeezed the trigger. When the hammer stopped at the half cock position, Jackson pulled it back, aimed again, and fired a shot which mortally wounded Dickinson. Though Tennesseans were not unfamiliar with duels, many viewed Jackson as a brutal, cold-blooded killer. Wounded or not, he could have ended the matter honorably without killing his young foe. Jackson appeared to be a "violent, vengeful man."

Just a few months after the Dickinson affray, Jackson was further embarrassed by his unfortunate connection with Aaron Burr, Thomas Jefferson's former vice president. A natural schemer, Burr had concocted a shadowy plan to raise a military force and seize Spanish territory in the Southwest—and perhaps pluck some other fruit as well. Jackson was smitten by Burr's charm and charisma, and he even had a business connection with him. Jackson also reveled in the prospect of leading his militia against the despised Spanish "Dons," expanding the American republic, and gaining military renown. But he was shocked when he heard rumors that Burr's plans possibly included seizing U.S. territory. Convinced of Burr's loyalty to the United States, Jackson suspected that General James Wilkinson, the commander of American forces in the Southwest, was responsible (and indeed, the wily and duplicitous general was involved). As the conspiracy unraveled, Jackson noisily proclaimed his patriotism and readiness to use his militia to undo any plot against the United States. The authorities arrested Burr—but not Wilkinson—and sent him to Washington on charges of treason. His trial, resulting in acquittal, was a sensation and featured a classic confrontation between President Jefferson, who hated Burr, and Chief Justice John Marshall. Because Jackson vehemently defended Burr and attacked the Jefferson administration, he found himself at odds not only with the president, but also with Secretary of State James Madison, who was clearly in line to succeed Jefferson. That was unfortunate for Jackson; the aspiring general from Tennessee could not expect Madison's support as the United States moved toward war with Britain.

In the meantime, Tennesseans were clamoring for more Indian cessions, and in this respect the Republican administrations of Thomas Jefferson did not disappoint them. The president had always had an intellectual and geopolitical interest in the West, and he idealized an expanding, agricultural republic of virtuous yeomen. To achieve such a society the United States would have to acquire more land from both Indians and foreign nations, neither of which should be allowed to threaten national expansion and security. The most dramatic manifestation of Jefferson's stance was the Louisiana Purchase of 1803. Spain had recently ceded the Louisiana country to Napoleonic France, and Jefferson and the Westerners feared that American rights in the Southwest would be jeopardized by their powerful French neighbor. Most Westerners, Tennesseans included, expressed confidence in Jefferson's ability to resolve the matter without resorting to military action, but they were prepared to fight if necessary. The president first instructed his emissaries in France to offer $10 million for West Florida and the city of New Orleans, but strategic developments led Napoleon to offer all of Louisiana at the bargain-basement price of $15 million. Despite constitutional questions and other misgivings, the deal was concluded in the spring of 1803.

With the acquisition of Louisiana, the United States overnight expanded from the Atlantic Ocean to the Rocky Mountains and from the Gulf of Mexico to Canada. The nation had doubled in size, gaining millions of acres of fertile land—enough for the expanding white population and even those Indians who might be persuaded to exchange their Eastern homelands for new tribal domains in the West. The purchase also meant that for the first time in its history Tennessee did not adjoin any foreign territory, did not play any direct diplomatic role. That change was symbolized by the altered U.S. military presence on the site of present-day Memphis. Just a few years earlier, the federal government had constructed Fort Adams there as a symbol of American sovereignty and a bastion against Spanish and French threats. In 1798 the installation was moved two miles southward and renamed Fort Pickering in honor of the U.S. secretary of state (a larger fort below Natchez was named for the president). After the Louisiana Purchase, however, these posts were almost superfluous. The Mississippi was now exclusively an American waterway. Fort Pickering was reduced to the role of controlling the Indian trade and domestic shipping, and after 1813 it no longer had even a garrison.

Of more immediate concern to Tennesseans than the acquisition of Louisiana was Jefferson's systematic policy of cajoling Indians into ceding additional lands within the state. The president authorized another conference with the Cherokees, which was held at Tellico in October 1805. Serving as United States commissioners were Return Jonathan Meigs, the federal agent to the Cherokees, and Daniel Smith, one of the Cumberland's oldest and most respected leaders. Thirty-three Cherokees including Doublehead represented the Cherokees. Two separate treaties were signed. The more important of the two included the cession of the remaining Cherokee lands in the Nashville Basin as far south as the Duck River and all of the Cumberland Plateau southward to the mouth of the Hiwassee. Most of Middle and East Tennessee were now joined, and the Cumberland Road was entirely outside the Cherokee domain. The Indians also allowed the United States to construct two other roads through their remaining Tennessee lands, one from the Murfreesboro area southeastward into Georgia, and the other from Franklin down to Muscle Shoals and on to the settlements in Mississippi Territory. Because Fort Southwest Point and the trading house at Tellico were no longer conveniently situated for conducting Cherokee affairs, the government obtained a site on the north side of the Tennessee River across from the mouth of the Hiwassee, where a new Cherokee agency was soon opened.

The second treaty, concluded two days after the first, included a Cherokee promise not to restrict travel over a proposed road from Knoxville through Cherokee lands to New Orleans. More interestingly, the Cherokees surrendered the valuable land occupied by the soon-to-be-defunct Fort Southwest Point, supposedly because Tennessee intended to establish a new state capital there. But the announcement of that plan was a mere ploy. Later that year the general assembly dutifully decreed that it would hold its next meeting at Southwest Point, but it did so for only one day (September 21, 1807) and adopted only a single resolution—that the capital be moved back to Knoxville. The compensation for the Cherokee cessions in the two treaties of 1805 totaled $3,000 in merchandise, an annuity of $3,000, and $12,600 in money or, if the Indians preferred, in agricultural or industrial implements. Within a year additional treaties with the Cherokees and Chickasaws cleared overlapping tribal claims to the area between the Duck River drainage and the Tennessee River in Alabama. The acquisitions of 1805 and 1806 cost the United States about one and a half cents an acre, the average price for Indian cessions of the time. Afterward the only remaining Indian land within the eastern half of the state was the southeastern corner, which was still occupied by the Cherokees; the Chickasaws retained claims to a small part of Middle Tennessee as well as all of West Tennessee.

The treaties of 1805 and 1806 represented major concessions by the Cherokees and created much internal discord. Giving up their extensive hunting domain on the Cumberland Plateau and in adjoining portions of south-central Tennessee and northern Alabama signified an admission by certain tribal leaders that hunting was no longer a viable occupation. Hunting and all of its related activities, ritual, and core of belief, which had been so central to Cherokee culture, were now superfluous as the tribe embarked on the road to civilization. To many Indians ceding their hunting grounds was a terrible repudiation of their heritage. Even as more and more males accepted their role as farmers, others viewed the hunting lands as a cherished possession that offered a brief escape from the white man's world. Those lands carried memories of prouder days, when hunting and warfare defined the Cherokee male identity. The loss was more than just real estate; it was a cultural diminution.

To make matters worse, a number of village chiefs had conspired to use the cessions as a means of enriching themselves. Foremost among these was Doublehead. Once a fearsome Chickamauga leader, he, along with other chiefs of the Lower Towns in northern Alabama, had become a calculating proponent of the white man's civilization. Doublehead had used his position as speaker of the Cherokee national council to appropriate for himself and like-minded chiefs a grossly disproportionate share of treaty annuities and other federal perquisites. In 1803, when the Cherokees reluctantly agreed to allow construction of the Federal Road through their lands between Nashville and Augusta, Georgia, they stipulated that "our beloved chief Doublehead" would have control of the important ferry at Southwest Point. He was a wily schemer who often played both sides, seeming to uphold Cherokee rights and dignity while offering a helping—albeit grasping—hand to federal authorities. Before the treaty of 1805 was signed, he was receiving extra credit at the government trading post and had been promised a special private reserve within the lands to be ceded. And in January 1806 he and thirteen other accommodating Cherokee chiefs received significant favors in Washington, D.C. when they signed the treaty giving up Cherokee claims between the Duck and Tennessee rivers. The most remarkable reward was "Doublehead's Tract," a one-hundred-square-mile grant on the north side of Muscle Shoals. In addition, a delighted President Jefferson awarded him $1,000 for "his active influence" in promoting civilization among the Cherokees, "for his friendly disposition towards the United States," and for helping him become an even more "useful example among the Red People." The fourteen chiefs decided to keep for themselves $2,000 of the $10,000 that Congress would pay for the latest cession and to allow Meigs to use the rest to pay off debts that they and other chiefs owed traders.

Doublehead had overplayed his hand. He had become arrogant, too confident of his own ability and power. His actions and those of his associates, most of whom came from the Lower Towns, infuriated many Cherokees residing in the more numerous Upper Towns of southeastern Tennessee and northern Georgia. The more remote Valley Cherokees in western North Carolina mostly remained aloof. The "younger" chiefs of the Cherokee Nation were primarily responsible for the rising tide against Doublehead and his collaborators. Some of these men may have been middle-aged or even older, but they would not be recognized as "old" chiefs until elected as such by the national council. This was not simply a dispute between full-blood traditionalists and mixed-blood advocates of "progress." Doublehead was a full-blood, while many of those opposing him and upholding Cherokee tradition were mixed-bloods. No, the dispute was more a matter of outrage toward Doublehead and his coterie (including Meigs) for their defiance of accepted tribal procedure in handling land matters and for their transparent self-interest. There was a growing perception that their identity as Cherokees depended on affirming tribal ownership of all lands; only this would prevent hasty and ill-considered cessions of a precious heritage belonging to all.

Amid Cherokee calls for a renunciation of the Treaty of Washington, Doublehead remained defiant. Finally in July 1807 a number of younger leaders secretly met and decided that the old chief should die for his transgressions. The drama played out in August at a stickball contest at Hiwassee Town, Tennessee. Amid the drinking, betting, and general excitement attending the competition, a Cherokee named Bone Polisher accosted Doublehead and called him a traitor. When Bone Polisher made a threatening move, the chief drew his gun, and Bone Polisher his hatchet. Doublehead killed him on the spot. Later that day one or more assailants shot Doublehead at a local tavern and left him for dead. Friends moved him to a nearby house, but three Cherokee conspirators found and killed him with knives, hatchets, and guns. One of the assassins was apparently The Ridge, later to become famous within the Cherokee Nation as Major Ridge. The death of Doublehead was a clear signal that many Cherokees would oppose any further cessions of tribal lands. Woe to those leaders who would sacrifice their common birthright.

The division among the Cherokees became even more apparent in 1808, when agent Meigs attempted to persuade residents of the Lower Towns to sell their portion of the tribal domain and move across the Mississippi to present-day Arkansas. Since the 1790s about one thousand mostly traditionalist Cherokees had willingly emigrated there on their own. Despite Meigs's earlier praise of Cherokee males for their strides toward becoming agriculturists, he now hoped to sway them by emphasizing the attractive hunting lands of Arkansas, where they could enjoy the old way of life. His contradictory stance simply reflected what everyone knew: acquiring the Indians' land was always more important to federal authorities than civilizing them. A number of the Lower Town chiefs agreed to discuss an exchange of lands, but only in Washington, where suspicious tribesmen could not follow their every move. Coincidentally, and unknown to Meigs, thirty-two Cherokees from some Upper Towns in Tennessee had just completed their own conversations in Washington with Secretary of War Henry Dearborn and President Jefferson himself. That they consulted neither Meigs nor chiefs of the Upper Towns in Georgia, shows that they trusted no one and had their own agenda. They apparently represented some of the Cherokees living between the Little Tennessee and Hiwassee rivers. Noting their recent strides toward civilization, they requested that the tribal domain be divided between the Lower and Upper Towns and that those who wanted to farm receive their own private lands. Because they were still untutored in the arts of civilization, they did not want to become individual citizens of Tennessee, but rather citizens and wards of the United States. Jefferson told them to discuss this with the Lower Towns and suggested that some Cherokees might want to follow the hunter's life in Arkansas.

Meigs continued to aggressively encourage tribal removal to Arkansas, and a number of people in the Lower Towns prepared to join friends and kinsmen there. As rumors of a general removal mounted, whites squatted on Cherokee lands in Tennessee and Georgia, expecting to have preemption rights when the United States concluded the necessary treaties. Late in 1809, with the encouragement of Meigs and Governor Willie Blount (half-brother of William Blount), the Tennessee legislature sent a resolution to President James Madison urging Cherokee removal. By then, however, the crisis had galvanized the chiefs of the Upper Towns in Georgia and some in Tennessee to take decisive action. At national councils in 1808, 1809, and 1810 they initiated a series of measures designed to prevent local or regional interests from disrupting the Cherokee polity. New laws affirmed the supremacy of the council and denied the right of any Cherokee individual to exchange any part of their common domain for new lands in the West. No longer would unscrupulous whites be able to pit Lower Towns against Upper Towns. Instead, annual national councils would rule on all major issues, and a national committee of representative chiefs would exercise authority when councils were not in session. The younger chiefs of the Upper Towns who had spearheaded these institutional changes achieved a united front by adding to the committee a number of "beloved old warriors" from the Lower Towns and Tennessee. Although some eight hundred Cherokees voluntarily emigrated to Arkansas in 1810, they left knowing that their fellow Indians refused to cede any of the lands they had occupied. These events mark the true emergence of a Cherokee Nation. Continuing a long heritage of shrewd adaptability, the Cherokees had rationally appraised the present crisis and selected a course of action that prevented both a mass removal to the West and further cessions of their lands. They had power, but how long could they retain it?

At least as perplexing to Tennesseans as Cherokee insistence on retaining their lands was the confusion over the lands already cleared of Indian title. How to determine the respective rights of Tennessee, North Carolina, and the United States and reach an equitable settlement? Well before Tennessee achieved statehood, North Carolina had already granted or sold many of the best lands there, including potentials located in unceded Indian territory. Even after Tennessee statehood, North Carolina's largesse with military grants continued. Tennessee argued that its new status implied a right to all remaining land within its limits, but both North Carolina and the federal government disagreed. The United States claimed title to all land in Tennessee not already subject to a valid claim, with the exception of North Carolina's right to meet future requests for military land bounties by its revolutionary veterans or their heirs. Tennessee naturally wanted as much land as possible to ensure its future growth and prosperity.

After a long and complicated series of negotiations between the three parties, they reached an agreement in 1806. One of the provisions was the creation of the Congressional Reservation encompassing all of Tennessee west of the Tennessee River and the southwestern portion of Middle Tennessee. All of the reservation west of the Tennessee still belonged to the Chickasaws, and when they finally ceded their claims, it would become part of the federal public domain. The potentials already located there under North Carolina law remained valid, but no new ones would be accepted unless there was insufficient land available elsewhere in Tennessee to satisfy North Carolina's future revolutionary claims. Tennessee controlled the rest of the state and would attempt to satisfy North Carolina's claims there, excluding the area south of the French Broad, east of the Tennessee, and north of the Little Tennessee, which North Carolina had conceded to the Cherokees in 1783. Any more claims in that region would hopelessly confuse the already bewildering status of property and squatter rights attending the Treaty of the Holston and its belated survey. When the Cherokees finally ceded their remaining lands within the state, Tennessee would have exclusive ownership. In return for the various concessions, the state agreed to set aside large tracts of land for the support of public schools, academies, and two colleges, one each in East and Middle Tennessee; these lands, with certain exceptions, would not be sold for less than the federal minimum price of $2 an acre. Though state leaders believed this arrangement ensured continued growth and income, they would prove susceptible to the political pressures of squatters who demanded the right of preemption and sometimes refused to pay anything at all for land. Worse yet, North Carolina's land grants in Tennessee continued to proliferate.

Amid all the confusion over Indian cessions and the conflicting state and federal claims, Tennessee continued to grow and even prosper. Knoxville and Nashville were the hubs of their respective parts of the state; the former was still politically dominant

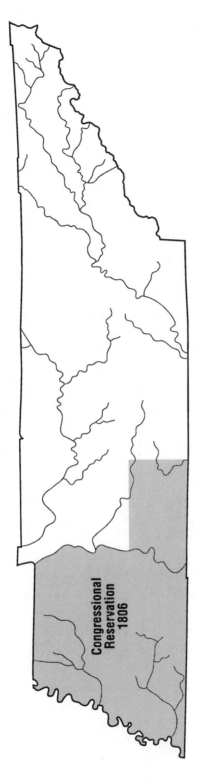

Congressional Reservation, 1806.

as the capital, but it was not growing as rapidly as Nashville. Knoxville attracted all the leading political figures within the state as well as many visiting dignitaries. Blount Mansion, the governor's residence, was a frontier bastion of sophistication. For most of the 1790s the *Knoxville Gazette* was the state's only newspaper, carrying international, national, and regional news, local chitchat, and sharp editorial opinion (especially on Indian policy). The Reverend Samuel Carrick was still the only teacher at Blount College, which by the early 1800s had moved from the reverend's home to a two-story frame building on the town square. The school's classical curriculum included studies in Greek, Latin, rhetoric, logic, and natural and moral philosophy. Tuition had risen to $8, room and board to $25. Many men of later prominence matriculated there, but the college's only known degree was conferred in 1806. The truth is that Blount College and its frontier counterparts were more like secondary schools than true colleges. By 1807, when the legislature renamed it East Tennessee College, its only legacies were the building, some former students, a curriculum, and an enduring problem of insolvency. No one could have imagined that after a long and troubled metamorphosis it would emerge as The University of Tennessee.

With the end of the Indian wars and completion of the Cumberland Road, Nashville began to grow. Its first newspaper, the *Tennessee Gazette*, began publication in 1797, the same year postal service was established from Knoxville. But by 1800 Nashville still had only 345 people—191 whites, 151 slaves, and 3 free blacks. As might be expected in a frontier community, the males greatly outnumbered females, 131 to 60. The town's inhabitants were also quite young; only eight white males and four white females were older than forty-five years. Clustered around the four-acre square fronting the river on Water Street were a few substantial business buildings, including an impressive but still unfinished stone edifice where that same year Bishop Francis Asbury, on his first visit to town, preached repentance to a crowd of sinners. Perhaps the most imposing building was the Talbot Hotel, which boasted nine rooms and twenty-three windows. It was the hotel of choice for visitors and a local favorite for conviviality and gossip. Nashville and Middle Tennessee soon experi-

Blount College in Knoxville, ca. 1807. COURTESY THE
UNIVERSITY OF TENNESSEE SPECIAL COLLECTIONS.

enced remarkable economic growth, and in 1808, eight years
after his first visit, Bishop Asbury found Nashville "greatly improved," with "an elegant court house." And in 1812 the town
won the coveted status of state capital from Knoxville. When Asbury returned that year, he complained that the stone house
where he had preached before had been razed to make room for
a new statehouse. But he admitted that the new building easily
surpassed the old in grandeur if not in sanctity. Knoxville again
became the capital in 1817, followed by Murphreesboro in 1819,
and then Nashville again in 1826, this time permanently.

Relocating the capital to Nashville was simply a political ac-
knowledgment that Middle Tennessee had surpassed East Tennessee in numbers and prosperity. Between 1800 and 1810 the
number of counties in Tennessee rose from eighteen to thirty-
seven, with those in Middle Tennessee increasing from seven to
twenty-one. The population from the Cumberland Plateau west-

ward to the Tennessee River had risen to 160,360, compared to 101,367 in East Tennessee. Davidson County, which had been divided to allow the creation of new counties, still had the largest population—15,608, including 9,173 whites, 6,305 slaves, and 130 free blacks. The slaves represented slightly more than 40 percent of the county's population, a proportion reflecting the increasing importance of slave-based commercial agriculture. Knox County, in contrast, ranked second among East Tennessee counties with a population of 10,171, including just 1,271 blacks (about 12.5 percent of the total). All of the counties in that part of the state had a total of only 9,376 blacks, barely 9 percent of the population. Campbell County, a poor area on the edge of the Cumberland Plateau, had just 4 percent. These demographic statistics clearly corresponded to the physiographic and economic disparities between East and Middle Tennessee.

By 1810, as trouble escalated between the United States and Great Britain, Tennesseans and other Westerners acknowledged—and even exulted in—the likelihood of war. Fighting for its life against Napoleonic France, Britain had resorted to a blockade of that nation and European ports under its control. It also renewed its despised tactics of the 1790s: stopping American ships on the high seas, inspecting their cargoes for contraband, and frequently impressing sailors into service for the Royal Navy. Napoleon responded by targeting American vessels trading with British ports. National pride was offended. Tennesseans, like other Americans, held mass protests in 1807 when a British warship fired on the USS *Chesapeake*, an American frigate, forced it to surrender, then took several of its crew. Beginning with the Embargo Act, the Jefferson and Madison administrations enacted measures designed to pressure Britain and France into respecting American rights. As good Republicans, Tennesseans supported those attempts and became more aggressive in denouncing Britain in particular.

Tennesseans believed a war with Britain would likely mean American annexation of present-day Canada, where the British had conspired with Indian leaders like Tecumseh, a militant foe of American expansion. War also carried the possibility that the United States would acquire the Floridas because Spain was a British ally against Napoleon; no longer would runaway slaves be

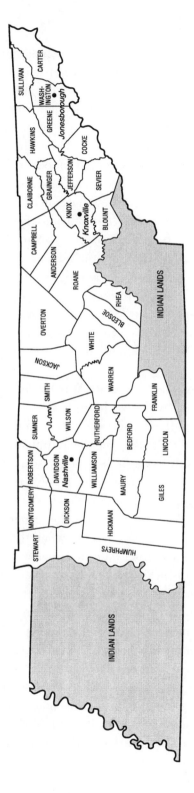

TENNESSEE, 1810. DEPARTMENT OF GEOGRAPHY AND THE CARTOGRAPHIC SERVICES LABORATORY AT THE UNIVERSITY OF TENNESSEE.

able to find refuge there. Tennessee's Congressman Felix Grundy reflected an impressive breadth of vision when he said he was "anxious not only to add the Floridas to the South, but the Canadas to the North of this empire." His comments were distinctly nationalistic in tone, rife with indignation over the affront to the American people and body politic. Other frontiersmen-cum-political leaders echoed his sentiments about Britain. As early as 1810 John Sevier said it was "high time that insolent and perfidious nation was chastised." Andrew Jackson agreed, spouting nationalist diatribes against both John Bull and the Spanish "Dons." When the Twelfth U.S. Congress convened in 1811, Tennessee's entire congressional delegation—including Grundy and the recently elected John Sevier—were among the frontier War Hawks who followed the lead of Speaker of the House Henry Clay, a dynamic young Kentuckian. Their agitation was important in securing a declaration of war on June 18, 1812, ironically after Britain had already decided to abandon its most objectionable maritime offenses.

Andrew Jackson was exultant. War at last! This was the long-awaited chance to prove himself. He immediately wrote President Madison offering to raise 2,500 volunteers under his command to fight the British, but the administration had no intention of allowing him to earn the glory he so avidly sought. This was especially galling because even before declaring war, the government had appointed James Winchester, Jackson's friend and subordinate in the militia, as brigadier general in the regular army. Jackson's chance came, though, when the federal government asked Governor Willie Blount to provide 1,500 men to support General Wilkinson in the defense of New Orleans. Blount ignored the suggestion that someone other than Jackson be in command and signed a commission appointing his friend major general of U.S. volunteers, a more prestigious rank than major general of state volunteers. Despite his misgivings about serving under the rascally Wilkinson, Jackson assembled almost 2,100 troops in Nashville and started toward New Orleans in the bitter cold of January 1813. He and most of his men went by boat while the cavalry and mounted infantry headed overland to meet them at Natchez. Upon his arrival there, Jackson received orders that he was to proceed no farther, and a bit later that he and his men were no longer needed and were thus discharged from service. Jackson was outraged. The government had abandoned him and his troops in Natchez. They were without necessary provisions, without pay, and far from home. His only recourse, he decided, was to lead them back to Nashville by way of the Natchez Trace. It required supreme will and leadership on his part to threaten and cajole them over those five hundred miles, but somehow he kept them going. He was strong, yet solicitous about his troops' welfare. His iron determination, his *will*, led his men to liken him to the toughest thing they knew—hickory wood. And because their respect was now mingled with affection, he became Old Hickory. By the time they returned to Tennessee, Andrew Jackson had proven himself a leader.

But leadership on the battlefield was another matter. By late 1813 few Tennesseans had actually experienced combat. General James Winchester, Jackson's old friend, was a notable exception. After recruitment duty for the U.S. Army in the Ohio Valley, he had received command of a force moving toward Detroit. They had succeeded in driving a detachment of British soldiers out of Frenchtown, a small settlement on the River Raisin a short distance south of Detroit, but a larger force of British troops and Indian allies attacked them on the morning of January 22, 1813. The Americans were routed and Winchester was among the officers captured. Not until the spring of 1814 was he released in an exchange of prisoners, and when he returned home, he vigorously defended his conduct at the River Raisin against the charges of General William Henry Harrison and others. Like Andrew Jackson, Winchester was a member of the frontier elite who was acutely sensitive about his honor. On another front in 1813, John Williams, the adjutant general of the Tennessee militia, led a force of about 165 East Tennesseans into Spanish Florida. A small detachment of regular U.S. soldiers accompanied them. After skirmishing with the Seminoles and burning several of their towns, the expeditionary force returned to American soil.

In the meantime, Jackson had finally found himself a war, a brutal sideshow of the conflict with Britain. It involved the "Red Sticks," a militant Creek faction in the Upper Towns of what is now south-central Alabama. The Red Sticks had long resented American inroads on their lands and native culture. By 1811 they were undergoing a religious revitalization that emphasized retention of their old ways and resistance to the civilizing efforts of Benjamin Hawkins, their federal agent. They also hated their accommodationist brothers living in the Lower Towns of eastern Alabama and Georgia. The real trouble began in October 1811 with the arrival of Tecumseh from the North. He had been unsuccessful in his attempts to persuade the Chickasaws and Choctaws to join his pan-Indian confederacy against American expansion, but the Upper Creeks proved more hospitable. Tecumseh's prestige as a Shawnee warrior, and the fact that his mother was a Creek, guaranteed a large audience when he made an impassioned appeal for unity against American aggression. His eloquence and logic stirred many, especially the younger warriors. They would remember his words.

Shortly after Tecumseh's departure, Mother Nature rumbled a dramatic accent note. Between December 1811 and early 1812 a series of earthquakes centered in the Mississippi Valley near New Madrid, Missouri, reverberated throughout the trans-Appalachian region, stirring apocalyptic and millennial visions among whites and Indians alike. Traditionalist Creeks saw cosmological and sacred significance in the quakes, signs that they should join Tecumseh's holy crusade. There was an unease throughout the Creek Nation, a waiting for something. The match that ignited this tinder was an American demand that the Creeks apprehend and execute several of their warriors who had killed some whites along the Ohio and Duck rivers. The Creeks did as they were commanded, but the Red Sticks were inflamed by the executions. Goaded by aggressive shamans, they initiated a civil war against tribal accommodationists. Rather than watch from the sidelines, frontier whites attacked some Red Sticks, and the result was a major war. The chief leader of the Creek insurgents was Red Eagle, a mixed-blood who was also known as William Weatherford. On August 30, 1813, he led 750 warriors in an attack on Fort Mims, a trading post about forty miles above Mobile. Inside the fort were 120 militiamen and some 300 whites, mixed-bloods, friendly Creeks, and blacks. In heavy fighting the

Red Sticks took the fort, leaving nearly 250 defenders dead. Most of those who survived were blacks. As word of the attack on Fort Mims spread, exaggerated tales of Red Stick atrocities circulated, as did rumors that Britain and Spain would back the Indians. The Creek War thus blended into the larger War of 1812.

The Creeks were a convenient, accessible foe. They owned millions of acres of fertile lands and controlled several promising overland and water routes between Mississippi Territory, Tennessee, Georgia, and Louisiana. Andrew Jackson was one of a number of Southern leaders who were anxious to dispossess them. As early as the spring of 1812, following the killing of whites on Duck River, he had written that "we are ready to pant for vengeance. . . . The whole Creek nation shall be covered with blood." The *Nashville Clarion* was less hyperbolic and more honest, saying that the murders by Creeks provided a convenient "pretext for the dismemberment of their country." The carnage at Fort Mims settled the matter. Self-preservation, honor, and the desire for land dictated a war against the Creeks. When the Tennessee legislature called for 3,500 volunteers, throngs of patriotic young men responded, and Jackson and Major General John Cocke of East Tennessee were soon leading two armies into Alabama. Altogether, counting both volunteers and U.S. troops, each army numbered about 2,500 men. Jackson was to assume overall command when the armies converged in northern Alabama, and the combined force would later link up with separate forces from Georgia and Mississippi Territory. The soldiers would build a series of secure forts and supply depots throughout the Creek homeland and ruthlessly carry the war to all hostile villages.

The first Red Stick town to fall to Jackson's forces was Tallussahatchee on November 3, 1813. Almost all of the defending warriors perished in the bloodbath. As a young recruit named Davy Crockett recalled many years later, "We shot them like dogs." He said one Creek woman was shot at least twenty times, and soldiers burned to death forty-six warriors who had taken refuge in a house. Crockett claimed that on the following day his comrades ate potatoes that had been taken from the house's cellar and stewed in the oil of the incinerated bodies. Despite the early victory, a critical lack of supplies made it impossible for

Jackson to bring the Creek War to a quick, decisive end. His soldiers were near starvation and threatening to return home. Jackson faced down repeated attempts at desertion before he gave up
and watched his fellow Tennesseans leave. By the end of 1813 he
was a general without an army.

And then, almost miraculously, Governor Willie Blount quickly
raised another force of volunteers and dispatched them to Alabama, where they combined with newly arrived U.S. infantrymen
to raise Jackson's force to nearly five thousand men. This time
the general was unyielding in his demands and discipline, even
to the extent of ordering the execution of an eighteen-year-old
militiaman on a flimsy charge of mutiny, an act that would dam-
age Jackson politically. Despite such distractions, Jackson's large
army, including friendly Cherokees and Creeks, soon marched
toward the main Red Stick stronghold of Tohopeka. Because of
its position within a loop of the Tallapoosa River, Tohopeka became known as Horseshoe Bend. The Creeks held a formidable
position, some one hundred acres on the peninsula in the bend
with a well-designed and solid barricade across the neck. The
defenses appeared impregnable, but at midmorning of March 27,
1814, Jackson ordered a frontal assault on the Creek breastworks.
In the meantime, some of his reserves and Cherokee allies across
the river from Tohopeka swam over to create a diversion in the
enemy rear and steal any canoes that might be used for escape.
At the breastworks there was heavy fighting before some of Jackson's soldiers managed to get over the top. One of the first was a
young officer named Sam Houston, who collapsed with an arrow
in his leg. He was followed by others who stormed into town,
firing at the retreating Indians. Houston, still lying on the
ground, ordered the arrow ripped from his leg, flesh and all, then
led his men against a cluster of Red Stick warriors. He was shot
twice in the shoulder, and one of the wounds would plague him
for the rest of his illustrious life. The fighting continued, chaotic
and deadly. No quarter was asked for or given. Not until evening
did the killing cease and Jackson's men have an opportunity to
savor their great victory. Some nine hundred Creek warriors had
been killed, while the victors had lost forty-one soldiers and
twenty-three Indian allies, with another two hundred or so of

wounded. The Battle of Horseshoe Bend brought an end to effective Creek resistance.

The Creek War and especially the Battle of Horseshoe Bend
made Andrew Jackson a military hero. The Madison administration, no longer reluctant to honor him, now awarded him the
rank of brigadier general in the U.S. Army and made him commander of the Seventh Military District, which included Tennessee and the rest of the Southwest. His first responsibility was to
conclude a peace treaty with the Creek Nation and secure a large
land cession as an indemnity for the recent war. He met with the
Creeks, former hostiles and allies alike, at Fort Jackson in August
and curtly demanded more than half the tribal domain—most
of Alabama and a large chunk of Georgia. He also insisted that
they cease any communications with the British and Spanish and
allow construction of roads and military installations in their remaining lands. Jackson's demands were extortionate and a
shameful betrayal of his former Creek allies. Of the thirty-five
chiefs who finally signed the infamous Treaty of Fort Jackson,
only one was a former Red Stick. Millions of acres of prime agricultural land—cotton land—now became available to white
settlers and speculators. Frontiersmen everywhere cheered Old
Hickory for his feats on both the battlefield and the council
ground. And soon he would gain even more renown, much more.

Many Americans considered the Creek War of little importance compared to recent disasters in the War of 1812. Most humiliating of all was a British military foray up Chesapeake Bay
in August 1814 that had led to an invasion of Washington, D.C.,
and the burning of the executive mansion and other public buildings. President Madison and his wife had to flee the capital to
avoid capture. Tennesseans were as horrified as other Americans
by the indignity, and some feared that the incompetence and
cowardice shown in Washington threatened liberties purchased
with the blood of 1776. Now, even while peace negotiations were
being conducted in Europe, rumors were circulating of British
plans to launch a massive invasion of the Southwest that would
enable them to drive up the Mississippi Valley and divide the
American nation in two. It was Brigadier General Andrew Jackson's task to foil such a plan, and there was no time for niceties.

Fresh from his triumph at the Fort Jackson treaty grounds, he fortified Mobile Bay, the anticipated invasion point, then led a force into Florida to prevent further Spanish cooperation with the British. He ignored the fact that Spain was still a neutral nation. After a brief battle Jackson captured Pensacola, where he lectured the Spanish governor about the perils of assisting America's enemy. Then he promptly returned to Mobile.

After receiving further intelligence on British plans, in December 1814 Jackson moved his base of operations to New Orleans, where he awaited thousands of additional volunteers from Tennessee and Kentucky. Later that month a large British force took a shortcut from Lake Borgne to the Mississippi River and suddenly appeared just a few miles south of New Orleans. Jackson's men quickly prepared a formidable battle line, and after some preliminary skirmishing the British launched a frontal assault on January 8, 1815. Jackson's well-entrenched sharpshooters and artillery men decimated the enemy. Sir Edward Packenham, the British commander in chief, was among those killed. Jackson chose not to pursue the withdrawing troops, and the threat of invasion ended. Ironically, diplomats had signed a peace treaty at Ghent, Belgium, two weeks earlier, but trans-Atlantic communications were too slow to prevent the battle. Though the treaty provided for a return to the status quo before the war, a British victory at New Orleans could have resulted in the loss of Louisiana. Because Britain had never recognized the legality of the Louisiana Purchase, it might well have insisted on returning that conquered area to Spanish sovereignty. Jackson's victory made that question moot. Tennessee's Old Hickory was a national hero, and the victory at New Orleans would ultimately propel him to the White House. Jackson, it has been argued, personified the ordinary man made good, the frontiersman triumphant. For ordinary Tennesseans the war evinced a rousing sense of nationalism, a fighting elan born of the frontier experience, a willingness to answer the call of duty. Jackson was Old Hickory, and ordinary Tennesseans would later become known as Volunteers.

After the war a minor embarrassment confronted the Madison administration. Article Nine of the Treaty of Ghent specifically provided that any lands taken by U.S. forces from British Indian

Andrew Jackson. COURTESY THE UNIVERSITY OF TENNESSEE
SPECIAL COLLECTIONS.

allies would be returned to those tribes. Thus the millions of acres extorted from the Creeks in the Treaty of Fort Jackson would remain in Creek possession. But General Andrew Jackson, supported by the vast majority of Westerners, angrily defied the British treaty. Those lands belonged to white America and had been earned by Jackson's leadership and the blood of his men. By now the Madison administration well understood both Jackson and the ethos of frontiersmen and made no attempt to enforce Article Nine. The British, concerned about a possible frontier threat to their Canadian possessions should they insist on American compliance with the article, chose to remain quiet. Both the Creeks and ultimately the Spanish in Florida were undone by this British and American realpolitik. There was no way to prevent white settlers and speculators from swarming onto Indian lands, a fact of life that had ironic consequences for one of Tennessee's leading frontiersmen. John Sevier, still in the House of Representatives, became one of the surveyors of the Creek lands acquired through the efforts of his old nemesis. His thoughts on this twist of fate are unknown. In September 1815 he died at age 70 while surveying the Creek boundary and legitimizing Andrew Jackson's legacy on the maps of American expansion.

10.

THE WESTERN DISTRICT: 1795–1840

By 1815 Middle and East Tennessee were at different stages of frontier evolution. In the Cumberland Basin a slave-based commercial agriculture thrived, and Nashville, bustling and confident, was the most important town between Lexington and Natchez. The only recent Indian fighting had been on the Creek frontier in Alabama; the last Indian attacks against Cumberland settlers were twenty years removed and were now just a memory of old-timers. No tribal claims remained to impede progress, nor even the presence of friendly Indians as daily reminders. The nearest Cherokee and Chickasaw towns were more than a hundred miles away. With the emergence of a viable market economy and an effective white hegemony, the basin was moving out of its frontier era. The Cumberland Plateau, however, remained largely undeveloped, still a tedious barrens through which travelers hastened on their way elsewhere. In East Tennessee, meanwhile, topography continued to define the economy and settlement patterns. The ridges offered few agricultural prospects and attracted few inhabitants, while the valleys featured small towns, small-scale farming, and livestock raising. Communities like Knoxville and Jonesborough offered the amenities of a quiet, civilized life but seemed mere eddies in the flow of humanity to more glamorous destinations. The Cherokees who still resided in the southeastern corner of the state posed no military threat, and their remaining lands, whites confidently believed, would soon be ceded. East Tennessee's frontier phase was winding down but had not yet ended.

Recent successes in the War of 1812 bolstered the confidence of all Tennesseans, engendered a strong sense of national identity, and made people expectant of new growth and accomplishments. For a few years an "era of good feelings" prevailed which would admit no sense of limitation. Tennesseans—and indeed, Southwesterners in general—anticipated Spain's surrender of Florida, either through war or unrelenting American diplomatic pressure. In the meantime men like Major General Andrew Jackson and John Coffee continued their time-honored speculations, especially in the newly opened Creek cession in Alabama. Jackson was also active as a federal commissioner in several important treaty conferences with Southern tribes, and his objective was always the same—to acquire more land and forcefully suggest Indian relocation west of the Mississippi. In 1817–1818, at the head of a large army which included many Tennessee volunteers, he again swept into Florida, burning Seminole villages, humiliating Spanish authorities, and executing two British nationals. Though such tactics were undiplomatic, they were effective, and Spain soon agreed to U.S. demands for the sale of Florida. Amid these momentous events Jackson and his friends cast a covetous eye on the Western District, the state's last major frontier.

The Western District, now known as West Tennessee, encompassed the area between the Tennessee and Mississippi rivers, some 10,700 square miles or a fourth of the entire state. All of it was within the Congressional Reservation created in 1806, as was the southwest quarter of Middle Tennessee. The latter part of the reservation had largely been cleared of Indian title. It was part of the public domain and was open to white settlement. The Western District, however, was not public domain. Rather, it was an enormous hunting area owned by the Chickasaws, whose villages were in northern Mississippi. (They also owned the adjoining territory in Kentucky bounded by the Tennessee, Ohio, and Mississippi rivers.) North Carolina had already sold or granted rights to much of the Western District, but these could not be located or developed until the Chickasaws formally ceded the region. Until this happened there was no need of direct westward access to the Mississippi from Nashville, and communication with New Orleans went by way of the Cumberland River or the Natchez Trace.

The Mississippi River had long had geopolitical significance, and the Chickasaw Bluffs, spaced at intervals along some sixty miles of riverfront, were four of its most strategic sites. The first and northernmost bluff is immediately above the mouth of the Hatchie, and the second is immediately below the mouth of that river. The third is about midway between the second and fourth bluffs, and the fourth, or lower, bluff is near the Mississippi state line. The bluffs had a commanding presence over a long stretch of the river where the surrounding terrain was otherwise uniformly flat and swampy. Military officers were especially impressed by the fourth bluff's strategic significance, but also commented on its potential as a town site. Thomas Hutchins, the English officer who also explored the Cumberland, reported in 1766 that the fourth bluff was an "airy, pleasant, and extensive situation for settlements." A bit later Colonel John Pope saw it as one of the most eligible sites for a town on the lower Mississippi.

Still, the bluff's military-diplomatic role was foremost. During the Revolution, Chickasaw warriors under James Logan Colbert, the famous Scots trader, used it as a base for attacking Spanish and American boats on the river. There, where the city of Memphis would arise, the French, Spanish, and U.S. armies successively constructed a series of forts to defend their claims to the heart of America. By the 1790s the Spanish backed a group of Chickasaws led by Wolf Friend against supporters of Piomingo, a traditionalist war leader who favored the Americans. The Colbert family of mixed-bloods, which was rapidly gaining in power, also supported the United States. The pro-Spanish faction relied on goods imported from Florida by the British firm of Panton and Leslie. In 1795, at the invitation of Wolf Friend, the Spanish built Fort Fernando de Barrancas (Fort Ferdinand of the Bluffs), the last non-American outpost on the fourth bluff. That same year, however, the Treaty of San Lorenzo transferred the bluffs to American sovereignty and shifted the boundary with Spain southward to thirty-one degrees latitude. Two years later the Spanish finally abandoned Fort Fernando, and Captain Isaac Guion of the U.S. Army established Fort Adams on the same site. That post was soon replaced by nearby Fort Pickering. During their relatively brief existence the two American forts hosted a number of noteworthy soldiers, including Meriwether Lewis and Zachary Taylor. The quiet, often miserable duty stations were enlivened by occasional civilian visitors and by the distribution of Indian goods. In October 1801 the infamous General James Wilkinson appeared for negotiations with seventeen Chickasaw leaders over widening the Natchez Trace for wagon traffic. By bribing George Colbert, Wilkinson received permission to "lay out, open and make a convenient wagon road through their land."

Beyond its geopolitical significance, the Mississippi was an ancient channel of commerce and culture. It had nourished sophisticated and thriving Mississippian centers like Cahokia and Chucalissa. By the late eighteenth century the river had played multiple roles: as part of a vast French fur-trading network stretching from New Orleans to the Illinois Country and beyond; as a remote theater of conflict during the Revolution; as an artery of commerce so vital to American frontier people that they considered allying with whichever nation controlled it; and as a commercial and administrative conduit for U.S. Indian affairs. Sometimes those roles overlapped. James Robertson, for example, opened a trading outlet on the bluffs when he served as Virginia's Chickasaw agent during the American Revolution. By the late 1780s perhaps as many as twenty-five American traders of varying reputation frequented the fourth bluff. Robertson became the first U.S. agent to the Chickasaws, though he continued to live on the Cumberland. In 1797 he was replaced by Samuel Mitchell, who became the first agent to reside in the Chickasaw villages in Mississippi. His agency was at Tokshish, strategically located at the junction of the Natchez Trace and a trail to the Chickasaw Bluffs. At both Tokshish and the bluffs Americans would exercise growing authority over the Chickasaws and ultimately over the Western District.

Federal Indian policy required Agent Mitchell and his successors to maintain the peace, supervise trade, promote Indian civilization, and encourage further tribal cessions of land. By 1800 there was little danger of the Chickasaws warring against either the whites or other Indians. Trade was the most immediate concern, and in 1802 the United States opened the Chickasaw Bluffs Trading House near Fort Pickering. Government trading posts also played a vital role in encouraging Indian land cessions, and President Jefferson was disarmingly candid in this regard. He urged the establishment of a Chickasaw post "for furnishing them all the necessaries and comforts they may wish (spirituous liquors excepted), encouraging them and especially their leading men, to run in debt for these beyond their individual means of paying." The Indians would then cede more lands to satisfy their obligations. The effectiveness of this policy was almost immediately apparent. In 1805 the Chickasaws ceded land in Middle Tennessee to offset a debt of $12,000. The Chickasaw Bluffs trading post continued to offer on credit an array of high quality goods—the Chickasaws were discriminating customers—and each year Indian indebtedness rose by several thousand dollars. Struggling to meet their material needs and financial obligations, Chickasaw males used their West Tennessee hunting lands to good effect. In 1809 the trading house at the bluffs ranked first among fourteen U.S. trading posts, with more than $12,000 worth of pelts. By 1815 that figure had risen to almost $24,000; the goods included thirty-six thousand deerskins as well as beaver, raccoon, fox, wolf, bear, panther, otter, and fox peltries. The federal trader sent the skins downriver to New Orleans and from there by sea to the Eastern United States. Tallow, beeswax, and wild game were also traded extensively. Chickasaw business with private traders boosted total production considerably. Clearly hunting was a much more integral part of the Chickasaw economy than for that of the Cherokees.

The trade was so important to the Chickasaws that within a few years they had two semi-permanent towns near the bluffs trading house—one a few miles inland and a smaller one, numbering about fifty Indians and their slaves, on a river terrace at the base of the bluffs. The latter village had several corn fields and a quarter-mile race track where the Chickasaws, noted horsemen, ran their horses. By 1819, however, the Chickasaws were paying exorbitant prices for manufactured items ($4 for a coarse blanket, for example), and in return they were receiving very low prices for their own goods (no more than twenty-five cents for a large goose or turkey or for a large cut of venison). Dissipation was a growing problem. Despite the federal prohibition against selling liquor to Indians, the Chickasaws were obtaining well-watered whiskey at the bluffs for $2 a gallon. At a camp not far from the trading house a visitor saw many Chickasaws who were drunk, though he said they "were generally well dressed, extravagantly ornamented, and, from the fairness of their complexions, and agreeable features, appear to have profited from their intercourse with whites." Some of them could speak English and, despite evidence to the contrary, a number were "making advances towards civilization."

Whether or not they were becoming civilized, the old hunting days were clearly ending for the Chickasaws because, like other Southern tribes, they faced constant pressures on their land base. The Congressional Reservation, consisting mostly of the Western District, totaled more than 6.8 million acres. By the time North Carolina ceded Tennessee in 1789, it had sold 942,000 acres in the reservation that were contingent upon eventual Chickasaw cession. Among the purchasers was John Rice, who appeared at the Hillsborough, North Carolina, land office in October 1783 and bought a 5,000 acre tract on the fourth Chickasaw Bluff. He paid $2,500 in money that had depreciated so much it was actually worth only about one-tenth that amount. It was a sweet deal. That same day fellow speculator John Ramsey bought 5,000 acres immediately south of Rice's acquisition. Rice's speculative interests became apparent in an advertisement he placed in a Maryland newspaper inviting prospective immigrants to consider settling at a new town he planned for the bluffs early in 1792. He claimed the area was in many respects better than Kentucky and the Cumberland. Families could buy land from him at $33.33 per 100 acres with a maximum purchase of 200 acres, or they could lease their land at low rates. Like many promoters, Rice was prone to exaggeration, especially when he stated that it was because of the Chickasaws' "repeated and pressing solicitations" that he planned his settlement. He also included some practical advice about the river trip from Fort Pitt and the distances involved. He claimed he already had support in Maryland, especially among Catholics, and in the Cumberland Basin, where he intended to obtain corn and livestock. General Wilkinson, in a secret letter to his Spanish masters in New Orleans, said Rice and his friends were "obscure individuals" who posed little danger. He was right. Rice died in 1791 and his plans would go unrealized for almost thirty years.

Still, throughout that long period, the fourth bluff remained a tantalizing prospect for speculators and town builders. In 1794 John Overton, a Nashville judge and one of the state's most prominent men, acquired John Rice's claim to the bluff. He quickly sold a half-interest to a less prominent friend who later far exceeded him in renown—Andrew Jackson. A series of complicated transactions during the next twenty years or so left Overton with a half-interest, Jackson an eighth, their mutual friend James Winchester a fourth, and the heirs of Winchester's brother an eighth. The machinations of Overton, Jackson, and the Winchesters coincided with North Carolina's continuing issuance of revolutionary land bounties and Tennessee's inability to satisfy those grants in the eastern and middle parts of the state. In 1811 North Carolina argued that all lands fit for cultivation had been taken outside of the Congressional Reservation and appointed a surveyor to begin locating warrants in the Western District. Tennessee nullified North Carolina grants made after 1806, then backed off because of the legal uncertainty.

This impasse, coupled with the fact that many of the North Carolina grants were now owned by Tennessee citizens, provided a powerful impetus for clearing Indian title to the Western District and opening the region to settlement. The Tennessee legislature and a host of grant holders petitioned the United States to open negotiations with the Chickasaws for this purpose.

As the pressure mounted, the *Nashville Clarion & Tennessee Gazette* asked in February 1818 whether "nothing is to be done with the Chickasaw Indians?" It said that almost half of the Chickasaws had already moved west of the Mississippi and that barely five hundred males remained, yet their domain fronted the Mississippi for three hundred miles and contained eight million acres "inferior to none in point of soil and convenience in the union." This included cotton lands so good that the United States would be able to raise at least $15 million from the sale of the Chickasaw domain. The Indians had made few improvements in Tennessee, and the cession of their lands to the United States was "of vital importance" to the state. It was likely that George Colbert ("an artful fellow") and a few other Chickasaws would oppose cession, "but they have so long lived on the crumbs of the Americans that as soon as they ascertain the government to be in earnest their opposition will cease." As "a prudent father sometimes has to mortify his loving children, so if Colbert's father the President should humble him a little, he as a good child will submit without a murmur."

The *Clarion* thus implicitly recognized how critical the support of prominent Chickasaw mixed-bloods was to cession. As was true in many other tribes, they served as cultural brokers between federal authorities and tribal traditionalists. Some were bilingual and reasonably well-educated, and most were shrewd businessmen. Among them were the Colberts, scions of James Logan Colbert, the Scottish trader who had married into the tribe in the early eighteenth century. Immediately preceding the War of 1812 the Colberts had been crucial in preventing Chickasaw defection when Tecumseh visited and eloquently called for united Indian resistance to American aggression. The Colberts and their followers had faithfully served Andrew Jackson in the Creek War, but first and foremost, the family looked after their own interests. If federal authorities hoped to be successful in dealing with the Colberts, the correct formula was, as Jackson put it, "touching their interest and feeding their avarice." This certainly applied to George Colbert, perhaps the wiliest member of the family. Bribing him and other tribal leaders followed the pattern of federal negotiations with Doublehead, the noted Cherokee wheeler-dealer. In an 1816 treaty Colbert was granted a personal reservation that included his lucrative ferry site where the Natchez Trace crossed the Tennessee River. Jackson also rewarded other Chickasaw leaders with gifts, money, food, and liquor. In exchange the Indians ceded large chunks of land in Alabama and south-central Tennessee. The bribes to Colbert and other mixed-blood leaders were, Jackson admitted, "the sole remedy in our power." He insisted on keeping the transactions secret because otherwise "the influence of the chiefs would be destroyed, which has been, and may be, useful on a future occasion."

The future occasion presented itself just a year later, when Jackson began pressuring the Monroe administration for permission to begin negotiations with the Chickasaws for all of their remaining lands in Tennessee and Kentucky. He admitted that settlers had no pressing need for the area but argued that its acquisition would protect commerce on the interior rivers and provide security for whites by extending the wedge between the Northern and Southern tribes. Besides, many whites held valid North Carolina grants in the Western District, and the United States had unconstitutionally denied their property rights so the Chickasaws could continue hunting there. Now, he incorrectly asserted, there was no longer sufficient game to justify Indian possession. Acquiring these lands would also demonstrate conclusively that Chickasaw claims and pretensions to tribal authority were secondary to the claims of the states in which they resided: "I have long viewed treaties with the Indians an absurdity not to be reconciled with the principles of our Government." They were an infringement on national sovereignty. Congress should extend to the Indians its "protection and fostering care" while legislating for them as it did for other residents of the United States. Jackson was sharpening many of the arguments he would later make in the White House.

The momentum for dispossession continued. In the spring of 1818 Congress authorized the state of Tennessee to issue grants and perfect titles in the Western District for all valid North Carolina claims that had not been located elsewhere in the state. Tennessee could use its existing land laws in accomplishing the task. Though the federal authorization stipulated that the state could not act until the Indian claims had been ceded, the intent of Congress was clear. There *would* be a Chickasaw cession. President Monroe agreed. He responded to Jackson's earlier advice by appointing Jackson and Isaac Shelby as commissioners to negotiate with the Chickasaws at their council grounds near Old Town, Alabama. When Jackson and Shelby arrived there in October, they discovered that nothing could proceed until they had bribed three of the Colbert brothers and two other tribal leaders. Then, Jackson addressed the assembled Indians, boldly asserting that the American government owned Chickasaw lands on the basis of early English grants to the Virginia and Carolina colonies and that these grants had been transferred to the United States after the Revolution. The government had allowed the Chickasaws to continue using the land for hunting, but now the game was gone and white settlers had a just right to it. He promised death to any "bad men" who threatened the lives of chiefs who agreed to a cession and said that the president would regard a refusal to sell the lands as evidence "of ill will and ingratitude."

Jackson's visage ranged from stern to wrathful, and the assembled Indians no doubt knew of the popular agitation against them in Tennessee. The *Nashville Clarion* was publishing anti-Chickasaw propaganda, focusing especially on threats made against tribal leaders who wished to accommodate the United States. The pressure was too great to resist. Acting upon the advice of the Colberts, the Chickasaws finally signed a treaty on October 19, 1818, selling all their Tennessee and Kentucky lands for a total of $300,000, which would be divided into fifteen annuities of $20,000 each. This amount did not include money spent on bribes, which were unmentioned in the treaty. Except for the reservation of a salt lick on the Sandy River, the cession included all of the Western District as well as the adjoining part of Western Kentucky. It represented about a fourth of the state of Tennessee and a tenth of Kentucky. As far as many Tennesseans were concerned, this was Jackson's finest hour. Upon ratification of the treaty in January 1819, the state had a new frontier, which was officially designated the Western District in 1820.

There were restrictions on this latest frontier. It was part of the public domain, and most of the land ostensibly belonged to the United States government, but the North Carolina sales of the 1780s, including those of choice lands like the fourth bluff, were officially recognized. Moreover, North Carolina retained the right to locate its unused revolutionary land warrants there, a right that it partly transferred to the University of North Carolina. These prior and future claims offered the most promising opportunities for speculators, and Tennessee had authority to issue titles in the district on all valid conveyances made by North Carolina. The rest of the land belonged to the United States, but its survey and administration would be under the existing land legislation of Tennessee. The state already had six land districts in East and Middle Tennessee, and it created two more in the portion of the Congressional Reservation that lay east of the Tennessee River.

In the Western District itself, the state established five smaller districts that were roughly equal in size and were defined by north-south and east-west lines. Each was further divided into square units that were five miles to a side. Thus the state was employing a system of survey similar to that of federal lands elsewhere (though the latter featured units that were six miles to a side). Where possible, claims would be located along the survey lines or adjacent to other claims already located along those lines. Certain preemption rights applied to people residing in the Western District before September 1, 1819. The principal surveyors of the smaller districts recorded all the valid warrants and the names of the current owners. Each owner would have a ticket with a different number, the highest number equaling the number of valid warrants. The surveyor would then place advertisements in Nashville and Knoxville newspapers describing the boundaries and regulations of the district, as well as the date when the land office would open for the filing of entries. Then, on the first Wednesday of December 1820, after a random drawing of all tickets, the surveyor would record each number next to the appropriate name in the surveyor's book. There were certain provisions for smaller claims, and arbitrators would rule on disputed claims.

Even while these administrative decisions were being made, speculators were busily at work within the district, and the hoopla about their prospects was assuming ridiculous proportions. A short time after the Chickasaw cession an informative essay appeared in the Raleigh, North Carolina, *Register* which said that some of the land already surveyed in the district was worth $10 or even $20 an acre, but that the spirit of emigration was so uncritical that "every rock, swamp and sandhill" was perceived as valuable. Near the Chickasaw Bluffs, the author conceded, a narrow elevated strip might be suited for "Hollanders" who could perhaps create an "amphibious town," but otherwise the country within ten miles of the Mississippi was annually inundated to a depth of four to ten feet. Reclaiming it by constructing dikes or levees "belongs to a future and perhaps distant age." For twenty to forty miles east of the inundated land the soil was excellent, but from there to the Tennessee River the uplands were mostly of a "poor gravelly soil." The *Nashville Clarion* vigorously disputed most of the essay, noting that flooding in the district "takes place but seldom," that upland soils were "equal to the best," and that the average price was $2 an acre or less.

Among the most enthusiastic promoters of the district was John Overton, who even before the Chickasaw cession was launching his long-standing plans to develop the fourth bluff. James Winchester and his sons were Overton's eager partners, while Andrew Jackson, with an eye on national politics, assumed a lesser role in the venture. In order to protect their investment on the bluffs, the three older partners took the precaution of organizing another partnership with three other men in the event they might have to buy the adjoining tract of five thousand acres acquired by John Ramsey. This would head off any threat of a competing town site, and though Overton obtained an interest in the Rice tract he and his associates apparently never felt the need to take any further steps toward establishing their "second contemplated company." They directed their energies toward developing the Rice tract and by early 1819 hoped Jackson's influence could secure federal mail service by way of the Natchez Trace and its branch trail from Tokshish. Winchester's experience as a surveyor fit neatly with his real estate interests, and it was probably no coincidence that he was appointed to survey the southern boundary of the district along the thirty-fifth parallel. This would also be the boundary between Tennessee and the new state of Mississippi. In the summer of 1819, after serious disputes with James Colbert and other Chickasaws, Winchester completed what he steadfastly considered an accurate survey along the appropriate parallel from the Tennessee River to the Mississippi. As expected, his survey placed the fourth bluff safely north of the thirty-fifth parallel, but both the Chickasaw Nation and the state of Mississippi protested that his line was actually south of the parallel. Years later, a resurvey showed that Winchester in fact had been too far north, so Tennessee gained about 440 square miles at the expense of Mississippi.

Even before Winchester began his work, his son Marcus and William Lawrence had started surveying the fourth bluff for a new town, laying out a few straight streets paralleling the river and intersected by shorter east-west streets. There were four public squares, 362 town lots, and a public promenade atop the bluff along the entire riverfront. The grid pattern was very much like that of other aspiring Western towns, reflecting the influence of William Penn's original plat of Philadelphia. Continuity was a powerful force on the urban frontier. The original town plat for Memphis was completed in May 1819, barely seven months after the Chickasaw cession. James Winchester, who was something of a classicist, characterized the Mississippi as America's Nile and proposed that the new town be named for one of ancient Egypt's most famous cities. Overton suggested the creation of a triangular new county that would encompass their town, but Winchester argued that a rectangular configuration was more practical; it would include more of the hinterland and might increase the value of town lots by 15 to 20 percent. Overton made the suggested adjustments, the handful of people in southwestern Tennessee dutifully petitioned for a new county, and in November the legislature created Shelby County, named in honor of Andrew Jackson's fellow commissioner in the Chickasaw Treaty of 1818. Because the name Memphis was still unfamiliar, the act designated "Chickasaw Bluffs" as the county seat. Shelby was one of four counties established that year in the Western District and the first entirely west of the Tennessee River. By 1823 there were fourteen counties throughout the area.

Overton was never content to leave anything to chance where his investment was concerned, and having presided over the creation of Memphis and Shelby County, he began a publicity cam-

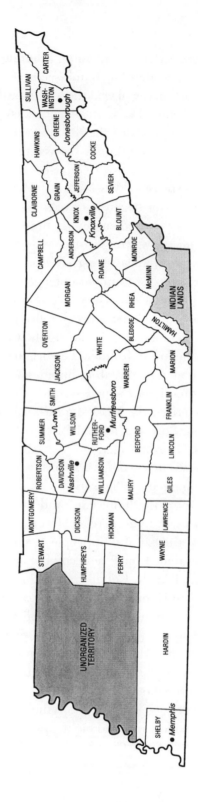

Tennessee, 1820. Department of Geography and the Cartographic Services Laboratory at the University of Tennessee.

paign to attract prospective inhabitants. His glowing, almost giddy description of the town and its prospects, along with information on the sale of lots, appeared in newspapers in Nashville, New Orleans, Natchez, St. Louis, Louisville, Cincinnati, and Pittsburgh. A popular Philadelphia magazine devoted several pages to a "Description of Memphis in 1820," and a Baltimore firm made an engraving of the town plat which was used to print perhaps two thousand copies. But people were not so easily swayed at the time because the Panic of 1819 was nearing its peak. Even though they offered free whiskey to would-be buyers, Overton and his associates were able to get only $30 to $100 each for their lots—not much considering that payments could be stretched over five years. In some cases they got nothing because they chose not to challenge the preemption claims of certain noisy squatters who had bought cabins directly from the Indians. Some of these men were veterans of the War of 1812, and the potential embarrassment they might create perhaps persuaded Andrew Jackson to trade his interest in the Memphis site for lands elsewhere. Looking toward 1824 and a likely run for the White House, the general, a man of the people, could ill afford to appear less than magnanimous toward his former underlings. Besides, he had never taken an active role in the Memphis venture.

Meanwhile preparations were underway to implement the recent legislation for surveying and entering the newly acquired lands. On May 1, 1820, the eleventh district survey office officially opened in Memphis, the same day that the county court first convened. Within a short time more than one hundred public and private surveyors were scattered throughout the Western District. One of these was Memucan Hunt Howard, who like many of his peers had crossed the Tennessee River at Reynoldsburg, a sickly yet "prosperous village" with a dozen or more stores to meet the needs of the district's newcomers. A minister accompanied Howard's party for about a week, offering evening prayers and making the woods ring with his singing of hymns. That was probably reassuring to the surveyors, who were terrified of wild animals, especially when wolves howled during the night. The surveyors frequently encountered Indians, who were enjoying a

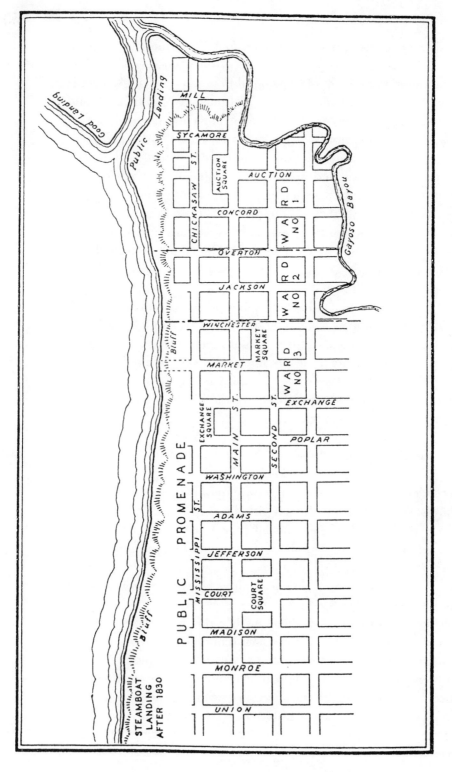

Plan of Memphis in the Late 1820s. From Gerald M. Capers, Jr., *The Biography of a River Town, Memphis: Its Heroic Age* (Chapel Hill, 1939).
COURTESY UNIVERSITY OF NORTH CAROLINA PRESS.

last opportunity to hunt their ancient lands. Sometimes whites could buy venison or other game from them for a pittance. The intensified hunting made the animals very wild and timid, increasing the surveyors' safety when they were alone and unarmed in the field. At such times they kept track of one another by blowing on trumpets. If Indian suppliers were unavailable, Howard's group went to the squalid little village of Memphis to buy flour, bacon, and other provisions from the store of Marcus Winchester and William Carr. Chickasaw hunters continued to take their game and pelts to the bluffs, where they bought watered-down liquor from the newly established Memphis merchants. James Winchester said that the few inhabitants of the town had the Indian trade as their common object, and his son Marcus attempted to buy as much cheap liquor as possible for his business. For more than ten years after the treaty, Chickasaws continued to trade in Memphis, where occasional gawking visitors watched them play their traditional games of stickball on a level area below Beale Street.

The initial influx of settlers into the district was modest in part because of bad timing. The major national depression that had begun in 1819 lingered well into the 1820s. Banks and markets collapsed, debt skyrocketed, and federal land sales plummeted. Newspapers in Middle Tennessee were filled with notices of indebtedness and of schemes such as lotteries to raise money to satisfy the IOUs. Immigration temporarily slowed throughout the trans-Appalachian frontier. People were painfully aware that they were part of an interdependent economy. Many speculators, especially town promoters, were victimized by their own foolish expectations and became targets of ridicule. In October 1819 the *Nashville Clarion*, formerly a staunch supporter of the district's prospects, satirized the town promoters there with a mock advertisement for a mythical "Skunksburg," the creation of three noteworthy entrepreneurs: "Andrew Aircastle, Theory M. Vision, and L. Moonlight, Jr. & Co."

The slow development of the district was only partly due to the national depression. For most would-be immigrants there was no legal way to obtain land except from the original holders of North Carolina claims or their heirs. Some of the largest and

most powerful claimants to lands in West Tennessee invited im-
poverished farmers and their families to settle on their estates,
improve the lands, and perhaps purchase them when times were
better. These claimants already owned the best real estate, and
the remainder, as public domain, belonged to the United States.
Because there was no prospect of the government selling these
lands anytime soon, many of the district's first white inhabitants
simply squatted on the public domain. Travelers in the district
often characterized squatters as dissolute and shiftless people,
enervated by stifling heat and humidity and spurred to action
only by the prospect of a good hunt. Tennessee had no incentive
to evict these people from the public domain, and in fact there
soon developed a significant lobby in the state legislature which
was devoted to protecting them. One of the strongest and most
colorful proponents of squatter rights was Davy Crockett, who
moved into the wild country of the northern part of the district
and, like many of his somewhat distant neighbors, spent more
time hunting than farming. More ambitious than most, and
much given to glad-handing and politicking, Crockett would
soon make a compelling case for his fellow squatters in the state
legislature and the halls of Congress.

Though the number of immigrants to the Western District
rapidly increased after 1825, Memphis's future appeared uncertain. Other sites on the Tennessee side of the Mississippi vigorously contested its ambition of dominating trade on the river between Natchez and St. Louis. Two of these would-be contenders
were short-lived: the proposed town of Fort Pickering south of
Memphis, and Ashport, at the mouth of the Forked Deer River.
The earliest true rival was Fulton, on the first Chickasaw Bluff,
above the mouth of the Hatchie. The proprietors of the site were
all visionaries who had sponsored other towns and then, almost
in the blink of an eye, shifted their affections. Fulton was laid out
in 1827 as "The Great Town of the West," but it quickly expired
because, its founders claimed, Memphians had unfairly ma-
ligned it. A far more fundamental problem for Fulton were two
islands in the Mississippi that made direct access to the town
inconvenient. Most boats steered to the opposite side of the islands and stayed there until passing Fulton entirely. Memphis

had a similar problem, a large sandbar which for years made landing difficult. This offered the perfect opportunity for Randolph, a town established in 1827 on the second Chickasaw Bluff just below the Hatchie's mouth. Its proprietors promised not to lie about the attractions of their town (a lie in itself), but by early 1828 Randolph still consisted of a solitary cabin. Nonetheless, the town developed a good river trade, though according to one disgruntled male, "not a single young lady of sort, size, or description" resided there. Randolph was a serious rival of Memphis because for part of the year the Hatchie was navigable as far inland as Bolivar, making Randolph the natural port for much of the hinterland's produce.

Meanwhile, despite Overton's persistent efforts, Memphis remained a backwater. Even after the advertising blitz attending the town's creation, its estimated population in 1820 was only 54 people, while that of Shelby County was 355, including 142 white males, 100 white females, and 113 slaves. Memphis's prospects were so uncertain that its founders feared the possibility that the county seat would be relocated elsewhere. Overton believed that whether Memphis retained that honor would determine if it "shall be a decent little town in our day (say in 20 or 30 years) or a harbor for a few drunken boatmen (besides those now there)." His fears were well founded, for the county court was soon moved to the new town of Raleigh, ten miles inland on the Wolf River. As a sop, the state legislature officially incorporated the town of Memphis in 1826, but some of the older residents, fearing taxes and other obligations, were far from elated. Memphis remained a scruffy town struggling to compete against confident rivals, a periodic haunt of drunken and violent flatboatmen.

Another problem for Memphis and other river towns was the belief that they were unhealthy. In 1673 the French priest and explorer Jacques Marquette had found the area around the fourth bluff mosquito infested and sickly, as did the Spanish and American garrisons at Fort Fernando and Fort Pickering more than a century later. Many soldiers died or were incapacitated by disease. The heat and humidity were oppressive and debilitating. The Chickasaws, while valuing the site for its strategic features and superlative hunting, preferred to live on higher ground in Mississippi because the bluffs area "leaked too much" as a result of periodic flooding and poor drainage. A British visitor in 1806 praised the beautiful high plain of the bluffs, but remarked that it was rather small "and subsides into ponds and swamps"—a definite health hazard. Indeed, Memphians of a later generation, like residents of other trans-Appalachian river towns, would endure malaria, yellow fever, and a host of other afflictions. During the first fifteen years of its existence Memphis experienced five epidemics: dengue fever, smallpox, yellow fever, and two bouts with cholera. By 1825 the town still had barely 300 people and only 663 in 1830. Its two major advantages would be apparent only later. First, although its location was unhealthy, Memphis was superbly situated for a growing trade in cotton. Second, Memphis benefited from the tenacity of John Overton, the often absent landlord, and Marcus Winchester, the town's first mayor and most distinguished citizen.

Mississippi River towns encountered natural dangers more terrifying and much more spectacular than disease. In December 1811, during the first of the massive New Madrid earthquakes, the few residents of the fourth bluff fled to higher terrain, one attributing the event to a recent comet that portended the possible end of the world. Their fear was understandable: the quakes rechanneled a portion of the Mississippi, created Reelfoot Lake, and toppled so many trees that parts of northwestern Tennessee became nearly impenetrable wilderness thickets. Fallen timber clogged many of the streams. Huge storms added to the chaos, and the area was colloquially known as The Hurricanes. Despite the obvious impediments to agriculture, the northwest part of the district was a splendid refuge for all kinds of game animals, and backwoods hunters like Davy Crockett would find it a paradise.

Most of the early growth in the Western District occurred on the gently sloping interior plateau where the land was fertile and the drainage better than along the Mississippi. One of the most popular areas was present-day Henry County, immediately west of the Tennessee River and adjoining Kentucky. The eastern part of the county offered easy access to Middle Tennessee. Its topography of broken and forested hills interspersed with small, fertile valleys, was familiar and reassuring. A north-south ridge served as a sharp demarcation between this part of the county and the more open uplands to the west. The entire county was well suited to the cultivation of tobacco, corn, and even cotton. At first the area was under the jurisdiction of Stewart County, and business was transacted at Reynoldsburg on the east side of the Tennessee. But after the General Assembly formally created Henry County in 1821, the pace of development accelerated, and by 1830 it was the most populous county in the Western District. Its new seat of government was the town of Paris, which arose on a carefully selected site in the middle of the county and was named for the native city of the Marquis de Lafayette, an enormously popular figure in the United States. When Paris was laid out in 1823, the lots around its public square sold for $200 each. A few months later Paris already had a log courthouse, five general stores, and three hotels; by 1830 it was the second largest town in the Western District with some eight hundred residents, and it could boast of schools, tree-lined streets, fine houses, a lyceum, and some local industries. Three years later, if one is to believe the *Tennessee Gazetteer*, its inhabitants included lawyers, physicians, clergymen, carpenters, bricklayers, cabinet makers, tailors, hatters, tanners, shoemakers, blacksmiths, tinners, saddlers, tavern keepers, and a silversmith. Visitors agreed that it was a lovely community—"Paris, beautiful Paris!"—or at least, as one traveler remarked, "much the handsomest town I have seen since I left Louisville."

During their early frontier period the towns of the Western District were more important than their counterparts in East and Middle Tennessee had been. The fertile interior of the district was even more isolated from the outside world than upper East Tennessee had been in the late eighteenth century. Many of the district's towns were surveying centers, established before there was a significant influx of settlers. They were the vanguard of civilization on the frontier, and the few roads in the district connected the towns with outlying areas. Communities like Jackson, Paris, and Dyersburg were centers of local government, merchandising, land transactions, education, and culture. Some had no particular natural advantage except that they were near the geographic center of a newly created county. In that sense towns in West Tennessee were creatures of the state legislature. But each town also reflected the aspirations of frontier entrepreneurs, men who saw their economic prospects tied not to their own farms but to the sale of town lots and to urban promotion. As in many other frontier areas, the competition among towns for political and economic preference was fierce throughout the district. Two merchants, William Armour and Henry Lake, hedged their bets by opening a store in Jackson, then a branch in Bolivar, and then others at several locations in the district, including Paris.

For some years the largest community in the Western District was Jackson, the seat of Madison County. Situated in an area of fine upland soils, Jackson was also on one of the main overland routes to the Mississippi. Robert Lake built the first brick house there, but William Armour outshone him with a mansion modeled after that of Charles Carroll of Carrollton, Maryland (Armour's wife wanted a tangible memory of her home state). Other prominent outsiders who moved to Jackson included the Bigelows of Massachusetts, who opened a school, a newspaper, and a store. By 1830 Jackson had about nine hundred inhabitants, and a decade later it supposedly was home to "ten distilleries, thirteen saw mills, fifteen flour mills, twenty-one grist mills, seven tanneries, two cotton factories with fifty-one employees, one tobacco factory, one wagon and carriage factory, one hat and cap factory, and an iron foundry."

There were problems in these towns, however, besides the fear that a rival community might prevail. Even in a promising town like Jackson there was little hard money, and barter was a common option. Sanitation was poor, and although local ordinances specified certain minimum health standards, citizens often disregarded even the most obvious of precautions. Urban growth also brought the danger of fire. Taxes were anathema, so West Tennessee towns copied other communities on the trans-Appalachian frontier by resorting to voluntarism to address their problems; volunteer fire companies were common in such towns. Municipal authority was more coercive when it came to slaves. Amid the paranoia surrounding Nat Turner's slave uprising in Virginia in 1831, citizens of Jackson instituted a mandatory slave patrol. All eligible males were expected to participate, and slackers could be fined one dollar for refusing.

Creating an adequate transportation network was one of the foremost problems for Tennessee and for the Western District in particular. Boosters in Randolph worked with those in Bolivar in behalf of a state-funded canal linking the latter town, on the Hatchie River, with the Tennessee River; it would enhance Randolph's economic role by providing a direct water link between Middle Tennessee and the Mississippi. Nothing came of the proposal, but Tennessee legislators often supported local, state, or federal subsidies for similar projects. One of the more ambitious legislative schemes for assisting the Western District was an 1836 resolution for a turnpike and railroad route stretching from Virginia to Memphis. It proposed a hard-surfaced macadamized road from Abingdon to the Tennessee River west of Nashville and then a railroad to Memphis. The scheme failed to get beyond the talking stage, but Memphis would long aspire to be a center of railway and riverboat traffic. Sometimes it was difficult for West Tennessee to get its share of attention because it was still sparsely populated and legislators tended to rationalize that it already had ready access to the Tennessee, Ohio, and Mississippi rivers. When Shelby County wished to clear the lower Wolf River channel, it had to raise money by imposing local taxes.

The great hope of frontier areas was that the United States government would undertake and finance important internal improvements. Substantial help came from this quarter in 1824, when Congress appropriated $15,000 to survey and construct a military road westward from Memphis to Little Rock in the Arkansas Territory. Over a period of years the road would be improved and provide an important link to the West. Its construction was a forthright recognition of Memphis's strategic location, something the town's boosters would continue to emphasize. And in 1829 Memphis gained a slight advantage over Randolph by obtaining U.S. mail service three times a week via Jackson. The mail was carried by four-horse coaches. Randolph had service once a week by horseback. Ironically, Memphians and other frontier people could expect little assistance from President Andrew Jackson, who adamantly opposed federal appropriations for internal improvements unless they represented a clear national need. Obviously qualifying in this regard was a U.S. naval shipyard established in Memphis in the early 1840s, but it proved a dismal failure.

The military road directed the attention of Memphians westward, and the Mississippi River pointed southward and northward, but what about connections between Memphis and points eastward? Adequate transportation continued to be a perplexing problem both within the Western District and between the district and the East. Roads in the district remained deplorable for many years, bridges were almost nonexistent, and ferries were few and sometimes dangerous. Even by the 1830s traveling the main overland route from Nashville to Memphis was an exhausting and frightening experience. In December 1831 two urbane and adventurous young Frenchmen abandoned their plans to go by steamboat from Louisville to New Orleans because the Ohio River was frozen solid. To Alexis de Tocqueville and Gustave de Beaumont it seemed a good idea to take a road to Nashville and then to Memphis and to continue their river journey to Louisiana from there. It was a bad idea. The road from Louisville to Nashville was challenging enough, but the real adventure began on the journey to Memphis. Temperatures were near or below zero (mystifying the travelers because Tennessee is at about the same latitude as Egypt), and the two were riding in a small public carriage which was open to the elements. There were only a few small villages between Nashville and Memphis. The road was rough, unbanked, and heedless of the terrain. The carriage traces broke, then a wheel, then the axletree. After some makeshift repairs, the passengers continued to the Tennessee River, which they crossed amid ice-floes on "a paddle-wheel boat operated by a horse and two slaves." Tocqueville became ill and the two travelers spent a ghastly few days at a wilderness inn which had no chinking between the logs. They nearly froze, despite the roaring blaze in a fireplace large enough to roast an ox. After Tocqueville felt better they caught a stage and bounced another two days and two nights before arriving at their destination.

"Memphis!!" Beaumont wrote, "What a fall! Nothing to see, neither men nor things." They fled on the first steamboat south.

Had Tocqueville and Beaumont cared to spend a few more days in Memphis, they could have visited the remains of Nashoba (the Chickasaw word for "wolf") near present-day Germantown. Nashoba had been established in 1825 on nearly two thousand acres by the remarkable English woman Frances Wright. Something of a dilettante, Wright envisioned the estate as a grand experiment in the education and gradual emancipation of slaves, whom she acquired by purchase and donation. Her prominent board of trustees included General Lafayette and reformer Robert Dale Owen. At first Wright was able to maintain cordial relations with prominent Memphians, and Nashoba became a must-see stopover for European and American intellectuals traveling down the Mississippi. Among her prominent guests was the irascible Frances Trollope, the notorious Englishwoman whose disappointments as a businesswoman in Cincinnati tainted her views of her adopted land, expressed in her book *Domestic Manners of the Americans*. Another visitor was Jeremiah Evarts, a prominent Quaker who would later become a leading opponent of forced Indian removal. A proper Philadelphian through and through, Evarts could not resist a few snide digs at his liberated hostess.

Many people found Wright's communitarian and racial ideas disquieting, but Nashoba quickly became even more famous for Wright's unorthodox views on sexual mores, leading some to characterize the community as a brothel. Nashoba was an antireligious particle amid a sea of Western District revivalism, and if God didn't directly threaten its destruction, some district residents no doubt believed some form of divine retribution was imminent. The Nashoba experiment ended less than a decade after it had begun. Wright was often absent, her trustees were not always competent, the finances were in disarray, and most important, Wright's interest waned. In 1830 she concluded the experiment by chartering a ship and taking the thirty-one Nashoba blacks to the Negro republic of Haiti, where they received land. Though Nashoba was a failure, it stands as an intellectual and philanthropic landmark of frontier Tennessee, one of a number of "Backwoods Utopias" that reformers created on the American frontier.

Memphians were interested in Wright's Nashoba experiment, but their real concern was first to ensure their own community's survival and second to gain ascendancy over rival communities within the district and along the Mississippi. When the town was founded, steamboat service was infrequent and erratic, though flatboaters by the hundreds continued to tie up at the waterfront until the Civil War. Although it took a while for Memphis to gain an edge in riverboat service, locals became involved in the business at an early date. Farmers near the river found a ready source of income in supplying steamboats with firewood cleared from their property, and Memphis became the collection point for rafts of hardwood logs which would be floated or towed downstream. But the real question was whether the town could become the dominant shipping point for the cotton that was increasingly being produced in Tennessee and adjoining parts of Alabama and Mississippi. In 1826 farmers in neighboring Fayette County, a region blessed with fine soil, managed to haul three hundred bales of cotton over the rudimentary road to Memphis and send them downriver. That modest fifteen thousand dollar shipment was a harbinger of future prosperity for Memphis and southwestern Tennessee. But Randolph remained a formidable rival for another decade; by 1834 as many as ten to fourteen steamboats called there each week. The editor of the local newspaper touted the town's virtues and said that despite the "neighborly frowns" of Memphis, Randolph was destined to "rise to great importance." By 1836, however, circumstances had changed radically in favor of Memphis, and the editor moved there himself, giving Randolph little more than a backward glance.

Probably the decisive events ensuring Memphis's ascendancy over other river towns were the Chickasaw treaties of 1832 and 1834, which cleared northern Mississippi of Indian title and would soon lead to the removal of the Chickasaws to present-day Oklahoma. Before those treaties Memphis's proximity to the Mississippi state line had been a liability because that line was also the boundary of the Chickasaw Nation. White speculators and cotton growers could only salivate at the prospect of gaining

those Indian lands. After the cession, cotton cultivation spread
rapidly to within a few miles of Memphis. The town began to
surpass other river ports because of its unrivaled proximity to a
large cotton-producing area which included not only the southwestern part of the Western District but northern Mississippi and
Alabama as well.

District cotton was among the highest quality. In 1850 it would
be recognized at the London Exposition as second only to the
Sea Island cotton of Georgia. By the mid-1830s it already brought
as much as two cents a pound more in New Orleans than cotton
from other parts of Tennessee. Assuming that the best cotton sold
for twenty cents per pound and that prime Western District land
produced from one thousand to five thousand pounds of cotton
per acre, a planter theoretically could earn gross receipts of
$100,000 for every one hundred acres. By 1840 Fayette, Harde-
man, and Haywood counties, all in the immediate hinterland of
Memphis, each produced more than three million pounds of cotton. Madison County produced more than two million pounds,
and Shelby and Tipton counties more than one million pounds
each. The basis of Memphis's cotton hegemony had been firmly
established.

Another example of the town's emergence as a trade center
came in 1842, when officials finally gained control of their own
waterfront in what has been characterized as the "flatboat war."
In an ugly confrontation with hundreds of boatmen over payment of wharf taxes, a strong-willed constable, backed by local
militia, prevailed. Memphis authorities had established an orderly, stable system for controlling the town's river trade. Memphis embarked on a boom, its population rising from just 1,799
in 1840 to 22,623 in 1860. During the 1850s the value of Shelby
County farms would soar from $3.2 million to $9.4 million, compared to only $6.7 million for its closest district rival.

The emergence of cotton cultivation should not obscure the
fact that the Western District had other major crops. In 1840
Henry County produced almost 9.5 million pounds of tobacco
with a valuation of $1.2 million, nearly four times the value of
Fayette County's cotton (partly because tobacco prices that year
were unusually high). No other West Tennessee county produced

even one million pounds of tobacco, though Weakley County would eventually surpass Henry County in output. The 1840 census figures show that the leading cotton counties produced significant quantities of other agricultural goods, but in the following two decades they understandably concentrated on cotton and acquired many of their foodstuffs from other counties. Even in 1860, however, diversified farming was important in the district. The value of Gibson County's cotton, tobacco, corn, wheat, and livestock exceeded the agricultural valuation of all other district counties but Shelby.

In both Middle and West Tennessee, cotton planters relied on slave labor. Gone were the early frontier days of East Tennessee and the Cumberland, when men like John Sevier and James Robertson would have personal, one-on-one relationships with trusty slaves who accompanied them on epic explorations or campaigns against hostile Indians. And gone were the days when there was an understood, yet undefined, arena in which a slave might exercise personal initiative and be accorded a measure of respect. Plantation slavery and the growing of staple products changed all that. Economic transformation and the racial problems in nearby states brought changes of attitude toward black slaves and free blacks alike. As late as the 1820s many Tennessee slave owners had been toying with notions of compensated, gradual emancipation and colonization of freed blacks in West Africa. That is why the leaders of Memphis could tolerate Frances Wright's racial experimentation at Nashoba, if not her unorthodox ideas on sexual behavior. But after Nat Turner's 1831 uprising in southern Virginia, many Southerners became paranoid; they tossed and turned in their sleep, tormented by nightmares of slave insurrections fomented by Northern abolitionists. And besides, slaves had become too valuable, too essential to cotton production for their masters to consider freeing them. Reasoned discourse on race and slavery largely ceased.

This turn of attitude is most apparent in the language of the new Tennessee constitution adopted in 1835. Most of the pressure for a constitutional convention came from the rural population of Middle and West Tennessee, which chafed at the unwarranted advantages elites had enjoyed since statehood in 1796. The new constitution was seen as the triumph of democracy, especially because it defined a more equitable system of taxation, but it stripped all blacks of their rights. The debate among the delegates regarding blacks had often been thoughtful and compassionate, but in the end the document prohibited the legislature from emancipating slaves without the consent of their owners, and for the first time since statehood adult free black males were denied the right to vote. Tennessee's free blacks joined their slave brethren among the permanently disfranchised. The emergence of commercial agriculture within the state had played a powerful role in redefining the status of blacks. They became entries in ledger books, representatives of profits and losses, and the occasional subjects of references by plantation overseers to particularly recalcitrant individuals. As a result, we know fewer personal details about the antebellum generation of blacks than about blacks of earlier periods. If, as Frederick Jackson Turner contended, the frontier fostered American democracy, in Tennessee it was a democracy that was now racially exclusive.

In addition to disfranchising free black males, the 1835 constitution recognized the former Western District as West Tennessee, one of the three grand divisions of the state. That status symbolized the district's new respectability and its continuing evolution from frontier to settled, civilized (or semi-civilized) region about to embark on a boom period of cotton cultivation. And yet despite the nascent domination of a slave-dependent planter elite, West Tennessee was still the abode of genuine frontier people. By the 1830s it was chiefly famous as the home of Davy Crockett, the quintessential American backwoodsman and droll politician who regaled Eastern sophisticates with tall tales of frontier adventure and accomplishment. Davy Crockett, far more than Andrew Jackson, represented the frontiersman made good, the uncommon common man rising above humble circumstances and becoming a national icon. He would eventually assume a mythic import that still rivals Jackson's.

Crockett's credentials as a Tennessee frontiersman were impeccable. His grandparents were early residents of the Rogersville area and were killed by Indians in 1777. One of their sons was John Crockett, an upright, though generally unsuccessful, resident of Washington and Greene counties. David was born to John and Rebecca Crockett in August 1786 near Greeneville. He was indifferent to schooling and sometimes ran away from parental authority, once leaving for two and a half years. But in 1806 he married and settled down to family life on a small farm in East Tennessee. Dissatisfied, he moved his family in the fall of 1811 to a fork of the Elk River in Lincoln County. That part of south-central Tennessee had only recently been cleared of Indian claims, and as David immodestly remarked in his famous autobiography, "It was here that I began to distinguish myself as a hunter, and to lay the foundation for all my future greatness. . . . Of deer and smaller game I killed abundance; but the bear had been hunted in those parts before, and were not so plenty as I could have wished." By early 1813 he had moved to Franklin County, between the town of Winchester and what is now the Alabama boundary. At the time, Indian country was on the other side of the line, and events there portended a change in Crockett's life.

The Creek War was just getting underway, the result of the Red Stick dissidents' slaughter of hundreds of people at Fort Mims. Crockett joined Tennessee volunteers and militia in Andrew Jackson's punitive expedition against the Creeks, serving with Colonel John Coffee. His experiences with Coffee and Jackson left him contemptuous of officers and critical of their disdain for ordinary soldiers. In his later political career he consistently supported volunteers against the regular army and attacked West Point as a bastion of aristocracy. He participated in the attack on the Creek town of Tallushatchee in November 1813 and in contrast to Coffee's official report viewed the carnage as a massacre. By the time Crockett's famous autobiography appeared in 1834, the mutual animosity between him and Jackson was well known, so his version of the Creek War was not entirely objective. Likewise, his story of brave soldiers defying General Jackson and returning home from that campaign is clearly exaggerated, if not erroneous. It does not credit Jackson's almost single-handed quelling of the incipient mutiny. Crockett left the army after his ninety-day enlistment expired in December, missing Jackson's decisive victory at Horseshoe Bend in March 1814.

The following September Crockett returned to service as a sergeant and participated in some minor mopping-up operations before returning to civilian life in March 1815.

Soon after Crockett's return to Franklin County his wife died, and in 1816 he married Elizabeth Patton, a widow. The following year he moved westward again, to what soon became Lawrence County; ironically, it was within an area recently ceded by the Chickasaws in a treaty negotiated by General Andrew Jackson. Crockett and his fellow pioneers set up their own ad hoc government until the state legislature officially organized the county and appointed him justice of the peace. Though he lacked legal training, Crockett was apparently fair and commonsensical in his decisions. As he boasted in his autobiography, no one ever appealed his decisions, and if they had, the decisions "would have stuck like wax" because he relied "on natural born sense, and not on law learning; for I had never read a page in a law book in all my life." The formula worked, and Crockett, employing his broad backwoods humor, soon won election as colonel of the county militia. He also became town commissioner for Lawrenceburg and in the summer of 1821 won election as state representative for Lawrence and Hickman counties. Whether or not Tennessee was prepared for him, a new kind of politician had arrived center stage, a true frontier politico, distinctly different from the aristocratic Jackson and prepared to address the need of common backwoods people. And their foremost need was land.

Beginning with his first term in the legislature Crockett took a keen interest in the Western District, and late in 1821 he moved to a remote part of present-day Gibson County. There on a fork of the Obion River he found an abundance of game; it was the sort of place where a mighty hunter could find satisfaction—and, coincidentally, gain mythic fame. Crockett planted some corn, but his real interest was hunting. His politics never suffered, for he was elected to the legislature from his new district and consistently supported the interests of squatters and other poor landholders in Tennessee. In 1825 he lost his first bid for a seat in Congress, then returned home and during one seven-month period, by his count, killed 105 bears. He also nearly drowned while attempting to take a flatboat of barrel staves down the Mississippi. His career took a more promising turn in 1827 when he was elected to Congress from West Tennessee's Ninth Congressional District.

During his first term in Washington Crockett expressed antipathy toward the administration of John Quincy Adams and, for a time at least, strong support for his erstwhile commander Andrew Jackson. He also supported the Tennessee Vacant Land Bill, a proposal that the United States give all of its vacant lands in Tennessee to the state, which would sell them to support education. Crockett apparently believed the state would sell the lands at very low prices in order to oblige his poor constituents, but he soon suspected that colleagues like James K. Polk intended to make more money by setting a much higher price. Crockett also came to believe that the law as drafted would dispossess a number of his squatter constituents. The squatters were true pioneers, the vanguard of American civilization, and deserved to retain both the lands they occupied and the improvements they had made. If a choice had to be made, then education be damned. When the bill came up later, Crockett offered an amendment which would have granted preemptions protecting squatters and their improvements. Both the bill and his amendment were tabled after extensive debate. Likewise, Crockett's later attempts to guarantee the landholdings of his poorer constituents met defeat, partly as a result of the efforts of Tennessee colleagues who viewed him as a traitor. But there is no doubt that Crockett was thinking of his constituents—the "real" Tennessee pioneers.

Reelected to a second term in 1829, Crockett was at first careful not to antagonize Andrew Jackson, who was now president. Jackson, after all, was almost as popular as Crockett in the latter's congressional district. Prior to Jackson's presidency, the only overt split between the two men had come in the early 1820s when Crockett had backed Colonel John Williams, a Jackson enemy, for re-election to the U.S. Senate. At the time he had apparently paid little attention to the larger implications of his action. Regardless of his earlier feelings, Crockett was actively opposing Jackson by early 1830, when he attacked Jackson's Indian Removal Bill and veto of the Maysville Road bill. Crockett was not being overly sympathetic to Indians; voters in the Western District, a frontier area, would never have supported such a candidate. He no doubt felt some empathy for individual Indians on a vague, abstract level, but his vote against the removal bill appears to have been more the result of his collusion with Eastern Whigs and his hatred of Jackson. Whigs could provide Crockett with powerful Eastern friends and perhaps rewrite his views in a form more palatable to a national audience. Crockett's stubborn opposition to Tennessee Democrats on the vacant land issue had lost him any organized support within his own party. For their part, Whigs reveled in the prospect of finding a colorful, genuine frontiersman—from Tennessee, no less—who would stand up to the frontier-common-man pretensions of Jackson. As for Jackson's veto of Kentucky's Maysville Road project, the president's arguments that federal money should be spent on internal improvements only if they had national importance carried little weight with many Westerners. How could newly developing areas mature without federally financed turnpikes, canals, and river-clearance projects?

Davy Crockett, it is clear, did not oppose Jackson solely on the basis of logic or governmental philosophy. He had come to hate the president, and that sentiment was reciprocated. Thus it was hardly surprising that William Fitzgerald, a prominent Jacksonian, opposed Crockett when he ran for his third term in 1831. Even with Jackson's backing and that of Polk's political machine, Fitzgerald managed to win by only a narrow margin. Crockett, however, was nothing if not resilient and in 1833 again won election to Congress, where he continued to support his version of a Tennessee vacant lands bill. Though he had insisted that he would never wear Andrew Jackson's collar around his neck like a pet dog, he had become a pet of the Whig Party. They touted his virtues, ghostwrote books attributed to him, and sponsored his speaking tours in the Northeast. Crockett apparently thought there might even be a chance that he would gain the White House. But in 1835 his uncompromising stance toward Jackson ended whatever dreams he may have entertained, and a Jacksonian defeated him (by barely two hundred votes) in his bid for re-election to Congress. Almost immediately Crockett began planning another move, this time from the Tennessee frontier to someplace more distant and exciting. He decided to undertake an expedition to Texas and to survey prospects there. It hardly mattered that there was a war underway between transplanted Americans and the forces of General Antonio López de Santa Anna. As he paused at Memphis before leaving Tennessee, Crockett reportedly took a swipe at his former constituents who had repudiated him: "You may all go to hell and I will go to Texas."

Texas, as it turned out, proved to be more of an adventure than Crockett had expected. It was perhaps characteristic and fitting that in March 1836 he and some friends found themselves at an old, abandoned mission just outside San Antonio. There they became partners in death with some 180 other men who, facing impossible odds, perished defying Santa Anna's army. The precise circumstances of Crockett's death at the Alamo are a source of great controversy. Some scholars contend that he and a few others hid in a storage area and were not discovered by Mexican troops until after the fighting was over and that Santa Anna then imperiously ordered their immediate execution. A far more familiar and popular version—especially among Texans— is that Davy Crockett fought to the end and was part of the heroic last stand at the Alamo. It was only fitting that six weeks later another erstwhile Tennessean frontiersman, Sam Houston, led the Texas army to its dramatic and decisive victory over Santa Anna at the Battle of San Jacinto. And it was Houston who became the first president of the Republic of Texas.

But Houston's legend could not match that of Davy Crockett, and only Daniel Boone's legend exceeded it. Boone, however, was a more remote, stoic hero representative of an earlier age that was little given to the exaggeration of the Jacksonian era. The contrast between Daniel Boone and Davy Crockett was much like that between George Washington and Andrew Jackson. Crockett was adept and eager in his self-promotion, and his stories— whether told by himself or others—were part of an emerging folklore about the frontier that carried into the post-frontier era of the Old Southwest. He was the quintessential frontier rustic, lacking formal education but possessed of intelligence, wit, and

Portrait of Davy Crockett. By John Gadsby Chapman.
COURTESY HARRY RANSOM HUMANITIES RESEARCH CENTER ART
COLLECTION, THE UNIVERSITY OF TEXAS AT AUSTIN.

common sense. He was a mighty hunter—or, just as good, said he was—who could shrewdly take the measure of any sophisticate in Nashville or Washington. His seat in Congress and political alliance with the Whigs ensured a large audience for his antics. And his, certainly more than Jackson's, was the true rags-to-riches story of the American frontier; he was a truer representative of the common man. Andrew Jackson was a speculator who advanced his own interests and those of other elites, but Davy Crockett supported squatter rights and cheap land.

Following the Alamo, the popular media in the United States increased its coverage of Crockett the legend, and his persona came to embody the Frontier Myth. He, Houston, and Jackson exemplified not only the Tennessee frontier, but also a larger national process. Even more than Boone, they represented the frontier transcendent, moving beyond localized and personalized experience toward a national identity that self-consciously gloried in the violence that hastened the realization of our Manifest Destiny. All three men were frontiersmen cum political leaders who reflected a marriage of myth making and politics. Today Houston's legend has perceptibly diminished, while Jackson's fame endures, but only Davy Crockett has inspired movies, television series, a craze for coonskin hats (Crockett abhorred them), and a song proclaiming him "King of the Wild Frontier." Jackson may have won the political wars, but Crockett prevails in American popular culture. Not bad for a Congressman from the cane-brakes of the Western District.

II.

Hegemony and Cherokee Removal: 1791–1840

For white Tennesseans, the Cherokee presence was always a visible reminder of their frontier heritage, of dreams unfulfilled. That tribe had once claimed more than half of the entire state, but through a series of cessions retained only the southeastern corner by the end of 1806. Whites coveted that region as well, but for more than a decade they were unable to make any legal inroads there. The Cherokees held them off, not through force of arms, but through wily maneuvering and remarkable selective acculturation. They were becoming "civilized" and thereby acquiring the means of retaining both their homelands and identity as a people. For many Cherokees, civilization was simply another strategy in a long process of creatively coping with whites and redefining what it meant to be Cherokee. Ironically, it was a strategy sanctioned by United States Indian policy.

Civilization was one part of the twofold U.S. policy regarding Indians. The other was to acquire their lands to accommodate an ever-expanding white population. Whenever the two objectives came into conflict, as of course they sometimes did, the latter always prevailed. The 1791 Treaty of the Holston was a blend of both objectives, authorizing a tribal land cession and instruction of the Cherokees in the ways of white society and agriculture.

The government would furnish agricultural implements, seed, and appropriate tutelage in the agricultural and mechanical arts. Cherokees would be encouraged to live like whites: replacing their matrilineal and matrilocal society with a patriarchal society; forsaking the extended, clan-dominated families for nuclear families; giving up tribal landholding and village society for individual, privatized property; forsaking the old religious beliefs and adopting Christianity; learning English; abhorring the old practices of blood revenge; and in general conforming to the norms of white Americans. The Cherokees were to become red-skinned whites. They were expected to conform to an idealized Jeffersonian society of humble yeomen and their families tending individual plots of land. That image and expectation for Indians would continue into the twentieth century.

The objective of the United States was never to physically exterminate the Native Americans; rather, its policy implied a cultural annihilation by demanding Indian acceptance of white normative values. To today's observer the policies of Washington, Jefferson, and others seem terribly ethnocentric, but in those days people assumed that Indians would *want* to change from what was clearly an inferior state—primitive and savage—to a more settled, aspiring existence. To a Jeffersonian, it was only rational to believe that a savage should be converted to civilization. Believing that people are but reflections of their environment, Jefferson assumed that with proper instruction Indians had the capacity to transform themselves and become assimilated into the larger, white-dominated society. He even believed for a time that racial intermarriage would promote that end and that the whole process would take only a generation or so. He was naive.

The first U.S. agent to the Cherokees was Leonard Shaw, who arrived in 1792 at Ustanali, the capital of the Upper Towns in northern Georgia (the Cherokee villages in Tennessee were included among those towns). Little Turkey, the nominal head chief of the Cherokees, was helpless to prevent continued raids by John Watts, Dragging Canoe's successor among the Chickamauga hostiles, nor could agent Shaw protect peaceable Cherokees from savage retaliation by white Tennesseans. When Shaw

277

HEGEMONY
AND
CHEROKEE
REMOVAL:
1791–1840

warned the Indians not to treat with Governor William Blount of the Southwest Territory, who as superintendent of Indian affairs was his superior, Blount requested his removal. His replacement was Benjamin Hawkins, who became agent to the Creeks as well as the Cherokees. Hawkins took up residence among the former tribe while his subordinate, Silas Dinsmoor, became the resident Cherokee agent. Together they began easing the tribes through a transition from hunting and the old female-dominated agriculture to a plow-based farming conducted by males. In an effort to encourage the domestic arts among Indian women, they distributed spinning wheels, looms, and cotton cards and hired white women to provide instruction in their use. Many Cherokee men, however, resisted Dinsmoor's efforts to get them to farm and attempted to sustain their traditional hunting practices. As late as 1804 almost all able-bodied males spent the winter hunting while women continued as before to do the spring planting. But game was rapidly dwindling on the hunting grounds of the Cumberland Plateau and northern Alabama. Return Jonathan Meigs, who became Cherokee agent in 1801, called the hunting lands "a nursery of savage habits" and wanted their cession so that Cherokees could embark wholeheartedly on plow agriculture. During 1805 and 1806, under great pressure, the Cherokees relinquished almost all their Tennessee lands except the area south of the Little Tennessee and Tennessee rivers.

Even with the decline of hunting, many Cherokee males were unhappy about becoming farmers. People do not give up traditional gender roles easily, and Cherokee men faced ridicule from their peers as well as the prospect of failing at plow agriculture. It seems likely that the disruptions in traditional life were at least partly responsible for the continuing threat of violence between the races. Occasional murders by whites and Indians continued to complicate relations, as did horse theft. Horses were a mobile, readily disposable form of wealth on the frontier. A Cherokee underground could steal them on the Tennessee frontier, sift them through the reservation, and sell them to whites in Alabama who were unlikely to ask many questions. Even law-abiding Indians might wink at such thievery, considering it one of the few available means of getting back at whites who, after all, were stealing their lands. As part of their civilization program Silas Dinsmoor and his successors encouraged more attention to this problem by the Cherokee National Council. Near the turn of the century the council approved a small mounted police force, the lighthorse patrol, which intermittently pursued horse thieves and other miscreants.

White aggression against the Cherokees was even more blatant. Besides putting constant pressure on the tribal land base, whites stole Cherokee horses and sometimes resorted to outright violence. In 1802 two white Tennesseans murdered a Cherokee man and took his horse. White authorities described the act as "wanton, unprovoked murder," but the two men went unpunished because no one would testify against them. Just a few months later another Tennessee Cherokee was killed by a white man, who claimed it was an accident. Though the National Council had tried to curb clan revenge, relatives of the slain Indian traveled to Sevier County, where they killed the white man's son as well as a woman in the family. Meigs persuaded the council to arrest the instigator of this clan retaliation and turn him over to the local U.S. military garrison, where he would be safe from a lynch mob. But it still turned out badly for the Indian; a white court tried him, disregarded the defense of clan retaliation, and hanged him. The message was clear to any Indian: laws on the frontier were not color blind. They operated to the advantage of whites. Eventually the federal government attempted to placate the Cherokees for such obvious inequities by paying $100 to $200 for each Indian murdered by whites.

The three-way land settlement in 1806 between the United States, Tennessee, and North Carolina, occurring about the same time as massive Cherokee land cessions, promoted the likelihood of more Indian-white violence. Under its terms the remaining Cherokee lands in Tennessee were not subject to North Carolina or U.S. claims and would therefore, in theory at least, be a valuable source of state revenue, especially for financing public education. But from the beginning Tennessee officials were more interested in satisfying the demands of their landless constituents than in meeting educational needs, and they did little as white intruders squatted on Cherokee lands in the years immediately preceding the War of 1812. Both Governor John Sevier and Governor Willie Blount advocated additional cessions, and agent Meigs became a co-conspirator by supporting an exchange of tribal lands for territory west of the Mississippi, where more than one thousand Cherokees already resided. But the United States and Tennessee refrained from pushing the issue, perhaps because nobody wished to antagonize the Cherokees at a time when Tennesseans were fighting both the British and the Creeks.

From the mid-1790s to about 1808 a fairly clear-cut political division existed among the Cherokees. There were the Upper Towns of southeastern Tennessee, southwestern North Carolina, and northern Georgia, whose National Councils met regularly at Ustanali. Rivaling them for influence were the Lower Towns situated farther down the Tennessee River toward Muscle Shoals. At first the latter towns were led by former Chickamauga intransigents like John Watts, but after Watts died in 1802, leadership was assumed by an oligarchy that included such former warrior chiefs as Doublehead and Bloody Fellow, who were renowned for their earlier resistance to white expansion. They were also allied with equally shrewd whites—mostly former British loyalists— who had married within the tribe. Prior to 1800 the strategic location of the Lower Towns and the personal prestige of their leaders gave them an advantage over the Upper Towns. Agent Meigs recognized this preeminence and attached more significance to the Lower Town meetings at Willstown in northeast Alabama than to those at Ustanali. He also believed he could negotiate more readily with men like Doublehead, who looked out for his own interests and those of his friends; the federal government could deal with such men. But Doublehead's many questionable activities led to his assassination by fellow Cherokees at Hiwassee in 1807.

Largely because of the devious maneuvers of Doublehead and his associates, including agent Meigs, successive National Councils at Ustanali had established by 1810 a rough framework for centralized tribal governance, complete with a thirteen-member National Committee that would handle matters arising between the annual councils and set the agenda for the councils. The National Committee reflected the traditional Cherokee emphasis on harmony and consensus; its members represented every important tribal faction. The tribe, now seemingly united, opposed any treaties not approved by the council and insisted that Meigs as their agent vigorously defend their rights. The National Council attempted to modify the custom of clan revenge in such a way as to placate both Indians and whites, but incidents of clan violence would continue for many years. The emergence of the National Committee marked the first significant step toward tribal nationalism and demonstrated the Cherokees' growing determination to retain their land and identity. The council's resolution of 1810 directly discussed the primacy of land: "The country left to us by our ancestors has been diminished by repeated sales to a tract barely sufficient for us to stand on and not more than adequate to the purpose of supporting our posterity." As for those Cherokee individuals who were moving across the Mississippi, the resolution expressed hope that the U.S. government would neither "be influenced by any straggling part of the Nation" nor agree to a cession "contrary to the will and consent of the main body of the Nation." To leave the Nation without its approval meant loss of tribal citizenship.

While the United States sought additional land cessions, it continued to support Cherokee education and conversion to Christianity. Despite what we today interpret as the constitutional separation of church and state, the United States encouraged Protestant denominations to minister among the tribes and eventually subsidized their efforts with annual appropriations. The evangelical Moravians were the first group to proselytize among the Cherokees in an organized way, approaching tribal leaders in 1799 with a proposal to set up a day school and model farm among them. After they established themselves at Springplace in north Georgia, it became apparent that they emphasized conversion, while the Cherokees were mostly interested in practical, secular education.

Gideon Blackburn, a Presbyterian preacher in Maryville, Tennessee, proposed an approach that was different from that of the Moravians. Instead of insisting on conversion before civilization, Blackburn would reverse the order. He wanted to establish several secular schools among the Cherokees and was confident the

Indians would convert to Christianity after becoming educated. In 1803, supported by Meigs and most of the leading men of the Upper Towns in Tennessee, he toured Eastern churches to solicit funds for Cherokee schools. With council approval he opened the first school near the Hiwassee River in 1804, and a second two years later. The Moravians, following suit, finally opened their own boarding school at Springplace in 1804. During the few years the Presbyterian schools operated, they supposedly instructed three hundred to four hundred Cherokee pupils, primarily mixed-bloods who already understood at least some English. But in 1809, only ninety-four Cherokee youths matriculated at Presbyterian schools. Blackburn's two institutions in Tennessee together accommodated sixty students, and a private tutor instructed eight others within the state. There were only two other small schools within the entire Cherokee Nation.

During the first two decades of the nineteenth century, the Cherokees made significant strides toward developing a settled, dispersed agricultural society. In 1809 agent Meigs reported that 12,395 Cherokees lived in the Southeast and owned more than 19,000 cattle, 6,500 horses, 19,700 hogs, and 1,000 sheep. They also had 567 plows, 429 looms, more than 1,500 spinning wheels, and 583 black slaves (compared to perhaps 100 in 1790). Thirteen gristmills and three sawmills served Cherokee needs, though there were still no cotton gins. The "hundreds of miles of roads" within the reservation linking Cherokees to each other and to regional centers beyond were another measure of tribal progress. The old town system, an essential feature of traditional tribal life, was already disintegrating as individual families and their kin scattered up and down the valleys in search of good land. Many families, however, still retained a town identity and gathered together at old council houses for ceremonial occasions or festivities. In 1809 and 1810 Major John Norton, a Scotsman and adopted Iroquois (who also claimed to be part Cherokee), found many aspects of traditional life throughout the tribal domain. He attended stickball games and council meetings, witnessed Eagle Tail dances, and even spent a few nights in traditional winter houses, still used in remote areas of the Cherokee Nation. But while evidence of the "old" Cherokee identity was abundant,

Norton also saw change and progress, and he believed that acculturation might enable the Cherokees to avoid removal to lands beyond the Mississippi.

Rapid change often produces feelings of fear and anxiety. It was no different for the Cherokees. In January 1811, according to one account, three spirit messengers appeared in the sky and told several Cherokees to warn their brothers against abandoning their unique identity because the Great Spirit had made Indians and whites different. Certain things offered by whites were useful, like reading and writing, while others, like their corn, religion, and medicine, were not. When the New Madrid earthquakes began the following December, many Cherokees believed the Great Spirit was angry. Indian homes were knocked off their foundations and large sinkholes appeared and filled with murky green water. Agent Meigs reported that some Cherokees "have thrown their clothing into the fire" as a rejection of white civilization, but he did not perceive any anger directed at missionaries or other whites. Fortunately, the excitement never assumed the bitter, intratribal nature of the contemporary Creek revitalization. Rather, it appears to have been an effort among some tribal members to adapt the new imperatives of civilization to the old mores. If a charismatic leader had appeared, the Cherokee renewal might have assumed the dimensions of Handsome Lake's revitalization movement among the Iroquois or that of Tenskwatawa and Tecumseh among the tribes of the Great Lakes. Instead, the younger political chiefs successfully channeled the fervor away from millennialism and into a Cherokee nationalism that focused on aggression against the Creeks.

When the Creek War got under way amid the War of 1812, some Cherokee leaders feared that its chaos would create similar divisions among their own people. They approached agent Meigs with an offer to lead a volunteer detachment of Cherokees against both the British and the Creek Red Sticks. Meigs was supportive because he believed such action would demonstrate conclusively the loyalty of his Cherokee clients to the United States. With the assent of the War Department and the legislatures of Georgia and Tennessee, Cherokee volunteers enlisted in frontier militias and were to receive the same equipment, pay,

and rank as the white soldiers. Eventually some six hundred
Cherokees joined the militia forces, and they were especially effective under Andrew Jackson at the Battle of Tohopeka (Horseshoe Bend) in March 1814. Cherokee tradition tells of Junaluska,
a noted warrior from North Carolina, who saved Old Hickory
from death in battle, an act of heroism Junaluska would later
regret. The Cherokees lost 36 warriors in their two engagements
against the Creeks, but their rewards included some 350 prisoners as well as a number of black slaves taken from the Creeks.

Unfortunately, the war proved almost as disastrous for the
Cherokees as for the defeated Creeks. At the Treaty of Fort Jackson the imperious General Jackson demanded a huge cession of
land from the entire Creek Nation—former hostiles and allies
alike—that included 2.2 million acres of *Cherokee* lands in
northern Alabama. (Jackson was never too careful when it came
to honoring tribal demarcations.) Beyond that, the federal government reneged on its promise and refused to pay Cherokee volunteers at the same rate as white militiamen. According to
Meigs's detailed records, the United States owed Cherokee soldiers more than $55,000, plus pensions for widows. To make
matters worse, the government insisted that Meigs use tribal annuities to repay the United States nearly $6,000 for blankets and
ammunition issued to Cherokee soldiers. A third grievance was
the widespread destruction of Cherokee property by white militiamen during the war. The worst offenders were soldiers from
East Tennessee who had had a lifelong aversion to Cherokees.
While on the march this rabble killed Indian livestock both for
the cooking pot and amusement, pillaged homes, and randomly
destroyed Cherokee personal property. Many officers admitted
their inability to control their troops. Meigs produced verified
claims for nearly $23,000 in damages and estimated that the true
total was twice that much.

President James Madison and Secretary of War William Crawford met with tribal representatives early in 1816 to discuss these
matters. The Cherokee evidence was persuasive, and Madison
agreed that they would retain their 2.2 million acres mistakenly
ceded by the Treaty of Fort Jackson. They would also receive
their full pay, pensions, and more than $25,000 in indemnities

for damages done by the Tennessee militia. The United States in turn received full authority to construct roads and navigate streams throughout the Cherokee Nation to facilitate trade among Tennessee, Georgia, and the Mississippi Territory. This Cherokee victory was short-lived. The frontier reaction against Madison's decision—abetted by the wrath of Andrew Jackson—forced the president to back step and insist on new negotiations to persuade the Cherokees to cede not only the 2.2 million acres just acknowledged to be theirs, but also 1.2 million acres north of the Tennessee River. The United States would provide a $6,000 annuity for the former and a single payment of $20,000 for the latter. Meigs, who had honorably defended the Cherokees' just claims, now believed the Indians should accede to the government's wishes. When the Cherokee council refused, he was furious, Jackson was furious, and the squatters who had already invaded those lands were furious. But they would get their way.

The solution was to emphasize what should have been obvious to the Cherokees and to all other Southern tribes: regardless of tribal boundaries, white expansion could not be stopped. Civilization among the Indians, even the Cherokees, had been at best a qualified success. Whites still believed that most Indians were wedded to a hunting lifestyle. The Indians' insistence on retaining their identity—not to mention their lands—called into question old, optimistic Jeffersonian assumptions about their assimilation into a white-dominated national culture. Jackson ridiculed the notion of treating tribes as sovereign entities and renewed the argument that Indians were mere "tenants at will" who lived under the sovereignty of the individual states. His pronouncements to Chickasaws and Cherokees alike were completely predictable: because they lacked sovereign rights, they should strike the best possible bargain for ceding their lands and move across the Mississippi, where game was abundant and a beneficent United States would provide them with ample land. Those relatively few Indians who had become civilized could remain in the Southeast if they chose, but they would be subject to state laws like any other residents. It would be best if they all moved west.

Although refusing to sell tribal lands in July 1816, the National

Council sent a delegation to a meeting between U.S. and Chickasaw delegates where a possible Chickasaw cession of a portion
of Alabama was being discussed. The fifteen Cherokees were to
observe the proceedings and ensure that the Chickasaws did not
give away any of the 2.2 million acres recently confirmed to the
Cherokees; some of those lands overlapped with Chickasaw
claims. The Cherokees had selected most of their delegates from
the Lower Towns because they were most familiar with the lands
at issue. General Jackson, who was one of the United States commissioners, realized that constant encroachments by white trespassers had renewed sentiment in the Lower Towns for removal
westward. Finding it "both wise and politic to make a few presents to the chiefs and interpreters," he persuaded the visiting
Cherokees to sign an agreement selling the 2.2 million acres for
$60,000, divided into annuities of $6,000 for ten years—less
than three cents an acre. The Cherokees would also receive
$5,000 for any improvements in the surrendered territory. This
agreement was made with the understanding that it was valid
only if approved by the National Council in October. Jackson
appeared at that council, and when he failed to persuade that
body to accept the sale, he gained the assent of a cabal of leaders.
The deal was concluded, and despite the protests of most Cherokee chiefs, the federal government accepted Jackson's treaty.
Tennessee Governor Joseph McMinn believed the acquisition of
these Alabama lands would open new markets for his constituents, but for the present he wanted the United States to concentrate on obtaining Cherokee cessions in Tennessee. Jackson
planned to do so.

The problem of white squatters on Cherokee lands played into
Jackson's hands, and he intended to leverage that advantage into
a tribal cession of lands north of the Tennessee River, including
large tracts in Tennessee. He believed Lower Town leaders would
make the deal, despite opposition from the National Council.
The rationale would be that the United States was entitled to a
share of tribal lands equal in size to lands made available for
Cherokees migrating to Arkansas. Meigs and Governor McMinn
supported this argument, and in January 1817 at the Hiwassee
agency in Tennessee the agent met secretly with Lower Town

leaders who had already decided to move to Arkansas (by this time approximately 2,500 Cherokees resided there). The Upper Towns were well aware of the plotting, and in May representatives from fifty-four towns met in council, denounced the idea of an exchange, and passed several measures aimed at strengthening the tribal government. The council also resolved that if more Cherokees moved westward, federal reimbursement for improvements should be available to women as well as men, and that if a woman chose to remain in the East while her husband left, the United States should not dispossess her. A final measure provided a means of amending the new framework of government, suggesting that these changes of 1817 represent the first constitution of the Cherokee Nation. The changes, William G. McLoughlin contends, were the result of "creative, collective statesmanship."

But nothing could deflect the juggernaut of Jackson, McMinn, Meigs, and the federal government. Willy-nilly, negotiations got underway at the Hiwassee agency in June 1817. Jackson, McMinn, and General David Meriwether were the U.S. commissioners, and Meigs was a more-than-interested observer. Many chiefs of the Upper and Lower Towns attended, as well as fifteen chiefs from Arkansas, including John D. Chisholm, the son of William Blount's co-conspirator. The Arkansas Indians were natural allies of the government and favored a cession large enough to equal the U.S. lands on which they already resided and any additional amount necessary for new Cherokee immigrants. Lower Town chiefs who intended to move agreed with their Western brothers. In their opening statements the commissioners alluded to the 1809 meeting between President Jefferson and some visiting Tennessee Cherokees who had advocated a division of lands between the Upper Towns, of which they were a part, and the Lower Towns, which, they said, were made up of individuals attached to the old ways. Now the United States wanted to facilitate such a division by encouraging most, if not all, Cherokees to move west. Those who chose to remain behind could have their own private reservations and would be eligible for U.S. citizenship. For eight days most chiefs argued, correctly, that the meeting with Jefferson hardly constituted a commitment by anyone, least of all the entire Cherokee Nation. Finally, sixty-seven chiefs

☙ 287

HEGEMONY
AND
CHEROKEE
REMOVAL:
1791–1840

prepared a memorial rejecting what could only be a second-class U.S. citizenship and expressing a desire to continue their progress toward civilization within their homeland.

Jackson would have none of it. He threatened, he cajoled, he prevailed. Early in July thirty-one chiefs from the Upper and Lower Towns, along with the remaining two Western Cherokee delegates, signed Jackson's treaty. The two delegates from Arkansas then obligingly signed by proxy the thirteen names of the Arkansas delegates who had returned home. Thus forty-six Cherokee names were affixed to the document, though the thirty-six chiefs who had signed the earlier protest remained adamantly opposed. No doubt some of those who signed believed that the treaty concessions did not deny Cherokees the right of remaining in the East if they so chose. Quite likely some of the signers also expected a quid pro quo. Despite President Madison's promises of the previous year, the Cherokees had received little compensation for their service in the Creek War. It can hardly be a coincidence that the day after the treaty was signed, Jackson wrote Secretary of War George Graham that it was always his understanding that the Cherokees were entitled to the same pay and emoluments as other troops: "I made this promise believing it was Just. I hope it will be complied with."

The treaty of 1817 stipulated that the following year the United States would prepare a census of the Cherokees living on both sides of the Mississippi, and future tribal annuities would be distributed proportionately between the two divisions. The Cherokees agreed to cede a tract in Georgia, almost all of the Sequatchie Valley in Tennessee (about 278,000 acres), and two small parcels in Alabama. In return the federal government set aside a tract on the Arkansas and White rivers for the Cherokees. The United States would compensate tribal emigrants for any improvements of "real value," but it would provide only a rifle, ammunition, and a few other items for "poor warriors" making the move. The federal government would also furnish flat-bottom boats and provisions for emigration. Any Indian head of household residing on tribal land ceded under this treaty could, if he wished, become a U.S. citizen and take a private reservation, or allotment, of 640 acres which would include his home and other improvements. Such individuals would become subject to state law.

The U.S. Senate ratified the new treaty in December 1817, despite the efforts of a Cherokee delegation and their supporters in Congress. Almost immediately agent Meigs set about enrolling as many Indians as possible for removal westward. Joseph McMinn's term as governor of Tennessee had just expired, and he now served as Meigs's assistant at the Hiwassee garrison, where he was responsible for implementing the treaty. Assisting McMinn was Sam Houston, who despite his personal attachment to the Cherokees, strongly supported their removal. Houston was instrumental in convincing several bands, including that of Oolooteka (John Jolly), his adoptive father and a prominent Tennessee Cherokee, to leave for Arkansas. (A few months later Houston served as interpreter for an Arkansas delegation in Washington and provoked the ire of Secretary of War John C. Calhoun by appearing in Indian attire.) Most Cherokees urged one another to remain on tribal lands, and warned that anyone enrolling for removal would lose tribal membership. Richard Brown, who had signed the treaty, was replaced as president of the National Committee by John Ross, who would become the foremost defender of Cherokee rights. On two separate occasions during this crisis Cherokee women's councils, perhaps inspired by the aged Nancy Ward, presented petitions to the National Council saying that their lands had been given to them by the Great Spirit. They urged the council "to hold out to the last in support of our common rights."

McMinn, hoping to destabilize and demoralize the Indians in order to spur emigration, refused to authorize the Cherokee census that was necessary for distribution of tribal annuities. The National Council responded by using the lighthorse patrol to collect debts owed by prospective emigrants, and sometimes nationalist Indians burned down their houses to deny them federal compensation for their improvements. McMinn retaliated by posting soldiers around the property of would-be emigrants until it could be appraised. Though uninvited, he attended a meeting of the council and was shocked by the hostility toward those Indians planning to move. He took particular offense at the council's declaration that "We consider ourselves as a free and distinct

289

HEGEMONY
AND
CHEROKEE
REMOVAL:
1791–1840

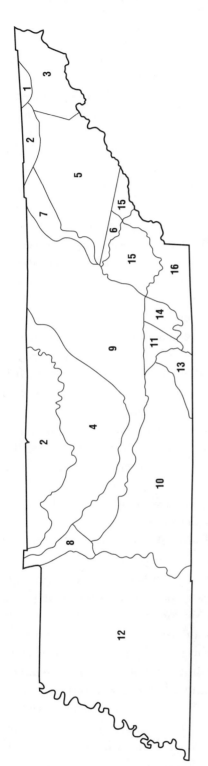

1. Treaty of Lochaber, 1770
2. Transylvania Purchase, 1775
3. Avery's Treaty, 1777
4. Treaty of Hopewell, 1785
5. Blount's Treaty (Holston), 1791
6–7. Treaty of Tellico, 1798
8. Chickasaw Cession, 1805

9. Treaty of Tellico, 1805
10. Dearborn's Treaty, 1806
11. Jackson & McMinn's, 1817
12. Great Chickasaw Cession, 1818
13–15. Calhoun's Treaty, 1819
16. Treaty of Removal, 1835

Indian Land Cessions in Tennessee. ADAPTED FROM CHARLES C. ROYCE, *Indian Land Cessions in the United States* (Washington: Government Printing Office 1900); WILLIAM R. GARRETT AND ALBERT V. GOODPASTURE, *History of Tennessee, its People, and its Institutions* (Nashville: Brandon, 1990); AND ALBERT C. HOLT, "The Economic and Social Beginnings of Tennessee," *Tennessee Historical Magazine*, 7 (October 1921).

nation," and that the U.S. government had no formal connection to them beyond "a friendly intercourse in trade."

By mid-1818 McMinn's work as enrollment agent was winding down, and he claimed that over 5,000 Cherokees had moved west, though his Indian opponents calculated the number at about 3,500. In either case, a significant minority had joined their fellow Cherokees in Arkansas. McMinn continued to insist that all Cherokees had to remove westward or become citizens and accept individual reservations. His description of the council's open hostility led John C. Calhoun, the new secretary of war, to authorize an offer of $100,000 for tribal cession of all Cherokee lands east of the Mississippi except for the private reservations. When McMinn presented this proposal in November 1818 before the National Council at the Hiwassee agency, it was rejected outright; the response was the same even when he upped the offer to $200,000. Angered, McMinn threatened to withdraw the troops protecting Cherokee lands; with hordes of intruders pouring in, mostly from Tennessee, the Indians might regret their intransigence. Bending somewhat, the council promised to send another delegation to Washington for further negotiations.

Fortunately for the Cherokees, they had acquired a powerful ally in the Boston-based American Board of Commissioners for Foreign Missions. The board was an umbrella organization that supervised the missionary activities of Congregationalist, Presbyterian, and Dutch Reformed congregations, and it had recently begun educating and proselytizing the Southeastern Indians, especially the Cherokees. With approval of the Cherokee National Council, the board's Reverend Cyrus Kingsbury established the Brainerd Mission in 1817 near Chickamauga Creek in present-day Chattanooga. The school was located on property acquired from the old Tory trader John McDonald, who went to live with his grandson John Ross. The Brainerd Mission would become the most famous school among the Cherokees (President Monroe even visited briefly), and Kingsbury and other board missionaries like Daniel Butrick and Samuel Worcester would emerge as staunch defenders of tribal rights. The American Board also had powerful, wealthy friends in business and politics—friends who had already begun speaking against the growing clamor for removal. These people, along with the missionaries, supported the original policy of civilizing Indians on tribal lands and eventually incorporating them into the larger fabric of American life.

By late 1818 the missionaries were increasingly involved in the Cherokees' political struggles, and Ross, a member of the delegation heading to Washington, was working at creating an alliance with them. But Joseph McMinn was enlisting his own allies, and by the time the twelve-member delegation left Knoxville on January 1 he had succeeded in bribing several of its members. The recent federal pressures had convinced many Cherokees that the Washington meeting was a prelude to removal. The delegation was given authority, if absolutely necessary, to cede all tribal lands under the best possible terms, but most of its members hoped to avoid this extremity by emphasizing the steps the tribe had taken toward civilization and promising that it would continue to move in that direction. Fortunately, and unknown to the Cherokees, outside circumstances now dictated a temporary end to federal efforts at total tribal removal. The entire sum appropriated by Congress for removal under the treaty of 1817 had been spent, and for a while at least, there would be no more. The Panic of 1819, moreover, was bringing a massive contraction of the economy. Nonetheless, Secretary of War Calhoun played his hand for all it was worth. He intimated to the delegation that the government might not demand all Cherokee lands east of the Mississippi, but would require at least a sizable chunk that would leave barely enough to meet the needs of those Indians who insisted on remaining. Surprised and relieved to learn that a total cession and mass exodus were not inevitable, the Indians quickly agreed to deliberate with Calhoun over the location and size of the tracts to be ceded.

Calhoun wanted most if not all of the land to be within Georgia, for one very good reason: Georgia's 1802 cession of its Western claims to the United States came with the proviso that the federal government remove the Indians from the state as soon as practicable. Now, nearly twenty years later, the Cherokees and Creeks were still very much present, and the state's political leaders were breathing fire. They wanted the Indians out—now. The Cherokees refused Calhoun's demand for a significant Georgia cession because some of their most important towns, including their capital, were there; in addition, they wanted their remaining lands to be contiguous to Creek holdings to the south. A wedge of white settlements between the Cherokees and Creeks would prove the undoing of both tribes. Calhoun and the delegates finally agreed that the best alternative lands were along the Tennessee River and its tributaries. Thus the Calhoun Treaty of February 2, 1819, resulted in a massive cession of parts of western North Carolina, southeastern Tennessee, northeastern Alabama, and a smaller parcel in Georgia. The sacrificed Tennessee lands included the Hiwassee District—almost everything between the Little Tennessee and Hiwassee rivers—and amounted to 1.54 million acres. The state eventually sold the Hiwassee District to settlers on a graduated scale ranging from $2 an acre downward. The surrendered Cherokee acreages in North Carolina, Alabama, and Georgia were 987,000, 739,000, and 536,000 respectively. These cessions fully compensated the United States for all past or future land grants that it made to the Western Cherokees. Like the treaty of 1817, the Calhoun treaty provided compensation for Indian improvements and allowed private reservations of 640 acres for individuals living on ceded lands who wished to remain in the East as citizens. What seemed clear—to the Cherokees at least—was the treaty's implied promise that there would be no more demands on the tribal homeland, that the Cherokees could continue their strides toward civilization without threat of dispossession. And for the present, the federal government allowed them to believe it.

For more than a decade after the 1819 treaty, the Cherokee Nation continued on its own path toward civilization and self-definition. The scope and nature of this civilization is difficult to gauge because missionaries and other reformers always gave the Cherokees a good press, using them as a sterling example of Indians' ability to progress within their Eastern homeland. Such portrayals naturally emphasized the accomplishments of mixed-blood businessmen and political leaders as well as the relatively few Indians who had converted to Christianity or chosen to attend mission schools. More traditionalist Indians, especially those in remote mountain areas, received much less attention.

One manifestation of white cultural inroads was the Chero-

293

Hegemony
and
Cherokee
Removal:
1791–1840

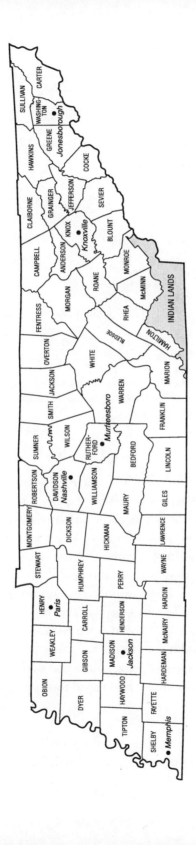

Tennessee, 1830. Department of Geography and the Cartographic Services Laboratory at the University of Tennessee.

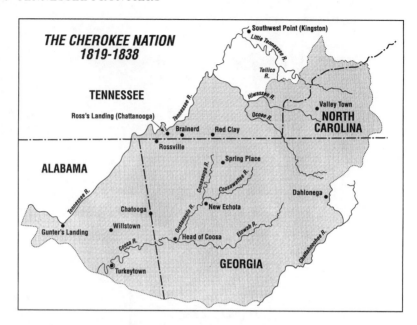

The Cherokee Nation, 1819–1838. ADAPTED FROM GARY E. MOULTON, JOHN ROSS, CHEROKEE CHIEF, © 1979 BY UNIVERSITY OF GEORGIA PRESS.

kees' changing gender roles. Like their middle-class white counterparts, Cherokee wives were now expected to be homemakers and keepers of the family hearth, not strong-willed individuals with significant political influence. Their proper functions included tending children, cleaning, spinning, weaving, cooking, and personifying domestic virtue and bliss. No longer were women to play the role of primary agricultural provider as they had always done. That was now a function assigned to tribal males. During the 1820s tribal laws reduced many traditional roles for women and favored the emergence of a patriarchal, patrilineal society dominated by acculturated males. Female participation in tribal politics nearly ceased to exist except perhaps in remote neighborhoods.

Cherokee males adapted as best they could to the new limitations and opportunities presented by civilization. The days of taking to the warpath were over, and federal and tribal authorities were pushing the old system of blood revenge toward extinction. For most men hunting was now a shadow of the past, a mere avocation. Horse-and-plow agriculture and stock raising were increasingly a fact of life. Male-dominated nuclear families continued to disperse throughout the countryside, but they often remained in close proximity to kin. Their log homes were little different from those of nearby whites. And yet, as always, Cherokee cultural syncretism blended the new ways with the familiar. In the Tennessee River Valley, for example, mixed-blood male elites became commercial planter-ranchers and used a system of herding that reflected European influences. But herding also incorporated certain features of the hunting tradition—like intimate knowledge of the landscape and a propensity to roam—and thus softened the transition to a market-based tribal economy.

Cherokee corn, tobacco, cotton, and livestock satisfied tribal needs, and surpluses often went to nearby regional markets like Knoxville, Nashville, Huntsville, and Athens. Individual Indians and their families might make the trip to market or, more often, middle men would do it for them. Predictably, the mixed-bloods were more skilled at farming and more focused on commercial production. The most successful had impressive plantations rivaling those of their wealthiest white neighbors, over whom Cherokee planters had a significant advantage because they did not have to buy any of the land they farmed. Instead, the tribe retained ownership, and any member could cultivate as much land as he wished as long as it was not already being used by fellow Cherokees and was not located too close to the improvements of others. The wealthiest Cherokee planters also relied on black slaves, whose number more than doubled between 1809 and 1825. Still, in the latter year over 90 percent of Cherokee families did not own a single black slave, and only thirty to forty families owned ten slaves or more. Among Cherokee slave owners—and among the tribe as a whole—there was a growing animus toward blacks, a perception that they were inferior by nature to both whites and Indians. Cherokees appear generally to have been less disposed than whites toward physical abuse of slaves; a notable exception was the wealthy mixed-blood James Vann, who when drunk tortured and even murdered his slaves.

In terms of slavery and racism, at least, "civilizing" the Cherokees had unfortunate consequences.

The mission schools, meanwhile, had a mixed record. In 1817 the only schools were at Springplace and Brainerd, which together taught fifty-one students—fewer than 2 percent of school-age Cherokees. By 1835, however, the Congregationalists under the Board of Commissioners had established ten new schools throughout the Cherokee Nation. The Moravians added another, the Baptists two, and the Methodists, relying on circuit riders, created six "itinerant schools." At any given time all of the schools together probably taught no more than 200 to 250 Cherokee children, and full bloods usually made up less than 40 percent of the total student body. As denominations increasingly emphasized preaching and conversion over secular education, many Cherokees became dismayed. Despite missionary efforts, by 1830 the four denominations claimed only 1,038 Cherokee members, 736 of them Methodists. Denominational rivals viewed the Methodists with distaste because of their meager requirements for conversion, their hopeful and democratic message, their outward equality with Indians, and the fact that some Methodists had married Cherokees. After 1830 Cherokee males assumed some of the preaching responsibilities for the various denominations, demonstrating that Indians could play prominent roles within the Christian fold. And yet the number of tribal conversions remained disappointingly low.

Only the Congregationalist-dominated American Board of Commissioners provided the Cherokees with educational opportunities beyond the reservation mission schools. A few bright, eager Cherokees, including Elias Boudinot and John Ridge, matriculated at the Cornwall Academy in Cornwall, Connecticut, where they quickly received a primer course on American racism. When Ridge married a local white woman, there were murmurs of community disapproval. But the real storm broke when Boudinot proposed to Harriet Gold, the daughter of a prominent citizen and official of the academy. Residents were scandalized by the idea that an Indian should seek the hand of a well-bred, Christian New Englander—and that she would accept! They became so threatening that Boudinot and Gold feared for their physical safety, but in March 1826 the couple proceeded with the wedding anyway. Cornwall Academy quickly closed its doors, ensuring there would be no future social disasters within the town's leafy confines. The residents, of course, were many of the same good folk who had reviled white Southerners for their lack of Christian charity toward Indians. Remarkably, Elias and Harriet Boudinot harbored no permanent resentment when they moved back to the Cherokee Nation, where they were strong proponents of civilization and Elias assumed great prominence.

An important objective of the civilization program was to teach the speaking, reading, and writing of English. Some Cherokees readily supported it while others viewed such instruction as a form of cultural imperialism that threatened traditional society. It was in this context that Sequoyah, one of Tennessee's greatest native sons, was to assume prominence. Sequoyah was born near present-day Vonore between 1760 and 1770 and was the son of a white man, purportedly the noted trader Nathaniel Gist of Virginia. His mother referred to the boy as George Guess or Gess and raised him among the conservatives of the Lower Towns. Whatever his origins, he was a traditionalist through and through, and he never learned to speak English. Sequoyah had always recognized the tremendous power that written language gave whites, and sometime around 1809 he began tinkering with the creation of a Cherokee alphabet. Despite frequent ridicule—and even suspicions that he was a witch—he completed a workable Cherokee syllabary by 1821. Each of eighty-six symbols (later eighty-five) stood for a Cherokee syllable. People who could speak Cherokee and remember the appropriate symbols could read and write in the language. By any standards the invention of a written language by a single individual was a remarkable achievement, and it repudiated any beliefs in the intellectual inferiority of Indians.

Within a short time many Cherokees had become literate in their own language, a development at first viewed with misgiving by some missionaries, who believed the syllabary would simply delay Indian learning of English. Before long, however, they recognized the impact of Sequoyah's invention and began translating scripture into the syllabary. In 1828 a tribal newspaper, the

Cherokee Phoenix, began publication. It was printed in both Cherokee and English and edited by Elias Boudinot. By 1835, even though fewer than one-third of the Cherokees could read in their own language, more than half of all tribal households had a member who could read either Cherokee or English.

The impact of Sequoyah's syllabary on Cherokee civilization depends on one's perspective. The increase in tribal literacy certainly helped missionaries to disseminate their theology and politicians to promote their points of view. However, the syllabary also enabled Cherokees to preserve in written form the wisdom of their elders and to maintain and communicate their worldview. By the end of the nineteenth century the Cherokee syllabary would be one of the most powerful means of preserving Cherokee traditionalism, an ethnic marker distinguishing Cherokees from others. And what of Sequoyah himself? Even while working on his syllabary, he was traveling back and forth between Tennessee and the Cherokee lands in Arkansas, and in the West he gained some prominence among his people. In 1842 he journeyed to Mexico in search of other Cherokee emigrants and died there from unknown causes.

The level of civilization varied from place to place within the Cherokee Nation. It was more prevalent among the *métis* who lived in fertile, accessible parts of the tribal domain and much less so among full-bloods residing in the mountains. Even among the former acculturation was often selective. For example, many parents of pupils at the mission schools supported secular education but resisted Christian proselytizing. Moreover, mixed-blood economic and political elites were careful to show proper deference to the full-bloods, who continued to dominate the National Council and many of whom remained profoundly traditional in outlook. During the mid-1820s there was a brief, nonviolent rebellion of conservatives against certain facets of acculturation, but cool diplomacy on both sides of the cultural spectrum smoothed over the differences.

The elusive nature of Cherokee civilization was most pronounced in remote areas where outward change belied a continuing traditional culture. It is not even clear to what extent the laws or other political processes of the Cherokee Nation had any

299

HEGEMONY
AND
CHEROKEE
REMOVAL:
1791–1840

SE QUO YAH

Sequoyah and Cherokee Syllabary. Portrait by Charles
Bird King, 1828. COURTESY THE UNIVERSITY OF TENNESSEE
SPECIAL COLLECTIONS.

impact in such places. In mountainous regions like southeastern Tennessee women adopted a subsistence style of farming and herding that subtly and creatively preserved certain aspects of their traditional roles as agriculturists and heads of household. Female-based clan strictures continued despite missionary disapproval, and the mythic story of Selu, the Cherokee cornmother, reinforced the significance of women. Female basket makers used familiar materials, patterns, and techniques, and later they would cleverly incorporate white technologies and styles into a craft that remained uniquely Cherokee. A woman who upheld traditionalist ways might also possess a spinning wheel or loom and attend camp revivals sponsored by the Baptists or Methodists. And male shamans might be conjurors one day and hellfire Christian preachers the next. The Cherokees continued to tell traditional stories, play traditional games like stickball, and perform traditional ceremonies. Civilization was a mixed bag indeed.

By 1827 Cherokee civilization was perhaps most apparent to outsiders on the political level. That year represents a watershed because of sweeping institutional changes designed not only to promote civilization but also to protect tribal lands and identity. A written constitution for the Cherokee Nation, modeled on that of the United States, provided for a new executive, legislative, and judicial structure. Permanent officers were chosen in 1828, and John Ross became the new principal chief, with powers and status analogous to those of the U.S. president. Cherokee leaders, most of them *métis*, had created a true national, centralized government. Its capital was New Echota, Georgia; the name honored the principal town of the eighteenth century and was a symbolic affirmation of the Cherokee renaissance. Likewise, the *Cherokee Phoenix*, first published in 1828, signified a people rising from the ashes. The laws of the Cherokee Nation, still respectful of certain tribal traditions, were nonetheless pushing the tribe toward a market-based economy and the adoption of bourgeois, maledominated sensibilities. Only free male citizens could vote, and the laws affirmed the institution of black slavery. Most startling was the bold assertion that the Nation was a sovereign entity subservient to no one. The Nation insisted that the United States uphold its many treaties, even—and especially—in the face of the rising Southern clamor for tribal removal. The Cherokees were determined to retain their land and identity.

Leading this movement of tribal nationalism was John Ross, only one-eighth Cherokee by blood and descended from three generations of Scottish-American traders. At the time he was chosen principal chief in 1828, he was almost thirty-eight years old. He had been born in Alabama, but his father, Daniel Ross, had finally settled in present-day Chattanooga, where he traded with whites and Cherokees alike. John eventually moved in with his grandfather, John McDonald, just a few miles away in what became Rossville, Georgia. He studied for a while under the Reverend Gideon Blackburn, both at Chickamauga and at an academy at Southwest Point. Daniel Ross made certain his son became familiar with Indian ways, but John never acquired fluency in the Cherokee language. He played an inconspicuous role in the Creek War and afterward became involved in a variety of business ventures, one with Timothy Meigs, the son of Cherokee agent Return J. Meigs. When Timothy Meigs died, Ross and his brother Lewis formed a partnership to provide supplies for the Cherokees and the U.S. government. Ross's Landing on the south bank of the Tennessee was a busy depot and a major stopover for boatmen and travelers taking the Federal Road between Nashville and Augusta. Ross also operated a ferry connecting his landing with Hamilton County, Tennessee, on the opposite side of the river. By the mid-1820s his growing tribal commitments led him to give up merchandising and move from Ross's Landing to the more centrally located Head of Coosa (now Rome, Georgia), where he became a leading planter-politician.

By creating a nation state, Ross and his fellow Cherokees had thrown down the gauntlet and boldly defied white attempts to force their removal westward. Their claim of national sovereignty outraged many white Southerners, especially Georgians, who were quick to point out that such a status directly contradicted the clause in the U.S. Constitution denying the right to create a state within the bounds of an existing state without the latter's approval. Whites also claimed—correctly—that the tribal constitution was the work of Cherokee elites and, furthermore,

John Ross, Principal Chief of the Cherokee Nation.
COURTESY THE UNIVERSITY OF TENNESSEE SPECIAL COLLECTIONS.

that it was designed to oppress more gullible traditionalists. Late
in 1827 Georgia affirmed its sovereignty over all lands within its
boundaries; regardless of treaties, Indians were mere tenants at
will and could be removed whenever the state chose. That same
year the Creeks, under enormous pressure, ceded all their remaining lands in Georgia. Now only the Cherokees remained defiant. Reacting to an evident crisis, President John Quincy Adams
tried a clever backdoor maneuver. Early in 1828 he negotiated a

treaty with the Western Cherokees which offered them much more land in present-day Oklahoma and offered incentives for Eastern Cherokees to move westward. The new treaty put enormous pressure on the Cherokee Nation by implicitly requiring them to make a major land cession to compensate the United States for the land in Oklahoma. From the perspective of white Southerners and Western Cherokees—not to mention politicians in Washington—the treaty made perfect sense. To leaders of the Cherokee Nation it represented a major threat.

Tennessee Congressman James C. Mitchell was among the politicians advocating Cherokee removal from the East under the 1828 treaty. He pushed for the enrollment of emigrants, but Ross and other tribal leaders traveled throughout the Nation, exhorting their people not to accept the government's offer. Few did, and most of those expressing interest were white men with Cherokee families who resided in Alabama or near the U.S. agency at Calhoun, Tennessee. Their demands for compensation were almost extortionate. An exasperated Adams complained that the only effect of civilization and Christianity on Indians was to encourage them to form their own communities and proclaim their independence and sovereignty. Southerners would have to find someone else to bring about the removal, and they confidently believed that the 1828 election of Andrew Jackson to the presidency would give them the right man. They were correct.

After Jackson's election but before his inauguration, the state of Georgia passed a law that would take effect on June 1, 1830. It called for the appropriation of all Cherokee lands within the state and the abolition of tribal law. Any remaining Indians would come under Georgia law and, "being savages, heathens, and people of color," they would be denied rights possessed by whites, including the right to be a witness in or party to any suit involving whites. Early in 1829, Jackson's secretary of war and fellow Tennessean John Eaton told a visiting Cherokee delegation that it was unrealistic to expect the president to act against Georgia's claim of sovereignty. It would be better for them to take advantage of the 1828 treaty and join their people in the West. Eaton was also secretly working with Tennessee's Governor William Carroll, asking him to visit the Cherokees to discreetly inquire about sentiments for removal. Because removal was "a work of mercy" by the federal government, Carroll might even bribe prominent Indians in order to promote emigration. President Jackson made his intentions clear in his first message to Congress in December 1829: he insisted that removal was a humanitarian measure. It was the only way Indians could preserve themselves and—if they chose—preserve their ways.

Jackson's grand scheme became apparent when his Indian Removal Bill was introduced early in 1830. The House and Senate each entrusted the matter to its respective Committee on Indian Affairs, and each was chaired by a prominent Tennessean—John Bell in the House and Hugh Lawson White in the Senate. The committees quickly found common ground, and on May 28 the Senate concurred with the House on a unified bill, which Jackson signed the same day. The act made it United States policy to encourage the removal of all tribes east of the Mississippi to new homelands on the other side of the river. The United States would also pay most of the costs associated with the move. No force would be used against those choosing to stay, but Jackson and his agents made it clear they were willing to do almost anything short of overt violence. The cornerstone of the removal policy was the assumption that each state had sovereignty over its resident Indians and that treaties were mere instruments of policy which could be abrogated or ignored at will. The policy generated great controversy across the United States, with most of the opposition predictably coming from the Northeast. Davy Crockett was one of the few Southerners in Congress to speak against removal. Three days after passage of the act and in accordance with its resolutions of 1828 and 1829, Georgia formally assumed jurisdiction over all 4.6 million acres of Cherokee land within its borders and over its Indian inhabitants.

During the next several years the state of Georgia engaged in a systematic campaign of intimidation. It raised a mounted Georgia Guard to harass and undermine tribal leaders, it abrogated Cherokee laws, it prohibited tribal councils from meeting in Georgia except to discuss removal, it closed the mission schools, it required loyalty oaths from missionaries and other whites residing among the Indians, and it surveyed Cherokee lands and distributed them to whites in a state lottery. Especially attractive were the estates of Cherokee leaders and the mining lots amid the recently discovered gold fields on tribal lands. After John Ross's family was evicted from their spacious mansion at Head of Coosa by lottery winners, they moved onto tribal lands a short distance over the Tennessee line. "Rich Joe" Vann also moved into Tennessee with over one hundred slaves after being evicted from his estate at Springplace. No longer permitted to meet at New Echota, the Cherokee Nation held its National Councils at Red Clay, in Bradley County, Tennessee, near present-day Cleveland. Here, in a beautiful cleared area that boasted a magnificent spring and a large open-sided council house, the Nation periodically convened until the exodus of 1838. But no state in the South offered a truly safe refuge for Indians. Alabama and Mississippi followed the lead of Georgia by declaring their jurisdiction over Indian lands, and Tennessee followed suit in 1833. None of those states, however, was as aggressive as Georgia; Tennessee, for example, readily conceded Cherokee property rights.

In mid-1830 President Jackson invited the Cherokees to meet with him in Nashville to discuss terms for tribal removal, but the National Council proclaimed their intention to remain in their homeland. They beseeched the president to uphold federal treaty commitments by protecting their lands and disbursing federal annuity payments, which Jackson refused to release to tribal officers. The Cherokees and their supporters needed that money to finance their efforts to sustain legal action against Georgia. Early attempts to get federal courts to rule against Georgia's actions failed, but the 1832 U.S. Supreme Court decision in *Worcester v. Georgia* appeared to be a Cherokee victory. The case involved Georgia's arrest and imprisonment of two missionaries, Samuel Worcester and Elizur Butler, who had continued to minister to Georgia Indians after refusing to swear allegiance to the state. The question was whether Georgia's laws superseded those of the Cherokee Nation within the boundaries of Nation—whether tribal law, exercised in accordance with federal treaties, prevailed over state law on the tribal domain. The court upheld the preeminence of tribal law in such circumstances, and in his written decision Chief Justice John Marshall elaborated upon his earlier interpretation of tribes as "domestic dependent nations"—

that is, polities subject to federal authority but not that of the states. But nothing came of this decision. Jackson supposedly said that John Marshall had made his decision and could now try to enforce it. Even if the president didn't utter these words, they reflected his sentiments perfectly.

The pressures exerted by the Jackson administration and by the states of Georgia, Tennessee, North Carolina, and Alabama were wearing down the Cherokees' will and power to resist removal. In April 1832 more than six hundred Cherokee emigrants headed west by way of the Hiwassee, Tennessee, Ohio, and Mississippi rivers. By the end of that year most of the missionaries had come to believe that, no matter how regrettable, removal was inevitable. They wanted John Ross to make the best deal possible. Some prominent Cherokees were coming to that conclusion as well. Elias Boudinot had already resigned as editor of the *Cherokee Phoenix* because he was not allowed to use the newspaper as a forum for both sides of the removal issue. In October 1832 John Ridge, president of the National Committee, introduced an unsuccessful resolution to send a delegation to Washington to discuss a treaty of removal. Even Andrew Ross, the chief's brother, attempted to interest a Red Clay council in such a treaty, only to be rebuffed. Some members of this evolving Treaty Party were in secret collusion with state and federal officials and received promises of special protection and private reservations—considerations not extended to opponents of removal. By 1833 and 1834 any pretense of tribal unity had disappeared, and the Treaty Party was openly advocating accession to the wishes of the United States and Georgia. The party's leaders were Major Ridge, his son John, and his nephew Elias Boudinot. Jackson's administration was eager to deal with the Treaty Party and attempted to protect its members from the Cherokee majority supporting Ross.

In anticipation of removal, the U.S. government undertook an extensive census of the Cherokee Nation in 1835, which revealed much about tribal population, wealth, literacy, and agriculture. Within the Southeast there was a total of 16,542 Cherokees living in 2,637 households. More than 77 percent of the Indians were full-bloods (though that term was never precisely defined). Residing among the Indians were 201 intermarried whites and 1,592 black slaves. The Nation had more than 44,000 acres under cultivation and produced over half a million bushels of corn. Much of this output went to regional markets. The dichotomy of relatively unacculturated mountain Cherokees and more acculturated valley Indians was apparent in Tennessee. The census listed 3,144 individuals living on tribal lands within the state; these included 2,528 Cherokees, 480 black slaves, 79 whites intermarried with Cherokees, and 57 others of mixed black or Catawba Indian heritage. More than four-fifths of the Cherokee families lived near the Tennessee River. Those in the more mountainous area to the east around Turtletown had the highest percentage of full-bloods; they had less education, fewer slaves, fewer material goods, and smaller, less productive farms. Southeastern Tennessee, perhaps better than any other part of the Cherokee Nation, reflected intratribal diversity.

The final act in Cherokee removal began in October 1835 when the Cherokees gathered at Red Clay to hear another removal proposal from Washington. It was rejected overwhelmingly, even by the Treaty Party. But when Ross then led a delegation to Washington in another effort to find common ground with the president, the Treaty Party arranged to meet with federal officials at the old council site of New Echota. There, protected by the Georgia Guard, they and their supporters would negotiate and sign a removal treaty. Upon Ross's advice, the vast majority of Cherokees refused to attend these proceedings and instead repudiated them. When Ross returned home before the New Echota meeting began, the Georgia Guard crossed into Tennessee, arrested him and his guest, the well-known author and composer John Howard Payne (of "Home Sweet Home" fame), and hustled them to a filthy Georgia jail, where they remained for almost two weeks. Georgia, a bastion of state sovereignty, had violated the sovereignty of a sister state, provoking a storm of anger in Tennessee.

But nothing could stop the proceedings at New Echota, where U.S. commissioners John F. Schermerhorn and former Tennessee governor William Carroll made their proposal. On December 29, 1835 a tiny percentage of the tribe representing the Treaty Party signed an infamous treaty ceding all tribal lands east of the Mississippi and promising to relocate in present-day Oklahoma, where the United States would provide them with an equal amount of land. The government would pay the Cherokees $5 million and additional compensation for their improvements, subsidize their transportation to the West, and provide for their subsistence during their first year of residence there. The Cherokees were required to complete their relocation within two years after Senate ratification of the treaty. They were also assured that their new lands would never come within the jurisdiction of any state or territory and that they could continue to hold their own councils and operate their own system of government. Twenty Indians signed the document, including the Ridges, Boudinot, and John Ross's brother Andrew. By doing so, the Treaty Party had opened themselves to the likelihood of violent retaliations; the long-understood penalty for selling the Cherokee homeland was death. For Major Ridge the situation reeked of irony. Back in 1807, as The Ridge, he had participated in the assassination of Doublehead as retribution for that chief's willingness to sign away tribal lands. And some years later, while a member of the National Council, he had strongly advocated a law specifying death for such an offense. The members of the Treaty Party were at least courageous. They insisted that they had simply done what was necessary to preserve their people. At the same time, however, it is clear that they received certain favors from Georgia and U.S. officials for their assistance.

Ross and his associates—indeed, almost the entire Cherokee Nation—reacted to these developments with shock and indignation. They heaped scorn upon the Treaty Party, pronounced the Treaty of New Echota invalid, and worked tirelessly to block Senate ratification. Impassioned speeches by Democrats and Whigs echoed through the halls of Congress. Long-winded discourse on constitutional theory mingled with moralistic appeals for justice to America's aborigines. Right up to the end it was apparent the vote on ratification would be close, razor thin close. Both Hugh Lawson White and John Bell assured Ross that the treaty would not be ratified. White, who was already distancing himself from Andrew Jackson, said he favored protecting the

309

HEGEMONY
AND
CHEROKEE
REMOVAL:
1791–1840

Cherokees but feared the consequences of disputing Georgia's sovereignty. On May 23, 1836, the bill received the necessary two-thirds approval by the margin of a single vote; White had finally voted for the treaty. It was mostly a party issue, and Jackson's obsession with the matter was decisive.

Most Cherokees refused to face reality and, following Ross's advice, made no effort to prepare themselves for moving. Ross meanwhile continued his hopeless campaign in Washington. As a precaution the U.S. Army and Tennessee militia were ordered to disarm the Indians and build stockades for their possible confinement. Officers were sympathetic to the Cherokees, acknowledging that the vast majority opposed the treaty and were well behaved. Brigadier General R. G. Dunlap, commanding a detachment of Tennessee volunteers, denounced "the lawless rabble of Georgia" and threatened to resign his commission because he feared dishonoring his state if was called upon to use "the point of a bayonet" to uphold "a treaty made by a lean minority" of Cherokees. The *Nashville Whig*, in a bit of self-serving sympathy, said that while Tennessee, North Carolina, and Alabama had been humane in their treatment of the Indians, Georgians had acted with "indecent haste in removing them." Despairing of the odds against them, some Indians decided to join the "Old Settlers" or "Cherokees West" who had already settled in eastern Oklahoma. Between 1836 and 1838 about two thousand left their homeland and headed west. Most went under federal supervision, some by boats from Ross's Landing and eventually up the Arkansas River, and others overland from the Cherokee agency at Calhoun through Middle Tennessee and the corners of Kentucky, Illinois, Missouri, and Arkansas. One of these detachments even paused at the Hermitage long enough for its leaders to pay their respects to Old Hickory, now in retirement. Another overland group consisted of some six hundred members of the Treaty Party who hoped to establish themselves in the West before Ross and his militant supporters arrived.

The last true National Council in the East took place at Red Clay in October 1837, as several thousand Cherokees huddled in a cold, driving rain to hear Ross outline his efforts to save their homeland. But their two-year grace period was about to expire, and federal authorities emphasized that the United States would enforce the treaty. A petition signed by 15,665 Cherokees protesting the treaty had little impact in Washington, nor did Ross's attempts to produce a compromise treaty allowing the Nation to retain a portion of its homeland. The Indians must leave. Defeated, Ross at last agreed.

Supervising the removal was Major General Winfield Scott, who had great sympathy for the Cherokees and ordered his troops to treat them with kindness. He divided the former tribal territory into districts and, assisted by state militia, began a forcible roundup of the Indians. His base of operations was Fort Cass, the site of present-day Charleston, Tennessee. Early that summer several large contingents of Indians left Ross's landing for the West, but their many hardships amid the oppressive heat and drought prompted a Cherokee plea that Scott defer the emigration until the weather improved that fall, when Cherokee authorities themselves hoped to supervise the removal. Scott agreed, but in the meantime many Cherokees remained confined in stifling stockades where food and medical attention were scarce.

Finally, during the fall of 1838, Ross and his associates oversaw the departure of some 90 percent of the remaining thirteen thousand Cherokees. The remainder either had prior rights to remain or hid out in the mountains. Many of their descendants are members of today's Eastern Band of Cherokee Indians. The first detachment of this renewed exodus stopped at Rattlesnake Springs just south of Charleston, Tennessee, on October 1 and by unanimous vote promised to re-create the Cherokee Nation in the West, a pledge they would keep. The multiple emigration routes to Oklahoma are collectively known as the Trail of Tears, and many are the stories of anguish associated with it. Between 1836 and late 1838 an estimated fifteen thousand to sixteen thousand Cherokees made the trek—or at least started it. Many perished in the army stockades, and others died on the trail, including Quatie, the wife of John Ross. A rough estimate is that the mortality rate during the removal was about 25 percent, or four thousand dead, though some demographers place the toll much higher. Nor did the dying end with resettlement in the West. Ross and his allies made up the overwhelming majority of the Chero-

📖 311

HEGEMONY
AND
CHEROKEE
REMOVAL:
1791–1840

"Trail of Tears." COURTESY WOOLARC MUSEUM, BARTLESVILLE,
OKLAHOMA.

kees in Oklahoma, much to the discomfit of the Old Settlers and
members of the Treaty Party, and just a few months after Ross
arrived, some of his followers assassinated the Ridges and Elias
Boudinot. The extent of Ross's involvement in the killings is unknown, but he must have taken some satisfaction in the deaths
of those who had dared violate tribal law and bargain away the
Cherokee birthright.

The treaty of New Echota marked the last cession of Indian
land in Tennessee. The state received title to an area bounded by
its southern and eastern boundaries, the Tennessee River on the
west, and the Hiwassee River on the north, as well as a narrow
strip running from the Hiwassee northward along the Great
Smoky Mountains to the Little Tennessee River. The acquisition
included all or part of six present-day counties. Following ratification of the treaty, Tennessee organized the cession as the Ocoee
District (named for a major tributary of the Hiwassee) and established procedures for white settlement after tribal removal.
After surveying the district, Tennessee sold the land on a graduated basis, from as little as one cent to $7.50 an acre; pro-

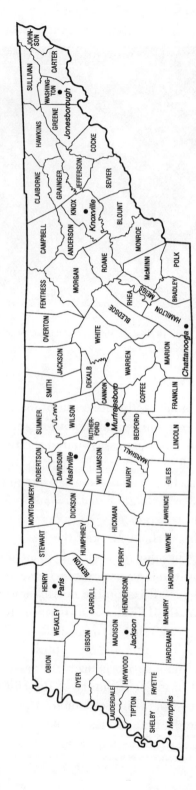

Tennessee, 1840. Department of Geography and the Cartographic Services Laboratory at the University of Tennessee.

ceeds supported internal improvements and the state's common school fund.

Even before the New Echota cession, whites had worked and resided in the Ocoee District, some as squatters and some with tribal approval. Across the Tennessee from the district was Hamilton County, created out of the Cherokee cession of 1819. The river had been at best a porous boundary between Hamilton County and the Cherokee Nation, and relations between the races were marked by "friendly intermingling and commercial activities." Whites thought nothing of crossing the river to do business or watch Cherokees play their frenzied and sometimes violent games of stickball. John Ross, who lived at Rossville, counted whites among his best customers at his nearby landing on the river. After moving to Head of Coosa in the mid-1820s, Ross sold his Rossville property to a white Methodist minister who was married to Ross's niece and could therefore own property within the Cherokee Nation. The minister went into partnership with another white and bought Ross's Landing and the warehouses associated with it. About the same time, Georgia's Wilson Lumpkin recognized the commercial and strategic importance of Lookout Mountain and became active in promoting a railroad to connect his state with that area. And in 1837, just a year after ratification of the Treaty of New Echota, John P. Long opened a store at Ross's Landing and received appointment as the community's first postmaster.

By the time Cherokee removal was underway in 1838, increasing numbers of squatters were moving into the Ocoee District to establish preemption claims. A new town was going up at Ross's Landing while barely half a mile away hundreds of Indians huddled within Camp Cherokee, a military stockade which served as their final home before they embarked on the Trail of Tears. In July of that year the *Hamilton Gazette*, a Whig weekly, achieved distinction as the first newspaper at the landing. Commissioners validated the entry claims of residents and hired an engineer to survey the town in a proper fashion. Then came the matter of deciding on a name for a town with so much promise. Lookout City seemed too pretentious to some, while Montevideo was rejected as being un-American. Why not *Chattanooga*, the Indian name for Lookout Mountain? Despite fears that the word was "too uncouth" and that outsiders might not know how to pronounce it, *Chattanooga* it was. The U.S. postal service recognized Ross's Landing as Chattanooga in November 1838, before all of the Cherokees had even begun their march westward. The irony seemed lost on the happy new community because white hegemony over the Indians had been a cumulative process, one of small accretions; the final victory went largely unrecognized. It was now possible to dispossess the Indians even while honoring them with a name.

CONCLUSION

History is never as sharply defined or divided as historians might like, and so it is when we discuss the end of the Tennessee frontier. Despite a common misconception to the contrary, removal of the Cherokees in 1838 did not mean that all Indians left. Approximately 1,500 individuals of significant degrees of Cherokee blood continued to live in the nooks and crannies of Tennessee, North Carolina, Alabama, and even Georgia. Today many thousands of their descendants remain in the old homeland and are not at all reluctant to proudly proclaim their Indian heritage. And so it has been with remnant groups of Seminoles, Miccosukees, Creeks, Choctaws, Houmas, and other Southern tribes. Despite the indelible stain on American honor that removal represents, the Native American presence remains vital throughout the region. Removal as a historical watershed is not a matter of the Indians disappearing, but of their losing their last large land base to whites. If the widely scattered lands of the small remnant groups had not been so marginal in value, they would have been taken as well.

By 1840 Tennessee had a population of 829,210. Almost half, 411,710, lived in Middle Tennessee, while 224,259 and 193,241 resided in East and West Tennessee, respectively. East Tennessee had grown only modestly since 1820, when it had 135,312 people, and it remained a region of small towns and diversified agriculture geared to nearby markets. Knox County was East Tennessee's largest producer in most important agricultural categories. The number of slaves in the region continued to be insignificant and represented barely 8 percent of the total population. In contrast Middle and West Tennessee had shown more substantial growth since 1820, when the former had a population of 287,501 and the latter had just been cleared of Indian title. By 1840 Middle Tennessee had grown some 43 percent, and West Tennessee already had almost as many people as East Tennessee. Nashville and Memphis were hubs of their respective areas, which were deeply enmeshed in America's expanding market economy. Though they produced many different crops, Middle and West Tennessee emphasized cotton and tobacco, which encouraged reliance on slave labor. Middle Tennessee's 107,735 slaves represented slightly more than 26 percent of its population, while West Tennessee's 56,610 slaves constituted 29 percent of its total. In almost every major category of agriculture, Middle Tennessee surpassed the other two regions; the major exception was in cotton production, where West Tennessee already led by more than 50 percent. Production of staple commodities in those two regions had made land itself the most valuable commodity.

Still, one should not be too literal in identifying 1840 as the emergence of a true market economy. Within some subregions— the Cumberland Plateau, for example—that point came later or perhaps never arrived at all. And in the micro-environment of Cades Cove in today's Great Smoky Mountains National Park, the transition from frontier to market agriculture and modernity was blurred by American popular culture. First settled by whites in 1818, when it was still Cherokee land, Cades Cove quickly became part of a larger America. Its people were relatively cosmopolitan; they traded regularly in regional centers like Maryville and Knoxville and were well aware of the latest national and international developments. The incredibly fertile soil produced a surplus of corn and other crops, and the period between 1840 and 1850 witnessed considerable prosperity. After the Civil War, however, all of East Tennessee was economically depressed, and Cades Cove, enveloped by mountains, became an especially in-grown community that was hardly an echo of its earlier days. The bonds of kinship hardened and discouraged demographic and economic fluidity.

Visitors to the cove, including some writers, were more en-thralled by its beauty and quietude than by its people, who ap-peared more and more anachronistic. Cades Cove and similar microenvironments gave rise to a distorted turn-of-the-century literature that depicted all of southern Appalachia either in ro-manticized premodern terms or as backward and often violent, the home of ignorant people. Either way, Appalachia was apart from the American mainstream, and the Southern mountaineer became a permanent frontiersman of the American mind. In this century the National Park Service has consciously abetted the romanticized, idyllic stereotype by tearing down the cove's frame houses, keeping the log cabins, and sustaining the Frontier Myth. Cades Cove, like some ancient insect encapsulated in amber, may forever be on view as an enduring Tennessee frontier. Similarly, the popular and historical fixation on Andrew Jackson, Sam Houston, and Davy Crockett has continued to identify Tennessee with an era of frontier volunteers.

What conclusions can we make regarding Tennessee's fron-tiers during the three hundred years we've looked at so briefly? First, Thomas Perkins Abernethy was at least partly correct in his path-breaking book *From Frontier to Plantation in Tennessee: A Study of Frontier Democracy* (1932). The desire to acquire land was the great engine which determined the course of the state's early history. There were certainly other important forms of eco-nomic opportunity—gold and other booty for de Soto, and slaves and deerskins for eighteenth century traders—but land was foremost. That was true for the earliest speculators such as Thomas Walker, was more true by the late 1760s, and remained true until well after removal of the Cherokees. Land was so es-sential an opportunity that many frontier residents had little emotional attachment to a particular area, town, or state. Some well-known figures in Tennessee history gained greater fame by going elsewhere, and many ordinary people did likewise, pulling up stakes and heading to Indiana, Illinois, the Missouri country, and all points west.

"Bounding" the land was one of the most important activities in frontier Tennessee. As the frontier's chief source of economic opportunity, land was a valuable commodity that required specific lines in specific plat books showing the distinction between "yours" and "mine." Speculators and ordinary frontier people alike were concerned about the validity of their land claims, a matter that was complicated by the confusing and imprecise metes-and-bounds system of survey. Sometimes, as in the case of the massive Revolutionary War land frauds, confusing surveys could be a good thing because unscrupulous individuals often had much to gain by messy overlapping claims. John Donelson's errant survey following the Treaty of Lochaber opened a vast new area to settlers, just as the lack of a survey for seven years after the Treaty of the Holston encouraged widespread violations of Indian lands by whites. While John Sevier was governor of Franklin, he hoped to extend the southern boundary of that dubious entity far enough to include Muscle Shoals. Fraudulent or confusing surveys could be helpful, but in most cases accuracy was more important. Richard Henderson wanted to be certain that the survey of the Virginia-Tennessee boundary would leave his massive claims in the Cumberland Basin within Tennessee, and forty years later James Winchester and his fellow speculators were betting that survey of the southern boundary of Tennessee (conducted by Winchester himself) would validate their claims to the fourth Chickasaw Bluff.

The hunger for good Tennessee land prompted elites to ally themselves with one another and, to a lesser extent, with their social inferiors both in North Carolina and in the transmontane region. Here I take exception to Abernethy's contention that the elites conspired against and exploited other whites, for I believe that men like John Sevier and William Blount *joined* with their underlings and led them toward mutually beneficial objectives. The fact that Blount, Robertson, and Sevier engrossed so much more land than most other whites does not mean their aims were

different from those of everyone else. The "little man," like the
speculator, would acquire all the land he could, and in any case
he still had opportunities to obtain lesser amounts; he also realized that the policies and leadership of his social superiors were
instrumental for the acquisition of land for himself.

But even in the earliest days of settlement in Tennessee, white
male society showed only conditional deference to elites. In neither Kentucky nor Tennessee, for example, were settlers willing
to abide for long the baronial pretensions of Richard Henderson.
William Blount realized that in order to retain influence in the
Southwest Territory he must break with George Washington's
Federalist administration; James Robertson undertook an unauthorized military expedition against the Chickamauga villages
because his militia and frontier constituents demanded it; and
John Sevier reluctantly became leader of the state of Franklin
because refusal would surely doom his reputation as the popular
Nolichucky Jack. Whatever their true feelings, governors William Blount, Sevier, Willie Blount, Joseph McMinn, and William
Carroll were all sympathetic to squatters. In Davy Crockett's case
we have a true frontiersman who gained political power, and
there can be no doubt that his efforts in behalf of the landless
poor were genuine. Many West Tennessee speculators encouraged people of limited means to settle on their properties and to
make improvements—not out of altruism, of course, but their
encouragement still enabled poor whites to gain a foothold. And
for better or for worse, when legislators had to choose between
funding education and sustaining squatters rights, the latter prevailed.

This obsession with land had an impact on government at all
levels. It was the catalyst for the speculators' exercise of political
clout in the North Carolina and Tennessee legislatures and for
their efforts to pressure the fledgling U.S. government for assistance. First and foremost the speculators wanted the United
States to negotiate with resident Indians and foreign nations for
massive cessions of land. When federal officials could not or
would not help, Tennesseans were not too proud to plot with
Spanish officials in New Orleans. The ad hoc creation of political
bodies like the Watauga Association, the Cumberland Compact,

the state of Franklin, and the new state of Tennessee all reflected a pervasive desire of elites and lesser citizens to facilitate and legitimize their acquisition of land.

Tennesseans considered it their just due when the United States purchased Louisiana from France, and later they pressured the government to force the Spanish "Dons" out of Florida by diplomacy or military force. Andrew Jackson performed a major service in this regard. Beyond that, Tennesseans expected the federal government to assume the major burden for protecting settlers from angry Indians who had been abused, from the threat of Spanish or French or British invasions, and ultimately from the consequences of the settlers' own actions. Once the settlers acquired land, they focused on creating adequate connections with the outside world. Only the U.S. government could provide effective assistance in making this transition from the frontier stage. Citizens wanted more and better roads (the federal roads were the most important); removal of navigational hazards from local rivers; and construction of canals and railroads. In this regard, at least, many Tennesseans repudiated the tenets of their hero President Andrew Jackson, who espoused fiscal restraint where internal improvements were concerned. Almost all frontier residents wanted to have their cake and eat it too, insisting on outside support but vehemently resisting outside control. Thus, just as their allegiance to elites was conditional, so was their allegiance to the national government. Tennesseans also made demands of the state government, but they were realistic enough to realize that the state's resources were insufficient to accomplish their objectives. At the county and community levels they depended on voluntarism and minimal rates of taxation.

Certainly one of the most important roles of the federal government was to protect backcountry populations during Indian wars, even though those wars often resulted from white aggression. This phase of the frontier experience emerged as the old trading frontier was disappearing. For much of the eighteenth century both the Cherokees and the Chickasaws had adapted to the trade through realpolitik and creation of a syncretic middle ground that enabled them to gain desired trading objects while retaining their identity and lands. The new economic relationships ultimately brought dependency, but the Indians' creativity and syncretism delayed the trade's most odious aspects for two generations. By the time of the American Revolution the settlers' frontier had reached Tennessee, and the growing need for land meant that a middle ground was no longer possible. Between the Revolution and 1794 American demands for Indian lands periodically provoked wars between whites and Tennessee Indians, invariably eliciting frontier requests for military protection and punitive expeditions against the Indians. At first Tennesseans sought support from their home colonies of North Carolina or Virginia while they raised their own militia units. Later they expected the new U.S. government to defend them, and if federal officials seemed reluctant, they undertook unauthorized militia campaigns. When the United States sometimes refused to pay the military for such actions, frontier people were furious and believed they had been betrayed.

In these military campaigns neither Indians nor whites attempted to fight according to "civilized" modes of warfare. In the eyes of whites, after all, Indians were the cultural "other"; they were by definition uncivilized. Indian wars, wherever fought, were savage and cruel. As Richard Slotkin has suggested, many Europeans saw migration to the New World as a path toward regeneration, a means of attaining a dignity and status impossible in Europe. Yet the New World was already occupied by Indians who as "others" would always be outside the possibilities imagined by the colonists. White regeneration therefore depended on the application of violence against native peoples, a theme which Slotkin argues is essential to an understanding of the frontier experience and its continuing mythic importance. Certainly Tennessee's frontier history abounds with examples of such violence, which was hardly one-sided.

Perhaps the most dramatic and profound of the federal government's many services was that of enabling frontier Tennesseans to fulfill their most persistent desire, the acquisition of all Indian lands within the state. This was part of a process that began with the Watauga leases of the early 1770s and continued with a series of treaties involving Richard Henderson and his company, the states of North Carolina and Franklin, the Southwest Territory, and the United States. From the 1790s on almost every treaty negotiated with the Cherokees and Chickasaws included a clause recognizing yet another territorial concession by the Indians. This process culminated with the 1835 Treaty of New Echota and the emigration westward of most Cherokees three years later. Almost always, despite complaining about frontier aggression against Indians, the United States government attempted to satisfy the demands of its frontier constituents.

Accompanying this dispossession was the insistence of the U.S. government that Indians become "civilized" by conforming to white standards of belief and behavior. Missionaries representing several denominations assisted in this Christian endeavor, and, outwardly at least, they enjoyed their greatest success among the Cherokees. But this tribal transformation was far more complex than federal officials, missionaries, or most modern writers have acknowledged. If anything, as President John Quincy Adams acknowledged, the attainment of civilization provided the means by which Indians could become more effective in protecting both their land base and their identity. In the end, of course, such matters were moot. The real objective of the federal government and its frontier constituents was to acquire tribal lands. Frontier whites did not want Indians civilized. They wanted them out. And this dispossession of Native Americans to suit the needs of white Americans is the central fact of Tennessee's frontier experience.

Essay on Sources

Abbreviations

AHR   American Historical Review
AHM   American Historical Magazine
ASPIA   American State Papers, Indian Affairs
ASPPL   American State Papers, Public Lands
CSRNC   Colonial and State Records of North Carolina
CVSP   Calendar of Virginia State Papers
ETHS   East Tennessee Historical Society
ETHSP   East Tennessee Historical Society Publications
GHQ   Georgia Historical Quarterly
JAH   Journal of American History
JCS   Journal of Cherokee Studies
JSH   Journal of Southern History
MVHR   Mississippi Valley Historical Review
NCHR   North Carolina Historical Review
THM   Tennessee Historical Magazine
THQ   Tennessee Historical Quarterly
TSLA   Tennessee State Library and Archives
WHQ   Western Historical Quarterly
WMQ   William and Mary Quarterly
WTHSP   West Tennessee Historical Society Papers

General Works

Standard works include Malcolm J. Rohrbough, *The Trans-Appalachian Frontier: People, Societies, and Institutions, 1775–1850* (New York: Oxford University Press, 1978); John A. Caruso, *The Appalachian Frontier: America's First Surge Westward* (Indianapolis: Bobbs-Merrill, 1959); Reginald Horsman, *The Frontier in the Formative Years, 1783–1815* (New York: Holt, Rinehart and Winston, 1970); Thomas D. Clark and John D. W. Guice, *Frontiers in Conflict: The Old Southwest, 1795–1830* (Albuquerque: University of New Mexico Press, 1989); Thomas P. Abernethy, *From Frontier to Plantation in Tennessee: A Study of Frontier Democracy* (Chapel Hill: University of North Carolina Press, 1932); Verner W. Crane, *The Southern Frontier, 1670–1732* (1929; reprint, New York: Norton, 1981); and W. Stitt Robinson, *The Southern Colonial Frontier, 1607–1763* (Albuquerque: University of New Mexico Press, 1979).

An excellent recent account of Tennessee history is Paul H. Bergeron, Stephen V. Ash, and Jeanette Keith, *Tennesseans and Their History* (Knoxville: University of Tennessee Press, 1999). Still popular are Robert E. Corlew, *Tennessee: A Short History*, 2d ed. (Knoxville: University of Tennessee Press, 1990); and Wilma Dykeman, *Tennessee: A Bicentennial History* (New York: Norton, 1975). See also Donald Davidson, *The Tennessee: The Old River—Frontier to Secession* (New York: Rinehart & Co., 1946). Several early accounts are still important: John Haywood, *The Natural and Aboriginal History of Tennessee up to the First Settlements Therein by the White People in the Year 1768* (1823; reprint, Jackson, Tenn.: n. p., 1959); idem, *Civil and Political History of Tennessee* (1823; reprint, Nashville: Publishing House of the Methodist Episcopal Church, South, 1891); J. G. M. Ramsey, *Annals of Tennessee to the End of the Eighteenth Century* (Charleston: Walker and James, 1853; reprint, Kingsport, Tenn.: ETHS, 1967); Philip M. Hamer, ed., *Tennessee: A History, 1673–1932*, 2 vols. (New York: American Historical Society, 1933); and Stanley J. Folmsbee, Robert E. Corlew, and Enoch L. Mitchell, *History of Tennessee*, 4 vols. (New York: Lewis Historical, 1960).

Overviews on Tennessee Indians include Ronald N. Satz, *Tennessee's Indian Peoples: From White Contact to Removal, 1540–1850* (Knoxville: University of Tennessee Press, 1979); and John R. Finger, "Tennessee Indian History: Creativity and Power," *THQ* 54 (Winter 1995): 286–305. For a broader view see Charles Hudson, *The Southeastern Indians* (Knoxville: University of Tennessee Press, 1976); and R. S. Cotterill, *The Southern Indians: The Story of the Civilized Tribes before Removal* (Norman:

University of Oklahoma Press, 1954); see also James H. O'Donnell III, *Southeastern Frontiers: Europeans, Africans, and Ameri-*
can Indians, 1513–1840: A Critical Bibliography (Bloomington:
Indiana University Press, 1982). An excellent work on geology is
Edward T. Luther, *Our Restless Earth: The Geologic Regions of
Tennessee* (Knoxville: University of Tennessee Press, 1977). For
the black experience see Lester C. Lamon, *Blacks in Tennessee,
1791–1970* (Knoxville: University of Tennessee Press, 1981); and
Edward Michael McCormack, *Slavery on the Tennessee Frontier*
(Nashville: Tennessee American Revolution Bicentennial Com-
mission, 1977).

Introduction

Frederick Jackson Turner's essay "The Significance of the
Frontier in American History" is in Frederick Jackson Turner,
The Frontier in American History (New York: H. Holt & Company, 1920); and in countless anthologies. The New Western Historians (no longer quite so new) include Patricia Nelson Limerick, who summarized and popularized much of the revisionist
canon in *The Legacy of Conquest: The Unbroken Past of the
American West* (New York: Norton, 1987). Her views, as well as
those of Richard White and Donald Worcester, have appeared in
many other forums, including Patricia Nelson Limerick, Clyde A.
Milner II, and Charles E. Rankin, eds., *Trails: Toward a New
Meaning for Western History* (Lawrence: University of Kansas
Press, 1991). See also William Cronon, George Miles, and Jay Gitlin, eds., *Under an Open Sky: Rethinking America's Western Past*
(New York: Norton, 1992). For the linkage of Turner with parallel processes in different frontier zones, see idem, "Becoming
West: Toward a New Meaning for Western History," in ibid.,
pp. 3–27.

Discussions of frontier historiography include Robert D.
Mitchell, ed., *Appalachian Frontiers: Settlement, Society and De-
velopment in the Preindustrial Era* (Lexington: University of
Kentucky Press, 1991); idem, "The Southern Backcountry: A
Geographical House Divided," in David Colin Crass et al., eds.,
The Southern Colonial Backcountry (Knoxville: University of

Tennessee Press, 1996); Andrew R. L. Cayton and Fredrika J. Teute, "Introduction: On the Connection of Frontiers," in Andrew R. L. Cayton and Fredrika J. Teute, eds., *Contact Points: American Frontiers from the Mohawk Valley to the Mississippi, 1750–1830* (Chapel Hill: Omohundro Institute of Early American History and Culture, 1998), pp. 1–15; and a newsletter, *The Backcountry: A Multidisciplinary Forum on Early American Frontiers* 1 (January 1995), Williamsburg, VA.

A wealth of literature addresses the Frontier Myth and its impact, but certainly among the most important works are Henry Nash Smith, *Virgin Land: The American West as Symbol and Myth* (Cambridge: Harvard University Press, 1950); and Richard Slotkin's trilogy, *Regeneration through Violence: The Mythology of the American Frontier, 1600–1860* (Middletown, Conn.: Wesleyan University Press, 1973); *The Fatal Environment: The Myth of the Frontier in the Age of Industrialization, 1800–1890* (Middletown, Conn.: Wesleyan University Press, 1985); and *Gunfighter Nation: The Myth of the Frontier in Twentieth-Century America* (New York: Atheneum, 1992).

1. Land, People, and Early Frontiers

Good overviews of human interaction with the Southeastern landscape are Timothy Silver's *A New Face on the Countryside: Indians, Colonists, and Slaves in the South Atlantic Forests, 1500–1800* (Cambridge: Cambridge University Press, 1990); Donald Edward Davis, *Where There Are Mountains: An Environmental History of the Southern Appalachians* (Athens: University of Georgia Press, 2000); and Margaret Lynn Brown, *The Wild East: A Biography of the Great Smoky Mountains* (Gainesville: University Press of Florida, 2000). For the impressions of a contemporary scientist, see William Bartram, *The Travels of William Bartram*, ed. Francis Harper (New Haven: Yale University Press, 1958).

In recent years there has been a lively debate over humankind's first appearance in the New World and the evolution of prehistoric cultures. See, for example, Joseph H. Greenberg, Christy G. Turner II, and Stephen L. Zegura, "The Settlement of the Americas: A Comparison of Linguistic, Dental, and Genetic Evidence," *Current Anthropology* 27 (December 1986): 477–497; Christy G. Turner II, "Teeth and Prehistory in Asia," *Scientific American* 260 (February 1989): 88–96; Luigi Luca Cavalli-Sforza, "Genes, Peoples, and Languages," *Scientific American* 265 (November 1991): 104–110; and Joseph H. Greenberg and Merritt Ruhlen, "Linguistic Origins of Native Americans," *Scientific American* 267 (November 1992): 94–99. A more recent revisionist analysis is Michael H. Crawford, *The Origins of Native Americans: Evidence from Anthropological Genetics* (Cambridge: Cambridge University Press, 1998). Both scholarly and entertaining is Brian M. Fagan, *The Great Journey: The Peopling of Ancient America* (London: Thames Hudson, 1987).

Southeastern archaeology is discussed in Hudson, *The Southeastern Indians*, and specialized works on Tennessee archaeology include Jefferson Chapman, *Tellico Archaeology: 12,000 Years of Native American History*, rev. ed. (Knoxville: University of Tennessee Press, 1994); Gerald F. Schroedl, ed., *Overhill Cherokee Archaeology at Chota-Tanasee* (Knoxville: University of Tennessee Department of Anthropology, 1986); idem, "Cherokee Ethnohistory and Archaeology from 1540 to 1838," in Bonnie G. McEwan, ed., *Indians of the Greater Southeast: Historical Archaeology and Ethnohistory* (Gainesville: University Press of Florida, 2000), pp. 204–241; Thomas M. N. Lewis and Madeline Kneberg Lewis, *Eva: An Archaic Site* (Knoxville: University of Tennessee Press, 1961); idem, *Tribes That Slumber: Indians of the Tennessee Region* (Knoxville: University of Tennessee Press, 1958); idem, *Hiwassee Island: An Archaeological Account of Four Tennessee Indian Peoples* (Knoxville: University of Tennessee Press, 1946; reprint, 1993); Charles H. Faulkner, *The Old Stone Fort: Exploring an Archaeological Mystery* (Knoxville: University of Tennessee Press, 1968); and Robert C. Maintfort Jr., *Pinson Mounds: A Middle Woodland Ceremonial Center* (Nashville: Tennessee Department of Conservation, Division of Archaeology, 1986). See also Vincas P. Steponaitis, "Prehistoric Archaeology in the Southeastern United States, 1970–1985," *Annual Review of Anthropology* 15 (1986): 363–404.

Related works include Jay K. Johnson, "Prehistoric Exchange

in the Southeast," in Timothy G. Baugh and Jonathon E. Ericson, eds., *Prehistoric Exchange Systems in North America* (New York: Plenum Press, 1994), pp. 99–125; Charles H. Nash and Rodney Gates Jr., "Chucalissa Indian Town," *THQ* 21 (June 1962): 103–121; Ronald K. Robinson, "Social Status, Stature, and Pathology at Chucalissa (40SY1), Shelby County, Tennessee" (master's thesis, University of Tennessee, 1976); Emmanuel Breitburg and John B. Broster, "A Hunt for Big Game," *The Tennessee Conservationist* 61 (July/August 1995): 18–26; Paul A. Delcourt, Hazel Delcourt, Cecil R. Ison, William E. Sharp, and Kristen J. Gremillion, "Prehistoric Human Use of Fire, the Eastern Agricultural Complex, and Appalachian Oak-Chestnut Forests: Paleoecology of Cliff Palace Pond, Kentucky," *American Antiquity* 63 (April 1998): 263–278; and Patricia Cridlebaugh, "American Indian and Euro-American Impact upon Holocene Vegetation in the Lower Little Tennessee River Valley, East Tennessee" (Ph.D. diss., University of Tennessee, 1984). Many significant articles also appear in the *Tennessee Archaeologist* and *Southeastern Archaeology*.

The Mississippian Era is a topic of enormous controversy. Among the important works used in this chapter are Timothy R. Pauketat and Thomas E. Emerson, eds., *Cahokia: Domination and Ideology in the Mississippian World* (Lincoln: University of Nebraska Press, 1997); John F. Scarry, ed., *Political Structure and Change in the Prehistoric Southeastern United States* (Gainesville: University Press of Florida, 1996); Chester B. De Pratter, *Late Prehistoric and Early Historic Chiefdoms in the Southeastern United States* (New York: Garland, 1991); Bruce D. Smith, "Mississippian Expansion: Tracing the Historical Development of an Explanatory Model," *Southeastern Archaeology* 3 (Summer 1984): 13–32; Gerald F. Schroedl, C. Clifford Boyd Jr. and R. P. Stephen Davis Jr., "Explaining Mississippian Origins in East Tennessee," in Bruce D. Smith, ed., *The Mississippian Emergence: The Evolution of Ranked Agricultural Societies in Eastern North America* (Washington, D.C.: Smithsonian Institution Press, 1990), pp. 175–196; and Patricia Galloway, ed., *The Southeastern Ceremonial Complex: Artifacts and Analysis* (Lincoln: University of Nebraska Press, 1989).

The last decade has witnessed a burgeoning scholarship on the
de Soto and Pardo expeditions, including Lawrence A. Clayton,
Vernon James Knight Jr., and Edward C. Moore, eds., *The De Soto Chronicles: The Expeditions of Hernando De Soto to North America in 1539–1543* (Tuscaloosa: University of Alabama Press, 1993); Paul E. Hoffman, "Hernando De Soto: A Brief Biography," ibid., pp. 421–459; Charles Hudson, *Knights of Spain, Warriors of the Sun: Hernando de Soto and the South's Ancient Chiefdoms* (Athens: University of Georgia Press, 1997); idem, *The Juan Pardo Expeditions: Exploration of the Carolinas and Tennessee, 1566–1568* (Washington, D.C.: Smithsonian Institution Press, 1990); idem, "The Hernando de Soto Expedition, 1539–1543," in Charles Hudson and Carmen Chaves Tesser, eds., *The Forgotten Centuries: Indians and Europeans in the American South, 1521–1704* (Athens: University of Georgia Press, 1994); Patricia Galloway, ed., *The Hernando de Soto Expedition: History, Historiography, and "Discovery" in the Southeast* (Lincoln: University of Nebraska Press, 1997); and Robin A. Beck Jr., "From Joara to Chiaha: Spanish Exploration of the Appalachian Summit Area, 1540–1568," *Southeastern Archaeology* 16 (Winter 1997): 162–169. An earlier, "official" description of de Soto's route is in *Final Report of the United States de Soto Expedition Commission*, 76th Cong., 1st sess., House Document 71 (Washington, D.C.: Government Printing Office, 1939; reprint, Washington, D.C.: Smithsonian Institution Press, 1985).

Arguments over the impact of Spanish expeditions on American Indians are fierce. A seminal work is Alfred W. Crosby Jr., *The Columbian Exchange: Biological and Cultural Consequences of 1492* (Westport, Conn.: Greenwood, 1972). Arguing for early pandemics are Henry F. Dobyns, *Their Number Became Thinned: Native American Population Dynamics in Eastern North America* (Knoxville: University of Tennessee Press, 1983); and Ann F. Ramenofsky, *Vectors of Death: The Archaeology of European Contact* (Albuquerque: University of New Mexico Press, 1987). Marvin T. Smith is more cautious about pre–de Soto disease, but stresses the radical consequences of later epidemics in *Archaeology of Aboriginal Culture Change in the Interior Southeast: Population during the Early Historic Period* (Gainesville: University

Press of Florida, 1987); and idem, "Aboriginal Depopulation in the Postcontact Southeast," in Hudson and Tesser, *The Forgotten Centuries*, pp. 257–275; see also Gerald T. Milanich, "Sixteenth Century Native Societies and Spanish Empire in the Southeast United States," *Archaeology of Eastern North America* 20 (Fall 1992): 1–18. Disputing the immediate impact of European diseases are Chester B. DePratter, "The Chiefdom of Cofitachequi," in Hudson and Tesser, *The Forgotten Centuries*, pp. 197–226; and John H. Hahn, "The Apalachee of the Historic Era," ibid., pp. 327–354. A different kind of Spanish-Portuguese impact is the subject of N. Brent Kennedy, *The Melungeons: The Resurrection of a Proud People* (Macon: Mercer University Press, 1995).

The Overhill Cherokees' role and geographic location during the earliest period of white contact is discussed in papers by Gerald F. Schroedl, Charles Hudson, and Roy S. Dickens Jr., in David G. Moore, comp., *The Conference on Cherokee Prehistory* (Swannoa, N.C.: Warren Wilson College, 1986); and Gerald F. Schroedl, "Cherokee Ethnohistory and Archaeology from 1540 to 1838." See also Peter H. Wood, "The Changing Population of the Colonial South: An Overview by Race and Region, 1685–1790," in Peter H. Wood, Gregory A. Waselkov, and M. Thomas Hatley, eds., *Powhatan's Mantle: Indians in the Colonial Southeast* (Lincoln: University of Nebraska Press, 1989), pp. 35–103; Russell Thornton, *American Indian Holocaust and Survival: A Population History since 1492* (Norman: University of Oklahoma Press, 1987); and idem, *The Cherokees: A Population History* (Lincoln: University of Nebraska Press, 1990). Creek and Choctaw changes are discussed in Vernon James Knight Jr., "The Formation of the Creeks," in Hudson and Tesser, *The Forgotten Centuries*, pp. 373–392; Patricia Galloway, "Confederacy as a Solution to Chiefdom Dissolution: Historical Evidence in the Choctaw Case," ibid., pp. 393–420; and idem, *Choctaw Genesis, 1500–1700* (Lincoln: University of Nebraska Press, 1995).

Samuel Cole Williams, *Early Travels in the Tennessee Country, 1540–1800* (Johnson City, Tenn.: Watauga Press, 1928), includes travel accounts of many early visitors to Tennessee, among them Captain Abraham Woods's version of the Needham and Arthur trip to Chota. Alan Vance Briceland, *Westward from Virginia: The Explorations of the Virginia-Carolina Frontier, 1650–1710* (Charlottesville: University of Virginia Press, 1987), offers a revisionist version of the Needham-Arthur route which is geographically plausible but undermined by archaeological and ethnographic evidence. Important aspects of early routes and Indian-white contacts are discussed in William E. Myer, "Indian Trails of the Southeast," in the *Forty-Second Annual Report of the Bureau of American Ethnology*, 1924/25 (Washington, D.C.: Government Printing Office, 1928); Helen Hornbeck Tanner, "The Land and Water Communication System of the Southeastern Indians," in Wood, Waselkov, and Hatley, *Powhatan's Mantle*, pp. 6–20; and Verner W. Crane, "The Tennessee River as the Road to Carolina: The Beginnings of Exploration and Trade," *MVHR* 3 (June 1916): 3–18.

For the Chickasaws and early French contacts, see John D. Stubbs Jr., "The Chickasaw Contact with the La Salle Expedition in 1682," in Patricia Galloway, ed., *La Salle and His Legacy: Frenchmen and Indians in the Lower Mississippi Valley* (Jackson: University of Mississippi Press, 1982), pp. 41–48; John Gilmary Shea, *Discovery and Exploration of the Mississippi Valley, with the Original Narratives of Marquette . . .* (Clinton Hall, N.Y.: Redfield, 1852); Marquette and La Salle materials in Reuben Gold Thwaites, ed., *The Jesuit Relations and Allied Documents*, 73 vols. (Cleveland: Burrows, 1896–1901); William A. Klutts, "Fort Prudhomme: Its Location," *WTHSP* 4 (1950): 28–40; and Daniel H. Usner Jr., *Indians, Settlers, and Slaves in a Frontier Exchange Economy: The Lower Mississippi Valley Before 1783* (Chapel Hill: Institute of Early American History and Culture, 1992).

2. Trade, Acculturation, and Empire

Primary sources include Samuel Cole Williams, ed., *James Adair's History of the American Indians* (Johnson City, Tenn.: Watauga Press, 1930); idem, *Lieut. Henry Timberlake's Memoirs, 1756–1765* (Marietta, Ga.: Continental, 1948); trader accounts in idem, *Dawn of Tennessee Valley and Tennessee History* (Johnson City, Tenn.: Watauga Press, 1937); William M. McDowell Jr., ed.,

Colonial Records of South Carolina: Records Relating to Indian Affairs, 1750–1754 (Columbia: South Carolina Archives, 1958); and idem, *Documents Relating to Indian Affairs, 1754–1765* (Columbia: University of South Carolina Press, 1970); and CSRNC.

Overviews on the Cherokees include Marion L. Starkey, *The Cherokee Nation* (New York: Russell & Russell, 1946); Henry Thompson Malone, *Cherokees of the Old South: A People in Transition* (Athens: University of Georgia Press, 1956); and Grace Steele Woodward, *The Cherokees* (Norman: University of Oklahoma Press, 1963). For tribal law see John Philip Reid, *A Law of Blood: The Primitive Law of the Cherokee Nation* (New York: New York University Press, 1970); and Rennard Strickland, *Fire and the Spirits: Cherokee Law from Clan to Court* (Norman: University of Oklahoma Press, 1975).

Among other excellent accounts of the Cherokees during this period are Gary C. Goodwin, *Cherokees in Transition: A Study of Changing Culture and Environment Prior to 1775* (Chicago: University of Chicago Department of Geography, Research Paper 181, 1977); Tom Hatley, *The Dividing Paths: Cherokees and South Carolinians through the Era of Revolution* (New York: Oxford University Press, 1993); David H. Corkran, *The Carolina Indian Frontier* (Columbia: University of South Carolina Press, 1970); idem, *The Cherokee Frontier: Conflict and Survival, 1740–1762* (Norman: University of Oklahoma Press, 1962); Louis De Vorsey Jr., *The Virginia-Cherokee Boundary of 1771: An Example of the Importance of Maps in the Interpretation of History* (Knoxville: ETHS, 1961); idem, *The Indian Boundary in the Southern Colonies, 1763–1775* (Chapel Hill: University of North Carolina Press, 1966); and John P. Brown, *Old Frontiers: The Story of the Cherokee Indians from Earliest Times to the Date of Their Removal to the West, 1838* (Kingsport: Southern Publishers, 1938).

The best work on Cherokee women is Theda Perdue's *Cherokee Women: Gender and Culture Change, 1700–1835* (Lincoln: University of Nebraska Press, 1998). See also Norma Tucker, "Nancy Ward, Ghighau of the Cherokees," *GHQ* 53 (June 1969): 192–200; Ben Harris McClary, "Nancy Ward: The Last Beloved Woman of the Cherokees," *THQ* 21 (December 1962): 352–64; Sara Gwenyth Parker, "The Transformation of Cherokee Appalachia" (Ph.D. diss., University of California at Berkeley, 1991); Clara Sue Kidwell, "Indian Women as Cultural Mediators," *Ethnohistory* 39 (Spring 1992): 97–107; and Hatley, *Dividing Paths.* For Indians' relations with blacks, see Theda Perdue, *Slavery and the Evolution of Cherokee Society, 1540–1866* (Knoxville: University of Tennessee Press, 1979); Rudi Halliburton Jr., *Red over Black: Black Slavery among the Cherokee Indians* (Westport, Conn.: Greenwood, 1977); and Gary B. Nash, *Red, White, and Black: The Peoples of Early North America*, 3rd ed. (Englewood Cliffs, N.J.: Prentice-Hall, 1992).

Discussions of French relations with Southern Indians include Daniel H. Usner Jr., *Indians, Settlers, and Slaves in a Frontier Exchange Economy: The Lower Mississippi Valley before 1783* (Chapel Hill: Institute of Early American History and Culture, 1992); Richard White, *Roots of Dependency: Subsistence, Environment, and Social Change among the Choctaws, Pawnees, and Navajos* (Lincoln: University of Nebraska Press, 1983); Arrell M. Gibson, *The Chickasaws* (Norman: University of Oklahoma Press, 1971); essays in Patricia Galloway, ed., *La Salle and His Legacy: Frenchmen and Indians in the Lower Mississippi Valley* (Jackson: University of Mississippi Press, 1982); and, broader in scope, Carolyn Keller Reeves, ed., *The Choctaw before Removal* (Jackson: University Press of Mississippi, 1985).

Analyses of other Southeastern Indians during the period include J. Leitch Wright Jr., *The Only Land They Knew: The Tragic Story of the American Indians in the Old South* (New York: The Free Press, 1981); James H. Merrell, *The Indians' New World: Catawbas and Their Neighbors from European Contact through the Era of Removal* (Chapel Hill: University of North Carolina Press, 1989); Kathryn E. Holland Braund, *Deerskins and Duffels: Creek Indian Trade with Anglo-America, 1685–1815* (Lincoln: University of Nebraska Press, 1993); R. S. Cotterill, *The Southern Indians: The Story of the Civilized Tribes before Removal* (Norman: University of Oklahoma Press, 1954); Daniel H. Usner Jr., *American Indians in the Lower Mississippi Valley: Social and Economic Histories* (Lincoln: University of Nebraska Press, 1998); James Taylor Carson, *Searching for the Bright Path: The Mississippi Choctaws from Prehistory to Removal* (Lincoln: University of Nebraska Press, 1999); and Claudio Saunt, *A New Order of Things: Property, Power, and the Transformation of the Creek Indians, 1733–1816* (Cambridge: Cambridge University Press, 1999).

The Indian trade is discussed in almost all of the general accounts of Indian-white contact, but more specific are John Philip Reid, *A Better Kind of Hatchet: Law, Trade, and Diplomacy in the Cherokee Nation during the Early Years of European Contact* (University Park: Pennsylvania State University Press, 1976); Joel W. Martin, "Southeastern Indians and the English Trade in Skins and Slaves," in Charles Hudson and Carmen Chaves Tesser, eds., *The Forgotten Centuries: Indians and Europeans in the American South, 1521–1704* (Athens: University of Georgia Press, 1994), pp. 304–324; Mary Rothrock, "Carolina Traders among the Overhill Cherokee, 1690–1760," *ETHSP* 1 (1929): 3–18; W. Neil Franklin, "Virginia and the Cherokee Indian Trade, 1673–1752," *ETHSP* 4 (1932): 3–21; idem, "Virginia and the Cherokee Indian Trade, 1753–1775," *ETHSP* 5 (1933): 22–38; accounts of traders in Williams, *Dawn of Tennessee Valley*; and Michael Morris, "The High Price of Trade: Anglo-American Trade Mistakes and the Fort Loudoun Disaster," *JCS* 17 (1996): 3–15. Alexander Cuming's career is the subject of William O. Steele, *The Cherokee Crown of Tannasy* (Winston-Salem: John F. Blair, 1977). For Christian Priber see Williams, *Dawn of Tennessee Valley*; Rennard Strickland "Christian Gottlieb Priber: Utopian Precursor of the Cherokee Government," *Chronicles of Oklahoma*, 48 (Autumn 1970): 264–279; and Knox Mellon Jr., "Christian Priber's 'Kingdom of Paradise,'" *GHQ* 57 (Fall 1973): 319–331.

The classic model of dependency theory is Immanuel Wallerstein, *The Modern World System: Capitalist Agriculture and the Origin of the European World Economy in the Sixteenth Century* (New York: Academic, 1974); *The Modern World System II: Mercantilism and the Consolidation of the European World Economy, 1600–1750* (New York: Academic, 1980); and *The Modern World System III: The Second Era of Great Expansion of the Capitalist World Economy, 1730s–1840s* (New York: Academic, 1989). This theory as applied to Indians is discussed in Martin,

"Southeastern Indians"; Bruce G. Trigger, "Early Native North American Responses to European Contact: Romantic versus Rationalistic Interpretations," *JAH* 77 (March 1991): 1195–1215; Wilma Dunaway, *The First American Frontier: Transition to Capitalism in Southern Appalachia, 1700–1860* (Chapel Hill: University of North Carolina Press, 1996); and White, *The Roots of Dependency*.

The original formulation of the middle ground is Richard White, *The Middle Ground: Indians, Empires, and Republics in the Great Lakes Region, 1650–1815* (Cambridge: Cambridge University Press, 1991). I have freely adapted White's ideas to my study of the Southeastern Indians.

Among the many works discussing British Indian policy in the Southeast are John Richard Alden, *John Stuart and the Southern Colonial Frontier: A Study of Indian Relations, War, Trade, and the Land Problems in the Southwest Wilderness, 1754–1775* (Ann Arbor: University of Michigan Press, 1944); Jack M. Sosin, *The Revolutionary Frontier, 1763–1783* (New York: Holt, Rinehart, and Winston, 1967); Corkran, *The Cherokee Frontier*; J. Russell Snapp, *John Stuart and the Struggle for Empire on the Southern Frontier* (Baton Rouge: Louisiana State University Press, 1996); Dawson A. Phelps, "The Chickasaws, the English, and the French, 1699–1744," *THQ* 16 (June 1957): 117–133; Philip M. Hamer, "Anglo-French Rivalry in the Cherokee Country, 1754–1757," *NCHR* 2 (July 1925): 303–322; Morris, "High Price of Trade"; and James C. Kelly, "Fort Loudoun: British Stronghold in the Tennessee Country," *ETHSP* 50 (1978): 72–91. See also Gregory Evans Dowd, *A Spirited Resistance: The North American Indian Struggle for Unity, 1745–1815* (Baltimore: Johns Hopkins University Press, 1992); and idem, "'Insidious Friends': Gift-Giving and the Cherokee-British Alliance in the Seven Years' War," in Andrew R. L. Cayton and Fredrika J. Teute, eds., *Contact Points: American Frontiers from the Mohawk Valley to the Mississippi, 1750–1830* (Chapel Hill: Omohundro Institute of Early American History and Culture, 1998), pp. 114–150.

For some leading figures of the period see James C. Kelly, "Notable Persons in Cherokee History: Attakullakulla," *JCS* 3 (Winter 1979): 2–34; idem, "Oconostota," *JCS* 3 (Fall 1979): 18–21; E. Raymond Evans, "Notable Persons in Cherokee History: Ostenaco," *JCS* 1 (Summer 1976): 41–54; idem, "Notable Persons in Cherokee History: Dragging Canoe," *JCS* 2 (Winter 1977): 176–189; William L. Anderson, "Oconostota," in Richard L. Blanco, ed., *The American Revolution, 1775–1783: An Encyclopedia*, 2 vols. (New York: Garland, 1993), 2:1261–1263; idem, "The Raven of Echota," in Blanco, *The American Revolution, 1775–1783*, 2:1374–75; Louis De Vorsey Jr., *De Brahm's Report of the General Survey in the Southern District of North America* (Columbia: University of South Carolina Press, 1971); and Richard G. Stone, Jr., "Captain Paul Demeré at Fort Loudoun, 1757–60," *ETHSP* 41 (1969): 17–32.

The now-standard account of Daniel Boone is John Mack Faragher's, *Daniel Boone: The Life and Legend of an American Pioneer* (New York: Henry Holt, 1992); but see also Stephen Anthony Aron, *How the West Was Lost: The Transformation of Kentucky from Daniel Boone to Henry Clay* (Baltimore: Johns Hopkins Press, 1996); Joe Nickell and John F. Fischer, "Daniel Boone Fakelore," *Filson Club Historical Quarterly* 62 (October 1988): 442–466; and especially Richard Slotkin, *Regeneration through Violence: The Mythology of the American Frontier, 1600–1860* (Middletown, Conn.: Wesleyan University Press, 1973).

For the Wataugans, see Moses Fisk, "A Summary Notice of the First Settlements Made by White People within the Limits Which Bound the State of Tennessee," *Massachusetts Historical Collections* 7 (1816), reprinted in *AHM* 2 (January 1897): 17–26; A. V. Goodpasture, "The Watauga Association," *AHM* 3 (April 1898): 103–120; Williams, *Dawn of Tennessee Valley*; Max Dixon, *The Wataugans* (Nashville: Tennessee American Revolution Bicentennial Commission, 1976); Carl Driver, *John Sevier, Pioneer of the Old Southwest* (Chapel Hill: University of North Carolina Press, 1932); Cora Bales Sevier and Nancy S. Madden, *Sevier Family History with the Collected Letters of Gen. John Sevier, First Governor of Tennessee* (1961; rev. ed., Beltsville, Md.: Columbia Planograph, 1982); James Morris Ransom, "The Life and Career of General James Robertson" (master's thesis, University of Tennessee, 1966); Paul M. Fink, "Russell Bean, Tennessee's

First Native Son," *ETHSP* 37 (1965): 31–48; and idem, "Jacob
Brown of Nolichucky," *THQ* 21 (September 1962): 235–250.

Other accounts include G. Melvin Herndon, *James Tatham,
1752–1819: American Versatile* (Johnson City, Tenn.: East Tennes-
see State University, 1973); Samuel Cole Williams, *William Ta-
tum, Wataugan* (Johnson City, Tenn.: Watauga Press, 1947); John
Allison, *Dropped Stitches in Tennessee History* (Nashville: Mar-
shall and Bruce, 1897); Pat Alderman, *The Overmountain Men:
Early Tennessee History, 1760–1795* (Johnson City, Tenn.: The
Overmountain Press, 1970); and Frank Merritt, *Early History of
Carter County, 1760–1861* (Knoxville: ETHS, 1950). On Richard
Henderson see Aron, *How the West Was Lost;* Archibald Hender-
son, *The Conquest of the Old Southwest: The Romantic Story of
the Early Pioneers into Virginia, the Carolinas, Tennessee, and
Kentucky, 1740–1790* (New York: Century, 1920); and William
Stewart Lester, *The Transylvania Colony* (Spencer, Ind.: S. R.
Guard & Co., 1935).

3. The Revolutionary Frontier
4. Expansion amid Revolution

Works related to society and cabin building are cited for chapter seven. Important documents on the Revolution in the backcountry are in CSRNC; CVSP; the Cherokee Collection, TSLA;
K. G. Davies, ed., *Documents of the American Revolution, 1770–
1783,* Colonial Office Series, 21 vols. (Shannon: Irish University
Press, 1972–82); and Lyman Copeland Draper Manuscripts (Tennessee and Kings Mountain), State Historical Society of Wiscon-
sin, available on microfilm. Important secondary accounts include Jerry Clyde Cashion, "North Carolina and the Cherokee:
The Quest for Land on the Eve of the American Revolution"
(Ph.D. diss., University of North Carolina, Chapel Hill, 1979);
James H. O'Donnell III, *Southern Indians in the American Revo-
lution* (Knoxville: University of Tennessee Press, 1973); idem,
The Cherokees of North Carolina in the American Revolution
(Raleigh, N.C.: Department of Cultural Resources, Division of
Archives and History, 1976); also Gregory Evans Dowd, *A Spir-
ited Resistance: The North American Indian Struggle for Unity,*

1745–1815 (Baltimore: Johns Hopkins University Press, 1992); John P. Brown, *Old Frontiers: The Story of the Cherokee Indians from Earliest Times to the Date of Their Removal to the West, 1838* (Kingsport: Southern Publishers, 1938); James Paul Pate, "The Chickamauga: A Forgotten Segment of Indian Resistance on the Southern Frontier" (Ph.D. diss., Mississippi State University, 1969); and Colin G. Calloway, *The American Revolution in Indian Country: Crisis and Diversity in Native American Communities* (Cambridge: Cambridge University Press, 1995).

On backcountry divisions and policy during the Revolution, see Ronald Hoffman, Thad W. Tate, and Peter J. Albert, eds., *An Uncivil War: The Southern Backcountry during the American Revolution* (Charlottesville: University of Virginia Press, 1985); John Richard Alden, *The South in the Revolution, 1763–1789* (Baton Rouge: Louisiana State University Press, 1957); idem, *John Stuart and the Southern Colonial Frontier: A Study of Indian Relations, War, Trade, and the Land Problems in the Southwest Wilderness, 1754–1775* (Ann Arbor: University of Michigan Press, 1944); Jack M. Sosin, *The Revolutionary Frontier, 1763–1783* (New York: Holt-Rinehart and Winston, 1967); John Haywood, *Civil and Political History of Tennessee* (1823; reprint, Nashville: Publishing House of the Methodist Episcopal Church, South, 1891); J. G. M. Ramsey, *Annals of Tennessee to the End of the Eighteenth Century* (1853; reprint, Kingsport: ETHS, 1967); Thomas P. Abernethy, *From Frontier to Plantation in Tennessee: A Study of Frontier Democracy* (Chapel Hill: University of North Carolina Press, 1932); idem, *Western Lands and the American Revolution* (1937; reprint, New York: Russell & Russell, 1959); Max Dixon, *The Wataugans* (Nashville: Tennessee American Revolution Bicentennial Commission, 1976); Samuel Cole Williams, *Tennessee during the Revolutionary War* (1944; reprint, Knoxville: University of Tennessee Press, 1974); and Rachel N. Klein, *Unification of a Slave State: The Rise of the Planter Class in the South Carolina Backcountry, 1760–1808* (Chapel Hill: Institute of Early American History and Culture, 1990).

Articles related to events during this time include Samuel Cole Williams, "The First Territorial Division Named for Washington," *THM*, ser. 2, 2 (1931–32): 153–164; Betty Anderson Smith,

"Distribution of Eighteenth-Century Cherokee Settlements," in
Duane H. King, ed., *The Cherokee Indian Nation: A Troubled
History* (Knoxville: University of Tennessee Press, 1979), pp. 46–
60; Helen Hornbeck Tanner, "Cherokees in the Ohio Country,"
JCS 3 (Spring 1978): 94–102; Philip M. Hamer, "John Stu-
art's Indian Policy during the Early Months of the Revolution,"
MVHR 17 (December 1930): 351–366; idem, "Correspondence of
Henry Stuart and Alexander Cameron with the Wataugans,"
ibid., 451–459; idem, "The Wataugans and the Cherokee Indi-
ans in 1776," *ETHSP* 3 (1931): 108–126; Randolph C. Downes,
"Cherokee-American Relations in the Upper Tennessee Valley,
1776–1791," *ETHSP* 8 (1936): 35–83; Thomas Lawrence Connelly,
"Indian Warfare on the Tennessee Frontier, 1776–1794: Strategy
and Tactics," *ETHSP* 36 (1964): 3–22; Robert L. Ganyard,
"Threat from the West: North Carolina and the Cherokee,"
NCHR 45 (Winter 1968): 47–66; Archibald Henderson, "The
Treaty of Long Island of Holston, 1777," *NCHR* 8 (January 1931):
55–116; Samuel Cole Williams, "Henderson and Company's Pur-
chase within the Limits of Tennessee," *THM* 5 (April 1919): 5–27;
Ronald Hoffman, "The 'Disaffected' in the Revolutionary South,"
in Alfred F. Young, ed., *The American Revolution: Explorations
in the History of American Radicalism* (DeKalb: Northern Illinois
University Press, 1976), pp. 273–316; Michael Kay, "The North
Carolina Regulation, 1766–1776: A Class Conflict," ibid, pp. 71–
123; Albert H. Tillson Jr., "The Localist Roots of Backcountry
Loyalism: An Examination of Popular Culture in Virginia's New
River Valley," *JSH* 54 (August 1988): 387–404; and Paul D. Es-
cott and Jeffrey J. Crow, "The Social Order and Violent Disorder:
An Analysis of North Carolina in the Revolution and the Civil
War," *JSH* 52 (August 1986): 373–402.

For the Chickasaws and West Tennessee see Arrell M. Gibson,
The Chickasaws (Norman: University of Oklahoma Press, 1971);
Lawrence Kinnaird, trans. and ed., *Spain in the Mississippi Val-
ley, 1764–1794: Translations of Materials from the Spanish Ar-
chives in the Bancroft Library, University of California, Berkeley,*
in *Annual Report of the American Historical Society, 1945,* 4 vols.
(Washington, D.C.: American Historical Society, 1946–49); James
Roper, "The Revolutionary War on the Fourth Chickasaw Bluff,"

WTHSP 29 (1975): 5–24; John W. Caughey, "Willing's Expedition down the Mississippi, 1778," *Louisiana Historical Quarterly* 15 (January 1932): 5–36; Kathryn T. Abbey, "Peter Chester's Defense of the Mississippi after the Willing Raid," *MVHR* 22 (June 1935): 17–32; Kathryn M. Fraser, "Fort Jefferson: George Rogers Clark's Fort at the Mouth of the Ohio, 1780–1781," *Register of the Kentucky Historical Society* 81 (Winter 1983): 1–24; Gilbert C. Din, "Loyalist Resistance after Pensacola: The Case of James Colbert," in William S. Coker and Robert Rea, eds., *Anglo-Spanish Confrontation on the Gulf Coast during the American Revolution* (Pensacola, Fla.: Gulf Coast History and Humanities Conference, 1982), pp. 158–176; and Robert S. Cotterill, "The Virginia-Chickasaw Treaty of 1783," *JSH* 8 (November 1942): 483–496.

General accounts of the Cumberland frontier include Harriet Simpson Arnow's classic books *Seedtime on the Cumberland* (New York: Macmillan, 1960); and *Flowering of the Cumberland* (New York: Macmillan, 1963). See also three books by Walter T. Durham, *The Great Leap Westward* (Gallatin, Tenn.: Sumner County Library Board, 1969); *Daniel Smith: Frontier Statesman* (Gallatin, Tenn.: Sumner County Library Board, 1976); and *James Winchester: Tennessee Pioneer* (Gallatin, Tenn.: Sumner County Library Board, 1979). Still quite useful is Albigence W. Putnam, *History of Middle Tennessee, or Life and Times of Gen. James Robertson* (1859; reprint, Knoxville: University of Tennessee Press, 1971). See also W. Woodford Clayton, *History of Davidson County, Tennessee, with Illustrations and Biographical Sketches of Its Prominent Men and Pioneers* (1880; reprint, Nashville: Charles Elder, 1971); Jesse C. Burt, *Nashville: Its Life and Times* (Kingsport, Tenn.: Kingsport Press, 1959); John Carr, *Early Times in Middle Tennessee* (Nashville: Parthenon Press, 1958); Haywood, *Civil and Political History of Tennessee;* and Ramsey, *Annals of Tennessee.* Pertinent articles include Archibald Henderson, "Richard Henderson: The Authorship of the Cumberland Compact and the Founding of Nashville," *THM* 2 (September 1916): 155–174; Wirt Armistead Cate, "Timothy Demonbreun," *THQ* 16 (September 1957): 214–227; Duane H.

King, "Long Island of the Holston: Sacred Cherokee Ground,"
JCS 1 (Fall 1976): 113–127; Louis De Vorsey Jr., "The Virginia-
Tennessee Boundary of 1771," *ETHSP* 33 (1961): 17–31; J. W. L.
Matlock, ed., "The Battle of the Bluffs: From the Journal of John
Cotten," *THQ* 18 (September 1959): 252–265; Katherine R.
Barnes, "James Robertson's Journey to Nashville: Tracing the
Route of Fall 1779," *THQ* 35 (Summer 1976): 145–161; and Rich-
ard Douglas Spence, "John Donelson and the Opening of the Old
Southwest," *THQ* 50 (Fall 1991): 157–172. Donelson's famous ac-
count of life on the *Adventure* is at the TSLA and appears in
Robert T. Quarles and R. H. White, eds., *Three Pioneer Docu-
ments: Donelson's Journal, Cumberland Compact, Minutes of the
Cumberland Court* (Nashville: Tennessee State Historical Commission, 1964).

The backcountry's most famous contribution to American
success in the Revolution is discussed in Wilma Dykeman, *With
Fire and Sword: The Battle of Kings Mountain* (Washington,
D.C.: National Park Service, 1978); Hank Messick, *King's Mountain: The Epic of the Blue Ridge "Mountain" Men in the American Revolution* (New York: Little, Brown, 1976); various personal
accounts in the Draper Collections (Tennessee and King's Mountain); and Lyman C. Draper, *King's Mountain and Its Heroes:
History of the Battle of King's Mountain, October 7th, 1780, and
the Events Which Led to It* (Cincinnati: P. G. Thompson, 1881).

5. Speculation, Turmoil, and Intrigue

Basic primary sources include ASPPL, ASPIA, CVSP, TSLA,
CSRNC, Cherokee Collection of the TSLA, Draper Papers, and
Lawrence Kinnaird, trans. and ed., *Spain in the Mississippi Val-
ley, 1764–1794: Translations of Materials from the Spanish Ar-
chives in the Bancroft Library, University of California, Berkeley,*
in *Annual Report of the American Historical Society, 1945*, 4
vols. (Washington, D.C.: American Historical Society, 1946–49).
For general accounts see Thomas P. Abernethy, *From Frontier to
Plantation in Tennessee: A Study of Frontier Democracy* (Chapel
Hill: University of North Carolina Press, 1932); John Haywood,

Civil and Political History of the State of Tennessee (1823; reprint, Nashville: Publishing House of the Methodist Episcopal Church, South, 1891); J. G. M. Ramsey, *Annals of Tennessee to the End of the Eighteenth Century* (1853; reprint, Kingsport: ETHS, 1967); Philip M. Hamer, ed., *Tennessee: A History, 1673–1932*, 2 vols. (New York: American Historical Society, 1933); Albigence W. Putnam, *History of Middle Tennessee, or Life and Times of Gen. James Robertson* (1859; reprint, Knoxville: University of Tennessee Press, 1971); Reginald Horsman, *The Frontier in the Formative Years, 1783–1815* (New York: Holt, Rinehart, and Winston, 1970); and Francis S. Philbrick, *The Rise of the West, 1754–1830* (New York: Harper & Row, 1965). Disagreeing with Abernethy in assessing democracy on the Tennessee frontier is John D. Barnhart, *Valley of Democracy: The Frontier versus the Plantation in the Ohio Valley, 1775–1818* (Bloomington: Indiana University Press, 1953). Indispensable for understanding the Blounts is William Henry Masterson, *William Blount* (1954; reprint, New York: Greenwood, 1969). See also Alice Barnwell Keith and William Henry Masterson, eds., *The John Gray Blount Papers*, 4 vols. (Raleigh: North Carolina Department of Archives and History, 1952–82).

Sources on Spain's troublesome presence along the Mississippi are cited for chapters three and four, but see especially Kinnaird, *Spain in the Mississippi Valley*. Quite useful is Arthur Preston Whitaker, *The Spanish-American Frontier, 1783–1795: The Westward Movement and the Spanish Retreat in the Mississippi Valley* (1927; reprint, Gloucester, Mass.: Peter Smith, 1962). More specific to Tennessee are D.C. Corbitt, "James Colbert and the Spanish Claims to the East Bank of the Mississippi," *MVHR* 24 (March 1938): 457–472; D.C. Corbitt and Roberta Corbitt, eds., "Papers from the Spanish Archives Relating to Tennessee and the Old Southwest," *ETHSP* 9–49 (1937–1977); Jack D. L. Holmes, "Spanish-American Rivalry over the Chickasaw Bluffs, 1780–1795," *ETHSP* 34 (1962): 26–57; Archibald Henderson, "The Spanish Conspiracy in Tennessee," *THM* 3 (December 1917): 229–249; and Arthur P. Whitaker, "Spain and the Cherokee Indians, 1783–1798," *NCHR* 4 (July 1927): 252–269.

Important for Tennessee's land history are "List of North Carolina Land Grants in Tennessee, 1778–1791," *File Microcopies of Records in the National Archives*, no. 68 (Washington, D.C.: National Archives, 1944); see also Goldene Fillers Burgner, comp., *North Carolina Land Grants in Tennessee, 1778–1791* (Easley, S.C.: Southern Historical Press, 1981); and for a good overview of a complicated subject, Daniel Jansen, "A Case of Fraud and Deception: The Revolutionary War Military Land Bounty Policy in Tennessee," *Journal of East Tennessee History* 64 (1992): 41–67. Related matters are in Albert V. Goodpasture, "Education and the Public Lands in Tennessee," *AHM* 4 (July 1899): 210–228; Thomas B. Jones, "The Public Lands of Tennessee," *THQ* 27 (Spring 1968): 13–36; Henry D. Whitney, comp. and ed., *The Land Laws of Tennessee* (Chattanooga: J. M. Deardoff, 1891); Billy R. McNamara, *Tennessee Land: Its Early History and Laws* (Knoxville: B. R. McNamara, 1997); and Arthur P. Whitaker, "The Muscle Shoals Speculation, 1783–1789," *MVHR* 13 (December 1926): 365–386. For the town most affected by the speculation of this period, see Anita Shafer Goodstein, *Nashville, 1780–1860: From Frontier to City* (Gainesville: University Press of Florida, 1989).

Quite useful are Samuel Cole Williams, *The Lost State of Franklin*, rev. ed. (New York: Press of the Pioneers, 1933); and Carl Driver, *John Sevier, Pioneer of the Old Southwest* (Chapel Hill: University of North Carolina Press, 1932). See also Pat Alderman, *The Overmountain Men: Early Tennessee History, 1760–1795* (Johnson City, Tenn.: The Overmountain Press, 1970); Paul M. Fink, "Some Phases of the History of the State of Franklin," *THQ* 16 (September 1957): 195–213; and William F. Cannon, "Four Interpretations of the History of the State of Franklin," *ETHSP* 22 (1950): 3–18. See also Samuel Cole Williams, "Western Representation in North Carolina Assemblies," *ETHSP* 14 (1942): 106–112. The most up-to-date biography of one of Tennessee's emerging leaders of this period is Robert V. Remini's *Andrew Jackson and the Course of American Empire, 1767–1821* (New York: Harper & Row, 1977); but still useful is Marquis James, *Andrew Jackson: The Border Captain* (Indianapolis: Bobbs-Merrill, 1933). For activities of Richard Henderson and other speculators see Stephen Anthony Aron, *How the West Was Lost:*

The Transformation of Kentucky from Daniel Boone to Henry Clay (Baltimore: Johns Hopkins Press, 1996); and Archibald Henderson, *The Conquest of the Old Southwest: The Romantic Story of the Early Pioneers into Virginia, the Carolinas, Tennessee, and Kentucky, 1740–1790* (New York: Century, 1920). See also Walter T. Durham, "Westward With Anthony Bledsoe: The Life of an Overmountain Frontier Leader," THQ 53 (Spring 1994): 2–19. A southwestern Virginian who was active in Tennessee affairs during the early period is the subject of Hartwell L. Quinn, *Arthur Campbell: Pioneer and Patriot of the "Old Southwest"* (Jefferson, N.C.: McFarland, 1990); see also James C. Hagy and Stanley J. Folmsbee, "Arthur Campbell and the Separate State Movements in Virginia and North Carolina," *ETHSP* 42 (1970): 20–46; and Lewis Preston Summer, *History of Southwest Virginia, 1746–1786, Washington County, 1777–1870* (1903; reprint, Baltimore: Genealogical, 1966).

For secondary accounts of Indian matters, see sources cited for chapters two through four, especially John P. Brown, *Old Frontiers: The Story of the Cherokee Indians from Earliest Times to the Date of Their Removal to the West, 1838* (Kingsport: Southern Publishers, 1938); R. S. Cotterill, *The Southern Indians: The Story of the Civilized Tribes before Removal* (Norman: University of Oklahoma Press, 1954); Tom Hatley, *The Dividing Paths: Cherokees and South Carolinians through the Era of Revolution* (New York: Oxford University Press, 1993); Randolph C. Downes, "Cherokee-American Relations in the Upper Tennessee Valley, 1776–1791," *ETHSP* 8 (1936): 35–83; and James Paul Pate, "The Chickamauga: A Forgotten Segment of Indian Resistance on the Southern Frontier" (Ph.D. diss., Mississippi State University, 1969). Important for understanding the U.S. military and its Indian campaigns during the period is Francis Paul Prucha, *The Sword of the Republic: The United States Army on the Frontier, 1783–1846* (1969; reprint, Bloomington: Indiana University Press, 1977). A basic source for United States–Indian relations is Charles J. Kappler, *Indian Affairs: Laws and Treaties,* 5 vols. (Washington, D.C.: Government Printing Office, 1904–1941). For extensive discussion of Cherokee treaties, consult Charles C. Royce, *The Cherokee Nation of Indians: A Narrative of Their Of-*

ficial Relations with the Colonial and Federal Governments, which appeared as the *Fifth Annual Report* of the Bureau of American Ethnology, 1883–1884 (Washington, D.C.: Government Printing Office, 1887), and is readily available as *The Cherokee Nation of Indians* (Chicago: Aldene, 1975). The most detailed maps are in idem, comp., *Indian Land Cessions in the United States* (Washington, D.C.: Government Printing Office, 1900). Early roads are discussed in Robert C. Kincaid, "The Wilderness Road in Tennessee," *ETHSP* 20 (1948): 37–48; idem, *The Wilderness Road* (Indianapolis: Bobbs-Merrill, 1947); and W. E. McElwee, "'The Old Road,' from Washington and Hamilton Districts to the Cumberland Settlement," *AHM* 8 (October 1903): 347–354.

6. The Southwest Territory

The most comprehensive works on the Southwest Territory are Walter T. Durham, *Before Tennessee: The Southwest Territory, 1790–1796* (Piney Flats, Tenn.: Rocky Mount Historical Association, 1990); and the more analytical William Michael Toomey, "Prelude to Statehood: The Southwest Territory, 1790–1796" (Ph.D. diss., University of Tennessee, 1991). These should be supplemented by the works of John Haywood, *Civil and Political History of Tennessee* (1823; reprint, Nashville: Publishing House of the Methodist Episcopal Church, South, 1891); J. G. M. Ramsey, *Annals of Tennessee to the End of the Eighteenth Century* (1853; reprint, Kingsport, Tenn.: ETHS, 1967); Albigence W. Putnam, *History of Middle Tennessee, or Life and Times of Gen. James Robertson* (1859; reprint, Knoxville: University of Tennessee Press, 1971); Thomas P. Abernathy, *From Frontier to Plantation: A Study of Frontier Democracy* (Chapel Hill: University of North Carolina Press, 1932); and John D. Barnhart, *Valley of Democracy: The Frontier versus the Plantation in the Ohio Valley, 1775–1818* (Bloomington: Indiana University Press, 1953). For William Blount's many machinations, see William Henry Masterson, *William Blount* (1954; reprint, New York: Greenwood Press, 1969); Alice Barnwell Keith and William Henry Masterson, eds., *The John Gray Blount Papers*, 4 vols. (Raleigh: North Carolina Department of Archives and History, 1952–82); and William Blount, *The Blount Journal, 1790–1796* (Nashville: Tennessee Historical Commission, 1955). Likewise, earlier cited biographies, especially Walter T. Durham's *Daniel Smith: Frontier Statesman* (Gallatin, Tenn.: Sumner County Library Board, 1976); and *James Winchester: Tennessee Pioneer* (Gallatin, Tenn.: Sumner County Library Board, 1979); and Robert V. Remini's *Andrew Jackson and the Course of American Empire, 1767–1821* (New York: Harper & Row, 1977) provide valuable insights, as does Nicholas Perkins Hardeman's *Wilderness Calling: The Hardeman Family in the American Westward Movement, 1750–1900* (Knoxville: University of Tennessee Press, 1977).

Providing a broader context for the Southwest Territory are Jack E. Eblen, *The First and Second United States Empires: Governors and Territorial Government, 1784–1912* (Pittsburgh: University of Pittsburgh Press, 1968); Peter Onuf, *Statehood and Union: A History of the Northwest Ordinance* (Bloomington: Indiana University Press, 1987); and Andrew R. L. Cayton, "'Separate Interests' and the Nation-State: The Washington Administration and the Origins of Regionalism in the Trans-Appalachian West," *JAH* 79 (June 1992): 39–67. See also Samuel Cole Williams, *Phases of Southwest Territory History* (Johnson City, Tenn.: Watauga Press, 1940); idem, *The Admission of Tennessee into the Union* (Nashville: Tennessee Historical Commission, 1945); idem, "The Admission of Tennessee into the Union," *THQ* 4 (1945): 291–319; Walter T. Durham, "The Southwest and Northwest Territories: A Comparison, 1787–1796," *THQ* 49 (Fall 1990): 188–196; idem, "The Southwest Territory: Progression to Statehood," *Journal of East Tennessee History* 62 (1990): 3–17; and the *Journal of East Tennessee History* 62 (1990) for other articles commemorating the bicentennial of the Southwest Territory by Paul J. Phillips, Michael Toomey, Tony Holmes, and Kent Whitworth. See also Robert E. Corlew, *Statehood for Tennessee* (Nashville: Tennessee American Bicentennial Commission, 1976); and John D. Barnhart, "The Tennessee Convention of 1796: A Product of the Old West," *JSH* 9 (November 1943): 532–548, which again takes issue with Abernethy, *From Frontier to Plantation in Tennessee.* Jo Tice Bloom discusses Tennessee's first territorial delegate in "Establishing Precedents: Dr. James White and the Southwest Territory," *THQ* 54 (Winter 1995): 325–335, and Kate White looks at another prominent individual in "John Chisholm, a Soldier of Fortune," *ETHSP* 1 (1929): 60–66.

The most important federal documents pertaining to the Southwest Territory appear in Clarence Edwin Carter et al., comp. and ed., *Territory of the United States South of the River Ohio, 1790–1796*, vol. 4 (1936) of *The Territorial Papers of the United States*, 28 vols. (Washington, D.C.: Government Printing Office, 1934–1975). See also ASPIA, ASPPL, and the Blount Papers, TSLA. Viewpoints of residents—and especially territorial leaders—appear in the territory's only newspaper, the *Knoxville Gazette*. The best sources for the territory's Indian Wars are cited for chapters three through five, especially John P. Brown, *Old Frontiers: The Story of the Cherokee Indians from Earliest Times to the Date of Their Removal to the West, 1838* (Kingsport: Southern Publishers, 1938); and James Paul Pate, "The Chickamauga: A Forgotten Segment of Indian Resistance on the Southern Frontier" (Ph.D. diss., Mississippi State University, 1969); see also Toomey, "Prelude to Statehood"; Randolph C. Downes, "Indian Affairs in the Southwest Territory, 1790–1796," *THM*, ser. 2, 3 (January 1937): 240–268; and Craig Symonds, "The Failure of America's Indian Policy on the Southwestern Frontier, 1785–1793," *THQ* 35 (Spring 1976): 29–45.

For Spanish activities and intrigues, see citations for chapters three through five, as well as Arthur Preston Whitaker, *The Mississippi Question, 1795–1803: A Study in Trade, Politics, and Diplomacy* (New York: Appleton-Century, 1934); Abraham P. Nasatir, *Spanish War Vessels on the Mississippi, 1792–1796* (New Haven: Yale University Press, 1968); Jane W. Berry, "The Indian Policy of Spain in the Old Southwest, 1783–1795," *MVHR* 3 (March 1917): 462–477; Jack D. L. Holmes, "The Ebb-Tide of Spanish Military Power on the Mississippi: Fort Fernando de las Barrancas, 1795–1798," *ETHSP* 36 (1964): 23–44; idem, "The First Laws of Memphis: Instructions for the Commandant of San Fernando de Las Barrancas, 1795," *WTHSP* 15 (1961): 93–104; idem, "Spanish-American Rivalry over the Chickasaw Bluffs, 1780–1795," *ETHSP* 34 (1962): 26–58; idem, "Fort Ferdinand of

the Bluffs: Life on the Spanish-American Frontier, 1795–1797,"
WTHSP 13 (1959): 38–54; idem, "Three Early Memphis Com-
mandants: Beauregard, Delville Degoutin, and Floch," *WTHSP*
18 (1964): 5–38; and Samuel Cole Williams, "French and Other
Intrigues in the Southwest Territory," *ETHSP* 13 (1941): 21–35.

Assessments of U.S. Indian wars during the period include
Francis Paul Prucha, *The Sword of the Republic: The United
States Army on the Frontier, 1783–1846* (1969; reprint, Bloomington: Indiana University Press, 1977); and Wiley Sword, *President
Washington's Indian War: The Struggle for the Old Northwest,
1790–1795* (Norman: University of Oklahoma Press, 1985). A
good discussion of an important federal outpost is Luke Henry
Banker, "Fort Southwest Point, Tennessee: The Development of
a Frontier Post, 1792–1807" (master's thesis, University of Tennessee, 1972); and idem, "A History of Fort Southwest Point,
1792–1807, *ETHSP* 46 (1974): 19–36. See also Samuel D. Smith
et al., *Investigations at Fort Southwest Point Archaeological Site,
Kingston, Tennessee: A Multidisciplinary Interpretation* (Nashville: Department of Environment and Conservation, Division of
Archaeology, 1993). For matters related to the territorial capital
(and capitol), see Stanley J. Folmsbee and Lucille Deaderick,
"The Founding of Knoxville," *ETHSP* 13 (1941): 3–20, and Stanley J. Folmsbee and Susan Hill Dillon, "The Blount Mansion,"
THQ 22 (June 1963): 103–122.

7. The Social Fabric

Again, my concept of cultural interaction between whites and
Indians borrows much from Richard White's *The Middle Ground:
Indians, Empires, and Republics in the Great Lakes Region,
1650–1815* (Cambridge: Cambridge University Press, 1991). For
backcountry leadership and the role of elites during the Revolution, see the sources cited for chapters three and four. I have especially relied on Jack P. Greene, "Independence, Improvement,
and Authority: Toward a Framework for Understanding the Histories of the Southern Backcountry during the Era of the American Revolution," in Ronald Hoffman, Thad W. Tate, and Peter J. Albert, eds., *An Uncivil War: The Southern Backcountry*

during the American Revolution (Charlottesville: University of
Virginia Press, 1985), pp. 3–36. See also essays by Rachel N.
Klein, A. Roger Ekirch, Jeffrey J. Crow, Emory G. Evans, and
Richard Beeman in that volume; Andrew R. L. Cayton, "Land,
Power, and Reputation: The Cultural Dimensions of Politics in
the Ohio Country," *WMQ*, ser. 3, 47 (April 1990): 266–286; Carl
Driver, *John Sevier, Pioneer of the Old Southwest* (Chapel Hill:
University of North Carolina Press, 1932); Robert V. Remini, *An-
drew Jackson and the Course of American Empire, 1767–1821*
(New York: Harper & Row, 1977); Walter T. Durham *Daniel
Smith: Frontier Statesman* (Gallatin, Tenn.: Sumner County Li-
brary Board, 1976); idem, *James Winchester: Tennessee Pioneer*
(Gallatin, Tenn.: Sumner County Library Board, 1979); James
Morris Ransom, "The Life and Career of General James Robert-
son" (master's thesis, University of Tennessee, 1966); Thomas
Edwin Matthews's somewhat limited *General James Robertson:
Father of Tennessee* (Nashville: Parthenon Press, 1934); Richard
Maxwell Brown, "Backcountry Rebellions and the Homestead
Ethic in America, 1740–1799," in Richard Maxwell Brown and
Don E. Fehrenbacher, eds., *Tradition, Conflict, and Moderniza-
tion: Perspectives on the American Revolution* (New York: Aca-
demic, 1977), pp. 73–99; Anita Shafer Goodstein, "Leadership
on the Nashville Frontier, 1780–1800," *THQ* 35 (Summer 1976):
175–198; and idem, *Nashville, 1780–1860: From Frontier to City*
(Gainesville: University Press of Florida, 1989).

Most of the books cited under "General Works" contain valuable information on frontier society, as do many of the more specific sources cited for previous chapters. Quite useful on a general
level is Everett Dick's *The Dixie Frontier: A Social History of the
Southern Frontier from the First Transmontane Beginnings to the
Civil War* (New York: Capricorn, 1964). For more specific topics
see Elliott J. Gorn, "'Gouge and Bite, Pull Hair and Scratch':
The Social Significance of Fighting in the Southern Backcoun-
try," *AHR* 90 (February 1985): 18–43; James I. Robertson Jr.,
"Frolics, Fights, and Firewater in Frontier Tennessee," THQ 17
(June 1958): 97–111; Neal O'Steen, "Pioneer Education in the
Tennessee Country," *THQ* 35 (Summer 1976): 199–219; James
Riley Montgomery, Stanley J. Folmsbee, and Lee Seifert Greene,

To Foster Knowledge: A History of the University of Tennessee, 1794–1970 (Knoxville: University of Tennessee Press, 1984); F. Garvin Davenport, "Culture vs. Frontier in Tennessee, 1825–50," *JSH* 5 (February 1939): 18–33; Buford C. Utley, "The Early Academies of West Tennessee," *WTHSP* 8 (1954): 5–38; A. P. Whitaker, "The Public School System of Tennessee, 1834–1860," *THM* 2 (March 1916): 1–30; and Louis B. Wright, *Culture on the Moving Frontier* (Bloomington: Indiana University Press, 1955).

Kentucky studies which are applicable to the Tennessee frontier are Arthur K. Moore, *The Frontier Mind: A Cultural Analysis of the Kentucky Frontiersman* (Lexington: University of Kentucky Press, 1957); Stephen Aron, "Pioneers and Profiteers: Land Speculation and the Homestead Ethic in Frontier Kentucky," *WHQ* 23 (May 1992): 179–198; and Elizabeth Perkins, "The Consumer Frontier: Household Consumption in Early Kentucky," *JAH* 78 (September 1991): 486–510. Outstanding on material culture is Lucy Kennerley Gump, "Possessions and Patterns of Living in Washington County: The 20 Years before Tennessee Statehood, 1777–1796" (master's thesis, East Tennessee State University, 1989); see also Miriam Fink, "Some Phases of the Social and Economic History of Jonesboro, Tennessee, prior to the Civil War" (master's thesis, University of Tennessee, 1934); and William Flinn Rogers, "Life in East Tennessee Near the End of Eighteenth Century," *ETHSP* 1 (1929): 27–42.

Almost all of the sources cited under "General Works" devote cursory attention to women. Typical of the usual depictions is Samuel Cole Williams, "Ann Robertson: An Unsung Tennessee Heroine," *THQ* 3 (June 1944): 150–155. More recent and specific accounts include Margaret L. Crawford, "The Legal Status of Women in Early Tennessee: Knox, Jefferson, and Blount Counties, 1792–1843" (master's thesis, University of Tennessee, 1992); and Lawrence B. Goodheart, Neil Hanks, and Elizabeth Johnson, "'An Act for the Relief of Females . . .': Divorce and the Changing Legal Status of Women in Tennessee," *THQ* 44 (Fall 1985): 318–339. For national overviews see Glenda Riley, *Divorce: An American Tradition* (New York: Oxford University Press, 1991); and Beverly Stoeltje, "A Helpmate for Man Indeed: The Image of the Frontier Woman," *Journal of American Folklore* 88

(January–March 1975): 25–41. The topic of frontier women has become important in recent years, fostering a wide-ranging scholarship that is refreshing, controversial, and often ideological. Perceptive overviews include Peggy Pascoe, "Western Women at the Cultural Crossroads," in Patricia Nelson Limerick, Clyde A. Milner II, and Charles E. Rankin, eds., *Trails: Toward a New Meaning for Western History* (Lawrence: University of Kansas Press, 1991), pp. 40–58; and Katherine G. Morrissey, "Engendering the West," in William Cronon, George Miles, and Jay Gitlin, eds., *Under an Open Sky: Rethinking America's Western Past* (New York: Norton, 1992), pp. 132–144. As part of this new literature, historians are also reassessing family life on the frontier, including the role of children. An example of the latter is Gary Shockley's "A History of the Incarceration of Juveniles in Tennessee, 1796–1970," *THQ* 43 (Fall 1984): 229–249.

The question of Celtic influences on the frontier has generated enormous controversy, especially since publication of David Hackett Fischer's *Albion's Seed: Four British Folkways in America* (New York: Oxford University Press, 1989). Besides Fischer, those arguing for the impact of various Celtic peoples include Forrest and Ellen Shapiro McDonald, "The Ethnic Origins of the American People," *WMQ*, ser. 3, 37 (April 1980): 179–199; Forrest McDonald and Grady McWhiney, "The Antebellum Herdsman: A Reinterpretation," *JSH* 41 (May 1975): 147–166; and Grady McWhiney, *Cracker Culture: Celtic Ways in the Old South* (Tuscaloosa: University of Alabama Press, 1989). Rodger Cunningham's *Apples on the Flood: The Southern Mountain Experience* (Knoxville: University of Tennessee Press, 1987) offers an original, provocative perspective on the subject. Somewhat dubious in sources and logic is Billy Kennedy, *The Scots-Irish in the Hills of Tennessee* (Londonderry: Causeway Press; Greenville, S.C.: Emerald House Groups, 1995). A sharp critique of those arguing for pervasive Celtic influence is Rowland Berthhoff, "Celtic Mist over the South," *JSH* 52 (November 1986): 523–546. Making claims for Finnish-Indian influences on the frontier are Terry G. Jordan and Matti Kaups, *The American Backwoods Frontier: An Ethnic and Ecological Interpretation* (Baltimore: Johns Hopkins Press, 1989). Among other things, Jordan and Kaups discuss backwoods architecture and cabin construction, as do James A. Crutchfield, "Pioneer Architecture in Tennessee," *THQ* 35 (Summer 1976): 162–174; James Patrick, *Architecture in Tennessee, 1768–1897* (Knoxville: University of Tennessee Press, 1981); John Morgan, *The Log House in East Tennessee* (Knoxville: University of Tennessee Press, 1990); Henry Glassie, *Pattern in the Material Folk Culture of the Eastern United States* (Philadelphia: University of Pennsylvania Press, 1968); and idem, "The Appalachian Log Cabin," *Mountain Life and Work* 39 (Winter 1963): 5–14.

For population mobility in East Tennessee, see David C. Hsiung, *Two Worlds in the Tennessee Mountains: Exploring the Origins of Appalachian Stereotypes* (Lexington: University of Kentucky Press, 1997); and excellent for the state as a whole, Thomas Allan Scott, "National Impact of Tennessee through Her Migrating Sons, 1830–1900" (master's thesis, University of Tennessee, 1966). Broader overviews are William O. Lynch, "The Westward Flow of Southern Colonists before 1861," *JSH* 9 (August 1943): 303–327; and James E. Davis, *Frontier America, 1800–1840: A Comparative Demographic Analysis of the Frontier Process* (Glendale, Calif.: Arthur H. Clark, 1977). John Ballenger Knox, *The People of Tennessee: A Study of Population Trends* (Knoxville: University of Tennessee Press, 1949), gives only cursory attention to the period before 1850.

African-Americans on the Tennessee frontier are discussed in Edward Michael McCormack, *Slavery on the Tennessee Frontier* (Nashville: Tennessee American Revolution Bicentennial Commission, 1977); Chase S. Mooney, *Slavery in Tennessee* (Westport, Conn.: Greenwood, 1957); Anita S. Goodstein, "Black History on the Nashville Frontier, 1780–1810," *THQ* 38 (Winter 1979): 401–420; James W. Patton, "The Progress of Emancipation in Tennessee, 1796–1860," *Journal of Negro History* 17 (January 1932): 67–102; and Lester C. Lamon, *Blacks in Tennessee, 1791–1970* (Knoxville: University of Tennessee Press, 1981). Related to the topic are John C. Inscoe, *Mountain Masters, Slavery, and the Sectional Crisis in Western North Carolina* (Knoxville: University of Tennessee Press, 1989); Bette B. Tilly, "The Spirit of Improvement: Reformism and Slavery in West Tennessee," *WTHSP* 28 (1974): 25–42; Richard B. Drake, "Slavery and Antislavery in

Appalachia," *Appalachian Heritage* 14 (Winter 1986): 25–33; and
Edward Hotaling, *The Great Black Jockeys: The Lives and Times of the Men Who Dominated America's First National Sport* (Rocklin, Calif.: Prima, 1999).

For religion see Walter B. Posey, *A Frontier Mission: A History of Religion West of the Southern Appalachians to 1861* (Lexington: University of Kentucky Press, 1966); idem, "Bishop Asbury Visits Tennessee, 1788–1815," *THQ* 15 (September 1956): 253–268; John B. Boles, *The Great Revival, 1787–1805: The Origins of the Southern Evangelical Mind* (Lexington: University of Kentucky Press, 1972); Peter Cartwright, *Autobiography of Peter Cartwright, the Backwoods Preacher*, ed. W. P. Strickland (1857; reprint, Freeport, N.Y.: Books for Libraries Press, 1972); Charles A. Johnson, *The Frontier Camp Meeting: Religion's Harvest Time* (Dallas: Southern Methodist University Press, 1955); Herman A. Norton, *Religion in Tennessee, 1777–1945* (Knoxville: University of Tennessee Press, 1981); Samuel Cole Williams, "Tidence Lane—Tennessee's First Pastor," *THM* 1 (1930–31): 40–48; and John R. Finger, "Witness to Expansion: Bishop Francis Asbury on the Trans-Appalachian Frontier," *Register of the Kentucky Historical Society* 82 (Autumn 1984): 334–357. Bishop Asbury's observations and thoughts are most readily available in Elmer E. Clark, J. Manning Potts, and Jacob S. Payton, eds., *Journal and Letters of Francis Asbury*, 3 vols. (London and Nashville: Epworth and Abingdon, 1958).

A massive literature exists on the Cherokees, and my indebtedness to William G. McLoughlin should be apparent. I have found especially helpful his *Cherokee Renascence in the New Republic* (Princeton: Princeton University Press, 1986) and *Cherokees and Missionaries, 1789–1839* (New Haven: Yale University Press, 1984). Other standard references include James Mooney's classic "Myths of the Cherokee," *Nineteenth Annual Report* of the Bureau of American Ethnology, 1898, 2 vols. (Washington, D.C.: Government Printing Office, 1900), most readily available as *Myths of the Cherokee and Sacred Formulas of the Cherokees by James Mooney* (Nashville: Charles and Randy Elder, 1982); see also Henry T. Malone, *Cherokees of the Old South: A People in Transition* (Athens: University of Georgia Press, 1956); and previously cited works, especially John P. Brown, *Old Frontiers: The Story of the Cherokee Indians from Earliest Times to the Date of Their Removal to the West, 1838* (Kingsport, Tenn.: Southern Publishers, 1938); R. S. Cotterill, *The Southern Indians: The Story of the Civilized Tribes before Removal* (Norman: University of Oklahoma Press, 1954); Theda Perdue, *Slavery and the Evolution of Cherokee Society, 1540–1866* (Knoxville: University of Tennessee Press, 1979); and idem, *Cherokee Women: Gender and Culture Change, 1700–1835* (Lincoln: University of Nebraska Press, 1998). See also William C. Sturtevant, "Louis-Philippe on Cherokee Architecture and Clothing in 1797," *JCS* 3 (Fall 1978): 198–205; and Gerald F. Schroedl, "Louis-Philippe's Journal and Archaeological Investigations at the Overhill Cherokee Town of Toqua," *JCS* 3 (Fall 1978): 206–219. Federal policy during this period is the topic of Francis Paul Prucha, *American Indian Policy in the Formative Years: The Indian Trade and Intercourse Acts, 1790–1834* (Cambridge, Mass.: Harvard University Press, 1962); and Ora B. Peake, *A History of the United States Indian Factory System, 1795–1822* (Denver: Sage, 1954). Most of the works dealing with Cherokee civilization will be cited for chapter eleven.

8. The Frontier Economy

All of the previously cited general works on Tennessee History include sections on economic development, as do the county histories. Harriet Arnow's *Seedtime on the Cumberland* (New York: Macmillan, 1960) and *Flowering of the Cumberland* (New York: Macmillan, 1963) are especially valuable in this regard for Middle Tennessee. (West Tennessee's early growth is the subject of chapter ten.) Two recent interpretive books with extensive analysis of the frontier and post-frontier economies are David C. Hsiung, *Two Worlds in the Tennessee Mountains: Exploring the Origins of Appalachian Stereotypes* (Lexington: University of Kentucky Press, 1997); and Donald Edward Davis, *Where There Are Mountains: An Environmental History of the Southern Appalachians* (Athens: University of Georgia Press, 2000). Davis is among those scholars taking exception to the arguments of

Wilma Dunaway in *The First American Frontier: Transition to*
Capitalism in Southern Appalachia, 1700–1860 (Chapel Hill:
University of North Carolina Press, 1996). Related to these works
is Christopher Warren Baker, "East Tennessee within the World-
Economy (1790–1850): Pre-Capitalist Isolation or Peripheral
Capitalism?" (master's thesis, University of Tennessee, 1991).
Lucy Kennerley Gump, "Possessions and Patterns of Living in
Washington County: The 20 Years before Tennessee Statehood,
1777–1796" (master's thesis, East Tennessee State University,
1989), also has useful raw data concerning economic developments. More wide ranging is Albert C. Holt, "The Economic and
Social Beginnings of Tennessee," *THM* 7 (October 1921): 194–230;
(January 1922): 252–313; and 8 (April 1924): 24–88, which appear
together as idem, *The Economic and Social Beginnings of Tennessee* (Nashville: George Peabody College, 1923). Of related interest is Eric Russell Lacy's *Vanquished Volunteers: East Tennessee Sectionalism from Statehood to Secession* (Johnson City,
Tenn.: East Tennessee State Press, 1965); see also Paul M. Fink,
*Jonesborough: The First Century of Tennessee's First Town, 1776–
1876*, 2nd ed. (Johnson City, Tenn.: Overmountain Press, 1989);
Miriam Fink, "Some Phases of the Social and Economic History
of Jonesboro, Tennessee, prior to the Civil War" (master's thesis,
University of Tennessee, 1934); and Samuel Cole Williams, ed.,
"Journal of Events (1825–1873) of David Anderson Deaderick,"
ETHSP 8 (1936): 121–137.

The decennial census of the United States provides vital statistics on agriculture and industry in every county. Almost every
general source previously cited at least touches on agriculture,
but also see Terry G. Jordan and Matti Kaups, *The American
Backwoods Frontier: An Ethnic and Ecological Interpretation*
(Baltimore: Johns Hopkins Press, 1989); and Grady McWhiney,
Cracker Culture: Celtic Ways in the Old South (Tuscaloosa: University of Alabama Press, 1989). Essential is Lewis Cecil Gray's
History of Agriculture in the Southern United States to 1860, 2
vols. (1933; reprint, Gloucester Mass.: Peter Smith, 1958), especially volume 2. More specific to the subject matter of this book
are Donald L. Winters, *Tennessee Farming, Tennessee Farmers:
Antebellum Agriculture in the Upper South* (Knoxville: Univer-

sity of Tennessee Press, 1994); Blanche Henry Clark, *The Tennessee Yeoman, 1840–1860* (Nashville: Vanderbilt University Press, 1942); Frank Owsley, *Plain Folk of the Old South* (Baton Rouge: Louisiana State University Press, 1949); Samuel B. Hilliard, *Hog Meat and Hoe Cake: Food Supply in the Old South, 1840–1860* (Carbondale: Southern Illinois University Press, 1972); idem, "Hog Meat and Cornpone: Foodways in the Antebellum South," in Robert Blair St. George, ed., *Material Life in America, 1600–1860* (Boston: Northeastern University Press, 1988), pp. 311–332; Edmund Cody Burnett, "Hog Raising and Hog Driving in the Region of the French Broad River," *Agricultural History* 20 (April 1946): 86–103; and Louis D. Wallace, ed., *The Horse and Its Heritage in Tennessee*, 3rd ed. (Nashville: Tennessee Department of Agriculture, 1951).

My discussion of distilling includes material from Thomas P. Slaughter, *The Whiskey Rebellion: Frontier Epilogue to the American Revolution* (New York: Oxford University Press, 1986); Mary K. Bonsteel Tachau, "The Whiskey Rebellion in Kentucky: A Forgotten Episode in Civil Disobedience," *Journal of the Early Republic* 2 (Fall 1982): 239–259; Kay Baker Gaston, "Robertson County Distilleries, 1796–1909," *THQ* 43 (Spring 1984): 49–67; Walter T. Durham, *Before Tennessee: The Southwest Territory, 1790–1796* (Piney Flats, Tenn.: Rocky Mount Historical Association, 1990); and Arnow, *Flowering of the Cumberland*. See also W. J. Rorabough, *The Alcoholic Republic: An American Tradition* (New York: Oxford University Press, 1979). A different aspect of economic development is discussed in Larry Schweikart's "Tennessee Banks in the Antebellum Period," *THQ* 45 (Summer 1986): 119–132 and (Fall 1986): 199–209.

Transportation is another subject discussed in most of the sources listed under "General Works" and many other previously cited works. Of specific utility were John Dawson Boniol Jr., "The Walton Road," *THQ* 30 (Winter 1971): 402–412; W. Calvin Dickinson, "Walton Road," *Tennessee Anthropologist* 20 (Fall 1995): 126–137; W. E. McElwee, "'The Old Road,' from Washington and Hamilton Districts to the Cumberland Settlement," *AHM* 8 (October 1903): 347–354; Robert C. Kincaid, "The Wilderness Road in Tennessee," *ETHSP* 20 (1948): 37–48; and idem, *The Wilder-*

ness Road (Indianapolis: Bobbs-Merrill, 1947). Lewis L. Laska
and Severine Brocki discuss a related matter in "The Life and
Death of the Lottery in Tennessee, 1787–1836," *THQ* 45 (Summer
1986): 95–118. For the Natchez Trace see Thomas D. Clark and
John D. W. Guice, *Frontiers in Conflict: The Old Southwest,
1795–1830* (Albuquerque: University of New Mexico Press, 1989);
and William C. Davis, *A Way through the Wilderness: The
Natchez Trace and the Civilization of the Southern Frontier* (New
York: HarperCollins, 1995). Still useful is George Rogers Taylor,
The Transportation Revolution, 1815–1860 (New York: Rinehart,
1951); and Stanley J. Folmsbee, *Sectionalism and Internal Im-
provements in Tennessee, 1796–1845* (Knoxville: ETHS, 1939).
See also idem, "The Beginnings of the Railroad Movement in
East Tennessee," *ETHSP* 5 (1933): 81–104; and Donald Davidson,
The Tennessee: The Old River — Frontier to Secession (New York:
Rinehart & Co., 1946).

An excellent account of the people who worked the rivers is
Michael Allen, *Western Rivermen, 1763–1861: Ohio and Missis-
sippi Boatmen and the Myth of the Alligator Horse* (Baton
Rouge: Louisiana State University Press, 1990); related works
include Walter Blair and Franklin J. Meine, eds., *Half-Horse,
Half-Alligator: The Growth of the Mike Fink Legend* (Chicago:
University of Chicago Press, 1956); Leland D. Baldwin, *The Keel-
boat Age on Western Waters* (Pittsburgh: University of Pitts-
burgh Press, 1941); Louis C. Hunter, *Steamboats on Western
Waters: An Economic and Technological History* (Cambridge:
Harvard University Press, 1949); Erik F. Haites, James Mak, and
Gary M. Walton, *Western Water Transportation: The Era of Early
Internal Development, 1810–1860* (Baltimore: Johns Hopkins
University Press, 1975); Erik F. Haites and James Mak, "Ohio
and Mississippi River Transportation, 1810–1860," *Explorations
in Economic History* 8 (Winter 1970): 153–180; and Harry N.
Scheiber, "The Ohio-Mississippi Flatboat Trade: Some Reconsid-
erations," in David M. Ellis, ed., *The Frontier in American Development: Essays in Honor of Paul Wallace Gates* (Ithaca, N.Y.:
Cornell University Press, 1969), pp. 277–298. Martin Dickinson's
journal of 1797–1799 is in the TSLA. Richard C. Wade's *The Urban Frontier: The Rise of Western Cities* (Cambridge: Harvard

University Press, 1959) remains a classic account of town growth and emerging elites on the trans-Appalachian frontier. Related to this are Anita Shafer Goodstein, *Nashville, 1780–1860: From Frontier to City* (Gainesville: University Press of Florida, 1989); and H. Phillip Bacon, "Nashville's Trade at the Beginning of the Nineteenth Century," *THQ* 15 (March 1956): 30–36.

The most acclaimed recent account of Meriwether Lewis, and the basis of my discussion, is Stephen E. Ambrose, *Undaunted Courage: Meriwether Lewis, Thomas Jefferson, and the Opening of the American West* (New York: Simon & Schuster, 1996).

The best overviews of industrial development are Hsiung, *Two Worlds*, and Davis, *Where There Are Mountains*, and among the more specifically focused articles are Paul M. Fink, "Bumpass Cove Mines and Embreeville," *ETHSP* 6 (1944): 48–64; Susanna Delfino, "Antebellum East Tennessee Elites and Industrialization: The Examples of the Iron Industry and Internal Improvements," *ETHSP* 56/57 (1984–85): 102–119; Samuel Cole Williams, "Early Iron Works in the Tennessee Country," *THQ* 6 (March 1947): 39–46; Raymond F. Hunt Jr., "The Pactolus Ironworks," THQ 25 (Summer 1966): 176–196; and Tyler Blethen and Curtis Wood Jr., "The Antebellum Iron Industry in Western North Carolina," *Journal of Appalachian Studies* 4 (1992): 79–87.

9. Statehood to Nationalism

Essential sources are the governors' papers, legislative papers, and the papers of many prominent individuals, all at TSLA; see also John H. Derwitt, ed., "Journal of John Sevier," *THM* 5 (October 1919 and January 1920): 156–194, 232–264; and Robert H. White, *Messages of the Governors of Tennessee*, vol. 1: *1796–1821* (Nashville: Tennessee Historical Commission, 1952). Almost all of the sources cited under "General Works" include important material on this period, as do various county histories, good examples of which are Inez E. Burns, *History of Blount County, Tennessee: From War Trail to Landing Strip, 1795–1955* (Nashville, 1957); and Ann Evans Alley, "Economic Development of Montgomery County between 1800–1820" (master's thesis, Austin Peay State University, 1986). Nashville's emergence as a re-

gional hub is discussed in Anita Shafer Goodstein, *Nashville,*
1780–1860: From Frontier to City (Gainesville: University Press of
Florida, 1989); and H. Phillip Bacon, "Nashville's Trade at the
Beginning of the Nineteenth Century," *THQ* 15 (March 1956): 30–
36. See also Betsey Beeler Creekmore, *Knoxville* (Knoxville: University of Tennessee Press, 1958). A brief overview of a physiographic area is W. Calvin Dickinson, Larry H. Whiteaker, Leo
McGee, and Homer T. Kemp, eds., *Lend an Ear: Heritage of the*
Tennessee Upper Cumberland (Lanham, Md.: University Press
of America, 1983). For Blount College, see James Riley Montgomery, Stanley J. Folmsbee, and Lee Seifert Greene, *To Foster*
Knowledge: A History of the University of Tennessee, 1794–1970
(Knoxville: University of Tennessee Press, 1984). An excellent
overview of William Blount's legal plight is Milton M. Klein's
"The First Impeachment," *Tennessee Bar Journal* 35 (February
1999): 11–13. In the case of Francis Asbury, I have taken verbatim
several passages from my "Witness to Expansion: Bishop Francis
Asbury on the Trans-Appalachian Frontier," *Register of the Ken-*
tucky Historical Society 82 (Autumn 1984): 334–357.

The accounts of visitors to Tennessee during the period are
numerous. Some appear in Samuel Cole Williams, *Early Travels*
in the Tennessee Country, 1540–1800 (Johnson City, Tenn.: Watauga Press, 1928); and in Reuben Gold Thwaites, ed., *Early*
Western Travels, 1748–1846, 32 vols. (Cleveland: A. H. Clark,
1904–1907). Other accounts appear in more complete form elsewhere, for example Francis Bailey's *Journal of a Tour in Unset-*
tled Parts of North America in 1796 & 1797 (London: Baily Brothers, 1856); Elmer E. Clark, J. Manning Potts, and Jacob S.
Payton, eds., *Journal and Letters of Francis Asbury,* 3 vols. (London and Nashville: Epworth and Abingdon, 1958); William Bartram, *The Travels of William Bartram,* ed. Francis Harper (New
Haven: Yale University Press, 1958); Gilbert Imlay, *A Topograph-*
ical Description of the Western Territory of North America, 3rd
ed. (London: J. Debrett, 1797); and Louis Philippe, *Diary of My*
Travels in America, trans. Stephen Becker (New York: Dela-
corte, 1977).

For the major players on Tennessee's stage, see Robert V. Remini, *Andrew Jackson and the Course of American Empire, 1767–*

1821 (New York: Harper & Row, 1977); Sam B. Smith and Harriet Chappell Owsley, eds., *The Papers of Andrew Jackson*, vol. 1: *1770–1803* (Knoxville: University of Tennessee Press, 1980); Harold D. Moser and Sharon McPherson, eds., *The Papers of Andrew Jackson*, vol. 2: *1804–1813* (Knoxville: University of Tennessee Press, 1984); Harold D. Moser, David R. Hoth, Sharon McPherson, and John H. Reinbold, eds., *The Papers of Andrew Jackson*, vol. 3: *1814–1815* (Knoxville: University of Tennessee Press, 1991); Carl Driver, *John Sevier, Pioneer of the Old Southwest* (Chapel Hill: University of North Carolina Press, 1932); James Morris Ransom, "The Life and Career of General James Robertson" (master's thesis, University of Tennessee, 1966); and Thomas P. Abernethy, *The Burr Conspiracy* (1954; reprint, Gloucester, Mass.: Peter Smith, 1968).

For the confused and complex state of U.S., North Carolina, and Tennessee land claims during this period consult the sources cited for chapter five, especially Henry D. Whitney, comp. and ed., *The Land Laws of Tennessee* (Chattanooga: J. M. Deardoff, 1891); and Thomas P. Abernethy, *From Frontier to Plantation in Tennessee: A Study of Frontier Democracy* (Chapel Hill: University of North Carolina Press, 1932).

Geopolitical and military affairs are discussed in Arthur Preston Whitaker, *The Mississippi Question, 1795–1803: A Study in Trade, Politics, and Diplomacy* (New York: Appleton-Century, 1934); Jack D. L. Holmes, "The Ebb-Tide of Spanish Military Power on the Mississippi: Fort Fernando de las Barrancas, 1795–1798," *ETHSP* 36 (1964): 23–44; James E. Roper, "Fort Adams and Fort Pickering," *WTHSP* 24 (1970): 5–29; Jay Leitch Wright Jr., *Britain and the American Frontier, 1783–1815* (Athens: University of Georgia Press, 1975); Joel W. Martin, *Sacred Revolt: The Muskogees' Struggle for a New World* (Boston: Beacon Press, 1991); Claudio Saunt, *A New Order of Things: Property, Power, and the Creek Indians, 1733–1816* (Cambridge: Cambridge University Press, 1999); and Frank Owsley Jr., *Struggle for the Gulf Borderlands: The Creek War and the Battle of New Orleans, 1812–1815* (Gainesville: University of Florida Press, 1981). Regarding Jackson's relations with the Indians, see citations for chapter eleven, and citations for chapter ten regarding Davy

Crockett and Sam Houston. For Indian treaties and cessions see Charles J. Kappler, *Indian Affairs: Laws and Treaties*, 5 vols. (Washington, D.C.: Government Printing Office, 1904–1941); and Charles C. Royce, *The Cherokee Nation of Indians: A Narrative of Their Official Relations with the Colonial and Federal Governments*, which appeared as the *Fifth Annual Report* of the Bureau of American Ethnology, 1883–1884 (Washington, D.C.: Government Printing Office, 1887), and is readily available as *The Cherokee Nation of Indians* (Chicago: Aldene, 1975).

10. The Western District

The most comprehensive overviews of West Tennessee for the period are Samuel Cole Williams, *Beginnings of West Tennessee, in the Land of the Chickasaws, 1541–1841* (Johnson City, Tenn.: Watauga Press, 1930); and Bette Baird Tilly, "Aspects of Social and Economic Life in West Tennessee before the Civil War" (Ph.D. diss., Memphis State University, 1974). For exploration, early contacts with Indians, and Spanish claims and occupations, see sources cited for chapters one, six, and nine. Especially useful is Lawrence Kinnaird, trans. and ed., *Spain in the Mississippi Valley, 1764–1794: Translations of Materials from the Spanish Archives in the Bancroft Library, University of California, Berkeley*, in *Annual Report of the American Historical Society, 1945*, 4 vols. (Washington, D.C.: American Historical Society, 1946–49); see also Arrell M. Gibson, *The Chickasaws* (Norman: University of Oklahoma Press, 1971); and Ronald N. Satz, *Tennessee's Indian Peoples: From White Contact to Removal, 1540–1850* (Knoxville: University of Tennessee Press, 1979).

The urban frontier was always important, and quite useful are James Roper, *The Founding of Memphis, 1818–1820* (Memphis: Memphis Sesquicentennial, 1970); idem, "The Founding of Memphis 1818 through December 1820," *WTHSP* 23 (1969): 5–29; and especially Gerald M. Capers, *The Biography of a River Town: Memphis, Its Heroic Age* (1939; reprint, New Orleans: Hauser-American, 1966). See also James D. Davis, *The History of Memphis, Being a Compilation of the Most Important Documents and Historical Events . . .* (Memphis: Crumpton & Kelly, 1873); and

James S. Matthews, "Sequent Occupation in Memphis, Tennessee: 1819–1860," *WTHSP* 11 (1957): 112–134. Useful for comparative purposes are Richard C. Wade, *The Urban Frontier: The Rise of Western Cities* (Cambridge, Mass.: Harvard University Press, 1959); and Daniel Boorstin's lively and persuasive account of frontier urban boosterism in *The Americans: The National Experience* (New York: Random House, 1965). Much documentary evidence on the founding of Memphis is in the Winchester and Overton papers, TSLA; in the James Roper Papers of the Mississippi Valley Collection of the University of Memphis; and in Walter T. Durham, *James Winchester: Tennessee Pioneer* (Gallatin, Tenn.: Sumner County Library Board, 1979).

Other primary sources include CSRNC, ASPIA, ASPPL, and the Middle and West Tennessee Papers, Lawson-McGhee Library, Knoxville. Newspapers for the period include the *Jackson Gazette*, easily the most informative on regional economic and social developments; the *Southern Statesman* (Jackson); the *Clarion and Tennessee State Gazette* (Nashville); the *Memphis Enquirer*; and the *Randolph Recorder*. See also Robert M. McBride and Owen Meredith, eds., *Eastin Morris' Tennessee Gazetteer, 1834, and Matthew Rhea's Map of the State of Tennessee, 1832* (Nashville: Gazetteer Press, 1971). For the Chickasaw cession of 1818, see Charles J. Kappler, *Indian Affairs: Laws and Treaties*, 5 vols. (Washington, D.C.: Government Printing Office, 1904–1941); Harold D. Moser, David R. Hoth, and George H. Hoemann, eds., *The Papers of Andrew Jackson, vol. 4: 1816–1820* (Knoxville: University of Tennessee Press, 1994); and Robert V. Remini, *Andrew Jackson and the Course of American Empire, 1767–1821* (New York: Harper & Row, 1977).

Early observers include John Bradbury, *Travels in the Interior of America, in the Years 1809, 1810, and 1811; . . .* , 2d ed, (London: Sherwood, Neely & Jones, 1819); Thomas Nuttall, *Journal of Travels into the Arkansas Territory, during the Year 1819, With Occasional Observations on the Manners of the Aborigines* (Philadelphia: P. H. Palmer, 1821), reprinted in Reuben Gold Thwaites, ed., *Early Western Travels, 1748–1846*, vol. 13 (Cleveland: A. H. Clark, 1904–1907); see also Richard E. Davis, "Views of Early West Tennessee As Seen through the Files of Ancient Newspa-

pers," *WTHSP* 6 (1952): 64–76; and Andrew S. Edson, "How
Nineteenth Century Travelers Viewed Memphis before the Civil
War," *WTHSP* 24 (1970): 30–40. Besides the many works on
Memphis, town and county studies include Ann McDonald
Meeks, "Whitehaven and Levi: The Evolution of Rural Commu-
nities in Southwest Shelby County, 1819–1970" (master's thesis,
Memphis State University, 1984); idem, "Whitehaven and Levi:
The Evolution of Rural Communities in West Tennessee, 1819–
1865," WTHSP 39 (December 1985): 10–25; Roger Raymond Van
Dyke, "A History of Henry County, Tennessee, 1820–1850" (mas-
ter's thesis, University of Tennessee, 1966); Roy W. Black, "The
Genesis of County Organization in the Western District of North
Carolina and in the State of Tennessee," *WTHSP* 2 (1948): 95–
118; Jay Guy Cisco, "Madison County," *AHM* 7 (October 1902):
328–348 and 8 (January 1903): 26–48; Perry Morton Herbert,
"Early History of Hardin County, Tennessee," *WTHSP* 1 (1947):
38–67; and Frederick M. Culp and Mrs. Robert E. Ross, *Gibson County, Past and Present: The First General History of One
of West Tennessee's Pivotal Counties* (Trenton, Tenn.: Gibson
County Historical Society, 1961). For farming see Lewis Cecil
Gray, *History of Agriculture in the Southern United States to
1860*, 2 vols. (Washington, D.C.: Carnegie Institution, 1933; reprint, Gloucester Mass.: Peter Smith, 1958); Donald L. Winters,
*Tennessee Farming, Tennessee Farmers: Antebellum Agriculture
in the Upper South* (Knoxville: University of Tennessee Press,
1994); Frank Owsley, *Plain Folk of the Old South* (Baton Rouge:
Louisiana State University Press, 1949); Blanche Henry Clark,
The Tennessee Yeoman, 1840–1860 (Nashville: Vanderbilt University Press, 1942); and Emma Inman Williams, "Jackson and
Madison County: An Inland Cotton Center of the Growing West,
1821–1850," *THQ* 3 (March 1944): 24–75.

Sources on specialized topics include Royal B. Way, "The
United States Factory System for Trading with the Indians,
1796–1822," *MVHR* 6 (September 1919): 220–235; Aloysius Plai-
sance, "The Chickasaw Bluffs Factory and Its Removal to the
Arkansas River, 1818–22," *THQ* 11 (March 1953): 41–56; James W.
Silver, "Land Speculation Profits in the Chickasaw Cession,"
JSH 10 (February 1944): 84–92; James E. Roper, "Isaac Rawlings,

Frontier Merchant," *THQ* 20 (September 1961): 262–281; idem, "Marcus Brutus Winchester, First Mayor of Memphis: His Later Years," *WTHSP* 13 (1959): 5–37; and idem, "Marcus Winchester and the Earliest Years of Memphis," *THQ* 21 (1962): 326–351. A good source on health problems is S. R. Bruesch, "Early Medical History of Memphis (1819–1861)," *WTHSP* 2 (1948): 33–94. See also Kate Born, "Organized Labor in Memphis, Tennessee, 1826–1901," *WTHSP* 21 (1967): 60–79; and Cecil C. Humphreys, "The Formation of Reelfoot Lake and Consequent Land and Social Problems," *WTHSP* 14 (1960): 32–73.

For the complicated matter of land legislation and policies, see the sources cited for chapters five and nine, especially Henry D. Whitney, comp. and ed., *The Land Laws of Tennessee* (Chattanooga: Deardoff, 1891); Thomas P. Abernethy, *From Frontier to Plantation in Tennessee: A Study of Frontier Democracy* (Chapel Hill: University of North Carolina Press, 1932); Thomas B. Jones, "The Public Lands of Tennessee," *THQ* 27 (Spring 1968): 13–36; Goldene Fillers Burgner, comp., *North Carolina Land Grants in Tennessee, 1778–1791* (reprint, Easley, S.C.: Southern Historical Press, 1981); and Memucan Hunt Howard, "Recollections of Memucan Hunt Howard," *AHM* 7 (January 1901): 55–68. A number of U.S. House and Senate reports and documents during the period discuss land issues in West Tennessee; see especially "Quantity of Public Land Remaining Unsold in Tennessee in 1829," House Document 763, 21st. Cong., 1st. sess.

Transportation was always a primary concern in West Tennessee, and useful studies include Ronald William Waschka, "Transportation at Memphis before the Civil War" (master's thesis, Memphis State University, 1970); Stanley J. Folmsbee, *Sectionalism and Internal Improvements in Tennessee, 1796–1845* (Knoxville: ETHS, 1939); W. Wallace Carson, "Transportation and Traffic on the Ohio and the Mississippi before the Steamboat," *MVHR* 7 (June 1920): 26–38; the insightful and entertaining Michael Allen, *Western Rivermen, 1763–1861: Ohio and Mississippi Boatmen and the Myth of the Alligator Horse* (Baton Rouge: Louisiana State University Press, 1990); George L. Sioussat Jr., "Memphis as a Gateway to the West," *THM* 3 (March 1917): 1–27, 77–114; Edward F. Williams III, "Memphis' Early Triumph over

Its River Rivals," *WTHSP* 22 (1968): 5–27; Addie Lou Brooks, "Early Plans for Railroads in West Tennessee, 1830–1845," *THM*, ser. 2, 3 (October 1932): 20–39; and Forrest Laws, "The Railroad Comes to Tennessee: The Building of the La Grange and Memphis," *WTHSP* 30 (October 1976): 24–42.

An excellent overview of Frances Wright and her Nashoba experiment is John Egerton, *Visions of Utopia: Nashoba, Rugby, Ruskin and the "New Communities" in Tennessee's Past* (Knoxville: University of Tennessee Press, 1977); see also O. B. Emerson, "Frances Wright and the Nashoba Experiment," *THQ* 6 (December 1947): 291–314; William H. Pease and Jane H. Pease, "A New View of Nashoba," *THQ* 19 (June 1960): 99–109; A. J. G. Perkins and Teresa Wolfson, *Frances Wright, Free Enquirer: The Study of a Temperament* (New York: Harper Brothers, 1939); J. Orin Oliphant, ed., *Through the South and the West with Jeremiah Evarts in 1826* (Lewisburg, Pa.: Bucknell University Press, 1956); and Frances Milton Trollope, *Domestic Manners of the Americans*, 2 vols. (London: Whittaker, Treacher & Co., 1832); see also Arthur E. Bestor Jr., *Backwoods Utopias: The Sectarian Origins and the Owenite Phase of Communitarian Socialism in America, 1663–1829* (Philadelphia: University of Pennsylvania Press, 1970). For Tocqueville see George Wilson Pierson, *Tocqueville and Beaumont in America* (New York: Oxford University Press, 1938).

The starting point for an appraisal of Davy Crockett is his own *A Narrative of the Life of David Crockett of the State of Tennessee* (Philadelphia: Carey & Hart, 1834) and its reprints: James A. Shackford and Stanley J. Folmsbee, eds., (Knoxville: University of Tennessee Press, 1973); and Paul A. Hutton, ed., (Lincoln: University of Nebraska Press, 1987). For factual information on Crockett's life, I have relied extensively on James Atkins Shackford, *David Crockett: The Man and the Legend*, ed. James B. Shackford (Chapel Hill: University of North Carolina Press, 1956). Among the many other relevant works I suggest Michael A. Lofaro, ed., *Davy Crockett: The Man, the Legend, the Legacy, 1786–1986* (Knoxville: University of Tennessee Press, 1985); Michael A. Lofaro and Joe Cummings, eds., *Crockett at Two Hundred: New Perspectives on the Man and the Myth* (Knoxville:

University of Tennessee Press, 1989); Walter Blair, "Six Davy Crocketts," *Southwest Review* 25 (1940): 449–460; Marvin Downing, "Davy Crockett in Gibson County, Tennessee: A Century of Memories." *WTHSP* 35 (1981): 54–61; Stanley J. Folmsbee, "David Crockett and West Tennessee," *WTHSP* 28 (1974): 5–24; Dan Kilgore, *How Did Davy Die?* (College Station: Texas A&M University Press, 1978); and for a lively yet balanced account of the Alamo, Walter Lord, *A Time to Stand: The Epic of the Alamo* (New York: Harper & Row, 1961). See also Richard Slotkin's comments in his trilogy: *Regeneration through Violence: The Mythology of the American Frontier, 1600–1860* (Middletown, Conn.: Wesleyan University Press, 1973); *The Fatal Environment: The Myth of the Frontier in the Age of Industrialization, 1800–1890* (Middletown, Conn.: Wesleyan University Press, 1985); and *Gunfighter Nation: The Myth of the Frontier in Twentieth-Century America* (New York: Atheneum, 1992).

Among the many accounts of Sam Houston are Marquis James, *The Raven: A Biography of Sam Houston* (Indianapolis: Bobbs-Merrill, 1929); Marion K. Wisehart, *Sam Houston: American Giant* (Washington, D.C.: Robert B. Luce, 1962); Randolph B. Campbell, *Sam Houston and the American Southwest* (New York: HarperCollins, 1993); and Marshall De Bruhl, *Sword of San Jacinto: A Life of Sam Houston* (New York: Random House, 1993). See also Jack Gregory and Rennard Strickland, *Sam Houston with the Cherokees, 1829–1833* (Austin: University of Texas Press, 1967); and Herbert L. Harper, ed., *Houston and Crockett: Heroes of Tennessee and Texas* (Nashville: Tennessee Historical Commission, 1986).

11. Hegemony and Cherokee Removal

Many previously cited authors who discuss the Cherokees address their strides toward civilization during this period, especially William G. McLoughlin, whose books include *Cherokees and Missionaries, 1789–1839* (New Haven: Yale University Press, 1984); the especially useful *Cherokee Renascence in the New Republic* (Princeton: Princeton University Press, 1986); *Champions of the Cherokees: Evan and John B. Jones* (Princeton: Princeton

University Press, 1990); and for the Cherokees' early experience in Oklahoma, *After the Trail of Tears: The Cherokees' Struggle for Sovereignty, 1839–1880* (Chapel Hill: University of North Carolina Press, 1993). McLoughlin's important articles include "Thomas Jefferson and the Beginning of Cherokee Nationalism," *WMQ*, ser. 3, 32 (October 1975): 562–580; and with Walter H. Conser Jr., "The Cherokees in Transition: A Statistical Analysis of the Federal Cherokee Census of 1835," *JAH* 64 (December 1977): 678–703, which discusses the most famous Cherokee census. That census is available as *Census Roll, 1835, of Cherokee Indians East of the Mississippi. With Index* (Washington, D.C.: National Archives), microfilm T496.

Other important works include Ronald N. Satz, *Tennessee's Indian Peoples: From White Contact to Removal, 1540–1850* (Knoxville: University of Tennessee Press, 1979); Grace Steele Woodward, *The Cherokees* (Norman: University of Oklahoma Press, 1963); Theda Perdue, *Slavery and the Evolution of Cherokee Society, 1540–1866* (Knoxville: University of Tennessee Press, 1979); idem, *Cherokee Women: Gender and Culture Change, 1700–1835* (Lincoln: University of Nebraska Press, 1998); and idem, "Southeastern Indians and the Cult of True Womanhood," in Walter J. Fraser Jr., R. Saunders, and Jon R. Wakelyn, eds., *Web of Southern Social Relations: Women, Family and Education* (Athens: University of Georgia Press, 1985), pp. 35–52; Henry T. Malone, *Cherokees of the Old South: A People in Transition* (Athens: University of Georgia Press, 1956); Mary Young, "The Cherokee Nation: Mirror of the Republic," *American Quarterly* 33 (Winter 1981): 502–524; John R. Finger, "Cherokee Accommodation and Persistence in the Southern Appalachians," in Mary Beth Pudup, Dwight B. Billings, and Altina L. Waller, eds., *Appalachia in the Making: The Mountain South in the Nineteenth Century* (Chapel Hill: University of North Carolina Press, 1995), pp. 25–49; Sarah H. Hill, *Weaving New Worlds: Southeastern Cherokee Women and Their Basketry* (Chapel Hill: University of North Carolina Press, 1997); Thomas Hatley, "Cherokee Women Farmers Hold Their Ground," in Robert D. Mitchell, ed., *Appalachian Frontiers: Settlement, Society and Development in the Preindustrial Era* (Lexington: University of Kentucky Press,

1991), pp. 37–51; Brad Alan Bays, "The Historical Geography of Cattle Herding among the Cherokee Indians, 1761–1861" (master's thesis, University of Tennessee, 1991); Douglas C. Wilms, "Cherokee Land Use in the State of Georgia, 1800–1838" (Ph.D. diss., University of Georgia, 1972); William R. Snell, "The Councils at Red Clay Council Ground, Bradley County, Tennessee, 1832–1837," *JCS* 2 (Fall 1977): 344–355; Brian M. Butler, "The Red Clay Council Ground," *JCS* 2 (Winter 1977): 140–153; Carl F. Klinck and James Talmon, eds., *The Journal of Major John Norton, 1816* (Toronto: Champlain Society, 1970); and Raymond D. Fogelson, "Major John Norton as Ethno-ethnologist," *JCS* 3 (Fall 1978): 250–255.

Works dealing with prominent individuals of the period include Gary E. Moulton, *John Ross: Cherokee Chief* (Athens: University of Georgia Press, 1978); idem, ed., *The Papers of Chief John Ross*, 2 vols.(Norman: University of Oklahoma Press, 1985); Thurman Wilkins, *Cherokee Tragedy: The Story of the Ridge Family and the Decimation of a People* (New York: Macmillan, 1970); Grant Foreman, *Sequoyah* (Norman: University of Oklahoma Press, 1938); idem, "The Story of Sequoyah's Last Days," *Chronicles of Oklahoma* 12 (March 1934): 25–41; Theda Perdue, ed., *Cherokee Editor: The Writings of Elias Boudinot* (Knoxville: University of Tennessee Press, 1983); Francis Paul Prucha, ed., *Cherokee Removal: The "William Penn" Essays and Other Writings by Jeremiah Evarts* (Knoxville: University of Tennessee Press, 1981); Robert V. Remini, *Andrew Jackson and the Course of American Empire, 1767–1821* (New York: Harper & Row, 1977); and Michael Paul Rogin's provocative and controversial *Fathers and Children: Andrew Jackson and the Subjugation of the American Indian* (New York: Knopf, 1975).

Excellent discussions of federal Indian policy during the period include Francis Paul Prucha, *American Indian Policy in the Formative Years: The Indian Trade and Intercourse Acts, 1790–1834* (Cambridge, Mass.: Harvard University Press, 1962); and sections of Prucha's *The Great Father: The United States Government and the American Indians*, 2 vols. (Lincoln: University of Nebraska Press, 1984). A standard account is Ronald N. Satz, *American Indian Policy in the Jacksonian Era* (Lincoln: Univer-

sity of Nebraska Press, 1975); see also Anthony F. C. Wallace, *The* ᴇssᴀʏ ᴏɴ
Long, Bitter Trail: Andrew Jackson and the Indians (New York: ꜱᴏᴜʀᴄᴇꜱ
Hill and Wang, 1993); Francis Paul Prucha's discussion of alter-
natives to removal in "Andrew Jackson's Indian Policy: A Reas-
sessment," *JAH* 56 (December 1969): 527–539; and Bernard W.
Sheehan, *Seeds of Extinction: Jeffersonian Philanthropy and the
American Indian* (Chapel Hill: University of North Carolina
Press, 1973), which is excellent on the vagaries and ironies of Jeffersonian Indian policy. Among the most important and convenient primary sources are ASPIA and Charles J. Kappler, *Indian
Affairs: Laws and Treaties*, 5 vols. (Washington, D.C.: Government Printing Office, 1904–1941). Charles C. Royce, comp., *Indian Land Cessions in the United States* (Washington, D.C.:
Government Printing Office, 1900), offers the most detailed
maps of cessions. For in-depth commentary on treaties, see
Charles C. Royce, *The Cherokee Nation of Indians* (Chicago: Aldene, 1975).

Many scholarly and popular works discuss Cherokee removal
and often reflect an ideological view. One of the most thorough
and sober accounts is an old one—Grant Foreman's *Indian Removal: The Emigration of the Five Civilized Tribes of Indians*
(Norman: University of Oklahoma Press, 1932). Specific to the
Cherokees is John Ehle, *Trail of Tears: The Rise and Fall of the
Cherokee Nation* (New York: Doubleday/Anchor, 1988); Rob-
ert C. White, *Cherokee Indian Removal from the Lower Hiwassee Valley* (Cleveland, Tenn.: Cleveland State Community College, 1973); and analyses of removal-related topics in William L.
Anderson, ed., *Cherokee Removal: Before and After* (Athens:
University of Georgia Press, 1991), including Anderson's his-
toriographical and bibliographical essay on Cherokee removal.
Another essay in the same collection is Russell Thornton's "The
Demography of the Trail of Tears Period: A New Estimate of
Cherokee Population Losses." Other good articles include Ronald N. Satz, "Cherokee Traditionalism, Protestant Evangelism,
and the Trail of Tears," *THQ* 44 (Fall and Winter 1985): 285–301,
380–401; and Kenneth Penn Davis, "The Cherokee Removal,
1836–1838," *THQ* 32 (Winter 1975): 311–330. Theda Perdue and
Michael D. Green, eds., *The Cherokee Removal: A Brief History*

with Documents (Boston: Bedford Books, 1995), is a superb volume of documents with excellent introductory commentary. Chickasaw removal is discussed in Arrell M. Gibson, *The Chickasaws* (Norman: University of Oklahoma Press, 1971)

For white settlement in the Ocoee District of southeastern Tennessee, see Gilbert E. Govan and James W. Livingood, *The Chattanooga Country: From Tomahawks to TVA, 1540–1976*, 3rd ed. (Knoxville: University of Tennessee Press, 1977); James W. Livingood, *Hamilton County* (Memphis: Memphis State University Press, 1981); Zella Armstrong, *History of Hamilton County and Chattanooga, Tennessee*, 2 vols. (Chattanooga: Lookout, 1931–1940); and Donald Davidson, *The Tennessee: The Old River — Frontier to Secession* (New York: Rinehart & Co., 1946).

Conclusion

The survival of "remnant" Indian groups in the post-removal Southeast has attracted much attention in the last twenty years. See, for example, John R. Finger, *The Eastern Band of Cherokees, 1819–1900* (Knoxville: University of Tennessee Press, 1984); idem, *Cherokee Americans: The Eastern Band of Cherokees in the Twentieth Century* (Lincoln: University of Nebraska Press, 1991); Sharlotte Neely, *Snowbird Cherokees: People of Persistence* (Athens: University of Georgia Press, 1991); Walter L. Williams, ed., *Southeastern Indians since the Removal Era* (Athens: University of Georgia Press, 1979); and J. Anthony Paredes, ed., *Indians of the Southeastern United States in the Late Twentieth Century* (Tuscaloosa: University of Alabama Press, 1992).

Most of the statistics for this chapter come from the agricultural and manufacturing tables of the Sixth U.S. Census, 1840. Durwood Dunn's *Cades Cove: The Life and Death of a Southern Appalachian Community, 1818–1937* (Knoxville: University of Tennessee Press, 1988), is a fine assessment of the interplay between people and land in one famous cove. Dunn joins a number of scholarly and popular writers who have said much about the images of Appalachia and its people. For an excellent interpretive and bibliographical assessment, see Dwight B. Billings, Mary Beth Pudup, and Altina Waller, "Taking Exception with Excep-

Studies of Appalachia," in Dwight B. Billings, Mary Beth Pudup,
and Altina Waller, eds., *Appalachia in the Making: The Mountain South in the Nineteenth Century* (Chapel Hill: University of
North Carolina Press, 1995), pp. 1–24. Recent additions to the
literature include Donald Edward Davis, *Where There Are Mountains: An Environmental History of the Southern Appalachians*
(Athens: University of Georgia Press, 2000); Wilma Dunaway,
*The First American Frontier: Transition to Capitalism in South-
ern Appalachia, 1700–1860* (Chapel Hill: University of North
Carolina Press, 1996); and David C. Hsiung, *Two Worlds in the
Tennessee Mountains: Exploring the Origins of Appalachian Ste-
reotypes* (Lexington: University of Kentucky Press, 1997).

Index

John R. Finger

is Emeritus Professor of History at the University of Tennessee, Knoxville.